INTRODUCTION TO

SOCIAL WORK

SOCIOLOGY SERIES
Edited by John F. Cuber

INTRODUCTION TO

SOCIAL WORK

Rex A. Skidmore

Milton G. Thackeray

both of University of Utah

NEW YORK

APPLETON-CENTURY-CROFTS

Division of Meredith Publishing Company

Preface

Social welfare and social work are significant components of modern society. Directly or indirectly they affect the lives of everyone. Learning about social welfare or social work is an important part of general education as well as a part of preprofessional preparation for the helping professions.

Social welfare depicts man as the center of the universe. In his associations with others his life is enriched; but he also encounters numerous problems. Social work is a professional attempt to help him to solve problems in social functioning and to strengthen his social relationships.

The purpose of this book is to help the student to understand, think, and feel about social welfare and social work; to help him to learn *about* social welfare and social work, not *how* to do social work. It focuses on the *why,* the *what,* the *who,* the *when,* the *where,* and—in an exploratory way—the *how* of social work.

This book is aimed at (1) junior and senior college students who want to increase their general understanding about social welfare and social work, and (2) those who have a preprofessional interest in social work. It can also be used in social work philosophy classes and as a reference text on the graduate level.

Social work is both a field and a method. This book attempts to present an introductory, integrated, overall view of both.

Up-to-date materials are included from the 1962 Social Security Amendments, the thirteen-volume Curriculum Study of the Council on Social Work Education, and from current activities and actions of the National Association of Social Workers and the Council on Social Work Education, including the 1962 Curriculum Policy Statement.

This text provides several unique areas of special emphasis including

v

chapters on Prevention, Aging, International Social Work, Social Work as a Profession, Social Work Education, and the Enabling Processes. In one sense this book encompasses the sociology of social work.

The fields of social welfare and social work are described and exemplified with case glimpses and cases. The traditional social work settings are discussed and illustrated. In addition, introductory materials are presented regarding the basic social work processes accompanied by case materials.

The book is composed of four main parts. The Introduction answers the question, "What Is Social Work?", defines and illustrates the problems of social functioning, and depicts the evolution of social welfare in America. Part II includes pertinent materials on social work services in the following settings: psychiatric, medical, school, public welfare, child welfare, corrections, international social work, group work, community organization, and services for the aged. The social work processes are introduced in Part III, with chapters on casework, group work, community organization, and on the enabling processes, including administration, supervision, consultation, collaboration, social action, and research. Part IV considers social work's professional development with emphasis on the sociology of the social work profession, prevention, education for social work, and a look at the future.

The authors are grateful to Mrs. Georgia W. Snyder, Mrs. Hulda V. Garrett, Miss Louise Browning, Miss Zella D. Allred, Mrs. Eleanor S. Stein, Miss Eva Hancock, Mr. Kenneth A. Griffiths, Mr. Gene Shumway, and Mr. Veon G. Smith, faculty, University of Utah, who read one or more chapters of the manuscript and made helpful suggestions on organization and content.

To the entire faculty of the Graduate School of Social Work, University of Utah, we express appreciation. Many of the ideas of this book have resulted from their encouragement, suggestions, and intellectual stimulation across the years.

A special note of commendation is due our secretaries, Mrs. Anne B. Jenson, Mrs. Sara S. Nicholson, Mrs. Mardon E. Erekson, and Miss Patricia Clark for their excellent assistance. Their accuracy and enthusiasm have been invaluable. We also appreciate the excellent art work— some of the illustrations—of Harold C. Secrist and Mardon E. Erekson.

The authors deeply appreciate the support and encouragement of their wives, Knell and Farol, who made many helpful suggestions, and devoted their time and talents to reading and improving the manuscript.

R. A. S.

M. G. T.

Contents

part **I**

Introduction

CHAPTER 1

What Is Social Work?

We live in a fast-moving, push-button, space age; yet, we find that people are still the center of the world and its values. The rocks, the stars, and the moon are important; but man is more important. As men and women live together, problems of relationship and interaction emerge. Personal problems, family problems, and community problems appear on the horizon of everyday living.

When serious difficulties in human relationships arise, the question immediately becomes "Can we get help?" The answer is usually "Yes." Many professions are ready to help, one of which is social work. What is social work? What is social welfare? What part do they play in this cosmonaut age?

Social work and social welfare are based upon three premises: (1) that man is important, (2) that he has personal, family, and community problems resulting from his interaction with others, and (3) that something can be done to alleviate his problems. An introductory case glimpse illustrates premises (2) and (3).

Joe had been in a state hospital for nineteen years, confined to one of the back wards. Those who had known him reported he was institutionalized because of tremendous emotional pressures due to a "shattered marriage." The attendants indicated he had talked to no one for several years, and that he apparently lived in a world of his own.

Then came a change. As a part of experimentation in treatment, a social worker was assigned to meet with Joe for thirty minutes daily with the goal of bringing him back to reality. The worker explained to Joe that she was going to see him regularly and was genuinely interested in him. For the first two weeks, he uttered nary a word. Then one day he surprised the worker by saying, "I like you."

The worker continued to spend about thirty minutes daily with Joe. She was sympathetic, interested in him, warm, friendly, and accepting. He responded steadily to her interest and efforts. Within six months, he was discharged from the hospital and had become established in his community. A follow-up two years later showed he had made a successful return to society and was an accepted, productive citizen.

When asked by a close friend, what had happened, Joe eagerly replied, but with seriousness, "The worker was just like a magnet— drawing me out of my shell. I couldn't resist her."

SOCIAL WELFARE

Social work and social welfare are often confused and sometimes used synonymously. Actually, social welfare has a broader meaning and encompasses social work and other related programs and activities. Social welfare, according to Friedlander,[1] "is the organized system of social services and institutions, designed to aid individuals and groups to attain satisfying standards of life and health, and personal and social relationships which permit them to develop their full capacities and to promote their well-being in harmony with the needs of their families and the community."

Vasey[2] explains that definitions of social welfare include two main characteristics: "(1) The utilization of welfare measures to support or strengthen the family as a basic social institution through which needs are met. Even those programs designed to aid the victims of broken homes or untenable family situations attempt to find the best possible substitute pending the return to or development of a good family situation. (2) The intent to strengthen the individual's capacity to cope with his life situation."

Social welfare, in a broad sense, encompasses the well-being and interests of large numbers of people, including their physical, mental, emotional, spiritual, and economic needs. Economically it is big business. For example, in 1955–56, about twenty-two billion dollars were expended for public welfare programs in the United States involving millions of Americans. The 1960 survey by the U.S. Bureau of Labor

[1] Walter A. Friedlander, *Introduction to Social Welfare*, 2nd ed. (Englewood Cliffs, N.J.: Prentice-Hall, Inc., 1961), p. 4.
[2] Wayne Vasey, *Government and Social Welfare* (New York: Holt, Rinehart & Winston, Inc., 1958), p. 11.

Statistics reflected there were 116,000 persons employed in social welfare, 42 percent more than in 1950.

Social welfare includes the basic institutions and processes related to facing and solving social problems, those problems which affect large numbers of people and which require some kind of concerted group effort to resolve. In this sense, social welfare includes not only qualified social workers but also untrained personnel who are employed in public welfare, in probation, and in other areas in which social problems are being faced and resolved. Present-day standards require a Master of Social Work degree as a minimum for the professional social worker, with at least two years of work experience under adequate supervision. Thus, social work is the upper professional echelon in the social welfare hierarchy.

A glance into the history of social welfare reveals that services have been provided across the centuries for disadvantaged persons and groups. Examples of such services include the care of the sick and the poor administered by the early Christian Church, and the provisions of the Elizabethan Poor Laws of the sixteenth and seventeenth centuries. Social services came first, and methods of social work developed out of social welfare. At the turn of the twentieth century social work was becoming more formalized, and within the next several decades emerged into a profession—a specialized, modern, segment of the totality of social welfare.

Social welfare is talked about today in the United States as it has never been talked about before. It is something that is of interest to political and religious leaders as well as citizens. The preamble of the Constitution of the United States includes the famous words to "promote the general welfare." Allport[3] typifies the increasing interest and status of social welfare:

Social service has a greater clarity of perspective than does politics or commerce. It can therefore press for the stabilizing reforms that are needed to make life rich, meaningful and just in a system of free initiative and individual liberty. By asserting its convictions more loudly than it has, social service can make itself not only the servant but also the prophet of democracy. And today, as never before, democracy needs both servants and prophets.

Social service has limits and limitations. But it has also the saving virtue of self-criticism, and is daily growing in shrewdness and sense of strategy. Its foundations are eternally valid. The balance, therefore, is in its favor.

SOCIAL WORK

The next question that follows is, "What is social work?" A current answer appeared in an editorial in the *New York Times:*

[3] Gordon W. Allport, *Personality and Social Encounter* (Boston: Beacon Press, 1960), p. 292.

A new profession has been growing to maturity under our noses. It is social work. Once thought of as basket-on-the-arm assistance to the poor, it now is a discipline, scientific in method and artful in manner, that takes remedial action on problems in several areas of society. It ministers to families in economic or emotional difficulty. It helps communities to bring their welfare and related services into good balance. It works in medical, group and school situations. It seeks to correct the causes underlying delinquency and adult criminality.

A much-used definition of social work appears in the Curriculum Study, sponsored by the Council on Social Work Education: "Social work seeks to enhance the social functioning of individuals, singly and in groups, by activities focused upon their social relationships which constitute the interaction between man and his environment. These activities can be grouped into three functions: restoration of impaired capacity, provision of individual and social resources, and prevention of social dysfunction." [4]

The underlying assumptions of social work are: [5]

1. Social work like all other professions has problem-solving functions.
2. Social work practice is an art with a scientific and value foundation.
3. Social work as a profession came into being and continues to develop because it meets human needs and aspirations recognized by society. . . .
4. Social work practice takes its values from those held by the society of which it is a part. However, its values are not necessarily or altogether those universally or predominantly held or practiced in society.
5. The scientific base of social work consists of three types of knowledge: (a) tested knowledge, (b) hypothetical knowledge that requires transformation into tested knowledge, and (c) assumptive knowledge (or "practice wisdom") that requires transformation into hypothetical and thence into tested knowledge. . . .
6. The knowledge needed for social work practice is determined by its goals and functions and the problems it seeks to solve.
7. The internalization of professional knowledge and values is a vital characteristic of the professional social worker since he is himself the instrument of professional help.
8. Professional skill is expressed in the activities of the social worker. . . .

The Curriculum Study describes some of the essential values of social work which are important in defining this profession: [6]

1. Each person has the right to self-fulfillment, deriving from his inherent capacity and thrust toward that goal.
2. Each person has the obligation, as a member of society, to seek ways of self-fulfillment that contribute to the common good.
3. Society has the obligation to facilitate the self-fulfillment of the individual and the right to enrichment through the contributions of its individual members.
4. Each person requires for the harmonious development of his powers so-

[4] Werner W. Boehm, *Objectives of the Social Work Curriculum of the Future*, Curriculum Study, Vol. I (New York: Council on Social Work Education, 1959), p. 54.
[5] *Ibid.*, pp. 41–42.
[6] *Ibid.*, pp. 43–44.

cially provided and socially safeguarded opportunities for satisfying his basic needs in the physical, psychological, economic, cultural, aesthetic, and spiritual realms.

5. As society becomes more complex and interdependent, increasingly specialized social organization is required to facilitate the individual's efforts at self-realization. . . .

6. To permit both self-realization and contribution to society by the individual, social organization must make available socially sanctioned and socially provided devices for needs satisfaction as wide in range, variety, and quality as the general welfare allows.

According to the Curriculum Study, "These values constitute a minimum commitment for the social worker. They imply definition of human freedom as conditioned by the exigencies of modern living."

The goal of social work, according to the Curriculum Study, is the enhancement of social functioning wherever the need for such enhancement is either socially or individually perceived. "The patterns, directions, quality and outcomes of man's social relationships (social interaction) in the performance of his various roles (social functioning) become the professional concern of social work. A problem presented in the area of social interaction whether raised as a problem by the individual or by a group in the community, calls for the professional services of the social worker."

The basic functions of social work—restoration, provision of resources, and prevention—are intertwined and interdependent. Restoration of impaired social functioning may be subdivided into curative and rehabilitative aspects. Its curative aspects are to eliminate factors which have caused breakdown of functioning, and its rehabilitative aspects, to reorganize and rebuild interactional patterns. Illustrations of restoration would include assistance in obtaining a hearing aid for a partially deaf child or helping a rejected, lonely child to be placed in a foster home. The rehabilitative aspect might be helping the one child to psychologically accept and live with the hearing aid and supporting the other child as he adjusts to the new foster home.

Provision of resources, social and individual, for more effective social functioning may be subdivided into developmental and educational. The developmental aspects are designed to further the effectiveness of existing social resources or to bring to full flower personal capacity for more effective social interaction. An example would be the services of a Family Service Society which help Mr. and Mrs. X, through individual and conjoint interviews, to understand each other better and to open the channels of communication between them for the first time in their twelve years of marriage. The educational spectrum is designed to acquaint the public with specific conditions and needs for new or changing social resources. Again, this could be illustrated by public talks given by staff members of a Family Service Society in which counseling services are described as a resource in alleviating marriage and family problems.

The third function, prevention of social dysfunction, involves early discovery, control, and elimination of conditions and situations which potentially could hamper effective social functioning. The two main divisions are prevention of problems in the area of interaction between individuals and groups, and second, the prevention of social ills. Premarital counseling would be an example of an attempt to prevent individual and social problems in relation to social functioning. Hopefully, through this process couples will be able to anticipate possible difficulties in marital interaction and, through adequate consideration and understanding, avoid the problems that might ensue otherwise. Prevention of social ills ordinarily falls within the area of community organization. An example of this function is the Community Welfare Council approach to the reduction of juvenile delinquency through the utilization of all community organizations and economic resources (e. g., to build a new Youth Center and provide it with a professionally trained staff to work with boys and girls who are near-delinquent or who live in "delinquency areas"). An overall conclusion in the Curriculum Study states, "that the focus on social relationships, however, is suggested as the *distinguishing characteristic* of the social work profession."

Bartlett claims that social work is "a configuration of elements none of which is unique but which, in combination, represent a contribution quite distinct from that rendered by any other profession." [7]

Social work may be defined as an art, a science, a profession which helps people to solve personal, group (especially family), and community problems and to attain satisfying personal, group, and community relationships through use of certain methods including casework, group work, community organization, and the enabling processes of research and administration. Social work not only helps people to solve problems, but also assists them to prevent problems and enrich daily living.

Certainly the main focus of the social worker is upon helping people to improve their social functioning, their ability to interact and relate to others. On the other hand, there are many in the related helping professions who also assist with interactional problems. In addition, social workers sometimes help individuals to solve individual and personal problems. The social worker ordinarily works with clients on a conscious level, helping them to face realities and to solve problems without delving into the realm of the unconscious. Social work is an art because it requires great skills to understand people and to help them to help themselves. It is a beginning science because of its problem-

[7] Harriett M. Bartlett, *50 Years of Social Work in the Medical Setting, Past Significance/Future Outlook* (New York: National Association of Social Workers, 1957), p. 24.

WHAT IS SOCIAL WORK?

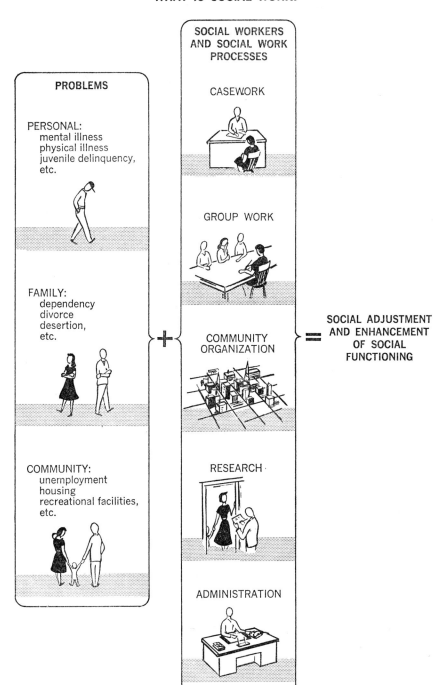

PROBLEMS

PERSONAL:
  mental illness
  physical illness
  juvenile delinquency,
  etc.

FAMILY:
  dependency
  divorce
  desertion,
  etc.

COMMUNITY:
  unemployment
  housing
  recreational facilities,
  etc.

**SOCIAL WORKERS
AND SOCIAL WORK
PROCESSES**

CASEWORK

GROUP WORK

COMMUNITY
ORGANIZATION

RESEARCH

ADMINISTRATION

**SOCIAL ADJUSTMENT
AND ENHANCEMENT
OF SOCIAL
FUNCTIONING**

solving method and its attempt to be objective in ascertaining facts and in developing principles and operational concepts. It is a profession because today it encompasses the attributes of a profession, although in its first stages in some regards.

DISTINGUISHING CHARACTERISTICS OF SOCIAL WORK

Comprehension of social work may be enhanced by consideration of some of its distinguishing characteristics, which follow:

1. Focus is on the wholeness and totality of the person—encompassing the person, environmental factors, and his behavior. Social work stresses the total person in the total environment.

2. Emphasis is on the importance of the family in molding and influencing behavior. Social workers attempt to understand the principles underlying family interaction and to work with the family as the basic unit of improving social functioning, recognizing that most social problems inhere in inadequate or imbalanced family relationships. The family is usually regarded as the *case* in social work.

3. Utilization of community resources in helping people to solve problems is very important. Social workers have a comprehensive knowledge of community resources and are able to tap them to meet the needs of their clients. They help to get "Mrs. Jones to the clinic," to the agency which can help the most in the solution of her particular problems. Making referrals is a major service of social workers.

4. Use of the supervisory process provides for guidance and direction of inexperienced workers and for continuing growth of the experienced. Both in graduate study and in practice, social work provides supervision by qualified, professional personnel to help the worker to continue to grow professionally and to acquire increased knowledge and abilities. The supervisor is available regularly to help the worker to do a better job and to increase his understandings and skills in working with people. This process is particularly important because the social worker, himself, is the tool in helping troubled persons, and he needs to grow professionally, keeping abreast of new knowledge and skills.

5. Social work has a unique educational program involving classwork and practical field work experience which go hand in hand. To obtain a Master of Social Work degree requires two years of graduate training in one of the sixty-three graduate schools in the United States and Canada. This program includes both academic classes and live field experiences in working with clients which gives an integrated combination of theory and practice.

6. Social work uses three basic methods: casework, group work, and community organization. Casework involves a close, face-to-face relationship, mainly on an individual to individual basis, in working with

people and their problems; group work utilizes the group as the tool to bring about desired changes in social functioning with troubled persons; and community organization is the *intergroup* approach toward facing and solving social pathologies. All three are utilized by social workers in helping people with personal, family, and community problems.

7. Social work has distinctive professional bodies: The National Association of Social Workers (NASW), and the Council on Social Work Education (CSWE). NASW was established in 1955, after careful study, and brought together several smaller professional social work groups into a unified, dynamic organization. Its membership has increased rapidly and in 1963 it enrolled more than 39,000 social workers. This organization is doing much to raise the standards of social work practice, to recruit qualified persons for professional training, and to interpret practice and values of social work to the public. The Council on Social Work Education, originated in 1952, is doing a considerable amount to improve training facilities, standards, and programs as well as helping with recruitment, public relations, and strengthening social work practice.

8. The *relationship* is the key in the social work process. Everything that is a part of the interview is important, but to the social worker, the feeling tones between the worker and client are particularly important. The social worker attempts to make it possible for the client to face and solve his problems through this warm, accepting, understanding relationship.

9. Social work has an orientation in psychiatric concepts and places considerable stress upon understanding people. The social worker is particularly interested in how the client feels about himself and his relationships with others. The worker possesses considerable understanding of the basic knowledge and concepts of psychiatry which assist him in dealing with human behavior.

10. The *social* in social work emphasizes stress on social interaction and resultant social functioning and malfunctioning. Significant principles from sociology and social psychology, as well as from group dynamics, are woven into the artful fabric of social work, and are utilized in understanding relationships of people and in helping them to resolve their conflicts.

11. Most social workers are employed in agency settings. Although the number of social workers in private practice is increasing, most of them operate within the famework and policies of agencies; this gives them structural backing and support which strengthens their services in many ways. Supervision, consultation, and collaboration, inherent in agency settings, provide many positive resources for the worker.

12. The basic aim of social work is to help the client to help himself.

Contrary to what many people believe, the social worker does not listen to a client and then prescribe a "social-psychological pill"—even though many clients ask for this. He endeavors to help a person to improve his understanding of himself and his relationships with others, and to tap his own and community resources in solving his problems. The social worker operates under the premise that most people have ego strengths to solve their own problems when they really bring them out into the open and understand what they are. Whereas several professions are primarily concerned with the pathological, social work endeavors to stress and utilize strengths, individual and social, to effect desired changes in behavior.

13. Money is used primarily for the agency and services, not to increase the income of the professional person. Since most social workers are employed in agencies and are on a fixed salary, fees are utilized for the welfare of the agency rather than for an increased income for the workers. Income from all sources is used to enhance the total agency's services rather than to increase the individual worker's income.

14. A social worker is particularly effective in developing and using the team approach, bringing about coordination of services and activities. Many professional workers regard the social worker as the catalyst who has the ability and responsibility to help the professional team to work together and function in optimal fashion. The social worker often acts as coordinator for the team effort.

SOCIOLOGY AND SOCIAL WORK

How are sociology and social work related to each other? Admittedly, they share much in common, but are also different in many ways. Sociology has been defined by early American sociologists as follows: by L. F. Ward as the "science of society," and by F. H. Giddings as "the scientific study of society." A. W. Small said that sociology "is the study of men considered as affecting and as affected by association." Cuber explains that "sociology may be defined as a body of scientific knowledge about human relationships." [8] Gillin and Gillin state that "sociology in its broadest sense may be said to be the study of interaction arising from the association of living beings." [9]

Sociology and social work are both interested in people, their interactions, and understanding these interactions. The sociologist is particularly concerned about the *how, when,* and *why* people behave as they do in association with others. He aims to pinpoint the social problems,

[8] John F. Cuber, *Sociology, A Synopsis of Principles,* 5th ed. (New York: Appleton-Century-Crofts, 1963), p. 4.

[9] John Lewis Gillin and John Philip Gillin, *An Introduction to Sociology* (New York: The Macmillan Company, 1942), p. 3.

conduct research, and do everything possible to understand interaction in human associations. He is particularly interested in the *why* of human interaction.

The social worker is certainly interested in understanding people, how they behave in association with others; but he is particularly concerned about helping these same people to solve problems which they have, to improve their social functioning. Whereas the sociologist generally spends most of his time in study and in ferreting out the facts, the social worker tries to understand the client, make appropriate diagnosis, and proceed with treatment, helping to solve the problems and change the situations in order to bring about better adjustment.

PSYCHIATRY AND SOCIAL WORK

The social worker is not a junior psychiatrist. The roles of the social worker and psychiatrist are different, but are of coordinate status. The psychiatrist and the social worker are frequently both members of the professional team and each has unique contributions to make professionally.

Noyes and Kolb define psychiatry "as that branch of medicine which deals with the genesis, dynamics, manifestations and treatment of such disordered and undesirable functionings of the personality as disturb either the subjective life of the individual or his relations with other persons or with society." [10] Psychiatry is a relatively new medical specialty.

The founding of the American Psychiatric Association, first known as the Association of Medical Superintendents of American Institutions for the Insane, took place in 1844. Great strides have been made during the intervening years, and today the approximately 12,000 psychiatrists in the United States are making significant contributions in increasing understanding of the dynamics of family life, of human personality and how it functions, and in helping many individuals with various kinds of personal and emotional disturbances.

One psychiatrist states that the major difference between psychiatry and social work is that the psychiatrist deals mainly with depth in regard to personal and social problems, and the social worker with breadth. The psychiatrist places stress on intrapersonal dynamics, often delving into and handling unconscious motivation and related factors, whereas the social worker utilizes environmental resources and usually operates within the conscious level of behavior.

Psychiatry and social work have many things in common. They both work with people who possess personal and social problems. They both

[10] Arthur P. Noyes and Lawrence C. Kolb, *Modern Clinical Psychiatry* (Philadelphia: W. B. Saunders Co., 1961), p. 1.

help people to improve their relationships with others. They both have considerable interest in, sensitivity, and ability to understand and direct feelings and emotions.

Several differences stand out between social work and psychiatry. The social worker tends to utilize the total community resources, sometimes tapping many material resources, economic and otherwise, in improving social relationships. The psychiatrist deals with patients on a medical basis, prescribes medication and hospitalization, if needed, and tends to focus on the unconscious, intrapsychic factors, working particularly with individual personality reorganization. The social worker often works with the marriage and/or family as a whole, rather than just the individual person. Ordinarily, serious mental disturbances are handled only by the psychiatrist; yet social workers use psychiatric understandings in diagnosis and treatment, and sometimes work directly with seriously disturbed individuals and families. The psychiatrist is particularly interested in the internal dynamics of individual behavior. The social worker is especially concerned about social functioning involving social and community factors and interactions.

PSYCHOLOGY AND SOCIAL WORK

The psychologist and social worker are often members of the same professional team, particularly in treatment clinics and related settings. Nevertheless, many people raise questions about the overlapping and the differences between these two. LaPiere and Farnsworth point out that the psychologist "has historically been interested in the nature of the individual human being endeavoring to discover the processes involved in his adjustments to his environment, the machinery and processes of learning and the like." [11] The psychologist is particularly interested in understanding the individual and his behavior.

Psychology and social work operate on some common grounds. They are both interested in the behavior of people, in their interactional patterns in particular, although the psychologist focuses on individual behavior and the social worker on social functioning. They both seek the thinking and feeling processes of people.

In regard to differences, the psychologist has an area entirely unto himself in the field of testing and measurements. He also studies biological factors as well as social factors related to individual behavior. He is particularly interested in the individual attributes of people, and aims to understand their characteristics and behavior. On the other hand, some psychologists, particularly clinical psychologists, go beyond the study phase and work directly with people in the helping process.

11 Richard T. LaPiere and Paul R. Farnsworth, *Social Psychology*, 2nd ed. (New York: McGraw-Hill Book Co., Inc., 1942), p. 5.

These activities overlap some with social work, and yet the focus seems to be different when considered as a totality. The psychologist usually works with individuals on a rather intensive basis and sometimes becomes a psychotherapist. On the other hand, the social worker is particularly interested in the social functioning and relationships of his clients and in utilizing community resources to meet their personal and social problems.

A clarifying tribute was paid to social work by the graduate student who reported:

> It may sound naive, but I was most impressed by the philosophy underlying the principles used. I am in psychology, and while I am certain psychology operates from the same philosophy, this had never been spelled out. What I am referring to is emphasis on human worth and dignity which would seem to stem from a Christian ethic and also the belief in democratic processes and an attempt to make this work at the community level—not only in community organization, but in case and group work as well.

COUNSELING AND SOCIAL WORK

Some people confuse the role and functions of the counselor with that of the social worker. There are many kinds of counselors, but only three are mentioned here: the school counselor, the marriage counselor, and the rehabilitation counselor.

The school counselor is usually trained in educational psychology. He ordinarily works with students on a short-term basis, helping them particularly with vocational choices and academic problems. He and the social worker share much in common. The social worker tends to be more intensive, works with the client longer, focuses more on the family constellation, and utilizes community resources. The school counselor also uses testing to advantage in many situations.

The marriage counselor may receive his basic training from any of ten main graduate fields of study, only one of which is social work. He is then required to have clinical experience under supervision. In one sense, then, social work is a part of marriage counseling. In another sense, marriage counseling is one particular emphasis in social work. The differences arise across the variations in graduate training and professional experiences.

The rehabilitation counselor is one who is usually trained in educational psychology, is skilled in the use of testing, and focuses his attention and abilities on the individual and his immediate problems of vocational rehabilitation. In situations where both a counselor and social worker are part of the team in rehabilitation, the counselor ordinarily helps with the testing, the short-term counseling, and related activities. The social worker usually assists with the emotional and/or family problems, has fewer cases, and works with clients more intensively. The counselor is particularly interested in the vocational factors and the social worker helps especially with feelings attaching to personal, social, and emotional problems.

SOCIAL WORK IN THE WORLD TODAY

Social work is emerging as an important profession in the modern world. Of the 116,000 persons engaged in social welfare at the present time, more than 39,000 are members of the National Association of Social Workers, the professional body of social workers. In December, 1961, provision was made for professionally trained and experienced social workers to become members of the Academy of Certified Social Workers which gives them additional professional status. In August, 1962, more than 20,000 had so qualified.

Social work today is utilized in a variety of settings and agencies. Some of the important ones are psychiatric, medical, marriage and family counseling, the school, rehabilitation, corrections, public welfare, and child welfare. Schools of social work train a student to work in any agency, giving him the basic understandings, skills, and attitudes which make it possible for him to function adequately.

Social work is becoming more and more important, because thousands of persons are tasting of its services and are telling their friends and associates who have problems of its many values and services. People are not only being helped with personal and family problems, but also with neighborhood, national, and even international difficulties. A prominent American, who recently returned from a trip abroad, made the statement that what the United States needs most of all to improve its foreign policy and relations is to have trained social workers as state department attachés where each of the official government representatives works and lives. Trained social workers in foreign countries would understand the people and work with them where they are, helping them to help themselves and interpreting the United States in a much more favorable light than in the past.

NASW News, August, 1962, reflects that the Board of Directors of NASW approved the following proposal for consideration by the Delegate Assembly for action:

Our government should maintain a comprehensive social welfare attaché program as an integral part of its policy and operation. Limited experience in the past has proved the value of the social welfare attaché in assisting embassy staffs as a consultant on social welfare problems, interpreting United States social welfare developments abroad, and providing valuable information about social welfare in other countries for use by governmental and non-governmental agencies in the United States.

In March, 1963, the National Association of Social Workers announced that a qualified social worker had taken the oath of office as Social Welfare Attaché at the United States Embassy in Brazil. This appointment was the first tangible result of the work done by NASW in cooperation with the U.S. Department of Health, Education, and Welfare since the two positions for Social Welfare Attachés, established in 1947, were discontinued.

Current evidence indicates that social work is here to stay and that in the years and decades ahead it will grow and expand its services, helping more people with personal, family, and community problems, especially related to adequate social functioning.

SUMMARY

1. However fast-moving, and uncertain today's world may be, people are still at its center and core.

2. People have problems which invite professional assistance: personal, family, and community.

3. Social welfare is an important aspect of the modern way of life.

4. Social work is an emerging profession which focuses particularly on helping people to solve their personal, family, and community problems through enhancing social functioning.

5. Sociology and social work have much in common; however, the sociologist is primarily interested in studying about human associations and the social worker is interested in helping to treat people with their problems.

6. The psychiatrist helps people on an intensive, deep, intrapsychic level, whereas the social worker assists particularly with the conscious, realistic factors, tapping social and community resources and assisting especially with interactional problems.

7. The psychologist shares many things with the social worker, but mainly stresses understanding and measuring individual human behavior and vocational guidance, whereas the social worker focuses on the emotional factors, particularly in relation to social functioning.

8. School counselors and vocational rehabilitation counselors provide services which overlap with social work in many ways. However, they help particularly with individual problems and ordinarily operate more on a short-term basis. They use tests and work mainly with individuals in facing and solving academic and vocational adjustment problems. The marriage counselor may be a social worker or a person trained in a related but different discipline. He functions rather similarly to the social worker. He usually is not as well versed about community agencies and resources, but may have superior knowledge regarding sociological, legal, or psychological factors related to marriage and the family.

9. Social work is becoming increasingly important in the present world.

QUESTIONS FOR DISCUSSION

1. What is social work? Formulate your answer in your own words.
2. Why is there a greater need for social workers today?
3. What are some of the distinguishing characteristics of social work?
4. Give an example or case history to illustrate social work services.
5. Define and illustrate the meaning of *social functioning*.
6. Differentiate between social work and social welfare.
7. Compare and contrast the disciplines of social work, sociology, psychiatry, psychology, and counseling.
8. Describe and illustrate the three main functions of social work.
9. Why is social work developing rapidly as a profession?
10. Does the social worker usually "give advice" or "help a person to help himself?" Discuss.

SPECIAL ACTIVITIES

1. Visit a social work agency and talk with one of the workers about the services of the agency.
2. Read one or more social work cases found in one of the casebooks that are available.
3. Visit your local Community Welfare Council and learn about all the social work agencies in operation in your community.
4. Prepare a written or oral report on the history of social work.

SELECTED REFERENCES

BISNO, HERBERT, "How Social Will Social Work Be?" *Social Work,* Vol. 1 (April, 1956), pp. 12–18.

BOEHM, WERNER W., *Objectives of the Social Work Curriculum of the Future,* Curriculum Study, Vol. I (New York: Council on Social Work Education, 1959).

COHEN, NATHAN E., *Social Work in the American Tradition* (New York: Holt, Rinehart & Winston, Inc., 1958).

EATON, JOSEPH W., "Whence and Whither Social Work?" *Social Work,* Vol. 1 (January, 1956), pp. 11–26.

FRIEDLANDER, WALTER A., ed., *Concepts and Methods of Social Work* (Englewood Cliffs, N.J.: Prentice-Hall, Inc., 1958).

KADUSHIN, ALFRED, "Prestige of Social Work—Facts and Factors," *Social Work,* Vol. 3 (April, 1958), pp. 37–43.

REGENSBURG, JEANETTE, "Some Thoughts on Being a Professional Social Worker," *Social Casework,* Vol. 40 (April, 1959), pp. 200–226.

VASEY, WAYNE, *Government and Social Welfare* (New York: Holt, Rinehart & Winston, Inc., 1958).

CHAPTER 2

Problems of Social Functioning

Social work is an enabling profession which seeks to help individuals with personal problems and their human relationships. To be successful, enabling must be rooted in the unswerving conviction of man's preeminence and worth, and in relevant knowledge and skill in helping people. The social work profession provides training to facilitate the enabling process.

Social work is not antiseptic. It neither purports to make life sterile—free from stress-producing problems—nor to relieve people of responsibility for their problems. Such objectives would be as undesirable as they are impractical, as life without any problems would be meaningless. Problems are building blocks to the progress and creativity of free men everywhere.

Generally, people struggle successfully, and often with imagination and ingenuity, with their everyday concerns. Many persons learn to cope with stress and to take minor crises in stride. Some, spurred on by handicaps, rise to great heights. In other situations, however, the individual is faced with problems which he cannot solve by himself. Some of these problems are personal and result from weak egos or poor native endowment; some are family induced and conditioned; and others result from community pressures and failures. Income loss due to unemployment, accidents, or illness may force dependency for periods of short or long duration.

Abandoned, neglected, and deprived children are incapable of functioning normally and require the help of adults. Many individuals become dependent upon their families or society as they advance in years and must rely upon help to meet their basic needs. No age group, economic class, or society is ever completely free of problems which more or less interfere with the role performance of some of its members.

The intervention and aid of social work is indicated when the individual cannot cope with social obligations and commitments by himself. The help of social work is appropriate when the individual's problems are social and block or distort such relationships which exist for him within the family, at school, on the job, and in other social groupings. The aim of social work is to improve and enhance social functioning of individuals, singly and in groups.

SOCIAL FUNCTIONING DEFINED

Social functioning "designates those activities considered essential for performance of the several roles which each individual, by virtue of his membership in social groups, is called upon to carry out. . . . All role performance requires reciprocal activity, or social interaction, between individual and individual, individual and group, and individual and community." [1]

All professions take cognizance of the *wholeness* of man. However, because life is complex and science is specialized, each profession must confine itself to some aspect of man's functioning as a focus of its efforts and activities. Medicine, for example, except for the fields of public health and preventive medicine, confines itself largely to work with the ill. Education is focused on teaching methods, learning theory, motivation, and other aspects of pedagogy. The rites and ordinances of the church and scriptural exposition are functions of the ministry.

Social work has chosen to place its primary attention on man's relationships with other human beings. The social work focus is upon how and with what effectiveness the person performs his various social roles. Threats to, or actual impairment of, role-function are the situations to which the profession of social work addresses itself. "In dealing with the problem, the social worker must examine the particular social relationship (or area of interaction) in which it arises and address himself to the factors in it that block social functioning. To this end, the social worker's activities are directed both to relationships among individuals and to relationships between individuals and the organized social resources of the community." [2]

A fairly typical example of a block to social functioning is an illness causing inability of the wage earner to work, or to work efficiently. Illness can result in loss of employment and income for the family, and even in breakdown in family and employee-employer relationships. Social

---

[1] Werner W. Boehm, *Objectives of the Social Work Curriculum of the Future*, Curriculum Study, Vol. I (New York: Council on Social Work Education, 1959), p. 46.
[2] *Ibid.*, p. 47.

work, called upon to intervene, concerns itself with the fact of unemployment, rehabilitation of the wage earner, the family's income maintenance needs, and the shift in role relationship within the family due to the individual's illness.

A second illustration involves a patient who, relieved of disabling symptoms, was discharged from the hospital to her family. When readmitted a few months later she was as incapacitated as ever. Social study disclosed that her home was making her sick and that improvement in her marital and family relationships would have to develop before lasting benefits from medical treatment could be expected.

PROBLEMS OF SOCIAL INTERACTION AND FUNCTIONING

The problems of a democratic society in the twentieth century calling forth the knowledge and skill of social work are many. Any list of major problems is not comprehensive but includes family disorganization, mental illness, crime and delinquency, and the need for public assistance, illustrative of the many stresses of modern living. Following is a list of some of the major problems confronting many families today:

Family disorganization	Sickness and accidents
School adjustments	Physical defects
Mental illness	Mental deficiency
Crime and delinquency	Aging
Destitution and poverty	Community disorganization.
Unemployment	

Some examples of the problems of social interaction, numerous and dissimilar, are:

FAMILY DISORGANIZATION

It is generally agreed that no institution is more vital to the welfare of a nation than marriage. The home produces many of the most satisfying and enduring of all associations and the family is truly the mainspring of human action. When the individual's performance within the family is impaired, activities in other social groups may suffer.

Is the institution of the family breaking up? Although the answer is "No," nevertheless, there are signs of stress, and many American families are staggering under blows from without and within. The large number of divorces in 1963, about 400,000, amounted to a ratio of one divorce for every four marriages; it was also estimated that more than 50,000 desertions took place. That same year more than a million men, women, and children were affected directly by divorce. In 1958, of the 25.8 million family units in the United States with children under eighteen years of age, 2.8 million were broken by death, divorce, or desertion. Children have need for both parents and while most (87 percent) under eighteen have a home with two parents, a substantial number do not. Many children have known stress and conflict for months or even years prior to the loss of parents through divorce, desertion, or separation. Not infrequently they are pawns of bickering, forced into devastating alliances, and asked to take sides on issues which they cannot know or understand. Their security is undermined and they are torn in their loyalties. They are often shunted from one set of parents to another, to other members of the family, or placed with foster families or in institutions.

A disproportionate number of children of divorced parents are dependent upon public assistance, counseling, rehabilitation, or other means of restoration and assistance. Divorced parents are censured and sometimes humiliated and embarrassed by friends and foes, and they frequently experience guilt, loneliness, and self-recrimination.

Substitute family care in the form of day nurseries and day care centers has mushroomed. It is not uncommon, in any metropolitan community, to see a substantial number of preschool children being hurried to these private and public care centers as mothers dash to work. Unfortunately, many of these centers provide only physical care for their charges and some inadequately, although there are licensing and *some* standards in centers in metropolitan communities. Staff and activities geared to the intellectual, emotional, and social needs of the healthy growing child are often neglected in the nursery. Physical needs and safety are well cared for, generally—but developmental activities and experiences are often lacking. At home, parents are frequently weary and likely to devote little time to compensate for the deprivation.

It is a disturbing experience for many growing children to have their mothers occupied outside the home. Failure of deprived children to fully reach their potential is sometimes referrable to separation from the mother at a time when emotional ties are the mainsprings of psychological growth. Poorly devised substitute family care can become a seed bed for many of the ills of society. It takes careful and wise planning on the part of parents and the community to prevent problems. Community services, on a scale hardly before imagined, need to be developed and continually improved to protect the increasing number of children spending eight to ten hours a day in substitute families or child care centers.

Many changes affecting the family have occurred in the social roles and role expectations of individuals. In a relatively stable society, where social change is gradual, children learn the requirements of the group by imitation and observation. Their tasks tend to be simple and concrete rather than abstract. In America in 1850, when 85 percent of our total population lived in rural areas, and only 5 percent in cities of 100,000 or more, children were valued for their work and productive effort. What a change in the picture approximately 100 years later, when about 60 percent of our total population was living in 168 metropolitan areas.[3]

Few children today have the opportunity to learn industrial skills by working with their parents, and most are rarely regarded an economic asset. Today the variety of activities, roles, and the models from which youth may choose is infinite. But variety of choices and the rapidity of social change have resulted in bewilderment, loss of identity, and role confusion.

Confusion of roles has also resulted for women who today compete with men in industry and the professions and who often find themselves simultaneously in the dual major roles of housewife and employee. More than one-third of the 73,000,000 labor force is composed of women and seven and one-half million of these are mothers with children under eighteen. These include nearly 3 million mothers with children under six. At the turn of the century approximately one-sixth of all workers were gainfully employed females.

Female youth in contemplating the future are often faced with marriage and children and/or a career or suitable occupation. Their lot is made more complex by the fact that although they prepare for work or professions, and employers beckon and compete for their services, they are often censored for accepting employment while rearing their children. Many married women seen by marriage counselors present the mixture of feelings, of wanting employment or a profession and their emoluments while possessing a strong sense of responsibility to remain at home with their families. Furthermore, because of modern advertising and the status symbols of consumers' goods, many families believe they cannot manage without this income.

MENTAL ILLNESS

Perhaps no failure of social functioning in modern life is more pervasive than mental illness. It is estimated that nine million people in the United States today suffer from some form of mental illness serious enough to warrant treatment. It is estimated that one child in ten in grade school will be mentally ill at some time during his life.

In World War II, rejection before induction and discharges from the services for mental illness deprived the armed forces of 2,564,184 young men in the prime of life. Forty percent of our medical disability losses were due to psychiatric disorders—a group large enough in size to make 177 army infantry divisions.

The amount of manpower loss from mental illness in terms of indus-

---

[3] *Children in a Changing World* (Washington, D.C.: U.S. Interdepartmental Committee on Children and Youth, 1960), p. 8.

trial productivity is also staggering. "In terms of industrial productivity, at least one million man-years are lost each year because of mental illness. This is an economic loss of several billion dollars a year in wages, and several hundred million dollars a year in lost federal income taxes." [4] More than 600,000 resident patients were in hospitals for prolonged psychiatric care in 1963.

In 1955 patients in mental hospitals cost the nation more than five and one-half billion dollars before they died or were returned to society. If that illness could have been prevented or cured before hospitalization, "these people could have earned more than sixteen billion over the eight-year hospital span, and they would have paid Federal income taxes totaling several hundred million dollars on these earnings." [5]

Nothing is so disorganizing to the individual or his family as prolonged mental illness. Until very recently, little hope was offered to the mentally ill. They were literally "put away" by members of their families or civil authorities. The help provided for them in institutions has been woefully lacking, and as recently as 1955, Dr. Mesrop A. Tarumianz observed at a Governor's Conference: "Conditions in our state mental hospitals are rotten. For want of a more adequate word, and I do not know that I can find a more adequate word, I can only tell you the state mental hospital system stinks." [6]

Families whose wage earners become mentally ill are frequently deprived of needed income. They often experience repeated frustration by the difficulty or long delay in obtaining help and the many strains resulting from having to live with prolonged and baffling illness.

There are about seventy million adult users of alcoholic beverages. Some take one or two drinks upon two or three occasions throughout the year; others drink daily. Some drink heavily over weekends; and there are five million alcoholics who are unable either to abstain or control their drinking habits. [7]

Unfortunately many alcoholics fail to seek help because of their sense of shame, humiliation, and defeat. They cannot or will not admit that they have a problem, nor will they voluntarily seek help. They feel social disapproval, and well they might; for there is no group more stigmatized. Many state mental institutions refuse to admit alcoholics; and others that do admit them, keep them only long enough to sober and return them to a hostile family and community. Actually, most authorities agree that alcoholism is a disease requiring the attention of medical and social

---

[4] Mike Gorman, *Every Other Bed* (Cleveland: The World Publishing Company, 1956), p. 24.

[5] *Ibid.*, p. 27.

[6] *Ibid.*, p. 28.

[7] Raymond G. McCarthy, "History of Drinking Customs, Social Attitudes, and Controls." *Proceedings of Conference on Education About Alcohol* (Topeka: December, 1960), p. 32.

science. Social workers are helping many men and women with this disruptive problem; but relatively little is done in relation to the need.

CRIME AND DELINQUENCY

The crime rate is one index of the failure of individuals and groups in their social relationships. Crime is rapidly increasing in the United States. In 1961 serious offenses amounted to 1,926,090, an increase of 3 percent over the previous all-time high recorded in 1960, or 63,410 more serious crimes than the previous year. This was 98 percent more crime than in 1950. The crime clock shows four serious crimes every minute. The number of arrests of persons under eighteen years of age has more than doubled since 1950, while the population of youths ten to seventeen has increased by less than one-half. Since 1957 the population increase has been 7 percent; crime is up 34 percent.[8]

In 1958 between one and one-half and two million youngsters were arraigned by the police for misbehavior. More than 600,000 different children came before the juvenile courts for alleged delinquent behavior, including traffic offenses. In the same year about 20 percent of the children arrested were charged with serious offenses—burglary, auto thefts, robbery, aggravated assault, and criminal homicide.[9] From 1948 to 1957 delinquency cases more than doubled while the estimated child population rose only 27 percent.

One out of two cities of 10,000 or more population has no special juvenile police officer. Detention services for children are woefully inadequate. Each year one hundred thousand children are held in jails for adult offenders. Five out of ten counties throughout the United States have no juvenile probation services. Six out of ten juvenile court probation officers have no social work training. Three out of ten state training schools have no staff social workers, while four out of ten have no staff psychologist.[10] The need for trained social workers in the field of corrections is tremendous.

POVERTY AND DEPRIVATION

The Conference on Economic Progress described the U.S. problem of poverty dramatically:[11]

[8] *Uniform Crime Reports—1961* (Washington, D.C.: Federal Bureau of Investigation, U.S. Department of Justice, 1961), pp. 1–5.

[9] *Report to Congress on Juvenile Delinquency* (Washington, D.C.: U.S. Government Printing Office, 1960), p. 3.

[10] *Children in a Changing World, op. cit.*, p. 25.

[11] *Poverty and Deprivation in the U.S.* (Washington D.C.: Conference on Economic Progress, April, 1962), pp. 2–3.

In 1960, more than 77 million Americans, or more than two-fifths of a nation, lived in poverty or deprivation.

In poverty were almost $10\frac{1}{2}$ million multiple-person families with annual incomes under $4,000, and almost 4 million unattached individuals with annual incomes under $2,000—approximately 38 million Americans, or more than one-fifth of a nation.

In deprivation, above poverty but short of minimum requirements for a modestly comfortable level of living, there were almost $10\frac{1}{3}$ million families with incomes from $4,000 to just under $6,000, and more than 2 million unattached individuals with incomes from $2,000 to just under $3,000—more than 39 million Americans, or also more than one-fifth of a nation.

With less than half the income required to place them above poverty, there were almost $3\frac{1}{3}$ million families under $2,000, and about $1\frac{3}{4}$ million unattached individuals under $1,000—more than $12\frac{1}{2}$ million Americans.

Not everyone would agree with the definitions of "poverty" and "deprivation" deduced from the above figures and the conclusion that seventy-seven million Americans can be thus classified. Nevertheless, it is generally recognized that the home often falls short of being a self-contained economic unit and is incapable of providing the total income for its members. This fact is soberly emphasized by public welfare statistics. In March, 1963, public assistance was administered as follows: Old Age Assistance was given to 2,214,000 people; Aid to Families with Dependent Children was extended to 3,990,000 children and adults; Aid to the Blind to 99,000; Aid to the Permanently and Totally Disabled, 446,-000; and there were 1,020,000 recipients of general assistance.[12]

Not all of these individuals were experiencing failure of social functioning; however, poverty and destitution were familiar to many, and few recipients or their families, even with the help of public welfare, enjoyed living conditions which would not be considered substandard.

Because of our traditional values having to do with the family as a self-contained economic unit, many receiving public assistance experience humiliation, embarrassment, and a deep sense of personal failure. Public assistance for the able-bodied is demoralizing and should continue only during such times as it is necessary for the recipient to find other employment or to retrain and relocate him. Others having personal, emotional, and family problems frequently require casework services, medical and psychiatric care, and counseling.

In the United States there are recurrent fluctuations in the economic field. This has meant waste of resources which could have been used for consumption or future growth. It has meant the demoralization of those who could not find jobs. The number of unemployed workers has been placed between 4 and 6 percent of the total labor force except in times of recession and serious depression, as, for example, in 1932, when this number soared to a high of 25 percent of the labor force.

12 *Health, Education, and Welfare Indicators*, U.S. Dept. Health, Education, and Welfare (Washington, D.C.: U.S. Government Printing Office, June, 1963), p. 40.

Prolonged unemployment is a serious threat to the economic security of the nation and frequently results in loss of income, poverty, sickness, and disease. Social workers play a major role in helping persons and families with poverty and other economic problems by referral to income maintenance resources and other services.

SPECIFIC PROBLEMS OF SOCIAL FUNCTIONING

BRAIN DAMAGE

The James [13] case is an example of social dysfunction within a family group and the role distortion resulting from the birth and care of a brain-damaged child. This case also illustrates the not uncommon dilemma faced by a parent who does not know where to turn for help, and later the effective use of community resources.

The James family was having trouble. It was not the dramatic kind that makes newspaper headlines, nor the kind that deeply concerns neighbors and friends. Yet, all members of the family were affected, though they were unable to define their problems, even to themselves.

Mr. and Mrs. James had been married twenty years. The first ten years had been pleasant and satisfying. Two lovely children were born; Mrs. James was a good homemaker and mother. Mr. James received regular promotions in his employment.

Then, their third child, Steven, was born. The joy which they had felt in anticipation of this child turned to worry and concern. The parents were told by the doctor that the brain undoubtedly had suffered some damage during birth, and only time would reveal how severe. Mrs. James was so apprehensive and fearful the baby would suffocate that she devoted herself entirely to his care, kept him by her night and day, and would not permit anyone else to do anything for him. As he grew and gained strength, she still would not leave him, believing only she could give him the attention he needed. At the end of one year he could not walk, or even crawl, and because of his size she felt he was too heavy for anyone else to carry. Each succeeding year brought new problems. Lacking muscular coordination, he was unable to feed himself without spilling; because he could not articulate he made unusual sounds when he tried to talk. Mrs. James preferred not to have others around him because of these difficulties. She grew more and more attached to him, and became increasingly reluctant to ask anyone else to help care for him.

Having been a school teacher before her marriage, Mrs. James felt adequately trained to teach Steven, whose mental development had

[13] All names used in cases in this book are fictitious and enough facts have been altered to protect the identity of persons involved.

not been seriously impaired, when he was old enough. As years went by, he learned to do some things for himself and Mrs. James had more time to devote to the others in the family; yet they all felt that Steven always came first.

The two older children learned early that they had to find solutions to their problems elsewhere. It is true that they often resented Steven, but they overtly accepted the situation. Mr. James felt left out, but hesitated to voice his objections as he did not want to appear selfish and lacking in feeling for his handicapped son. Mrs. James, too, was not satisfied with their lives. She desired to be a more adequate mother and wished she were free to spend more time with her husband. She felt trapped.

Then came the turning point. Mr. James, an assistant manager of his firm, was asked to conduct the United Fund drive within his company. As he studied the publicity sent to him he was amazed to learn of the many services offered by the social agencies represented. He had known, of course, that welfare help was given to the poor and needy, that delinquent children were reported to probation officers working with the courts, and that alcoholics were helped by AA. But he had never thought of seeking help for himself or his family.

He was especially interested in the material about the Family Service Society and was surprised to learn that he could receive and pay for their specialized service.

He called for an appointment and was pleased to find understanding as he discussed his family situation and his personal feelings over the past ten years. Mrs. James also welcomed an opportunity to talk over her problems with the caseworker. She had long wanted to change the situation but honestly believed she had no choice.

In the weeks that followed, the parents learned of the many social agencies and services in their community which could help their son. They were referred to the Crippled Children's Service Society for speech, physical, and occupational therapy. About this time, Steven, too, expressed his dissatisfaction. One day he blurted, "You are my mother, my friend, my playmate, my nurse, and my teacher. Sometimes I get awfully tired of you."

This statement shocked Mrs. James and she earnestly began to reach out for the help which the community offered. Steven welcomed the opportunity to meet new people and to get out to see the world about him. Arrangements were made for him to attend a special class for handicapped children held in the public school, to spend a week at camp, and to attend Sunday School regularly. By use of a special wheel chair he learned to get around the house and to go places by himself.

It became possible for Mrs. James to see the loss to her husband and other children resulting from her extreme preoccupation with Steven;

and with casework help, to loosen her controls. She found more time to spend with her other children, who were in high school, to go out with her husband, and to become a part of community life. Gradually the favorable balance within the home was restored, together with an enhancement of the functioning of the entire family circle.

Oftentimes distortions occur in one's perception of role requirement. Hence, Mrs. James quite sincerely believed that it was her duty to do everything for Steven. She was unaware of the resources for special education, speech therapy, and counseling; and she mistakenly believed that she did not need the kind of help which these services offered. She neglected many importat activities of wife and mother and denied her own emotional and social needs, forgetting the fundamental reciprocal relationship between giving and receiving.

It was with these and other family matters that the social agency to which Mr. James appealed for help addressed itself. In gaining understanding and insight, Mrs. James was particularly helped to realize that Steven needed more freedom than she was giving to him along with the opportunity to develop to his capacity.

Problems are rarely personal in the sense that only one individual is affected. Frequently an entire family is disorganized by a member whose functioning has become impaired. Struggling to maintain its functional integrity in the presence of some breakdown within the group, the family marshals its resources and realigns its forces to cope with the threat to its stability. The James family illustrates the curtailment and redirection of the activities of the family because of Steven's handicaps. The objective of social work in this case was to restore family functioning through the utilization of community resources. The community is not wholly lacking in self-interest in the service it offers, for the health and safety of one, in no small degree affects the welfare of all members of a community.

The culture of a people has a strong element of control over the behavior of the group. Public attitudes, opinions, and beliefs may actually interfere with the helping process. Often these are inconsistent with stated purposes and goals, and can become obstacles to restoration of function.

MENTAL ILLNESS

Mrs. Jane Lyman's illness was greatly exacerbated by the attitude of those who were trying hardest to help her. Improvement in her behavior followed a change in their attitude.

Mrs. Lyman, age 40, had been hospitalized for a period of five years in a state mental institution. At the time she became ill she had been

socially prominent in her community. The daughter of a well-known
family and wife of a prominent industrialist, she found life in a mental hospital to be a radical change in her pattern of living. Mrs. Lyman
had been a successful school teacher, with status in her community,
who had always taken pride in the fact that her family was educated,
influential, had money, and that she could accompany them and her
friends on trips abroad.

When she was hospitalized the change in her living situation was
overwhelming. As soon as she entered the institution the steward had
her remove her jewelry, including her engagement and wedding rings.
Her own clothing was stored away to be kept for her when she returned home. The wardrobe issued by the hospital did nothing to
distinguish her from 999 other patients. She was placed in a ward
behind locked doors with other patients whose behavior was very
strange and even frightening to her at times.

Everything which meant so much to her—family, profession, friends,
and status in the community—was taken from her, including her cher-
ished freedom.

In the months and years which followed, hospital care deepened
her disappointment, her sense of failure, and humiliation. She was not
prepared for shock treatment when it was prescribed, but was simply
"herded along" with the others and pushed, in a straight jacket, up
the ramp to the ward where the treatment was given.

Her husband who had been devoted and was deeply interested in
her welfare, was told at the hospital that there was nothing anyone
could do for Jane and that his visits were not helpful. As was to be
expected, his visits became less and less frequent until he stopped seeing her at all. Loss of contact with her husband was terribly defeating
to Jane. Hope gave way to despair and she became resigned to spending the remainder of her life inside the hospital.

The remarks of a volunteer hairdresser to other employees, Jane
later recalled as painfully humiliating. Because she was silent and
noncommunicative the hairdresser assumed she did not hear when
she talked in patronizing tones, and mistakenly assumed that "Jane
doesn't know what we are saying. She is out of contact."

For Jane, the institutional experience was typical of that which
thousands before her had known in state mental hospitals, under conditions described as "rotten." The "cure" was worse than the disease.
Finally, an aroused citizenry began to make demands for reforms, the
climate of the hospital improved, new programs were instituted, and
the hospital became more therapeutic rather than merely custodial.
Trained, professional personnel were added to the staff. As this change
was taking place Mrs. Lyman was asked to talk to the social worker at
regularly assigned intervals. Gradually she was able to communicate,

whereas before she had been passive and sullen. She discussed the bitterness in her feelings about the care and treatment she had earlier received—loss of contact with her family, being "pushed" into shock, having her clothes and personal effects taken from her—and in doing so freed herself to be more positive and to take a constructive look at her experiences and life. For the first time in years she was encouraged to hope for a recovery and to plan her release. She started to get well and renewed her contacts with family and friends. Finally the day came when she went home.

This case illustrates a change in attitude toward the care of the mentally ill in one hospital. It also points to the role of the professional social worker who, for a period of many months, took an active part in helping Mrs. Lyman to reestablish contact first with reality about her, to instill within her the desire to return to the community, and to reestablish the ability to reach out and find satisfaction in the associations she had all but given up. During the same period interviews with members of her family helped to dissipate their frustrations and anger, create understanding, and to prepare them for Jane's return home.

A PROBLEM FAMILY

Multiple-problem families are known to practically every social work agency or institution. These families frequently have several members whose needs are such as to require help, and whose problems are so varied as to require the use of not one, but several specialized services. In the Hein family, David was in trouble with the law. His brother was a nonreader, and the baby had a congenital heart disorder. The mother had a rheumatic heart condition as well as serious marital difficulties. Mr. Hein, overwhelmed by family pathology, was seeking escape in extramarital affairs.

Services of several agencies were utilized in helping this family: court and probation officer, the church, the school for remedial reading and casework, marriage counseling for the parents, and medical help for Mrs. Hein and the baby. Multiple-problem families often call for the use of more than one community service, and a social worker, with a knowledge of what is available and the skill of a "mobilizer" in the use of referrals, is able to bring together the needs of a burdened family with the provisions of the community to relieve distress and suffering.

David Hein, age 16, had been arraigned by police officers several times for minor offenses, and had always been released to his parents. But when he and two other boys "borrowed" an automobile from a used car lot "just to go for a ride," he was referred to Juvenile Court.

The caseworker assigned to him made a home call and talked with his mother. It was apparent that Mrs. Hein was genuinely concerned with the actions of her eldest son, and had been for some time, but had been at a loss to know where to turn for help. She knew he was associating with the wrong group of boys, and that he had too much free time. He had stopped going to church and spent little time on his schoolwork at home. He had just turned 16, and she hoped he would be able to find an afterschool job now that he was of "working" age. Previous attempts to find work had failed because he was not old enough.

There were other problems, too, within the family, and Mrs. Hein welcomed the opportunity to talk to the caseworker. Her husband had been having an extramarital love affair for several months. Although she had tried to keep this information from the children, Mrs. Hein was certain that David knew of his father's philandering. Her husband's actions were of great concern to her, not only because of her strong desire to have a normal family life for her children, but also because of a deep religious conviction concerning divorce.

Her modest home was neat and clean, and she was attractive, though frail. She told the worker that because of a recurrent attack of rheumatic fever during her last pregnancy, she was in need of heart surgery. This health problem had caused her a great deal of worry, and greatly curtailed her physical activity. It seemed to take all her strength to keep her house clean, clothes washed and ironed, and enough food cooked to satisfy her growing family. She realized that she had neglected her husband, and had not had sufficient energy to give to her family, but it had not been from choice. The baby had a congenital heart condition which would need to be corrected by surgery when he was older.

Even this was not all. Her second son, Paul, was also having trouble. At 11 he was bright enough, but had never learned to read. The policy of the school he attended was to keep him with the children his own age, but the handicap of being unable to read made his performance far from satisfying, either to his teachers or to himself. He was difficult to discipline both at school and at home, he stayed out too late at night, and she was afraid that he, also, would soon be in trouble with the law.

After getting a picture of the whole complex family problem, the caseworker suggested several avenues of help. The father and mother were invited to see a marriage counselor to secure assistance in working out their problems, and to discuss ways of making marriage satisfying to them both again. David was seen regularly by the Juvenile Court worker, and Paul was referred to a social worker at school who arranged for him to have both casework services and remedial reading instruction. Contact was made with the religious leader of the family who was told of their intricate problems. Through his interest, the boys again began participating in church activities, keeping them in contact with their own peer group through organized sports and supervised recreation.

With encouragement from the caseworker the mother arranged for heart surgery for herself. Fortunately the family had adequate medical insurance so that this did not cause a financial hardship. When the baby was old enough, he also had the surgery which he needed.

As the overall family situation improved, tensions were relaxed and the father terminated his outside romance. With a happier home life, more peer group involvement, and casework help, the children gave up their delinquent tendencies, found new interest in church and school activities, and a better family balance was established.

A SCHOOL PROBLEM

A combination of stress at home and in the classroom resulted in a problem for one fifteen-year-old girl. The Norris family was able to use the help of the school social worker and the counselor in effecting improvement in school performance and in the family relationships. The problem was centered mainly in the school and did not call for the marshalling of community services or the work of several agencies. However, there was a premium upon cooperation between the family and the school's personnel services.

Mr. and Mrs. Norris, parents of Julie, age 15, were waiting for the school social worker to come to his office to start the day's work. They were extremely upset over a note which they had found the previous evening from Julie:

> Dear Mom and Dad,
> I am on my way to California. I can't stand it here any longer. No one at school likes me, and Jane has been telling everyone I have been "making out" with the boys. It's a lie but they believe her. I can't go to school any more. Please don't make me come home.
>
> > Julie.

She had cashed a $30 check and boarded a westbound bus the evening before. The parents knew Julie had not been getting along well at school, or at home, but they had thought that fifteen was a "difficult age," and that she would "outgrow it" in a year or two. In school she was receiving grades of "C" and "D" although she had ability to do better work. There was no communication between them. She could not talk to her mother, and her father was busy with his business and away from home much of the time.

The parents had called the police who sent out an alert. Later that day Julie was back home. The parents were relieved, but the incident shocked them into realizing that they needed help.

In a series of interviews with the school social worker the parents were helped to understand Julie's problems and to more effectively communicate this understanding to her. At the same time, arrangements were made for Julie and a younger sister to meet regularly with a school counselor and a group of students for group work help. In this group students were encouraged to discuss their problems. They talked about dating, homework, extracurricular activities, family rules, communication with parents, parental control and responsibility, and other topics which were causing trouble.

Julie's school work improved. It was not long before she was receiving "A" and "B" grades. As the father took more responsibility for helping the girls, and utilized his time with them to better advantage, the relationship within the home improved. The mother was more relaxed with the girls and tried to see things from their point of view. The girls discovered that their mother could be understanding and helpful and began to discuss problems with her. The entire situation improved considerably.

INCOME PROVISIONS AND THE ALCOHOLIC

Public welfare, the backbone of relief in this country, is available to those who can meet eligibility requirements. The accidental death of the parents and failure in the efforts of the grandparents to provide income, forced the Lewis family to seek help from the County Welfare Department. Other services, somewhat similar to those used in the Hein case were also utilized.

The Lewis family was facing disorganization on several fronts. Mr. Lewis was a problem drinker and had lost his employment, resulting in loss of income for the family. Five years earlier they had taken their three grandchildren to rear when the children's parents had been killed in an automobile accident.

The family was brought to the attention of the community when the eldest boy, Richard, who was then age 14, was arraigned by the juvenile authorities for truancy and a series of car prowl thefts. The juvenile court worker, upon making a home call discovered that Mrs. Lewis had no means of subsistence, that the payment on the home was due, and that the power company was threatening to turn off the electricity for nonpayment of the bill. Mr. Lewis had been drinking and was asleep on the living room sofa.

The probation officer referred Mrs. Lewis to the County Welfare

Department. She received an emergency order for food and the Department arranged with the power company to continue service. Arrangements were made for the children to be included in Aid to Dependent Children (ADC) payments. In the next few weeks Mr. Lewis was helped to accept treatment at the Alcoholic Rehabilitation Center, which in his community was operated by the university medical school.

Probation officers continued to work with Richard, and Mrs. Lewis received casework help in addition to a regular ADC check of $137 a month for the three grandchildren, from the County Department of Public Welfare. This met subsistence needs and opened the door toward rehabilitation.

SUMMARY

Role performance and the reciprocal interaction between man and his fellow human beings are the aspects of social functioning which concern social work. Although problems can be challenges to greater effort and achievement, they often contribute to breakdown of social functioning. A major area of disorganization is the home and family. Mental illness, crime and delinquency, poverty, deprivation, and other social problems strike large numbers of individuals and produce family and social breakdown. In general, problems can be classified as personal, family, or community.

Specific problems of social functioning have been illustrated in five cases—a brain-damaged child, a mentally ill woman, a family with multiple problems, a welfare client, and a teen-age girl with problems. The cases illustrate various typical functions of social work: (1) to help people to adjust and make constructive uses of their opportunities and resources; (2) to assist them in using existing services, and, if need be, to help the community develop programs and resources to solve unmet needs; and (3) to aid in prevention of family breakdown and dissemination of social problems.

QUESTIONS FOR DISCUSSION

1. What is your understanding of social functioning?

2. Make a list of personal or family problems which, though they may not altogether impair functioning, nevertheless contain interactional elements of difficulty.

3. Describe the experiences of an acquaintance who has been particularly effective in solving personal or family problems and note the use of services provided by the community.

4. Which of the cases in this chapter best illustrates the provision of community resources?

5. Give examples in the case material of the three casework functions of restoration, provision of services, and prevention.

6. In the case of Mrs. Lyman, what part did ignorance of mental illness and destructive attitudes of people around her play in delaying her recovery?

7. Why is seeking help with a personal or family problem an embarrassing or humiliating experience?

8. In what manner can a brain-damaged child result in an entire household's becoming disorganized?

9. List three social or personal problems with which social work is professionally concerned.

10. Evaluate changes in the function of the family in the last fifty years which have resulted in greater demands on social services and social work.

SPECIAL ACTIVITIES

1. Report on the life of one of the following men or women. List (1) those obstacles which, to the person or to you, appeared particularly formidable to social functioning; and (2) the strengths he or she marshalled in overcoming the obstacles:

> Booker T. Washington
> Helen Keller
> Ludwig van Beethoven
> Clifford Beers

2. Familiarize yourself with the problems of rearing a brain-damaged child. It is suggested that you contact your local association of parents of brain-damaged children, or the mother of such a child. Note problems of physical, mental, and social development in your community and the services, if any, which have been established and are used by parents needing help.

SELECTED REFERENCES

Action for Mental Health, Joint Commission on Mental Illness and Health (New York: Basic Books, Inc., Publishers, 1961).

BOEHM, WERNER W., *Objectives of the Social Work Curriculum of the Future,* Curriculum Study, Vol. I (New York: Council on Social Work Education, 1959).

GOODE, WILLIAM J., *After Divorce* (New York: The Free Press of Glencoe, 1956).

GORMAN, MIKE, *Every Other Bed* (Cleveland: The World Publishing Company, 1956).

GURIN, GERALD, VEROFF, JOSEPH, and FELD, SHEILA, *Americans View Their Mental Health* (New York: Basic Books Inc., Publishers, 1960).

KAHN, ALFRED J., ed., *Issues in American Social Work* (New York: Columbia University Press, 1959).

KEPHART, WILLIAM M., *The Family, Society, and the Individual* (Boston: Houghton Mifflin Company, 1961).

Poverty and Deprivation in the U.S. (Washington, D.C.: Conference on Economic Progress, 1962).

Social Work as Human Relations, Anniversary Papers of the New York School of Social Work and the Community Service Society of New York (New York: Columbia University Press, 1949).

Social Work Yearbook, 1960 (New York: National Association of Social Workers, 1960).

TOWLE, CHARLOTTE, *Common Human Needs,* rev. ed. (New York: National Association of Social Workers, 1957) .

WASHINGTON, BOOKER T., *Up From Slavery* (New York: Doubleday & Company, Inc., 1901).

CHAPTER 3

Evolution of Social Welfare in America

In 1962, for the first time in history, a president of the United States gave a message to Congress devoted solely to public welfare. President Kennedy declared to the 87th Congress: "Our basic public welfare programs were enacted more than a quarter century ago. Their contribution to our national strength and well-being in the intervening years has been remarkable.

"But the times, the conditions, the problems have changed—and the nature and objectives of our public assistance and child welfare programs must be changed, also, if they are to meet our current needs."

President Kennedy, in his statement to Congress, stressed the importance of the family unit and its preservation. He indicated that a united attack needs to be made on the problem of family breakdown; and then continued, "unless such problems are dealt with effectively, they fester and grow, sapping the strength of society as a whole and extending their consequences in troubled families from one generation to the next."

Inhabitants of the United States live in a land of freedom wherein democracy and democratic processes are prevalent. Stress is on the interdependence of men in society and it is generally recognized that the well-being of one person affects the well-being of his neighbors and brothers. The preamble of our Constitution, spelled out by the founding fathers, contains the immortal words, "to promote the general welfare."

The worth of the human personality and the importance of individual adjustment and well-being are significant aspects of the American way of life. The pages of American history, past and present, reflect that in a given society there are disadvantaged persons as well as those who have used their opportunities well. What has been done in the United States in the past to help them? What is being accomplished at present? Social welfare and, recently, social work, have arisen upon the American scene and provide some answers to these questions.

ECHOES OF THE PAST

The beginnings of social welfare were probably coexistent with the beginnings of man and his association with others. It is not difficult to imagine that even in the days of the caveman, neighborliness and helping one another with problems, both personal and family, were part of the daily living pattern. In all probability some of the wiser of these inhabitants had paths beaten to their dwellings by people seeking someone who would listen and help.

In primitive societies numerous kinds of plans and programs have often been in operation for helping people with social problems. Tribal customs and mores have provided for care of the sick, the aged, the deformed, and others who needed to be nurtured and given special attention. There has been a recognizance of the necessity to help one another to promote the welfare of all.

In ancient civilizations various and sundry attempts were made to care for the destitute, the poor, the sick, the unfortunate, and the handicapped. Many of these were handled on a family, neighborhood, or religious basis.

Bossard [1] indicates that social welfare was rooted in the distant past. In ancient China there were refuges for the aged, the sick, and the poor, free schools for poor children, free eating houses for weary laborers, associations for the distribution of secondhand clothing, and even societies for paying expenses of marriage and burial among the poor and destitute. In India, especially after the time of Buddha, considerable activity was related to giving to beggars. A saint with his bowl was one of the traditions of the Orient, and the emphasis in the religious teachings upon the obligation of almsgiving, not only made the holy men of that country a nuisance, but also encouraged imposters. The Greeks had no regular charitable organizations, but they did have institutions for the unfortunate and the sick. Gifts and assistance were publicly distributed at the time of the great festivals by men who were candidates for public office. There were asylums for wounded soldiers and for

[1] James H. S. Bossard, *Social Change and Social Problems,* rev. ed. (New York: Harper & Row, Publishers, 1938), pp. 673–674.

abandoned children; and in Athens a poor tax was levied and collected to help the destitute. The religion of the Hebrews laid great stress upon charity and helping those in need.

Vasey [2] summarizes the beginnings of social welfare activities as follows:

> Helping the distressed is a practice at least as old as civilization. It was general in ancient societies, even though not necessarily on a formal, organized basis. Ancient China had refuges for the aged and for the sick poor, and other provisions for distributing clothing and feeding the unfortunate. Both Greece and Rome had the xenodochia, or buildings for the custody and care of various classes of unfortunates. The act of almsgiving has been recognized by many religions as a duty, and many of them have considered acts of charity to be among the noblest expressions of sacred practices.

In medieval times the Church played a significant role in giving relief and in helping distressed persons. Monks and monasteries provided services to care for the indigent, the lame, the halt, and other unfortunate individuals. Bossard [3] indicates that

> All through the Middle Ages, the church was the one agency which attempted, in an organized way and on a comprehensive scale, to minister to the wants of the great mass of the needy. The monasteries became particularly important as charitable centers, distributing food and alms from the gate, and serving as refuges for pilgrims, soldiers, beggars and other wayfarers. The church, too, was active in the development of institutional facilities, such as the xenodochia, where miscellaneous groups of the needy were housed; hospitals devoted to the care of the sick; and institutions for foundlings, and orphaned and deserted children. All varieties of human need were recognized and, as time went on, orders of monks and nuns were instituted to specialize in their care.

Across the centuries there has been a shift from individualism to collectivism in helping those in need. Mutual aid has come to the fore particularly as populations have increased and moved into concentrated areas, and there has been additional need for societal programs to aid the disadvantaged.

EUROPEAN ROOTS

The roots of social welfare, and in a general sense of social work, reach a long way into the past. However, several significant developments in Europe have been particularly important in setting the stage and patterns for development of social welfare and social work in the United States. In 1536 a law was passed in England which provided that alms collected by local authorities and by churches on Sundays were to help to relieve the sick and the poor. This act, which is often

---

2 Wayne Vasey, *Government and Social Welfare* (New York: Holt, Rinehart & Winston, Inc., 1958), p. 24.

3 Bossard, *op. cit.*, pp. 675–676.

regarded as the beginning of the English poor law system, superseded the merely repressive measures of earlier legislation in an attempt to work out specific and definite provisions for relief. To deter people from openly begging, the law stipulated that "the mayor of every town and the Church wardens of every parish were to collect alms every Sunday, holiday or festival in common boxes," which were then to be utilized by those in need. Accounts were to be kept of the money collected and dispersed. The income was to be allocated so that poor, sick, impotent, and diseased persons, not able to work, might be helped and relieved. This law marked the shift in poor relief from an ecclesiastical to a secular system. The act had several significant provisions, including the illegality of begging, responsibility of society to help, assistance by and through the local community, and voluntary alms, with clerical assistance, but under the direction of the state.[4]

In 1572 overseers of the poor were appointed as civil officers. The Parliamentary enactment at this time provided for a direct public tax for the purpose of assisting the poor and destitute.

During the reign of Queen Elizabeth several laws were enacted which have been designated as the Elizabethan Poor Laws. Toward the close of the sixteenth century a civic sense of responsibility on a nationwide basis had developed in England. An act was passed in 1598 and revised in 1601 which provided a systematic plan for helping the poor and which established a system of public responsibility implemented through local care. The main provisions of the law remained in operation basically until 1834, and have played important roles in the development of social welfare in Europe, in the United States, and elsewhere. The act of 1601 established legislation which differentiated three classes of the poor: the able-bodied poor, who were to be provided with work, or with punishment in prison or the stocks if they refused to work; the impotent poor, who were to be kept in almshouses; and dependent children who were to be apprenticed unless parents or grandparents could support them. For the dependent children group, the boys were to be apprenticed until they were twenty-four years old and the girls until they were either twenty-one or married. Moneys to finance these laws were provided by taxes levied on lands, houses, and tithes, from money left for charitable purposes, and from fines levied for the breaking of certain laws. To carry out the administration of the system, the justice of the peace appointed civil officers in each parish, although nominations for these positions were made at a meeting of the parish church.

Many other laws have been passed in England and on the Continent to help the poor, and to provide other services for children, families, and individuals in trouble. The industrial revolution of the eighteenth

4 *Ibid.*, p. 678.

century, accompanied by urbanization, slums, and anonymity in living brought numerous situations which resulted in many persons with problems which called for help. Begging, almsgiving, charity, workhouses, orphanages, insane asylums, and jails became part of the culture of the times. Attempts to help people in a dignified manner were instigated and various programs, both public and private, came into existence.

The Elizabethan poor laws provided the basis for public social welfare in England with only minor changes until the Poor Law of 1834 was passed. This act provided for centralized administration with a pattern of uniformity throughout the country. It established a central authority consisting of three Poor Law Commissioners who were given regulatory powers over the local authorities. They could divide the country into districts, which were called Poor Law Unions, to replace the parishes as units of administration. Each unit was a district with an elective board of Guardians with salaried officers who were responsible for the administration of relief. The law also stipulated that the Guardians of each district were authorized to build or provide at least one workhouse, and all relief to able-bodied persons outside the workhouse was abolished.

In England in the 1860's, there was a considerable increase in the number of applicants for aid which focused attention on welfare and helping the poor. As a result there was revived concern in social reform and some individuals became interested in bringing about innovations and change. Such persons as Octavia Hill and Edward Denison pioneered in social welfare at this time. As a result of their efforts and those of others, a new type of social work organization emerged. In 1869 the "London Society for Organizing Charitable Relief and Repressing Mendicancy" was established and has generally been referred to as the London Charity Organization Society. The name of the new organization is descriptive of its purpose—the organization of relief rather than its creation or multiplication. As Bossard [5] reported, it proposed, in other words:

(1) the coordination of the work of the various charitable societies in London so as to prevent duplication; (2) an acquaintance by each of the work of other agencies; (3) a bureau of registry for all cases; (4) personal service to promote independence of spirit rather than the giving of material aid; and (5) a devotion to measures for the prevention of pauperism.

BEGINNINGS IN THE UNITED STATES

No attempt is made here to give a complete historical coverage of social welfare developments in the United States. Nevertheless, some highlights and examples of such developments are useful.

[5] *Ibid.*, p. 697.

In colonial days in America the basic pattern for assisting the poor and unfortunate followed the poor laws and activities of the mother country. Town and local governments provided services somewhat similar to those which had been instigated in the homeland. "Outdoor relief" was administered to the poor in their own homes initially. Placement or boarding out of dependents was also utilized both for children and adults. Almshouses were established as a means of "indoor relief." Extreme examples of the "farming out" procedure involved public auctions where orphans, neglected children, or disabled individuals were passed on to those who were willing to support them at the lowest cost to the community. The first almshouse for the care of the poor and indigent was established in Massachusetts in 1662. In 1685 it began to function both as an almshouse for the disabled and as a workhouse for the able-bodied poor. Another indication of community interest in providing services for the poor and needy was the establishment in 1644 of the Boston Latin School, which was supported in part by a land grant from that town. This was the beginning of free or charity schools in this country, and was the foundation underpinning free public education which developed decades later. In 1691, in Boston, the town leaders appointed the first "overseers of the poor" which was an initiatory step toward governmental centralization in the care of the destitute.

Lurie [6] states that before the establishment of the United States, the foundation of a comprehensive system of welfare services was in operation which included:

outdoor relief, almshouses, orphanages, hospitals, workhouses, prisons, and houses of correction. It was customary for the town government to assume basic welfare and economic responsibilities. For example, "When through rising prices due to grain shortages bread riots broke out in Boston in 1713, the Selectmen made regular purchases of grain which they sold during winter months below market price."

At the same time in the programs of public aid there was little distinction between the problems of dependency due to physical and mental disabilities and the poverty of the working population inherent in economic factors. Anyone who was in need of help for a shorter or longer period was a pauper irrespective of the reasons. For a long time the lack of a clear distinction between poverty and dependency was to confuse the development of social welfare programs.

Beginnings in the child welfare movement go back many years. In 1729 in New Orleans an institution was established by the Ursuline Sisters for children of parents massacred by Indians. In 1790 an orphanage was begun in Charleston, South Carolina, for children who had no living parents. By 1817 a school for the education of the "deaf and dumb" was in operation in Connecticut.

6 Harry L. Lurie, "The Development of Social Welfare Programs," *Social Work Yearbook, 1960* (New York: National Association of Social Workers, 1960), p. 22.

In early nineteenth century America people who were mentally ill were treated harshly, inhumanly, and often regarded as persons who had no sense of feeling either mentally or physically. In March, 1841, the famous Dorothea Lynde Dix by chance visited the East Cambridge jail and was shocked at the deplorable treatment of the insane inmates. She visited other jails and almshouses throughout the state and found all kinds of brutalities being practiced within them. On the basis of these experiences, she devoted the rest of her life to improving services for those who were mentally ill. She gave speeches, wrote letters, and contacted community and political leaders and others at home and abroad. As a result of her relentless campaign many state hospitals for the insane were established or enlarged and great improvements in treatment in poorhouses and jails took place. Through her activities and those of other dedicated leaders, the treatment of the mentally ill has shifted so that now they are more respected as other persons who are ill, and attempts are made to treat them and return them to their families and to society as quickly as possible. Today social work plays a major role in this rehabilitative service.

Likewise, in the area of the treatment of the juvenile delinquent and the criminal, the pages of history show significant developments related to social welfare and social work. In the latter part of the eighteenth century, in the very shadows of Independence Hall in Philadelphia, a new system of prison discipline, called the Pennsylvania System, was established. This innovation provided for individualized attention and treatment of prisoners accompanied by housing in separate cells. Prior to this time inmates were held in congregate rooms, sometimes twenty or thirty or even forty of them, day in and day out, often both men and women confined together. The new philosophy and practice was an attempt to treat and rehabilitate rather than merely to punish or seek retribution.

With the depression of 1873, after the Civil War in the United States, came chaos and many personal, family, and community problems. The Charity Organization movement in America was started, patterned in the main after European innovations. Across the decades this movement has resulted in the establishment of numerous private agencies and community welfare councils in most of the large population centers of this country. These councils, increasingly staffed by competent social workers, attempt to understand community needs, involve community leaders in studying these needs, make plans regarding them, and bring these plans to fruition.

The first Charity Organization Society in the United States was established in Buffalo in 1877. The coordinating function of this type of agency was urgent because of the numerous independent welfare agencies which were springing up and mushrooming in the population centers. In 1909 in Pittsburg and Milwaukee the first Community Welfare Councils—called Councils of Social Agencies—were established. These have grown and developed so that today one such council in a large metropolitan area has thirteen full-time persons working in research—collecting and interpreting information pertinent to community needs, problems, and solutions.

The charity organization movement in the United States was a significant one because it provided for private agencies which were interested in finding ways and means of organizing help to the poor through individualized services. These services included investigation of need, a registration bureau for charitable agencies for clearance to avoid duplication, friendly visiting, and other related activities.

Lurie indicates there were two types of agencies: those which were relief agencies and which raised funds for this purpose; and those which gave no relief but helped mainly with organization and coordination. Both types made efforts to find work for the unemployed and to solicit assistance from friends, relatives, churches, employers, or other sources. At first the workers were principally volunteers, but were later supplemented by salaried persons representing the society or agency. "The poor, it was believed, needed friendly guidance; they needed spiritual help, as well as material assistance." [7]

Closely allied to the Community Welfare Council movement has been the one for Federated Drives, collecting money for several agencies at one time. Historically the first such drive took place in Liverpool, England, in 1873, and the original one in the United States occurred in 1887, spearheaded by the Associated Charities in Denver. The latter involved twenty-three agencies which joined together and raised a total of $20,000. After World War I federated drives in this country were organized under the name of the Community Chest. By 1950 more than fourteen hundred such organizations existed in this country. In the last decade the trend has been toward establishment of United Fund agencies which have been organized on a broader base than Community Chests, the aim being to bring together as many of the local and national health and welfare agencies as possible in the collecting of funds.

Another significant development in social services in America has been that of the social settlement house. The first American settlement was organized in New York City in 1886; and three years later the most famous one, Hull House, was established by Jane Addams in Chicago. Similar neighborhood centers were instigated in many of the large cities in this country. Today these centers play a significant role in providing for the recreational, health, and welfare needs of boys and girls, youth, men, and women, particularly in deprived areas. They are also being used by the total citizenry, including the middle and upper classes, as

7 *Ibid.*, p. 29.

centers for providing social experiences, for taking care of recreational needs, and for solving personality problems.

There have been several pioneers in this country in social welfare. Many of these people have come from the upper classes and many have devoted their lives to helping disadvantaged people.

Social welfare services have developed so that today they reach out to practically every personal, family, and community need. As a result, research in welfare is being sponsored as never before.

PUBLIC ASSISTANCE AND WELFARE EMERGE

Almost from the beginning of the colonization of America there have been various attempts to provide governmental assistance to the poor and needy. For example, following the patterns of the Dutch, and later the English, New York City had a city physician for the poor as early as 1687.[8] Various other programs were established by towns and local communities in colonial America to provide for those who required different services.

Later laws were passed in states of the Union helping to provide financial and other services for the indigent, poor, destitute, and those with personal and family problems.

On the federal level the monumental Social Security Act of 1935 altered the total plan of helping persons in need. For the first time the federal government assumed a major role and responsibility in assisting the needy. The major provisions of the original act are summarized as follows:

1. A National old-age insurance system (OASDI), to be supported through taxes on payrolls, equally shared by the employers and employees. The survivorship provision was instituted in 1939, and at present nine out of ten gainfully employed workers in the U.S. belong to this system.

2. A federal-state unemployment insurance system, to be financed by a federal tax on payrolls. Liberal provisions were offered which encouraged the states to become partners in this system, and all states adopted unemployment acts soon after the law was passed.

3. Grants-in-aid to the states for old-age assistance, aid to families of dependent children, and aid to the blind.

4. Services for aiding maternal and child health, crippled children, child welfare, vocational rehabilitation, and public health measures.

Through increased federal services, children, families, and adults have been aided in many ways. Indicative of this situation, according to

[8] Leona Baumgartner and James R. Dumpson, "Health in Welfare: A Joint or a Divided Responsibility," *Public Welfare*, Vol. 20 (July, 1962), p. 155.

Oettinger, is the fact that on a single representative day in 1960, 361,000 children were receiving child welfare services from public child welfare agencies, which was one-third more than the number receiving service on a comparable day in 1950. This was a rise roughly comparable to the rise in child population during the decade.[9]

Reports from states to the Bureau of Family Services showed that 930,000 families with 2,811,400 children received aid to families with dependent children (AFDC) payments in July, 1962. There were 54,000, or 1.5 percent fewer recipients that month than in June. Medical assistance for the aged (MAA), the newest of the federal-state assistance programs, showed increases in numbers of recipients in both months. The gain in July was 1,300 recipients, or 1.2 percent. This brought the total of medically needy persons age 65 and over receiving MAA to 102,900. The August figures for recipients in other federally aided assistance programs were: old-age assistance, 2,228,400; aid to the blind, 100,000; and aid to the permanently and totally disabled, 420,500. In all, these five assistance programs reached 6,493,600 persons in August, 1962, with payments totaling $339,362,000.[10]

Major significant changes were made in social security legislation in the enactment of Public Welfare Amendments of 1962—Public Law 87–543. "Here for the first time the importance of preventive, protective, and rehabilitative services in public welfare was significantly recognized by providing a formula under which 75 per cent of the costs of such services would be met from federal funds. Here, for the first time since the Lanham funds of World War II, federal matching monies were authorized for day care."[11]

The provisions of this act[12] are numerous, including services for improvement in public welfare to prevent or reduce delinquency; improvement in administration through demonstrations, training, and public advisory groups; improvement of public welfare programs through extension of temporary provisions and increase in the federal share of public assistance programs; simplification of categories—optional combined state plans for the aged, blind, and disabled; and miscellaneous and technical amendments.

This bill provided that, effective September 1, 1962, federal matching in certain services and for the cost of staff training is increased from 50 percent to 75 percent. Effective July 1, 1963, a state that does not provide for the prescribed minimum self-care of self-support services

9 Katherine Oettinger, "Public Child Welfare Manpower Needs," *Public Welfare,* Vol. 20 (July, 1962), p. 151.

10 "News Release," Health, Education, and Welfare Department, Social Security Administration, Bureau of Family Services, Washington 25, D.C. (October 20, 1962).

11 *NASW News,* Vol. 8 (November, 1962), p. 3.

12 Wilbur J. Cohen and Robert M. Ball, "The Public Welfare Amendments of 1962," *Public Welfare,* Vol. 20 (October, 1962), pp. 191–197.

will receive federal matching on only a 50–50 basis for the cost of all services, training, and other administrative costs.

To further improve and coordinate services to children, another provision for a state plan is added to the requirements for the dependent children program, effective July 1, 1963. Each state plan must provide for the development of a welfare and related services program for each child recipient as may be necessary because of the home conditions and the special needs of each child.

The new law changes the name of Title IV to "Grants to States for Aid and Services to Needy Families with Children." The emphasis is to stress rehabilitation and related services. The law provides for coordination in community services and for an increase in training programs.

Another provision authorizes the state agency to provide counseling and guidance to the child's guardian in the use of the payment and the management of other funds. This is in order to insure that the child receives the money and other items which he requires. Aid also may be provided for both parents of a dependent child.

The secretary of the Department of Health, Education, and Welfare is directed by the law to appoint an Advisory Council in Public Welfare in 1964 to review the administration of public assistance and child welfare services and to make recommendations for improvement. This is to be a twelve-man council and to be representative of employers and employees, including representatives of state and federal agencies, of nonprofit social welfare organizations, together with other persons with special qualifications and members of the public. The findings of this Council are to be reported not later than July, 1966. Other provisions provide for a waiver of state plan requirements for demonstration projects and for an increase in adequately trained welfare personnel.

Improvement of public welfare programs is to be accomplished through extension of aid with respect to dependent children of unemployed parents or those in foster family homes, through increase of the federal share of public assistance payments, through extension of assistance to repatriated American citizens, and through federal payments for foster care in child care institutions. Increases are provided in payments to Puerto Rico, the Virgin Islands, and Guam and provision is made for payments to a relative of a child when the child is dependent. Income and resources are to be disregarded in determining the need of the individual for aid to the blind. Extension of child welfare services is provided along with day care services. Provisions are also made for authorized grants for training personnel in the field of child welfare.

As President Kennedy said when he signed the measure on July 25, "This measure embodies a new approach—stressing services in addition to support, rehabilitation instead of relief, and training for useful work instead of prolonged dependency. This important legislation will assist our States and local public welfare agencies to redirect the incentives and services they offer to needy families and children and to aged and disabled people. Our objective is to prevent or reduce dependency and to encourage self-care and self-support—to maintain family life where it is adequate and to restore it where it is deficient." [13]

The importance of public welfare was emphasized with the appointment of Dr. Ellen Winston of Raleigh, North Carolina, in January, 1963, as the first United States Commissioner of the newly-established Welfare Administration. She assumed the direction of Federal programs relating to child health and welfare, to needy families, and to the aging. In this new high-ranking position she becomes responsible for five major units in the Department of Health, Education, and Welfare:

1. The Bureau of Family Services, which administers the Federal grants-in-aid for public assistance to the States.

2. The Children's Bureau, which is responsible for investigating and reporting on all matters pertaining to the welfare of children.

3. The Office of Aging, which is responsible for coordinating and stimulating programs on aging.

4. The Cuban Refugee Program, which provides assistance to refugees from Cuba in the United States.

5. The Office of Juvenile Delinquency and Youth Development, which administers demonstration projects and training grants under the Juvenile Delinquency and Youth Offenses Control Act of 1961.

SERVICES OF VOLUNTEERS

Across the years many dedicated and interested persons have provided their time and money to help people in need. They have done this as individuals or as families rather than as citizens in a city, state, or federal community. These services have increased so that today thousands of volunteers are assisting in social welfare services in almost every kind of setting that could be mentioned.

Examples of current volunteer services include the following:

Twenty-five members of a Junior League in a middle-sized city spend one half day a week in assisting with activities in the local Mental Health Clinic. They provide their own cars and transport clients to and from the clinic. They "care" for the children in the waiting rooms and also spend time with some of the clients, on a friendship basis, helping them with routine problems and decisions. Their contributions to the overall services of the Clinic are considerable.

The Medical Wives Auxiliary in Jonestown invites its members to

[13] Wilbur J. Cohen, "The New Public Welfare Legislation," *News Release,* U. S. Health, Education, and Welfare Department (September 24, 1962).

spend half a day at one of the local hospitals performing a variety of kinds of tasks which facilitate total services. They work on telephone switchboards, care for children, and perform multitudinous other helpful services.

Volunteers from churches and religious groups minister to the sick, the poor, the destitute, and unfortunate in numerous ways. They cooperate with the professional disciplines to bring total, effective services.

SOCIAL WORKERS APPEAR

In the eighteenth and nineteenth centuries, with industrialization, greater mobility, and the increase in population and the accompanying social problems, it became apparent that both public and private social services needed to be increased if the problems and needs of the public were to be met.

Social welfare has developed slowly over several centuries. It is only within the past few decades, however, that social work has entered the scene as a major aspect of social welfare. In the latter part of the nineteenth century humanitarians and other dedicated persons, especially women, devoted their time and talents to helping the underprivileged, and began to lay the groundwork for the development of social work as a profession. In 1898 education for social work was initiated in a summer training course given by the Charity Organization Society of New York. This was a beginning impetus toward providing trained social workers. This course developed into a one-year program in 1904 within the New York School of Philanthropy. Other schools of social work developed and before long many men and women were calling themselves *social workers*. These were people who had obtained special training and experience to help people to help themselves. By 1921 the American Association of Social Workers was established, the first major professional social work body. In 1955 the National Association of Social Workers was created based on the amalgamation of seven smaller specialized social work associations. This professional body has grown in stature and in number so that it now enrolls more than 39,000.

Social workers today are employed in every kind of setting of social welfare. They are given, ordinarily, the more difficult tasks to perform and tend to gravitate to the administrative and supervisory positions. They are also used as consultants in helping to guide the work and activities of less trained social welfare aides and associates. Numerous county and state welfare departments now have many on their staffs who have received the Master of Social Work Degree, and the work being accomplished in these agencies is taking on a professional demeanor that was unknown in the past.

SUMMARY

The American way of life with its democratic emphasis has been conducive to the initiation and development of social welfare services. The pages of history reflect that, almost from the beginning of the colonization of this country, humanitarian men and women, both in public and private agencies and situations, have been interested in establishing and supporting services and activities to help distressed and unfortunate individuals and families.

The roots of social welfare in America had their beginnings in Europe, particularly related to the Elizabethan Poor Laws of England. Towns and local communities assumed responsibilities for aiding the unfortunate and disadvantaged.

Most of the other beginnings in social welfare were private in nature and involved philanthropic programs and activities. Gradually, civic-minded individuals and leaders proposed welfare programs financed by the tax dollar. Various state programs were started.

In 1935 the famous Social Security Act was passed in the United States, revolutionizing the total social welfare scene. The Act provided public assistance, social insurance, unemployment insurance, aid to dependent children, aid to the blind, and other special services.

In 1962 major modifications were made in the Social Security Act. These provide for additional federal participation, for liberalization of grants, and for safeguarding the rights of children and families. They also place considerably greater emphasis upon rehabilitation and preventive social welfare. The aim is not only to provide relief but to understand the causes of the problems and to remove them. The modern goal is to break the cycle of dependency and to assist the problems in melting away.

A major step in the development of social welfare has been the rapid rise of the profession of social work. Since the turn of the twentieth century the number of trained social workers has increased rapidly, and in the last decade the growth has been almost phenomenal. Social work now has a unified professional body, the National Association of Social Workers, and has a national educational body for setting standards, the Council on Social Work Education.

QUESTIONS FOR DISCUSSION

1. How does social welfare fit into the scheme of a democratic country and government?

2. Why do you think social welfare has developed so rapidly in the United States during the past three decades?

3. Trace the roots of social welfare in this country which had their beginnings in Europe.

4. Evaluate the provisions of the Elizabethan Poor Laws.

5. Compare and contrast the functions and effectiveness of private and public welfare programs.

6. What is the significance of increased appropriations for research regarding social welfare programs in the United States?

7. Describe the main provisions of the Social Security Act of 1935 and also of the 1962 amendments.

8. In the evolution of social welfare, where does social work appear and what part does it play today?

SPECIAL ACTIVITIES

1. Interview a professionally trained social worker who is in practice and report to the class your impressions of the social work profession.

2. Do a library study of the Elizabethan Poor Laws and give an oral report to the class on your findings.

3. Talk to some of the "old timers" in your community and prepare a report on early developments of social welfare services in your area.

SELECTED REFERENCES

ABBOTT, EDITH, *Some American Pioneers in Social Welfare* (Chicago: University of Chicago Press, 1937).

BURNS, EVELINE M., *The American Social Security System* (Boston: Houghton Mifflin Company, 1951).

BURNS, EVELINE M., *Social Security and Public Policy* (New York: McGraw-Hill Book Co., Inc., 1956).

COHEN, WILBUR J., and BALL, ROBERT M., "The Public Welfare Amendments of 1962," *Public Welfare,* Vol. 20 (October, 1962), pp. 191–198, 227–233.

QUEEN, STUART A., *Social Work in the Light of History* (Philadelphia: J. B. Lippincott Co., 1922).

TAYLOR, HASSELTINE BYRD, "The Nature of the Right to Public Assistance," *The Social Service Review,* Vol. 36 (September, 1962), pp. 265–267.

VASEY, WAYNE, *Government and Social Welfare* (New York: Holt, Rinehart & Winston, Inc., 1958).

WEISSMAN, IRVING, *Social Welfare Policy and Services in Social Work Education,* Curriculum Study, Vol. XII (New York: Council on Social Work Education, 1959).

WOODROOFE, KATHLEEN, *From Charity to Social Work* (Toronto: University of Toronto Press, 1962).

part II

Social Work Services

CHAPTER 4

Psychiatric Social Work

A fourteen-year-old boy, perspiring freely, clutched his mother's arm nervously intuiting her dread and sharing her fear of the moment when they would be separated while he talked to the psychiatrist and she would go for an interview with the social worker at the child guidance clinic.

A young wife, unable to tolerate the growing strain resulting from her husband's habit of staring blankly into space, his long periods of silence, and preference for being alone, listened eagerly as the social worker at the Veterans Administration hospital answered her questions about hospitalization and explained what she might do to assist with the medical and psychiatric care her husband needed to help him recover from his illness.

Seated around a table were three social workers, a psychologist, a psychiatrist, and a psychiatric nurse in a case conference at the community mental health center. They were about to formulate a treatment plan, based on diagnostic material each had presented, for an eleven-year-old boy who, two weeks earlier, had been referred from the school following an outburst of symptomatic behavior.

Attention is drawn in the above examples to three kinds of agencies in which psychiatric social workers function. The first is a child guidance clinic; the second a mental hospital; and the third a community mental health center. Social work has been established in psychiatric divisions of general medical and surgical hospitals, mental hospitals, psychiatric clinics for adults and children, residential treatment centers, and special schools for mentally handicapped children. In some areas throughout the United States, traveling clinics provide mental health services to rural populations, and have developed programs of mental health which include direct services to the mentally ill, community planning, training, consultation, and other activities that result in the creation, improvement, and expansion of facilities which prevent mental illness. Social workers who are involved in these kinds of activities work with individuals, groups, coordinate community activities, serve in consultant roles, and teach other social workers.

Who is the psychiatric social worker? Schools of social work educate and train men and women of high caliber for the general field of social work practice. The curriculum is *generic* with concentrations in the methods of casework, group work, and community organization. How, then, do graduates become psychiatric social workers?

In the first place, although the training for psychiatric social work is generic, it is customary for some schools to offer a *focus* seminar to students who express an interest in psychiatric social work, and, generally, psychiatric clinics or hospitals are used for their field work practice experience. The research—study, thesis, or project—is also focused upon the area of student interest.

Upon completing two years of graduate work leading to the Master's degree, the student further *specializes* when he accepts employment in a psychiatric facility, doing the work of the psychiatric social worker under qualified supervision which, for certification, must cover a two-year period and provide repeated and specific application of broad generic concepts and principles. He further rounds and deepens his knowledge of pathology and clinic entities and, through repeated experiences, learns how to function as a member of an interdisciplinary team. He becomes knowledgeable about the special problems of the mentally ill, their families, the attitude of the community toward the mentally ill, the culture of the hospital or clinic, commitment procedures, admission and intake policies, programming, and collaboration.

After being awarded the Master's degree and completing two years of supervised practice, the candidate becomes eligible for full membership in the National Association of Social Workers and certification. Members are no longer certified for sections or fields of practice.

One definition of psychiatric social work emphasizes the qualitative nature of practice regardless of the setting. Under this definition, psychiatric social work is a practice possessing qualities deriving from knowledge of psychiatric concepts and from the ability to adapt them to the social work process. The prefix *psychiatric* has been interpreted by some social workers to mean greater depth in knowledge of psychopathology and *dynamic* quality of practice.

The position of the Psychiatric Social Work Section of the National Association of Social Workers (NASW) is that the word *psychiatric* refers only to the setting where the social work is practiced rather than to any quality in the practice of social work.[1]

Psychiatric social work has been defined as "social work practiced in direct and responsible working relations with psychiatry. Psychiatric social work practice occurs in hospitals, clinics, or under other psychiatric auspices, the essential purpose of which is to serve people with mental or emotional disturbances." [2]

Education today for social work is largely generic and the curriculum for all matriculants consists of knowledge, techniques, methods, and attitudes. Early in the development of social work the curriculum offered courses in psychiatry and required special seminars for students wanting *psychiatric* social work. More recently the special seminars have been eliminated or made elective in many schools and psychiatric content is an integrated and required subject for all students.

Competence in psychiatric social work is based on graduate level training leading to the Master's degree and consisting of two years of graduate class and field instruction and research. Instruction includes knowledge of people derived from social work practice and from findings in the social sciences, medicine, economics, and law. Knowledge of social institutions forms a part of the base from which modern social work derives. In addition, the preparation includes knowledge of values, ethics, of techniques, and skills in working with people as individuals, in groups, and in various social situations.

BEGINNINGS IN PSYCHIATRIC SOCIAL WORK

Important changes had to be made in public opinion concerning the mentally ill to prepare the way for social work in the modern era. Exorcising, a barbaric and medieval method of treatment, made sense to those who believed that the mentally ill were possessed by demons, as did some means of cleansing and propitiation to those who saw sin as the cause of the malady. Such methods of treatment seem absurd now in the light of physical, psychological, and social theories of causation. Nevertheless, it makes interesting speculation to contemplate how social work, or any other professional discipline, would relate to these outdated theories of causation removed completely as they are from present understanding. Needless to say, such ignorance blocked all ameliorative effort. It was further assumed that once a person became mentally ill, he would always be mentally ill, a belief that persisted until early in the nineteenth century.

[1] "What is 'Psychiatric' Social Work?" *Canada's Mental Health*, Vol. 10 (October, 1962), p. 21.

[2] *Education for Psychiatric Social Work* (New York: American Association of Psychiatric Social Workers, 1950), p. 11.

Early attempts at care were crude and inhuman. The mentally ill were housed in overcrowded insane asylums, in almshouses with criminals and degenerates, and not infrequently, in jails and prisons. Bloodletting was one of the regular treatments along with starvation, blistering, purging, surprise baths, and whippings. For a small fee, curious visitors to insane asylums were entertained by "baiting" the madman.

As care became more humane and as leaders took initiative to improve the conditions of the care for the mentally ill, humanitarians realized that something could be done to relieve the suffering and distress of these forgotten castoffs. Dorothea Lynde Dix, an outstanding crusader, worked untiringly to awaken public opinion to the suffering and the needs of the mentally ill; and many others have pioneered in the mental health movement.

Kraepelin, Freud, Meyer, Sullivan, to name a few tireless workers, began to penetrate the causes of mental illness. Study, diagnostic, and treatment programs began to supplant antiquated practices, until today in many parts of the world much is being accomplished for the mentally ill. Causation is much better understood. Hope has pushed despair into the background; and it is believed by some that mental illness may actually be conquered.

Both facts and theory are used to explain mental illness, and it is reliably understood that many causal agents and etiological factors exist. Some of these are organic and include disease, trauma to the central nervous system, atrophy of the brain, and toxicity.

Mental illness, in numerous instances, appears to be rooted in such social institutions as the family, and, generally has an impact upon many others. It has been observed that parents often adversely influence their children, are in turn influenced by them and each other, that the community is often responsible for conditions leading to mental illness and is in turn weakened by it. With this understanding, the stage has been set to employ in the treatment of the mentally ill, individuals who work with families and with the community in getting at the source of the difficulty for purposes of prevention and treatment.

The first social workers were considered "handmaidens" to psychiatry. Jessie Taft, presenting the characteristics of the psychiatric social worker at a conference in 1919, typified the attitude at that time:

The born psychiatric social worker, as I see her has to be a maternal sort of person even if she is only twenty. She has to have genuine liking for people and their troubles. It won't do for her to be at bottom cynical, carping or critical. She needs a warmth and spontaneity and a whole-hearted interest that renders the making of good contacts simple, natural and inevitable.[3]

[3] *Proceedings of the National Conference of Social Work* (Chicago: National Conference of Social Work, 1920), p. 599.

The first psychiatric social workers were ancillary to medicine. They took histories for the psychiatrists and had very little autonomy, in contrast to their coordinate status as members of psychiatric teams in hospitals and clinics today. The social worker in the psychiatric setting is now more often a man. In 1932 the number of students who completed training in social work in Canada and in the United States was only 166, and 6 percent of these were men. The number completing training in 1962 by contrast was 2,476, nearly half of whom were men.

In the United States the first social workers in the mental health field worked in hospitals. Social work became a service at the Manhattan State Hospital in New York in 1906, and in the Boston Psychopathic Hospital in 1910. Smith College developed special training for psychiatric social workers in 1918, and this was followed by a similar program established in the New York School of Social Work in 1919.

In 1919, after the close of the First World War, the Surgeon General asked the American Red Cross to establish social work in the federal hospitals. The Red Cross assumed this responsibility and by January, 1920, social service departments had been organized in forty-two hospitals. The Red Cross continued this program until 1925 when the United States Veterans Bureau made social work a part of the medical service in veterans' hospitals.

The Child Guidance Movement, with its beginnings in the work done with juvenile delinquents by Dr. William Healy, was also an important step in psychiatric social work. A few child guidance clinics had been established before 1922 but this movement made its greatest advance after that time when, under the support of the Commonwealth Fund, demonstration clinics were established in Norfolk and St. Louis. In the next twenty years social work expanded rapidly in mental health activities, and although the hospitals were the first to make use of social work, the practice in clinics expanded more fully. Approximately 30 percent of social workers in the mental health field in 1932 were in hospitals. This percentage has increased since 1940, but the lack of trained workers for hospitals remains a problem.

World War II dramatically brought to the nation's attention the need for some program of treatment for the men of World War II who were disabled because of mental illness. It is now estimated that at least 10,000 psychiatric social workers are needed to provide the necessary services in clinics and hospitals. The National Mental Health Act, passed in 1946, contained provisions with which to establish, expand, and improve programs of training in psychiatry, clinical psychology, psychiatric nursing, and psychiatric social work. The number of schools of social work receiving this support was small in 1948, but by 1963 all accredited schools of social work in the United States were receiving financial support for training under the provisions of the National Mental Health Act.

Schools offering the Master's degrees, a third year, and doctoral program, were receiving such help for these programs.

The American Association of Psychiatric Social Workers (AAPSW), established in 1926, was the professional organization of Psychiatric Social Workers until 1955 when each of the *specialty* groups merged and became the National Association of Social Workers (NASW). One of the functions of AAPSW was that of approving sequences in psychiatric social work. Its publication, "The Statement of Essentials in Professional Education for Psychiatric Social Workers," was used by schools as a guide to curriculum building in class and field instruction. The Association also published *Newsletter* and its successor, the *Journal of Psychiatric Social Work,* which continued until 1956. With the merger of the several professional organizations, NASW began the publication of *Social Work* which is used today as the official organ of all the *sections*—psychiatric, school, medical, group work, and research. Before the merger, the AAPSW sponsored important conferences and meetings, including the Dartmouth Conference in 1949; and, in collaboration with the National Institute of Mental Health, it sponsored two institutes at Atlantic City, one in 1955 and one in 1957, on education for practice in psychiatric social work.

As training in all schools of social work became generic, psychiatric social work, as such, was deemphasized. Much of the course content "essential" for practice in psychiatric social work was integrated within the generic program, and by 1960 accreditation of all specialties was eliminated.

PSYCHIATRIC SOCIAL WORK PRACTICE

The psychiatric social worker studies, observes, and appraises the problem brought to the hospital or clinic by the individual and evaluates the role of the family; assesses the meaning of the findings resulting from the study; helps the individual and his family to use the treatment of the service organization; and assists them in solving their problems. O'Keefe explains that the psychiatric social worker

... carries responsibility in relation to both the patient and his family through all phases of diagnosis, care, treatment, and rehabilitation. . . .

In direct service the psychiatric social worker collaborates with members of other professions in the treatment program recommended for the patient. The primary focus of his treatment efforts may center in his relationship with the patient or may be directed largely into work with the family or other key figures. He assists the patient and/or his family to understand the meaning of the patient's illness and their reaction to it; to accept the need for treatment as a corrective measure; to determine and work toward the resolution of specific problems and stresses in the environment which impede treatment or interfere with adequate social functioning; to develop healthy, satisfying interpersonal relationships; to modify undesirable and unrealistic attitudes; and to facilitate use of the patient's own assets to strengthen his efforts toward a more satisfying adjustment.[4]

Social work is geared to helping the individual, family, or the community in meeting needs in ways which will result in improved individual performance at home, within the family unit, on the job, in the community, and in other social situations. The social worker's role clearly is not one of giving medication; it is not one of doing psychological testing; nor is it one of providing physical care for the patient. Rather, it is one of effecting social adjustments and assisting the individual to solve personal, family, and social problems.

PSYCHIATRIC SOCIAL WORK IN THE HOSPITAL SETTING

Admission is an essential aspect of psychiatric hospital practice, and one in which the psychiatric social worker has important responsibilities in relation to the following: [5]

a) To assist in interpretation of the hospital's facilities and program to the patient and his family.

b) Assistance to the family with problems arising from the patient's admission to the hospital, amelioration of the family anxieties in relation to the threat of having a mentally ill relative, interpretation to the family of the hospital's treatment procedures.

c) Formulation of plans, with the assistance of other community social agencies, which might make admission less urgent or occasionally prevent unnecessary or ill-advised admissions.

d) Establishing a relationship with the family which will encourage them to maintain a positive, non-rejecting attitude throughout the period of care, and ultimately help them to receive the returning patient with understanding and acceptance.

The patient who is admitted to the hospital for the first time invariably possesses attitudes regarding the institution and the program of care which are inimical to his best interest in the hospital. Furthermore, members of the family bring with them preconceived and distorted notions which seriously interfere with their efforts to assist in treatment plans. To many, the mental hospital is the "end of the line." The idea persists that to hospitalize is to "put away" and that "once insane, always insane." For some, hospitalization means loss of freedom. Many, if not most, state mental hospitals today have closed wards and locked doors. The denial to the patient of normal, simple pleasures is real. One patient said she disliked the hospital, not because she was mistreated or because the food was bad, but because she couldn't water her flowers or walk along the country lane. Many patients, hospitalized for the first

[4] Daniel E. O'Keefe, "Psychiatric Social Work," *Social Work Yearbook, 1960* (New York: National Association of Social Workers, 1960), p. 454.

[5] "The Psychiatric Social Worker in the Psychiatric Hospital," Group for the Advancement of Psychiatry, Report No. 2 (January, 1958), p. 3.

time, fear other patients; they are apprehensive of attack, seduction, or lack of identity. The lonely and deprived patient feels rejection and a depth of loneliness deepened by the isolation of hospitalization. At intake, the worker who interviews the patient can do much to allay these fears, can help the patient to become oriented to the hospital, and ease the pain of separation. In a similar way the social worker helps the family to accept hospitalization and the program of care for the patient. Families thus assisted support treatment efforts and hasten the day when the patient can be discharged.

Sometimes families believe that hospitalization is a solution to their family problems. They have been living with the problem, frequently for long periods of time, and their tolerance may have broken down, particularly when mental illness is accompanied by death, loss of employment, economic reversals, or other serious stress. These families need help to accept the fact that the mentally ill can be successfully treated and returned again to their homes, and that disturbed family situations can be adjusted and made to function acceptably to all concerned.

The ill individual is able to respond to treatment best when he has the assurance that his family continues to be involved in his welfare and cares about him. As the family is helped to mobilize its strengths, it can look ahead to reunion and the return to health of the ill member. The child who is hospitalized recovers more quickly when he knows that the separation from his family resulting from the hospital experience is not permanent.

The social worker studies the family, becomes knowledgeable about its strengths, weaknesses, and needs, and uses this knowledge in treatment.

It is vital that the social history be considered as a constantly reformulated body of information. It consists of material revealed as an outgrowth of a purposeful relationship of the psychiatric social worker with the patient, members of his family, physicians and agencies acquainted with the patient, and other community resources with which the patient may have had some experience, or which may be helpful in future planning. This dynamically developed social history provides a foundation for a continuing relationship of the psychiatric social worker to the patient and his family and community, within the total treatment process, and also makes a very important contribution to total treatment itself.[6]

There was a time when families were tolerated in hospitals as visitors, but not really welcome. They were told there was nothing they could do, and their interest was discouraged. More recently, the importance of the family in rehabilitation is emphasized and families are increasingly involved in the treatment program for the patient.

Treatment involving a family has many ramifications. Initially some families simply cannot bring themselves to think about the sick member's return home. A wife, for example, who has been severely traumatized by

6 *Ibid.*, p. 4.

the sickness of her spouse may be reluctant to have him rejoin the family circle. A patient who hallucinates may not be welcome by the family because she "hears voices" and talks to unseen audiences. A family and a neighborhood need help to understand and accept hallucinatory behavior.

Recently in a metropolitan community, citizens angrily protested when they learned that patients from a state hospital were to be placed in rest homes in their area. They wrote letters to the local newspaper, circulated protest petitions among neighbors, held meetings with city officials, and forced reconsideration of the hospital's plan. Another property owner built a high wall around his yard to isolate it from patients living in a nearby nursing home. Citizens need help to understand patients, their illnesses, and their capacity to again lead normal lives in the community. In recent years nursing and foster home care of mental patients have become an important part of the treatment. These programs are defeated, however, when patients are not given the freedom of the community.

Family care, placing hospital patients in private homes, is one example of a method of treatment with which the social worker is closely identified. Unfortunately, many patients are never considered for family care because its use is not developed in hospitals. Practical problems of such care have not all been solved. Many hospitals do not have social workers or staff to develop family care programs, which include finding homes for patients, making home studies, and supervising the placement of patients in homes. Families can accept the patients for whom the necessary preparation for family living is made but they must be assured of the continuing support of the hospital and the social worker.

Admission to a hospital is not always indicated. Community resources exist to keep patients at home and in the community. If the problem is aggravated by economic pressures, and financial assistance is needed to help the family maintain itself, this sometimes can be arranged through the use of the community's resources. If it is medically determined that hospitalization is necessary, the social worker helps the family with the arrangements.

It is desirable that a positive relationship with the family be formed and kept alive during hospitalization. Unfortunately, in some hospitals patients who have been institutionalized for many years are lost to their families. One of the writers called on the family of an elderly patient who had been hospitalized for thirty years. Her daughter, a middle aged woman, excused herself and returned to the door a moment later with the explanation that she did not want her son in the room while she talked to the worker about her mother. She had sent him on an errand. He and the other children had been told that their grandmother was dead. For nineteen years, and possibly longer, the family had kept the illness of this woman hidden, fearing disgrace. It is not easy for a patient to be received into his home or community when a family is driven to hide the fact of illness, and strongly unfavorable attitudes will have to change before headway is made in the treatment of the mentally ill.

The social worker is concerned with all aspects of the patient's relationships within the hospital, as well as to his family and community. Patients use treatment best when they understand and cooperate with it, and can trust the staff responsible for its administration. Rehabilitation can be best achieved when patient interest in his family, employment, and the community is sustained while he is in treatment; and the social worker is often the key person to assist him in maintaining sound interpersonal relationships. It is also the social worker who assists the patient in using the family and community resources for protection and restoration to normal activities.

A fascinating example of the role of the social worker in the mental hospital is depicted by Schmidt.[7] She was given the assignment, in a modern psychiatric hospital with about 2,700 patients, to test the hypothesis that even the most regressed patients, the "zombies" of the mental hospital world, could, with professional help, be reeducated, resocialized and return to society, or, at least, achieve enriched, less lonely lives. There were thirty-seven men with whom she began to work. The hospital had been their home, their only home, for an average of twenty years. They were the almost-forgotten, neglected individuals in the back wards of the hospital, representative of perhaps a quarter of a million men and women in similar settings. Privacy was an unknown commodity, and Schmidt's first impression was that the patients were "a faceless mass of mechanized robots." As she became acquainted with them, however, they became thirty-seven individual men, each with unique characteristics and emotional ingredients. She checked the hospital records carefully and began to understand each patient. She met with patients and encouraged them to talk about leaving the hospital. At first many would not discuss this at all. She arranged group conferences and also weekly individual interviews with the men. She talked with them about the things they could understand, very simple things at first, such as the broken bedsprings, "the need for paint to spruce up the drab walls and furniture. Wouldn't they like to have towels to dry their hands on instead of that sheet? Didn't they sometimes wish there was more than one mirror? Wouldn't some pictures on the wall look pretty?"

She encouraged them to complain, to raise questions, and to make suggestions. At first they did not even understand what the word "home" meant. It was incomprehensible to them. So she talked about "a place

7 Pansy Schmidt, "Assignment: Democracy's Scrapheap," *Journal of Social Work Process* (Philadelphia: University of Pennsylvania Press, 1961), pp. 73–93.

to stay" where there would be a bed, clean clothing, and something to eat. She took a warm, accepting, personal interest in each of these men and did everything possible to help each to rebuild lost dignity and self-respect. The physician began to make weekly ward rounds for the first time in the history of this service.

The social worker's assignment lasted about a year and a half. What were the results of this experiment? Eighteen of these sullen, scared men had left the hospital and become citizens in good standing in their communities outside the gates. After five years had elapsed the record showed that most of the eighteen who had left the hospital were still on the outside making satisfactory adjustments, and those in the hospital were getting along better. Schmidt observed that social workers can help mental patients, even those in the back wards in hospitals, if they use their professional knowledge, skills, and techniques. She made a final appeal for more help for persons who have been "consigned to the scrapheaps of our democracy," and, she concluded "a democracy can neither tolerate nor afford human scrapheaps." [8]

SOCIAL WORK IN THE PSYCHIATRIC CLINIC

In clinics, social workers make interpretations of the functions of the clinic, complete intakes, make studies of individuals in family situations, and assist with diagnosis and treatment. The patient is helped to decide whether to use the clinic, whether something more appropriate might be the answer to his problem, and whether the clinic services fit his needs. If the client is a child, the decision for use of the clinic must be shared with his parents. A study of a group of adult clinics in New York determined that "in clinics using psychiatric social workers for intake, patients were selected with greater discrimination, and there were fewer broken appointments. The average duration of treatment per patient increased and there was a higher percentage of successful treatment results." [9]

Study and exploration is followed with treatment, and the plan formulated is diagnostically rooted. In the study period:

It is essential to have pertinent information on such matters as the patient's physical health, intellectual capacity, vocational adjustment, family life, and social, ethnic and religious background. Knowledge of earlier or current attempts of the patient to solve his problems by recourse to other professional help, or in some other way, is also essential. . . . Among these skills are a disciplined use of interviewing techniques. . . . The skilled social worker also is accustomed to resourceful and selective use of environmental aids and to extending his activities in the interest of the patient outside the clinic walls, if desirable.

[8] *Ibid.*, p. 93.
[9] "Psychiatric Social Work in the Psychiatric Clinic," Group for the Advancement of Psychiatry, Report No. 16 (September, 1950), pp. 3, 4.

. . . Social caseworkers follow the principle of respect for the privacy, dignity and independence of the individual. . . .

In many clinics the psychiatric social worker also coordinates, for the patient and his family, the medical and other services set in motion within and outside the psychiatric clinic.[10]

There are many different kinds of clinics and services provided. Although they have the common objective of helping a disturbed child or mentally ill adult, some clinics are only for children; more often clinics serve both children and adults.

Psychiatric social workers serve on boards of agencies, they give talks, and interpret the needs for services for the mentally ill. They represent their particular area of competence on the clinic team. They maintain their professional identity through staff development programs, professional associations, and other contacts within their profession. They attend local, regional, and national meetings and conferences in the field of social work. The professional social worker helps to perpetuate his work by his contributions to training, education, writing, and research. He may be asked to assist in the training of other psychiatric social workers as a staff member, a field instructor of trainees, or by affiliating with a school of social work. To assure themselves of a regular supply of qualified personnel, clinics and hospitals make substantial investments in training. They provide staff for supervision, office space, and other facilities needed in training. Those agencies which train students are more generally favored with a pool from which they may recruit and maintain personnel levels and thus assure themselves of social work competence.

Social workers engage in various scientific studies and, increasingly, there is an emphasis in social work upon research. Research projects, under social work auspices, have recently been established by the Vocational Rehabilitation Administration and National Institute of Mental Health, and public funds are being made available for research in psychiatric social work in the mental health field to those studying for advanced degrees. There is a critical need for research personnel of ability to give direction to a wide variety of projects. Research is the means employed by a profession for building a foundation body of knowledge, for improvement of practice, and for use in preventive work.

Among the functions of the social worker in the clinic are the following described by O'Keefe:[11]

. . . the promotion and organization of community mental health programs and activities. In such programs he may carry a leadership or collaborative role directed toward: the integration of psychiatric programs with community health and welfare programs; provision of consultation to community health,

10 *Ibid.*, p. 3.
11 O'Keefe, *op. cit.*, p. 455.

education, and welfare services; and education of the community in mental health concepts.

The psychiatric social worker carries out his functions by the use of case-work, administration, consultation, community organization, and research with each appropriately applied to the mental health setting.

COMMUNITY MENTAL HEALTH

The work of the social worker in the community mental health program is always a team venture. The social worker represents one of several disciplines in a county, municipal, state, or regional organization combining such functions as program, organization and development, supervision, and consultation. Staff members serve as educational specialists and mental health consultants and their role is to stimulate program interest and development. The community approach is largely one of prevention. In a community in Minnesota, which consists of three counties and a population of approximately 68,500:

The energies of the board and staff of the Tri-County Mental Health Center are directed towards strengthening the efforts of the people of these three counties to improve their mental health and to prevent and to cope with mental illness. . . . The current and future mental health needs of all of the people can best be served if all individuals and groups concerned with promoting mental health and with caring for mentally ill assist each other and that the whole community will gain the greatest ultimate value from programs aimed at positive stimulation of mental health and prevention and early interception of illness.[12]

In yet another community developing mental health facilities:

The broad objectives of such a program can be specified as providing the adequate clinical and community mental health services for the community. Clinical services would include complete diagnostic and treatment plans for psychiatric problems of all sorts for individuals determined by policy to be eligible. Community services would include (1) consultation to other agencies, (2) mental health education in the community, (3) in-service training of appropriate groups, (4) research in mental health including a special aid in community planning through surveys of needs and program recommendations.[13]

Mike Gorman states: [14]

From the time of the establishment of the first state mental hospital in Williamsburg, Virginia in 1773 up until very recently, we were still living in what I have often referred to as "The Age of Banishment." This age is coming rapidly to a close and I think it is fair to state that we are on the threshold of a new era—the treatment of mental illness in the heart of the community.

12 Frank Kiesler, "Programming for Prevention in a Rural Area" (Grand Rapids, Minnesota: Tri-County Mental Health Center, 1961), p. 1; mimeographed paper.

13 "Community Mental Health Centers in the Salt Lake Area" (Unpublished paper, March 21, 1960), n.p.g.

14 Mike Gorman, "The Community—The New Mental Health Frontier," Speech at The Bulletin Civic Service Committee on Mental Health (October 15, 1956), pp. 2, 14.

As we have over the past several decades built a magnificent hospital and medical care system for the treatment of physical ills within the confines of our community, so shall we in the next several decades do the same for mental illness. . . .

It is gratifying to note that the states are on the march in the provision of tremendously expanded community mental health services. In a survey completed in November, 1955, the Council of State Governments reported that many states have doubled, and in some cases tripled, their appropriations for community mental health services. As all of you probably know, New York has led the way with the community mental health program which is currently budgeted at approximately $13,000,000.

CHANGING ROLE OF THE SOCIAL WORKER

In the past, the state hospital has stood for the efforts of the nation to treat and rehabilitate the mentally ill. These efforts have been dismal and characterized by neglect and banishment. Somewhat typical was one state hospital removed geographically from the community, isolated by mountains guarding one approach and a large swamp another.

The present trend is a far cry from the "swamp" psychology of the immediate past. Psychiatry and social work are moving out of the hospitals into the community. Patients are being treated in the community and the general practitioner in medicine is practicing more and more psychiatry.

There is considerable evidence of greater community understanding and acceptance of human beings. A petition signed by neighbors who had opposed the return of a patient to the community at an earlier time was torn up and the hand of welcome extended by these same aloof, hostile neighbors because as one of them said, "Our Neighborhood Council decided that we could not afford to put barriers in the way of people, that we could solve our problems in a more healthy way than by building barriers."

Programs are being developed for ex-patients, and for patients who are borderline and not in need of hospitalization, but who can be treated in the community. "These include emergency psychiatric services, mental health consultation, psychiatric sections in general hospitals, open hospitals, interaction 'prescriptions,' member-employee work programs, volunteer services, therapeutic communities, halfway houses, sheltered workshops, and foster family care programs."[15]

With a greater effort to treat the mentally ill at the onset of the illness, to utilize resources closer to home, and to mobilize the community, social work grows in importance; for the family, the community, and the impact of one upon the other, have always occupied the center of the social work stage.

[15] *Action for Mental Health,* Final Report of the Joint Commission on Mental Illness and Health (New York: Basic Books, Inc., Publishers, 1961), p. 169.

There is work yet to be done. While much is being accomplished for the mentally ill, much is yet in the blueprint stage. "This is a field where fads and fancies flourish. Hardly a year passes without some new claim, for example, that the cause or cure of schizophrenia has been found. The early promises of each of these discoveries are uniformly unfulfilled. Successive waves of patients habitually appear to become more resistant to the newest 'miracle' cure than have the group on which the first experiments were made."[16]

Manpower shortages continue to be critical. Much knowledge is yet to be gained. The present efforts to expand research and training through various organizations hold something of promise for the future in what in the past has been an all too dismal outlook for the mentally ill. There are many attitudes inimical to the mentally ill which will have to be modified before a real breakthrough can be expected. Attitudes which prevent effective treatment within the community, and which continue to be characterized by a psychology which has not kept pace with the new insights and hope, are most detrimental. *"These necessary preconditions are funds for personnel, training, and research; the replacement of political by professional controls in mental health programs and agencies; and the development of a community atmosphere that is receptive to new ideas for the treatment of mental patients."*[17]

SUMMARY

Psychiatric social work is social work in responsible relation to psychiatry and the field of mental health. It emphasizes cooperation with psychologists, nurses, and other individuals who are variously engaged in working in this field.

It has its roots in the mental health and child guidance movements, and in the emerging profession of social work. Its knowledge base is social work and the sciences of human behavior.

World upheavals—wars, depressions, and societal stresses and tensions—have given impetus to psychiatric social work. The National Mental Health Act and the Institutes of Health in Bethesda, Maryland, have made important contributions. Psychiatric social workers have affirmed their professional interest: in various policy statements, accreditation activities, educational and business conferences, special educational institutes, and last but not least, in the publications of the *Journal of Psychiatric Social Work* and *Social Work*.

The practice of psychiatric social work consists of knowledge, techniques and skill, attitudes, and a philosophy of prevention, rehabilitation, and restoration of the mentally ill. Methods and techniques in-

16 *Ibid.,* p. 189.
17 *Ibid.,* p. 192.

clude intake, interpretation, study, exploration, treatment planning, work with families, research, education, training, and community health.

The field of psychiatric social work is an integral part of social work with aims, goals, objectives, and a code of ethics shared in common. As treatment of the emotionally disturbed focuses on the family and the community, the role of social work grows in importance.

Greater knowledge and manpower are yet needed to combat mental illness. Research and training will have high priority in the immediate future and many professional people will need to pool their efforts to solve the destructive, perplexing problems of mental ill health.

QUESTIONS FOR DISCUSSION

1. What is psychiatric social work?
2. What justification is there for the prefix *psychiatric* to social work?
3. Is a psychiatric social worker different qualitatively or quantitatively from social workers in other fields of practice?
4. What new developments have led to the practice of psychiatric social work? How do you assess these developments in terms of their relative importance?
5. What are some of the elements of social work practice in a hospital? A psychiatric clinic?
6. Identify the bodies of knowledge and a few of the skills which a social worker requires for practice in a state hospital.
7. What particular skills will be needed in conducting an interview with a patient who is mentally ill, or a member of his family?
8. Compare and contrast the community approach to mental illness with the clinical approach.
9. How far has your community moved toward a community-centered mental health program?

SPECIAL ACTIVITIES

1. With the help of colleagues, write a script that embraces the essential features and steps in the development of the Mental Hygiene Movement. Dramatize this production for the benefit of the class.
2. List the facilities within your community for the care, treatment, and prevention of mental illness. Evaluate the support of treatment programs as compared with programs designed to prevent the spread of mental illlness.
3. Arrange for a supervisor of social work students in a psychiatric setting to discuss the training of social workers for the mental health field.
4. Make a list of public media which during the semester or quarter carried news items and information about mental health. Assess the value of these accounts in terms of your knowledge of what is required for a good mental health program for your community.

SELECTED REFERENCES

Action for Mental Health, Joint Commission on Mental Illness and Health (New York: Basic Books, Inc., Publishers, 1961).

BELLSMITH, VIRGINIA, GABELL, MARCENE P., KNEE, RUTH I., and SCHROEDER, DOROTHY, eds., *The Case Method in Teaching Social Work* (New York: National Association of Social Workers, 1959).

BELLSMITH, VIRGINIA, KNEE, RUTH I., and SCHROEDER, DOROTHY, eds., *Teaching Psychiatric Social Work* (New York: American Association of Psychiatric Social Workers, Inc., 1955).

Education for Psychiatric Social Work, Proceedings of the Dartmouth Conference (New York: American Association of Psychiatric Social Workers, 1950).

FINK, ARTHUR E., WILSON, EVERETT E., and CONOVER, MERRILL B., *The Field of Social Work,* 4th ed. (New York: Holt, Rinehart & Winston, Inc., 1963).

GORMAN, MIKE, *Every Other Bed* (Cleveland: The World Publishing Company, 1956).

GRINKER, ROY R., MACGREGOR, HELEN, SELAN, KATE, KLEIN, ANNETTE, and KOHRMAN, JANET, *Psychiatric Social Work: A Transactional Case Book* (New York: Basic Books, Inc., Publishers, 1961).

HAMILTON, GORDON, *Psychotherapy in Child Guidance* (New York: Columbia University Press, 1948).

KNEE, RUTH, ed., *Better Social Services for Mentally Ill Patients* (New York: American Association of Psychiatric Social Workers, Inc., 1955).

CHAPTER **5**

Medical Social Work

The doctor queried of the hospital superintendent, "Why have social service in this hospital?" The administrator answered with deep conviction and feeling, "The hospital provides the patient with heat, food, and medication, why shouldn't it take care of his social needs? They, too, are important." He went on to explain that the social problems and needs are often particularly significant in the total care and treatment of a patient; and if they are not considered, many times medical treatment fails.

What is medical social work, and in what social institutions is it practiced? What special knowledge and skills are required of a medical social worker? Answers to these and related questions appear in this chapter.

Medicine and social work joined hands in 1905 with the establishment of medical social work at the Massachusetts General Hospital in Boston under the enthusiastic, able encouragement of Dr. Richard Cabot. He and others recognized the need to understand more about social factors related to illness and its treatment, and to utilize social and community resources in comprehensive patient care.

The introduction of social workers into hospital and other medical settings has been slow but steady, so that today many hospitals have professional social workers on their staffs. Massachusetts General Hospital, itself, has expanded its social services to include forty-five workers. Social workers have also been gaining a foothold in public health settings and to a limited degree in medical clinics.

The American Association of Medical Social Workers (AAMSW) was established in 1918 with the goal of giving support and strength to this embryonic development. By 1946 a total of 2,095 social workers belonged to this Association. In 1955 this group joined with other social work organizations to create the National Association of Social Workers. The Medical Social Work Section of this Association has remained active in relation to practice and education and has sponsored several regional institutes to raise the level of practice in medical settings.

DEFINITION OF MEDICAL SOCIAL WORK

Medical social work is social work practiced in collaboration with another profession, medicine, and "public health within the structure of programs of health and medical care."[1] It is the application of social work knowledge, skill, attitudes, and values to the field of health and medicine. Medical social work addresses itself to illness brought about by or related to social and environmental stresses which result in failures of social functioning and social relationships. It is an ally to medicine and the healing arts and intervenes with medicine and related professions in the study, diagnosis, and treatment of illness at the point where social, psychological, and environmental forces impinge on role effectiveness.

Medical social work relates itself "to the goals and functions of such . . . social and health institutions as official health agencies (local, state, federal), voluntary health agencies (for example, the National Foundation), rehabilitation centers, and medical care divisions of public welfare agencies."[2]

Medical social work is practiced in those social institutions known to the public for their medical service emphasis; namely, public health at the local, state, federal, and international levels; general medical hospitals both public and private; T.B. sanatoria; county and state health departments; crippled children's hospitals; out-patient clinics; university teaching hospitals; and others.

The social workers in the medical setting employ and adapt the methods of casework, group work, community organization, consultation, teaching, and research in assisting individuals, groups of individuals, and communities in solving personal and family health problems, and to create, add to, strengthen, and improve the medical services of the community. Medical social work is often the vanguard of protective and preventive health measures.

Medical social workers engage in research and add to a professional body of scientific knowledge, which is used for treatment and prevention

[1] Eleanor E. Cockerill, "Medical Social Work," *Social Work Yearbook, 1960* (New York: National Association of Social Workers, 1960), p. 375.
[2] *Ibid.*

of illness. They assist inexperienced workers in their efforts to develop scholarship and skill through supervision and teaching, teach on faculties of schools of social work and in student training units as *field* instructors, and participate in workshops, institutes, and conferences, assuring perpetuation of professional purposes and a future of competence. Medical social workers also assist in teaching other disciplines employed in medical and health services and disseminate knowledge which permits greater cooperation and coordination of effort among all members of the team.

What, if any, are the distinguishing knowledge and skill characteristics of medical social work practice? Medical social work is uniquely a practice of social work in medical settings and institutions in responsible relation to medicine. Its concern is with the welfare of *patients* and the causal, contributing interrelationships of illness, family failures and breakdown, social stresses, and environmental pressures and influences.

Medical social work is shaped and guided by the attitudes, beliefs, knowledge, and acceptable ways of doing things of professionals serving in medical institutions and by the philosophy and practice of modern medicine. It requires a knowledge of illness and of the psychological and social impact of disease on the individual, his family, and the family interrelationships; it calls for the application and adaptation of social work concepts, principles, and ideas to the special needs of hospital and clinic clientele.

The knowledge gained in a two-year graduate course of study and the Master's degree is for *beginning* practice. The profession expects that the essentials of skill and knowledge will be implemented in practice as in other fields of social work. The graduate going into social work is required to practice for two years under competent, qualified supervision that will round his knowledge and sharpen his skills, before becoming a member of the Academy of Certified Social Workers.

The social worker collaborates with medicine in medical settings but retains his professional identity. Social work has a coordinate, rather than subordinate or ancillary role to medicine and is responsible to the institution and the supporting public. The practice of social work is regulated by a code of ethics, values, and standards of practice. In the medical setting the doctor is the clinical and medical authority and is held responsible under the law for medical practice. He is clinically responsible for patients and enjoys the authority of his medical knowledge, professional training, and medical competence. The medical social worker, likewise, is responsible for his area of professional competence.

Occasionally, in social work practice and particularly with students in training, the "aura" of the doctor creates a "halo" effect which inspires the trainee to make demands upon the doctor which he is ill-equipped to handle. This is understandable considering the high pres-

tige of medicine today and the doctor's role in modern society of pre-
scribing for patients and telling them what to do. Student social workers
who bring their attitudes about doctors with them into training, overwhelmed by the setting and the size of the job to be done, often seek
the doctor's views and expect decisions from medicine which are really
within the realm of their own profession. A staff physician asked a
student social worker, "Is the home ready to take Jimmy back?" The
reply, "I don't know, Dr. Jones, you didn't ask me to *find out*." The
teaching point made in Dr. Jones' retort is classic, "And, you didn't
ask me to *find out* about Jimmy's rheumatic heart." There are some
things for the social worker to know and to do, and some things for the
doctor; and these are determined by the role and competence of each.

FUNCTIONS OF MEDICAL SOCIAL WORK

Medical social workers perform numerous services in hospitals today.
Doctors and others are asking for help from the "social laboratory" as
never before. The specific functions of the medical social worker have
been spelled out by the Joint Committee of the American Hospital Association and the Medical Social Work Section of the National Association of Social Workers as follows:[3]

1. Aiding the health team in understanding the significance of social, economic and emotional factors in relation to the patient's illness, treatment
   and recovery.
2. Helping the patient and his family in their understanding of these factors to enable them to make constructive use of medical care.
3. Promoting the well-being and morale of the patient and his family.
4. Participating in the educational programs of other members of the
   health team.
5. Assisting the hospital in giving better patient care through its various
   services.
6. Facilitating the productive utilization of community resources to meet
   the needs of patients and their families.

It is estimated that about half of all patients who see doctors come
with psychosomatic illness involving personal, emotional, and family
problems. Thus, it is apparent that persons who are qualified to help
with social factors are important members of the comprehensive treatment team. Their services are related to (1) direct help to the patient,
and (2) indirect aid through assistance to the family and/or others. Help
to the patient is related to (a) intake, (b) hospitalization, (c) release, and
(d) aftercare. The social worker can be most valuable at the time a
patient is admitted to a medical setting. Through use of his skills and
knowledge he can assist the patient to adjust better to his medical en-

[3] *Essentials of a Social Service Department in Hospitals and Related Institutions*
(Chicago: American Hospital Association, 1961), p. 1.

vironment and treatment as well as offer help with financial arrangements when necessary. While the patient is in the hospital, the social worker can be of considerable assistance in providing an opportunity for the patient to talk to someone who will listen and who cares. This is usually therapeutically sound and helps in the total treatment plan. If a patient is worried about some problem, he is likely to feel better if he verbalizes his anxieties.

The social worker can perform a most important service when the patient is about to leave the hospital both in regard to healthy attitudes and toward realistic provisions which may need to be made on the outside. For example, a doctor, upon releasing a mother with a newborn baby, recommended that she drink a great deal of orange juice. When she left the hospital she went to her poor, dilapidated house with half the windows broken and partially covered with cardboard. To get any orange juice at all, she had to go to the store and sometimes wait for hours until the prices were reduced or the fruit was nearly spoiled. A social worker could have bridged the gap between the recommended treatment and the resources of the patient. This, of course, leads to the fourth aspect of helping the patient, aftercare. Again, social workers can be of considerable assistance in this regard.

Medical social workers also assist the patient through working with the family before, during, and after hospitalization and medical treatment, as part of the total comprehensive care program. A few examples illustrate these services. One mother who had given birth to a baby girl did not grow well enough to leave the hospital. When the social worker talked to her, it became evident immediately that she was concerned about her marital relations. The social worker talked with the husband a few times, and with the wife, and soon she was able to leave the hospital as the relationship became strengthened and improved. The family balance had been restored through the efforts of the social worker.

Recently, a young woman, about 24, was admitted to the emergency ward of a hospital when she attempted suicide for the third time. Because this was a hospital where there was no social service department, the administrator transferred her to a county hospital where this service could be provided. The main problem for this woman was familial, involving an alcoholic, mentally disturbed husband. It was only after the social worker gave help to the husband and family as a whole that this young woman could live with her situation.

A fifteen-year-old girl was hospitalized in the psychiatric ward of a private hospital. Part of her problem concerned her relationships with her mother and father. The psychiatrist worked with the girl in the hospital, and the social worker helped the mother and father to understand their daughter better, her needs, their relationships, and what could be done to open the door for communication among them. Through joint guidance of the psychiatrist and social worker, the girl was able to leave the hospital and return to an emotional climate at home which was more conducive to satisfactory daily living than it had ever been before.

DEFINITION OF ILLNESS

Illness has different meanings to different people. It encompasses medical, social, economic, and even spiritual components. Illness affects people in many ways, directly and indirectly, and is of particular consequence to individuals, families, and communities. The social worker plays a major role in interpreting illness to people and in helping them to muster their personal and social resources toward physical and mental well-being.

Webster's *International Dictionary* defines illness as a state of being ill or sick, bodily indisposition, disease. An ill person is one of "inferior quality, bad in condition, wretched, impolite, improper, incorrect, bad morally, evil in nature or character, malevolent, wicked, vicious, wrong." The word *disease* literally means want of ease, uneasiness. Dis, from the Latin prefix, means apart or asunder, and ease in a state of comfort or rest. The diseased person is a person wanting in ease. An invalid, on the other hand, is someone who is not valid, someone no longer able to bear the burdens of life, or who, for temporary or prolonged periods of time simply cannot function.

As defined by doctors, disease is extremely objective. Causation relates to agents which can be stained, tested for chemical qualities, measured, and described. The laboratory procedures used by medical personnel in hospitals, clinics, and in doctors' offices are objective devices used to determine the degree or seriousness of disability or pathology resulting from disease processes. Determinations are made of organic states such as result from bacteria, viruses, trauma, cellular dysfunction, and various circulatory disturbances.

Broadly speaking, illness—impaired role function—may result from factors not wholly organic, but social, psychological, cultural, and economic. Anything affecting the total well-being of the patient may support the illness and render the patient incapable of normal role performance. Illness may destroy a person's self-image. It forces dependency, reduces his usefulness to the family and other significant people. It cuts off the individual's access to normal enjoyment and satisfaction. The social worker, in addressing himself to other than organic factors, studies and defines illness in its cultural and environmental matrix and assists with the removal of barriers to health from these sources.

THE MEANING OF ILLNESS TO THE SICK PERSON

Illness means many things to many people and is always highly individual. For many, illness destroys the self-image. Illness forces dependency upon relatives and society, which may be difficult for the ill person to accept. The Essei Japanese man, for instance, whose rearing emphasizes the interdependence of family members, may develop symptoms, become immobilized, or resort to self-destruction when he can no longer count on a comfortable place of eminence within the family and is forced to accept relief or nursing home care.

Illness often minimizes the usefulness of the individual to his family and loved ones. When it interferes with the bread-winning function of the wage earner, illness can result in disorganization of the entire family, and for the wage earner in a loss of self-respect, feelings of helplessness, and despondency. The enjoyment of many of the normal functions of the individual is denied to the ill person, whose responses are often distorted and detrimental to normal social relationships.

The small child who is ill, who has to be hospitalized for extended periods of time, may lose the feeling of closeness to his parents and experience separation trauma. Some children who are separated even for short periods of time, particularly under unfavorable circumstances for which no preparation is made, carry a scar for many years, if not for a lifetime. Infants and young children who have been hospitalized and separated from their families for long periods of time, who lack the closeness of a vital tie to an adult parent or other significant person, may suffer irreversible physical and emotional damage, become autistic, distrustful of others, and encounter difficulties in relationships all their lives.

The adolescent who suffers from a prolonged illness, who is confined and obliged to curtail his activities, may lose peer group support at a time when peer support is greatly needed in his struggle for autonomy and independence. A wage earner suffering from a "nervous breakdown" who had been on relief, clung desperately to symptoms for fear he would be asked to return to work and a job he could not manage. He recovered only with skilled medical and social work help when he was assured that his welfare check was not contingent upon his illness and that he would recover and be able to work again and support his family.

The aged may use sickness as a method of forcing their children to give them care and attention. A mother, for example, who during her childbearing period was preoccupied with the task of rearing and educating her children, in middle age and retirement found her usefulness often questioned, if not by others, by herself. Her children, long since established in their own homes, were independent and did not have the same need for their mother as when they were younger. She sensed that she was not needed and that her role in the family had changed. She chose illness as an escape from the feeling that she was no longer useful, to force her children to live with and care for her. Unconscious regression to earlier states of dependency, helplessness, and illness are common reactions to stress. It is expected that the ill person will be dependent, helpless, and under the care of others; nevertheless, the sick are also expected to cooperate with the hospital and other individuals who are responsible for assisting in their care and treatment.

ILLNESS WITHIN THE FAMILY

A family is often controlled by its "sickest" member, with household activities revolving around the unhealthy individual. Small children are asked to curtail their natural exuberance when a parent or an elderly grandparent is ill, and older children are required to perform certain household tasks which previously may have been undertaken by the adults in the family. The family's entire way of life may be reorganized or drastically altered by the sickness of one of its members, and not infrequently, considerable family dysfunctioning results from the illness.

An illustrative case follows:

REFERRAL TO A NURSING HOME

Mrs. Jones, an elderly mother, became an invalid when she broke her hip. Following a short period of hospitalization a plan was made by her and her children for her to live in succession with several of her daughters. This plan was intended to provide variety for Mrs. Jones and to relieve the nursing care responsibility of any one of the daughters. A soft spot began to appear in the arrangement when Mrs. Jones decided that she did not wish to be shunted from one home to another, that she wanted more permanency in her old age than this plan provided, and that her preference was to remain in one place. The children agreed, which meant that as Mrs. Jones became increasingly dependent and bedridden the full burden of nursing care had to be carried by one daughter. It was no longer a shared family experience.

Despite her illness and dependency, Mrs. Jones, nevertheless, continued to exercise the authority of a parent over the daughter, ordered her about, made demands upon her, and made the other members of the household uncomfortable, creating such an impasse with the grandchildren that they began to develop symptoms. The family was weakened and threatened with disorganization and finally, with social work help, a plan was made for Mrs. Jones to move into a nursing home.

Frequently, with the help of services within the community, it is possible for a family to mobilize its resources to care for a sick or handicapped child or adult. While it is true that illness can foster family disorganization, it can also result in a constructive use of the family to achieve family unity and goals. Social agencies are available for use by families in this way. Many a handicapped or retarded child can be cared for by his own family, either by arranging its own resources, by using services within the community, or by a combination of family and community resources. Such resources as child guidance clinics, family service agencies, and many others can be called upon to strengthen and support the efforts of families to discharge their functions. In her role as a community mobilizer, the medical social worker performs a function which supports the medical care given to a sick person and in so doing realistically appraises the needs of the family and the "assets and liabilities" within the family and community for meeting these needs.

It is the purpose of social work to support and strengthen family life. In doing this the social worker makes use through referrals of existing services or assists in mobilizing the untapped potential of the community to prevent illness or to restore the sick and disabled to health and usefulness.

The case of Peter Simpson illustrates the social and psychological components of illness and the function of the social worker in relation to dysfunctional elements of personality.

PERSONALITY DYSFUNCTION

Peter Simpson, a thirteen-year-old boy, was treated for stress at the out-patient clinic of a general hospital. His response to the usual medical regimen for ulcer patients was unsatisfactory. The medication and diet did not bring his ulcers under control, and when he began bleeding internally, a full investigation of his circumstances was ordered. The social worker assisting with the investigation determined in an interview with the mother that Peter was the only remaining child living at home and that his father had died three years previously. Left alone following the death of the husband and the move of the older children from the home, Mrs. Simpson turned to Peter for comfort and advice. She assuaged her loneliness by talking to him and consulted him about living expenses, budget, and the family income. She often referred to him as the "man of the house," and expected him to shoulder the responsibilities of husband and father. Her affectional demands on the boy were heavy and unusual. She had him sleep with her at night because alone she was "nervous and uneasy."

Medical care brought no relief of symptoms to Peter because of a totally unrealistic home situation. Catapulted into the head position of a family and made the object of impossible affectional demands at 13, Peter collapsed. The social worker arranged for Peter to live with an older married brother and sister-in-law and referred him to the child guidance clinic for treatment at the same time. His symptoms were relieved almost immediately, when with professional help a change was made in his home situation.

Mrs. Simpson was able to accept the plan for Peter as she was helped to form new affectional interests and secure her economic position. Her relationship with the social worker served as an introduction to an ever widening circle of friends and to financial independence. She surmounted an extremely difficult hurdle when, at 53, with the help of social service, she decided to go to work. She had not been on the labor market at any time in her life and her decision now was filled with apprehension and doubt. However, she was healthy and intelligent, and able to complete training needed to qualify for work in a sportswear manufacturing plant. Her beginning salary was double her AFDC check of $120 per month and the gains to her from employment of financial independence, association with others, and a growing self-actualization, opened an entirely new life for her.

The medical care for Peter in this instance was aided by social services: first, through study and diagnosis which focused the social and emotional components of his illness; second, by a radical shift in living arrangements for Peter which his mother was helped to support; third, by referral to and use of child guidance; fourth, job training and employment for Mrs. Simpson resulting in financial independence and greater personal satisfaction.

Other cases spell out the meaning of illness and roles of the social worker. Mrs. Vincent was a tubercular patient who was helped by social services to accept hospitalization:

HOSPITALIZATION OF A TUBERCULAR PATIENT

Mrs. Vincent, age 38, hospitalized in a sanitarium with an active tuberculosis infection, refused to remain at the hospital. Because of her infection she was a health hazard to her children and to the community and by her refusal to stay in the hospital also placed her own life in peril by interrupting the treatment procedures outlined by the doctors. Repeated attempts to hold Mrs. Vincent in treatment had failed. She argued that her home and family required her presence. An intelligent woman, she was aware that in her condition she could infect the children, but this she believed was the risk she would have to take as the children and her husband needed her at home.

The social worker determined that Mr. Vincent, who had attempted to take over the management of the home, was too involved in his work as well as being inadequate in coping with household problems. Arrangements for neighbors to care for his preschool daughter and provide supervision for his two older children had fallen through. He did not know where to turn and, becoming increasingly discouraged by failure in his attempts to solve his problems, he began to stay away from home, comforting himself by drinking at the club.

The medical social worker addressed herself to the problem of care for the children and to Mrs. Vincent's feeling about being needed. She referred Mr. Vincent to a family agency in the community which helped him to secure a professional homemaker who managed the home and cared for the children. Not having to worry about the children, Mr. Vincent got over his despondency and more fully accepted his parental role and the need for his wife to be in the hospital. Mrs. Vincent was reassured about her own importance to the family by a plan of regular visits and communication with them. The result was that Mrs. Vincent remained in treatment until cured of her infection.

A case of release of a youth from a hospital, after his family had been prepared to receive him, follows:

HOSPITALIZATION FOR RHEUMATIC FEVER

John Rolf, age 10, was hospitalized for rheumatic fever. He responded to treatment and after several weeks of hospitalization was returned home. A short time later he was readmitted to the hospital. Under treatment, he was relieved of symptoms and returned to his home. This in-and-out pattern was repeated and before long he was in the hospital a third time. This time the case was picked up by social services for investigation into the circumstances of John's home.

Social study revealed that John lived in a home which included a bedroom with a dirt floor where he slept at night. This was damp and unsuitable for any boy, and especially one with rheumatic fever. Moreover, the family had not followed the regimen of rest, diet, care, and antibiotics prescribed by the doctors. Neither the family nor the environmental situation supported the medical care of this boy.

John's visits to the hospital stopped after the medical social worker brought the attention of the family's problem to the public welfare worker, who made arrangements for the Rolfs to live in a more suitable home. The public agency also assisted the Rolfs temporarily with the problems of income. This meant a supplementation of their budget to provide special diet and medical care for the boy. Over a period of time public welfare helped the family to work out a plan for increasing their income through gainful employment, better budgeting, and a firmer attachment to the labor market.

ILLNESS AND THE COMMUNITY

A community is a society of individuals which for mutual advantage plans for the welfare of its members. No community can afford to disregard the needs of people who are ill or who might require medical care if the family, unaided, cannot bear the burden. Recognizing various motives the community must take steps to protect the health of its members. It is known that the community will not permit sick people to go unattended because of the harm everyone would suffer by such a policy. The sick person, the handicapped, the disabled who cannot get the care he needs cannot be a healthy, contributing force within the community, and the community must therefore, in its own self-interest, provide hospitals, clinics, and other health services for him.

The community acts through its elected representatives and through such voluntary organizations as churches and federated fund-raising groups. The medical social worker is often one of the first to recognize the need for services, and, as a community mobilizer, assists those whose efforts are directed toward the improvement and strengthening of health services. In this country, with the rapidly expanding population and mushrooming suburbia, new resources are needed to care for the growing population and to identify its needs. The medical social worker, working at the grassroots, can be among the first to make community needs known.

Social and medical services generally follow residential and business developments in a community and precede professional activities. Too often the planning for a community is merely an afterthought and social workers need to take more initiative in planning ahead for the needs of a community in a growing economy.

To the community, illness means hospitals, clinics, and services for care of citizens. It means the organization of resources into units which can effectively dispense services as they are needed. It means the selection and training of personnel who have the requisite qualifications and the skill for the job to be done. To the community, illness means that some members in periods of illness will function less well than in times of health, with uncounted numbers of man-hours lost each year to the production of goods and services. To the school, illness means the loss of educational opportunities, and planning will need to take into consideration the loss and the handicap that will result from the illness of a school child. To medical social work, nursing, and other helping professions, illness means pointing up need, and making interpretations to the community as to what a community requires in the area of health. It means interprofessional collaboration and dedication to the ideals and purposes of the professions; namely, to have people enjoy the optimum of health.

SUMMARY

Medical social work is social work in responsible collaboration with medicine. It is practiced in hospitals and clinics and in those settings which we commonly identify with the practice of medicine. The clientele of medical social work are those whose needs are social and psychological, and whose functioning has been or is in danger of becoming impaired because of illness, disease, or disability.

The ill person, to the medical social worker, is the person who is not performing adequately in the various social roles appropriate for him. There are many factors to illness and in his work with the ill person the social worker addresses himself to those bearing directly upon the person's performance in his various roles—employee, employer, husband, wife, or child.

Illness has various and different meanings for the individual, his family, and the community. The family's activities are often centered around the sick person who is in a position to control the activities of the household.

Medical and health agencies within the community are established to assist the family in the performance of role. The meaning of illness to the community lies largely in the need of the community to promote the health of its citizens. Social workers, particularly those in medical settings, are in strategic positions to give direction to the development of services in communities.

QUESTIONS FOR DISCUSSION

1. What are the essential characteristics of medical social work?

2. What is the rationale for the prefix *medical* to medical social work?

3. Identify factors of illness to which the medical social worker would logically address himself.

4. Explain the kind of training a medical social worker would require as contrasted to the training, for example, of a physician.

5. What is unique or different about the definition of illness as it would be made by the medical social worker from the definition used by a physician?

6. List factors from the case illustrations bearing on the illness of the individual which are not medical in the strictest sense.

7. Compare and contrast the meaning of illness to: (a) the sick person; (b) his family; and (c) the community.

8. What are the major functions of the social worker in the hospital setting?

9. Are the services of the medical social worker related to prevention? Discuss.

SPECIAL ACTIVITIES

1. Study the history of medical social work and report the steps which have led to the use of the social worker in the medical setting.

2. Schedule a visit to a hospital or clinic in your community where the practice of medical social work has been established, and ask for an interview with the Chief of Social Services for purposes of determining the role and function of social work in that particular hospital or clinic.

SELECTED REFERENCES

BARTLETT, HARRIETT M., *Fifty Years of Social Work in a Medical Setting* (New York: National Association of Social Workers, 1957).

————, *Some Aspects of Social Work in a Medical Setting* (Chicago: American Association of Medical Social Workers, 1940).

COCKERILL, ELEANOR E., "Medical Social Work," *Social Work Yearbook, 1960* (New York: National Association of Social Workers, 1960), pp. 375–382.

Essentials of a Social Service Department in Hospitals and Related Institutions (Chicago: American Hospital Association, 1961).

FREEMAN, HOWARD E., LEVINE, SOL, and REEDER, LEO G., eds., *Handbook of Medical Sociology* (Englewood Cliffs, N.J.: Prentice-Hall, Inc., 1963) .

KING, STANLEY H., *Perceptions of Illness and Medical Practice* (New York: Russell Sage Foundation, 1962).

Selected Papers and Reports, Fiftieth Anniversary Celebration, Social Service Department, Massachusetts General Hospital (Boston: Massachusetts General Hospital, 1958).

CHAPTER 6

Social Work in the Schools

In a special message to Congress, January 29, 1963, President Kennedy underscored the values of education in a democracy, when he said:

Education is the keystone in the arch of freedom and progress. Nothing has contributed more to the enlargement of this nation's strength and opportunities than our traditional system of free, universal elementary and secondary education, coupled with widespread availability of college education.

Recognizing the importance of education in today's changing and challenging world, it is pathetic that, according to estimates, seven and one-half million students will leave school before they graduate from high school during the decade 1960 to 1970.[1] Considering the role played by school dropouts in the labor market, in crime and delinquency, and on welfare and relief rolls, as well as the great loss of potential talents and abilities both to the individuals and society, there is no question as to why this school problem becomes of utmost importance.

Statistics are depressing when comparing school dropouts with the economic and social problems facing this nation. Most dropouts work at unskilled or semiskilled jobs, and the number of such jobs is rapidly diminishing with increased automation and technological advances. Of all jobs, only 5 percent will be unskilled by 1970, compared with 56 percent in 1900. Even in farming the picture is bleak, for only one boy in ten who now lives on a farm will be able to earn a living at farming.

In the ranks of the unemployed, the rate is three times higher among

[1] Bernard A. Kaplan, "The Battle Shaping Up!" Newsletter, Visiting Teachers Association of Louisiana (Baton Rouge, Louisiana, April–May, 1963), p. 8; mimeographed.

male school dropouts than among high school graduates, and five times higher than for the total labor force. The unemployment rate for dropouts ranges from 20 percent to 30 percent; and in the slum areas of large cities, it is much higher. Of the five million in the labor force now unemployed, close to one million are youth between the ages of 16 and 20.

In the area of crime and delinquency the following gives a picture of the relationship to school attendance: "While most dropouts are not

UNEMPLOYMENT IS HIGHEST FOR YOUNG WORKERS AND THOSE WITH LEAST SCHOOLING

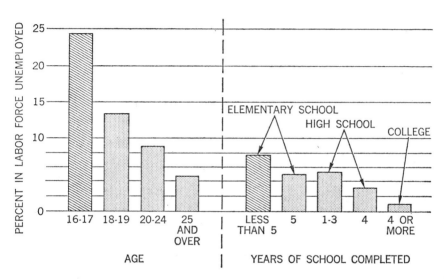

SOURCE: Interdepartmental Committee on Children and Youth, *Children in a Changing World*, Chart Book (Washington, D.C.: Golden Anniversary White House Conference on Children and Youth, 1960), p. 33.

juvenile delinquents, most juvenile delinquents tend to be dropouts. The rate of delinquency is 9–12 times higher among dropouts than among stay-ins. It has been estimated that 95 per cent of the 17-year-old delinquents are school dropouts, 85 per cent of the 16-year-olds, and 50 per cent of the 15-year-olds are dropouts." [2]

Surveys show that to a large extent adults on welfare and public assistance are school dropouts. For example, a study made in Chicago indicated that 90 percent of the adults receiving public aid had not finished high school. In an attempt to train these people to make them available to the labor market, it was found that a large majority were

[2] *Ibid.*

severely handicapped because they were deficient in rudimentary skills and fundamental education.

School administrators have not sat idly while this problem has been growing, and the holding power of the schools more than doubled during the period 1931–1961, even with the substantial increase in student enrollments. Nevertheless, the dropout problem continues to grow because there are more students enrolled in schools today than ever before. In 1960 there were 2.6 million boys and girls reaching age 18; by 1965 there will be 3.8 million; and by 1970 the number will have doubled to 5.2 million. Even with a higher percentage of students graduating, larger *numbers* will probably drop out. Thousands of students will discontinue their education in the middle of high school, or even earlier, because of economic, social, and emotional problems which may have little or no relationship to the curriculum or their ability to master recommended studies.

President Hoover's White House Conference in 1930 pledged:

For every child an education which, through the discovery and development of his individual abilities, prepares him for life; and through training and vocational guidance prepares him for a living which will yield him the maximum of satisfaction.

For every child such teaching and training as will prepare him for successful parenthood, home-making, and the rights of citizenship.[3]

When one considers that there will probably be more than seven million dropouts in a decade, and when he envisions the ominous threat to American society posed by those frustrated, floundering, unhappy, unskilled, uneducated, and unorganized youth, it becomes clear that there is still work to be done to bring American ideals to fruition.

Yet, an education for "all the children of all the people" is a generally accepted goal, echoed by White House Conferences before and since 1930 and uttered by statesmen, politicians, legislators, school administrators, and everyday rank and file Americans. Who are "all of the children?" Certainly the dropouts, who are an important segment of them, along with the mentally retarded, the hard of hearing, the deaf, the gifted, the epileptic, the arthritic, the encephalitic, the brain-damaged, the paraplegic, the emotionally disturbed, the dependent and neglected, the delinquent, the children of minority ethnic and religious groups, the cardiac, the economically deprived, those with orthopedic handicaps, the paralytic, and the children with speech disorders and hearing difficulties. Yes, these and others—the "normal" and the "not quite so normal"—are the children whose education is of national concern.

Not all children can use the facilities and regular resources of the school and its standardized curricula. Special equipment is often re-

[3] *White House Conference, 1930* (New York: Appleton-Century-Crofts, 1930), p. 47.

quired for the handicapped child—rest spaces for the cardiac, hearing aids for the hard of hearing, and stand-up tables for the crippled. Special teachers and staff are needed to work with the blind, the deaf, and the mentally retarded, while visiting teachers take the benefits of education to the homebound child. Perhaps, above all, to make the American dream a reality, it is necessary for teachers, physical therapists, orthopedic doctors, specialists with exceptional children, social workers, the parents, the community, all to believe and to recognize that children do have capacities which are trainable and that opportunities for education in America can be made operational in the lives of all children.

Some schools do see the need and do try to make provision for the whole child. These schools and school systems have added various specialists to their staff—speech and reading therapists, psychologists, psychiatrists, teachers of remedial work, physiotherapists, orthopedic physicians, nurses, and others to work with the handicapped, retarded, the physical disabled, and those children who, without specialized help, would be unable to use the regular school curriculum. Among the specialists who are part of this core of experts, is the school social worker.

BEGINNINGS IN SCHOOL SOCIAL WORK

Social work services were first established in the schools of Boston, Hartford, and New York in 1906–07, under the sponsorship of community agencies in those cities. The public school system of Rochester, New York, in 1914 became the first system to finance school social work from its regular budget.

Impetus was given to school social work in the twenties by the Commonwealth Fund, which supported a demonstration project in thirty communities widely distributed throughout the country. When financial support was withdrawn by the Fund in 1930, twenty-one of the original communities continued school social work services at local expense.

By 1930 there were 244 school social workers in thirty-one states, and by 1944 there were 266 cities with these services.

In recent years stimulation has been given to school social work by social workers and educators, and by such interested groups as the American Association of University Women and the Junior League through their studies of school dropouts, school attendance, and delinquency. While it is still too early to predict the outcome of financial aid supporting training in school social work by the National Institute of Mental Health, gains are certain to be made because of this effort.

The American Association of Visiting Teachers, organized in 1919, and the successor organizations—the National Association of School Social Workers, incorporated in 1945, and the National Association of Social Workers established in 1955—have, in turn, represented school social work. These associations have formulated standards for professional training, defined the function of the school social worker, stated qualifications of workers, described practice, sponsored workshops, interpreted the need for social work in the schools, and advanced school social work in various other ways. Since the merger of the professional organizations of social work in 1955, a School Social Work Section has continued to study and improve practice, plan speakers and meetings for the annual forum on social welfare, and participate in meetings of such educational groups as the Association for Supervision and Curriculum Development and the International Council for Exceptional Children.

The School Social Work Section of the NASW has a present membership of more than 1,000. Undoubtedly this number will grow as new recruits are selected and trained since the importance and need for this important service are increasingly recognized.

THE NEED FOR SCHOOL SOCIAL WORK

School social work is a service to children who have social and emotional problems which interfere with child-school adjustment. Sources of such adjustment difficulties can be inferred from such facts as:

1. We live today in a highly mobile society. Americans are constantly on the move. Laborers, artisans, managerial personnel, professional and white collar workers, and others with their families, are uprooted once, twice, as many as twenty or thirty times in a lifetime. Families move from one state to another, from city to city, and the children are expected to adapt themselves to new, strange, and sometimes frightening circumstances, which often and understandably are identified with their school experiences. One child, anticipating a move, told his parents wistfully that he wished he could take his "school, the teachers, and all the kids" with him. All children experience anxiety and concern when separated from that which is familiar and known. Too frequent or poorly planned separations can seriously interfere with a child's school performance.

2. Schools are not all guided by the same educational philosophy nor do they have the same curriculum. Children must adapt to a totally new educational subculture, when, for instance, they transfer from the pragmatic to the idealistic school. Not infrequently the classroom experience at one school lags behind or is ahead of another, or the content of the two fails to dovetail. Fortunately, in some school systems, provision is made to determine "where the child is" who is new to the system. The child can make the change more easily when properly oriented and indoctrinated. Where such steps are not taken, the integration of the child into the new program can prove difficult, if not actually traumatizing.

3. Curricular patterns become standardized in school systems, and more or less, make the same intellectual demands of all children of the same age. Actually, children are never the same. Precocious, richly-endowed youngsters learn rapidly; slow learners struggle to keep from being outdistanced by their brighter classmates. Some children have aptitude for certain subjects, some for others. Many, if not most children, are able to use the standardized curriculum; some fail and are lost without special attention.

4. Some children are ready for school at age six. Others will benefit by a longer period of time to mature socially and emotionally before entering school. The classroom is a traumatizing experience for the child who is not ready to accept group association and activities. Such a child may require the help of a social worker in adjusting to the group.

5. Forced attendance and compulsory school laws have implicit within them the responsibility of society to make education available and worthwhile to the child by removal of barriers to learning. The child whose learning is halted because he cannot read is entitled to special remedial help. Since reading is basic and the child who does not read is seriously handicapped, reading impairment, whenever possible, should be corrected. The nonreader may be the child for whom the reading curriculum was not adequate or the child who could not use the curriculum. Whatever the reason, role performance may be adversely influenced, and the need for restorative measures indicated. The role performance of the individual child is a primary concern of the school social worker.

6. All children have personal and family problems. Many of them are severe enough to prevent the children from taking advantage of their school opportunities. For example, a third-grader whose parents are rejecting him and withholding their love and affection may find he is immobilized and failing in his schoolwork. The social worker may step in to help the child and his parents to understand and accept each other, and to establish meaningful relationships between them.

THE SOCIAL WORKER IN THE SCHOOL

The social worker is not a teacher in the classroom with special groups or to the homebound. The designation *visiting teacher* denoting social work is becoming less commonly used. The term visiting teacher is usually used to describe the instructor who goes to the homebound child. The methods employed by school teachers and educators to stimulate and motivate learning, to involve pupils in learning experiences, to work with groups in the classroom, and to determine the specific use of subject matter, all belong to the art and science of teaching. The preparation, knowledge, skill, and training of the social worker is not that of a teacher. The social worker is not learning-focused. The function of social work in the school is diagnostic, evaluative, centered on the individual, and oriented toward treatment. The social worker is an enabler. He assists with the moving of barriers to learning, the enhancement of ego strengths, and in mobilizing resources for learning purposes. Social work intervenes when the learner is overwhelmed or threatened by the impingement of social forces destructive to or blocking the learning process.

It is the function of school social workers to assist the child with problems which interfere with his performance in school. "Children referred," according to Opal Boston, include "those who express their difficulties in school by aggressiveness, shyness, or withdrawn behavior; they may be failing academically without obvious cause; they may be hungry or ill; they may be truant; or there may be many other symptoms. These problems may reflect conflicts in family relationships, unwholesome community conditions, financial difficulties, and other social or emotional problems." [4]

The following materials illustrate the need for school social work. A youngster with high potential was doing below average work. The efforts of his parents and teachers to have him do better went unheeded. A study conducted by the school social worker shed light upon the reason for the pupil's indifference and failure to use his endowments. The members of his particular peer group not only did not strive for good grades, they actually placed a value on poor grades and poor academic achievement. Status in his group could be achieved only at the expense of his schooling, and status for this fourteen-year-old boy was important as he struggled with identity and feelings of emancipation from his parents. His problem, and that of the other boys, was corrected through a social group work approach which involved these students in a discussion of their antithetical and regressive value system.

Adolescents, in particular, strive for good standing with their peer groups. They have learned that their parents are not omnipotent and cannot be a bulwark and protection against all threats, not even if they wanted to be. While this realization is likely a dynamic of emancipation, it is painful to many and eased only by the acceptance and approval of the adolescent's peers. The social worker can help adolescents to weather the emotional storms which arise.

Frequent moves, relocation of the family, the transfer of allegiance, interest, and loyalty from one school to another, have resulted in a splintering and fragmentation of the educational experience for many children. One school child, who sat quietly most of the day discon-

---

4 Opal Boston, "School Social Work," *Social Work Yearbook, 1960* (New York: National Association of Social Workers, 1960), p. 523.

solately preoccupied with her own thoughts, had attended class in fifteen different schools in a period of three years. She made no effort to involve herself in learning until she was helped at the community child guidance clinic by a social worker to trust and find satisfaction in people.

In evaluating the social performance of a particular boy or girl, the social worker makes a diagnosis of the problem, identifies the area of difficulty, and formulates treatment which may center either in the school, the family, or in community services. If the school is the focus of disturbance, the corrective measures may have to come from or be initiated by the school, conceivably in curricular changes, improved orientation procedures, sounder programming, greater understanding on the part of student and teacher, ad infinitum.

The home situation may not be conducive to acceptable school performance. Relating himself to the social situation, the social worker sees the family as a center of motivation and the mainspring of the child's behavior. Broken homes, family stress and discord, economic factors which bear upon the effectiveness of the family all may influence a child and militate against his use of the educational experience. When the home environment is not conducive to the best performance of a pupil in the classroom, corrective measures are applied to the family to alter the imbalances.

The social worker helps the child to use the educational experience by working directly with the child and indirectly through others, principally the teacher and the family. The social worker enlists the services of others as their help is required, and is frequently the mobilizer of psychological guidance, nursing services, vocational counseling, medical diagnosis and consultation within the school, and a wide array of services outside. The social worker recognizes that all of the specialists are in a sense ancillary to teaching, and have subordinate roles. The primary purpose of the school is education, and the specialists who serve in the school system other than teachers must relate themselves to the educational purposes of the classroom teacher. It is not compatible with the aims of education to overlook any resource which can be brought to bear to achieve the goal of maximum educational benefit for each educable child.

TEACHER-SOCIAL WORKER ROLE

The teacher and the social worker are a team and their contact with each other is frequent. The teacher in the classroom is usually the first person to perceive the pupil's difficulty, and in making referrals defines and focuses the child's problem as she sees it in its academic context.

The school social worker uses the teacher's referral information in making the social diagnosis and keeps the teacher apprised of pertinent developments and the use of various corrective or restorative measures. The teacher is frequently the first to observe any changes or improvement in the behavior of the child resulting from treatment measures and she reports these to the social worker.

The teacher and the social worker are in communication throughout the period of treatment, exchanging information, offering suggestions, and, in general, assisting each other in helping the child to effect an adjustment—the teacher through pedagogy and the social worker by casework, group work methodology, and by the use of his knowledge, skills, and techniques.

Discussing school social work, Boston said:

As a member of the school staff, the social worker also offers consultation to teachers with whom he may share his professional knowledge and his understanding of the meaning of children's behavior. The teacher uses this help to increase her own effectiveness in her work with the children in her room.

School social workers also contribute to the school program through participation in faculty meetings, parent study groups, in-service training programs, and in school committees. In addition the school social worker plays an important role in a liaison capacity between the school and other community social agencies which helps the school and the other resources to be mutually helpful to each other.[5]

THE SOCIAL WORKER-PARENT ROLE

Most parents strongly desire academic success for their children, and are disappointed in failures within a culture which places a high premium on the value of schooling and accomplishment. A mentally retarded or physically handicapped child may present particular difficulties for the child or his parents. One parent whose child had suffered brain-damage experienced great frustration in repeated failures to have the child enrolled in school. The disappointment was heightened when the child who saw the children in the neighborhood enrolling in school year after year begged and pleaded with his mother to be permitted to attend. The pressure on the child from his peer group was a serious and disorganizing experience, both for the child and his parents, and pointed to the woeful lack of staff and facilities in the school for the handicapped, but educable child.

To assist with the problem the school social worker introduced the parents to others facing similar problems who, by working with the school social workers, teachers, the PTA, the League of Women Voters, and various legislators finally succeeded in having provisions made in the public schools for their handicapped children. By tapping various resources these parents were able to bring scouting, summer camping, and other kinds of activities into the lives of their children when pre-

5 *Ibid.*, p. 523.

viously all such educational and character-building activities had appeared to be covered with "off limits" signs.

Sometimes vital resources simply do not exist in communities, particularly in rural areas, and the social worker may take the lead in developing them. In one sense, the social worker serves as the community's conscience by calling attention to deprivation, need, and suffering, while always holding out the hope for something better. The school social worker actively hopes for school improvements and encourages parents and others in an effort to enact these improvements so that all children may gain maximum educational benefits within the limits of their own capacities.

A specific case illustrates some of the parent-child factors of concern to the social worker:

> One boy who had been truanting, had been told by the principal that if he persisted in his truanting he would be suspended and would not be permitted to attend school. In addition to missing school he had been arraigned by the local constable for stealing and driving a government truck. The matter had been referred to the Juvenile Court, and the judge told the boy that either he must stop truanting and stealing or he would be sent to a foster home or the state correctional institution for boys, and that he must see a psychiatrist.

> When seen by the school social worker he said, "I don't want to go into a foster home; I have a home. Foster homes are for children who don't have homes." He also said, "I don't want to go to reform school. I'm not a criminal." And again, "I need a psychiatrist about like I need rocks in my head." On investigation it was disclosed that all communication between this boy and the school principal had been blocked, and that his relationships with his teachers had suffered as a result. The boy had difficulty expressing himself, largely because of lack of trust in others and confidence in himself. After five interviews with the school social worker during which confidence and trust had been reestablished, he was ready to face the principal and teachers again, and to tackle and resolve the classroom problem, which he did successfully.

Some youth and some parents cannot communicate with educators and other authority figures. They do not only lack communication skill, but they have difficulty because of their emotions which result in failure to relate and transmit ideas and viewpoints. The social worker, through his study and evaluation of the situation, is often helpful in solving school problems.

Many parents hesitate to use community services because of their resistance to accepting help. Some parents go hungry and permit their children to become malnourished because seeking help is too threatening to them. To some parents seeking assistance represents failure on their part in rearing their children. Their feelings occasionally run so high that without help with their emotions they can never bring themselves to utilize services. For these threatened individuals the social worker is often a connecting link between the service and the need.

The social worker notes the existence of services and helps those who stand to benefit to tap their use with interviewing and relationship skill aimed at breaking down barriers. The worker thus renders a service in helping the parent to use the school, and in so doing, lays the groundwork for more effective and efficient use of the educational experience by the child. The social worker is ever alert to the fact that the family's influence upon children is the mainspring of their behavior; that there are various physical, social, psychological, and cultural forces which impinge upon the individual and which result in behavior which may or may not be conducive to learning and the sound use of the educational experience.

The classroom teacher had observed that Steven Colby was apathetic, listless, unmotivated, sat staring for long periods of time at his feet or out the window, and was unresponsive to the group or the classroom activity. The teacher made a referral to the social worker who, upon investigation, discovered that the Colby family urgently needed help. For months the family income had been depressed and their means were wholly inadequate for subsistence. The family, literally starving, was referred by social service to a relief-giving agency where they received income augmentation and budget management help. Within a few weeks Steven was responding with interest in his class and other school activities.

A high school junior who had become pregnant out-of-wedlock was referred to a children's agency providing services to girls and to their families. In making the referral, the school social worker was a friend and a source of reliable information to the girl. Learning that she could talk about her problem in confidence and not be condemned, the girl was able to seek help and accept it when proferred, and finally, to contact an agency established to assist girls in her situation.

An eight-year-old boy, self-conscious because he was unable to articulate clearly, was referred by the social worker to a speech clinic for corrective speech. At the end of six months he could pronounce, not only his "s" sounds and other difficult consonants, but he no longer was singled out by his peers for unkind remarks or equally distasteful solicitation and sympathy.

A medical clinic was used for an eye examination of a five-year-old boy with a *lazy eye*. This child had a visual defect, which, if not corrected in his early childhood, would have resulted in permanent loss of vision. The social worker in this instance made the referral and conferred with the family about the importance of keeping the *good* eye covered for many months.

The school social worker brings to his work comprehensive knowledge of community resources. He knows their existence, their background and history, their structure in the law, and the philosophy and policy guiding their administration. It is the school social worker who helps the troubled child and family to use local resources as a means of achieving optimum educational experiences for each child. He is the one who makes referrals to social agencies and is instrumental in bringing to pass a blending of needs and services.

THE SOCIAL WORKER AND THE SCHOOL CHILD

Casework and group work are both employed in the school setting. The following cases illustrate casework in a public school and in a university setting:

CASEWORK IN THE PUBLIC SCHOOL

Byron Farr, an intellectually superior sixth-grader was referred to the social worker because he was failing in school. His classmates avoided him and he "played and clowned" during regular class and study periods.

The teacher felt defeated. She had tried everything she knew to motivate Byron, but had gotten nowhere. Sensing the boy's need for social acceptance and peer group status, the teacher had resorted to various maneuvers to get his classmates to "make Byron one of them," but the students had not responded to her efforts. The students considered him a snobbish, intellectual pedant, for when he was not clowning he was trying to impress them with talk about world history and "space technocracy." The teacher understood Byron's behavior, yet felt frustrated because she was unable to help him to utilize the superior intellect he possessed.

When the social worker interviewed Mrs. Farr, she found an emotionally drained woman burdened with the care of seven children under eleven years of age, the demands of managing a home, many community activities, and helping her husband to work toward his Ph.D. She admitted to dispiritedly saying, "no" to Byron without hearing what he was asking, and to denying his requests because she lacked the energy to reach a decision. Not secure in her marriage, she would rise to her husband's defense at the suggestion that he should play a father's role by demanding "does his father always have to do what Byron wants?" From Mrs. Farr's report, it was clear that

Byron saw his father as an eminent, powerful figure, one whom he would like to imitate; but when he reached out for him, he was rebuffed. His failure to find satisfaction at home carried over to the classroom where, facing problems, he gave up without trying.

In addition to teaching history in a junior college, Byron's father was working towards his Ph.D. and had heavy commitments to community activities. Mrs. Farr, whose career had been interrupted by marriage, was silently resentful of the children, having to rear them without much assistance from their father. The excuses she made for his failures were thinly disguised and unconvincing, and clearly showed that she and the children were competing unsuccessfully for his time and attention.

To some extent, Mrs. Farr understood that Byron was a lonely, unhappy boy, who was striving for the status of his peers; nevertheless, she continually pushed him into more adult roles because he was precocious, the oldest child, and because she had nowhere else to turn for her own dependency needs.

Psychological tests and interviews revealed much about Byron's failure to function adequately within the school system. His IQ was 162. Rorschach tests indicated that the things he encountered in the world were rich in significance for him. He did not just see rocks, for example, but rocks of a definite kind, similar to others in some ways and different in other ways. He used verbal imagery to solve problems as social scientists often do, and at the same time used visual imagery as do the physical scientists. Testing also revealed that he was distractable and fantasied activity which obviously interrupted his performance, resulting in poor use of his potential for classroom work. By achieving satisfaction through intellectual mechanisms and their exploitation and fantasy, he had become isolated socially from his peer group.

When he talked to the social worker he described how boring schoolwork was. Asked if possibly a more important problem was that he did not have friends who shared his interests, and if he did not feel lonely, he began to cry and said, "Yes, and another thing I don't have is a BB gun."

In his desperate search for the approval of adults and classmates, Byron had been using his intellectual ability; but behind this facade was a very lonely boy. Basically he wanted to enjoy the dependent relationship of a child to his parents and other adults; but most of all he wanted status among his classmates.

The help provided for this boy involved the school, parents, social worker, and psychologist. The teacher, who had believed she was failing because she was unable to motivate a bright boy, was shown that the problem essentially was not school focused. She was encouraged in her efforts to individualize her work with Byron and to consider realistically how to help him to bridge the gulf between himself and his classmates. The teacher was more helpful when she realized that Byron's problem did not result from her failure to provide a challenging curriculum for a precocious boy. She learned that basic to his success in school was a close relationship with a significant adult, and that this relationship was the mainspring of social, emotional, and intellectual growth.

With help the teacher was able to give approval for Byron's scientific and intellectual interests, and to respond to his achievements and expressed desires. The social distance was bridged with his peers, in part, when their school's science display was given an "outstanding" rating at the science fair. Under the teacher's supervision, Byron had directed the building of the display which had given him a chance to work with the class members, to gain their esteem by his helpful demonstration of his scientific knowledge, and to share their satisfaction in the rating of merit awarded to their school by the judges.

During five conferences Mrs. Farr was given an opportunity to express feelings about her own situation as well as her relationship to Byron. In a supportive and understanding relationship with the caseworker she felt accepted, gained a sense of importance, and became less needful with the result that she was able to see that Byron was only a child and was not ready for peer relationships with adults, however bright he might be. After she understood his symptomatic behavior and realized that he needed more of her attention and love, she reversed herself by not only relieving him of much of the care of the younger children, but also by giving him some of her time and really listening to his problems. She had failed in the past by equating intelligence with emotional and social maturity, and had not allowed time for the satisfaction of normal dependency needs and mothering. She had failed by expecting too much of him too soon, and by turning to him for her own satisfactions and needs.

Mr. Farr, whose view of himself was that of helping and advising others, rather than of being in need of help himself, was given a comprehensive review of the evaluation of the boy's problem. He acknowledged the problem and actively entered into plans to correct the difficulties. It was pointed out to him that Byron saw him as powerful and strong, and that when his son read history books and talked to him of situations beyond his years it was his way of trying to gain attention from his father. From this he began to understand what was needed in terms of a relationship with his boy. He was able to shift in his view of the problem as one of meeting educational need to one that would require personal contact and development to make up the loss which the boy had felt. He was helped without becoming guilty, inordinately anxious, or resentful.

During the three months of interviews Byron's behavior began to change. He gave up much that was symptomatic in the classroom and found satisfactions through associations with classmates, thus developing peer group standing. As evidence of this he was elected to a class office for the first time.

His clowning and intellectualizing, his tendency to belittle efforts of classmates for self-enhancement, and to act superior to other pupils were lessened. He was able to make jokes on himself. At home, as the mother found easement from her chores of rearing the children through having some of them attend nursery school, she found more time for Byron and would talk to him in the evening when the other children were in bed. She no longer felt the need to compete with him, and with greater satisfaction in her own life, she fit into his schedule more easily. Mr. Farr learned ways to communicate his interest to Byron and to utilize their time together in ways that resulted in understanding and rapport. They would swim and hunt together and engage in activities at a level commensurate with Byron's interest and activities. His response to treatment was salutary and his school performance showed a marked improvement.

CASEWORK IN THE UNIVERSITY SETTING

Social work in the university setting is not common. However, Mrs. K. is an example[6] of casework with a married couple which aimed at strengthening the family unit and helping Mrs. K. with problems related to her role performance in school. Occasionally a mismated couple whose conflict may be complicated by parenthood needs help, not only to end an unhappy, destructive marriage, but to solve serious economic and social problems which are interfering with their academic work.

Mrs. K., a senior majoring in office administration in the College of Business, was failing in school. During her intake interview at the Bureau [7] she complained about her marriage. After a series of interviews it became apparent to her and to the social worker that her marriage was unworkable. Mrs. K. thought that her husband was too weak, too easily dominated, eccentric, and a poor provider. She further felt that marriage had proved far too large an undertaking for him, particularly since in marrying her he had assumed responsibility for her three children by a previous marriage—a boy, age 5, and two girls,

[6] Adapted from Milton G. Thackeray and Rex A. Skidmore, "Casework Service in a University Setting," *Social Casework*, Vol. 43 (February, 1962), pp. 69–70.
[7] Bureau of Marriage and Family Counseling, University of Utah.

ages 6 and 15. When Mr. K., also a student, came to see the worker, he readily acknowledged his limitations as a husband and father, and suggested a divorce.

Mrs. K. had also thought of divorce, but the idea of taking this action was distasteful to her. She had projected the failure of her marriage onto her husband. She felt that it was dangerous to be with him, and she was afraid that he might kill himself or do violence to her or their neighbors. She was certain that at any moment he was going to "brutally assault" her fifteen-year-old daughter.

In the staff conference it was concluded that, although Mr. K. was weak and ineffectual in marriage, at school, and on the job, he was not likely to become physically violent. Rather, this was a case of Mrs. K.'s having had enough of marriage and, in her frustration, trying to avoid the pain of failure by blaming her husband. Moreover, she was strongly motivated to finish her schooling. She believed that a college degree would increase her earning power.

As she became secure in her relationship with the worker, Mrs. K. confided, "I have been married and divorced not once but twice before. I'm a two-time loser. My friends must think I am awful!" She worried about what they would think if they were to learn that her third marriage was on the rocks. She was also concerned about what the worker thought of her. The worker's perception of Mrs. K.'s feelings, communicated to her within a relationship of trust, and his acceptance of her as an important individual, made it possible for her to talk about what she would have to do. Once the issues were brought into the open and discussed with her husband, her relatives, and her minister, she experienced great relief. She could then realize how destructive her marriage had become.

Finally, through individual and joint interviews, Mr. and Mrs. K. were able to agree to separate and to consult an attorney who would secure a divorce for them. Mrs. K. was referred to a day nursery which could give afterschool care to her two youngest children until she finished her schooling. She was also helped to accept psychiatric treatment in regard to the intrapersonal problems related to her unsuccessful marriage.

When Mrs. K. had first come to the Bureau, her disturbance had been acute. Her disorganized emotional state was evidenced by her psychological defenses, her psycho-physiological disturbances, and her many projections. Her suicidal and homicidal feelings were masked by her fear of her husband's violence. Continuing the marriage would have resulted only in even greater stress. At the end of the academic year, Mrs. K. graduated and found a suitable job. Mr. K. continued his schooling.

GROUP WORK IN THE SCHOOL

Work with groups is less commonly found, although growing in importance in some school systems because some problems are more easily solved with a group approach. In one high school, social group work was introduced by having the student leaders of the school meet weekly to discuss school and social problems. These students learned methods of solving personal, family, and other problems which were blocking the learning process. One of the students asked, "When did I first start disliking school?" Another confessed, "My problem started when I was in the kindergarten!" Together they discussed important causes for their attitudes. One student identified an important transition problem having to do with students transferring from the elementary school to junior high. Students in the elementary grades had been in a class where only one teacher taught. The responsibility of students was to relate to one, not to several teachers, and when they moved into junior high, they had a different teacher for each class period. In the elementary schools, the student group was relatively small and closely knit; in junior high it was large and impersonal, making orientation to the new surroundings and new friends a big hurdle. Finally, they mentioned that in the primary grades they had not been required to study at home, but in junior high school they were required to do an extensive amount of work at home. In fact, one student said facetiously, "Why bother to go home? When I have so much schoolwork to do at home, why not stay at school all the time?" As a result of this open discussion and the focusing of their problems, the school modified old programs and developed new ones to assist students through the orientation and transition period.

In still another group situation, students raised questions about dating excesses and school performance. Students seemed to feel that parents should set limits to their dating experiences. One student said, "If we don't date, our parents become unhappy and they are unhappy when we do." They talked about steady dating, the time dating took from their studies, and finally arrived at a solution which improved the academic and social climate for the entire school.

In one school system, children were brought together to discuss peer group difficulties and other classroom problems. Some were withdrawn, some shy, some too aggressive, and some in conflict about sex roles and in confusion about their own sexual identity. Many related poorly, if at all, to teachers and other adults. In almost every case, the children were unhappy in school, basically because of their poor relationships with adults and other children.

They were brought together in groups of six to eight for meetings which lasted for an hour once or twice each week. These activities consisted mostly of play and table games, followed by refreshments and group discussions. Few limits were set. They were told that they could not destroy school property, that they were not to harm one another, or to leave the room without permission. The results, after a few months, were significant in helping the children to develop appropriate relationship skills, to identify and relate to their own sex roles, and to express feelings about adults and become comfortable in relationships with adults and in the classroom situation.

PREVENTION

In no other institution is greater opportunity afforded for prevention of personal and social problems than in the schools. Educators are among the first to spot incipient, symptomatic behavior, and many teachers, if not most, would refer children to special services before serious damage occurs, if such services were available and if the attitudes of parents, children, and the public toward these services were less apathetic or hostile and more receptive.

There can be little question, for example, that problems of adjustment could be avoided if every school system had the organizational machinery and trained personnel to properly induct new students into the school system. The truant should be identified immediately and given specialized help on the fairly safe assumption that his truanting reflects personal or social malaise. Theft, arson, listlessness, disinterest in school, and shyness may all portend difficulties of small proportions which, if not handled early, might become serious problems.

The organization within the school for vocational guidance, health services, psychological and psychiatric services, and social services when used as a preventive tool holds promise of averting the kind of difficulty which leads to school dropouts, delinquency, vandalism, and other failure of youth to reap maximum benefits from their school experiences. The school social worker, in particular, is in a strategic position to work with children, families, and communities on a preventive level.

SUMMARY

School social work has grown out of the mandate to the schools to educate and train all of the children of all of the people to the maximum of their potential and capacity. It is a corollary to compulsory school attendance, since not all children, unaided, are able to fit into the traditional educational mold.

Recently specialists have been added as adjuncts to the school for the purpose of helping the child to use the educational experience. These specialists include social workers who in their functions relate themselves to the role performance of the child and his social imperatives and needs.

The school social worker focuses on social functioning and on the needs of the child to make an adaptation to the school. His work is addressed to the fact that forces within and outside the child, and often outside the school itself, may impinge in ways to block the use which the pupil is able to make of the school experience. The social worker intervenes to remove roadblocks to learning, and in doing so, may work with individuals or with groups of students.

The school social worker relates himself to the teacher, the principal, to the pupil, and to the parents. Frequently he works with the teacher and principal, striving for greater understanding of the difficulty which confronts the pupil. He has interviews with the student to aid him in accepting provisions of the school and the educational experience, depending upon circumstances which are diagnostically determined.

The school social worker becomes an adjunct to the families in helping them to accept the purposes of the school and the needs of the pupil and in bringing the two together. Parents frequently function inadequately, simply because of needs and unsolved problems in their own lives. The school social worker contributes to the solution of problems which interfere directly or indirectly with the pupil's schooling. The social worker works with the team—teachers and other specialists— to bring about the maximum educational benefits to all of the children of all of the people.

QUESTIONS FOR DISCUSSION

1. Defend the statement that school social work is a corollary to compulsory school attendance.

2. Which children in the school are potential candidates for school social work?

3. Explain why the need for school social work is suggested by social mobility, diversity of curriculum and school philosophy, and learning proclivities.

4. When is the home not an ally of learning?

5. What are the social-psychological elements in the diagnostic formulation of a school social work problem?

6. Cite examples from your own experience which would justify the function of a school social worker in the public school system.

7. What would militate against the teacher's performing the role of a school social worker?

8. In the Byron Farr case, what were the factors impinging upon the efficient and effective use of the school experience by Byron?

9. Outline how you would see the functions of the school social worker in the university setting.

SPECIAL ACTIVITIES

1. Invite a social worker from the public schools to discuss the role of a school social worker.

2. Outline the essential features of a school program for atypical children. Mention particularly your understanding of the kind of special equipment which would be needed by the school, staff requirements, and the relationship between the equipment and the school's educational objectives and philosophy.

3. List and briefly describe the essential functions of services within your community which might be arrayed or mobilized on behalf of the schoolchild in achieving a maximum utilization of the educational experience.

SELECTED REFERENCES

BARAUCK, ALICE W., BRANGWIN, LORNA C., and HAMILTON, JEANNE E., "Casework for Troubled Parents," *Social Casework,* Vol. 31 (March, 1950), pp. 112–116.

BOWER, ELI M., *Early Identification of Emotionally Handicapped Children in School* (Springfield, Illinois: Charles C. Thomas, Publisher, 1960).

JOHNSON, ARLIEN, *School Social Work* (New York: National Association of Social Workers, 1962).

KIRK, SAMUEL A., *Early Education of the Mentally Retarded* (Urbana: University of Illinois Press, 1958).

LEE, GRACE, *Helping the Troubled School Child* (New York: National Association of Social Workers, 1959).

NESBIT, ELSIE, GUILBEAU, GWENDOLYN, and LANDRUM, ELIZABETH W., "The Triangle—The Parent, The Teacher, and The Visiting Teacher," *The Bulletin of the National Association of School Social Workers,* Vol. 30 (June, 1955), pp. 3–15.

POOLE, FLORENCE, "An Analysis of the Characteristics of School Social Work," *Social Service Review,* Vol. 23 (December, 1949), pp. 454–459.

"School Social Work Practice," *Proceedings* of the Lake Forest Workshop (New York: National Association of Social Workers, 1958) .

SIKKEMA, MILDRED, "An Analysis of Structure and Practice of School Social Work Today," *Social Service Review,* Vol. 23 (December, 1949), pp. 447–453.

SMALLEY, RUTH E., "School Counseling as Social Work," *The Bulletin of the National Association of School Social Workers,* Vol. 30 (June, 1955), pp. 21–34.

THURMAN, ARCH, "School Social Work as it Relates to Community Services," *The Bulletin of the National Association of School Social Workers,* Vol. 31 (September, 1955), pp. 13–28.

CHAPTER 7

Public Welfare

What is public welfare? Public welfare means different things to many people and what it means depends somewhat on who these people are, and through what lens they view the picture.

A happily married couple in their late twenties are jubilant when told by the judge that they are now the proud and legal parents of their one-year-old son placed with them earlier by a child welfare worker. Public welfare for them is an affirmative answer to their longing and oft repeated question, "Will we ever have babies of our own to love and rear?"

To Mrs. Pignelli, public welfare means she can be at home with her children in their infancy when they most need her, for she can "get by" on the monthly check from the public welfare department. Many of her friends prefer to work and to place their children in the day care center, the meaning of public welfare to them. Some disapprove of Mrs. Pignelli's attitude about "taking relief"; nevertheless, this is what she prefers, and although the welfare check pays only for "essentials," she manages because her parents supply her with vegetables and meat from the farm, and she uses hand-me-down clothes given to her by the "relief society" sisters of her church. When the children are older, and all are in school, she will go back to her old job at the bank.

Mrs. Trimble is dying of cancer. She, her two children, some of her neighbors, and the postman on her route know that a check from "Social Security" is the basic means of financial support for the family since she stopped working. None question her "right" to receive the Social Security check and no derisive or objectionable comments are heard about it; yet, the social security check, public assistance to Mrs. Pignelli, and the adoption service are all public welfare and share a public concern for the income and other personal and social needs of the population.

To some, public welfare is the "garbage heap" for human wreckage— the idle, the shiftless, the sick and decrepit, the transient, loafers, malingerers, unemployables, beggars, and certain ne'er-do-wells.

Experts and professionals see public welfare in different ways. "Some, for example, see it as an aggregation of quite distinct programs, grouped together by most states and localities for administrative convenience in a public welfare department but quite independent from each other in purpose, origin, criteria of performance, and logic of development. Others by contrast . . . see public welfare evolving toward organic unity of function and purpose, a single whole in which the parts, however specialized in their functioning, derive their vitality and character from the parent body."[1]

Public welfare includes the public insurance systems; other income maintenance programs for the aged, the blind, the disabled; aid to families for the care of their children; medical care to the indigent and aged; and services of various kinds to these and other groupings of men, women, and children.

GOVERNMENT'S RESPONSIBILITY FOR WELFARE

Basic responsibility of government for welfare was established in England with the Elizabethan poor laws, and relief under the provisions of those laws was a local matter, limited to specialized kinds of need, and extended only to those whose claims of settlement could not be legally disputed.

Residual elements of relief in kind, public responsibility for only certain kinds of need, and work and residence requirements, characteristics of colonial relief, are still found in various welfare provisions of state and local governments. Although many of these measures were repressive, it is well to remember that they do, nevertheless, affirm the principle of governmental responsibility.

The *federal* government's responsibility for welfare started in the earliest days of the Republic when in 1785 Congress made grants of public lands to states for schools. Other responsibilities were extended when the people, through their elected representatives, added other agencies such as the Federal Office of Education, the Children's Bureau, and the Vocational Rehabilitation Administration; but a comprehensive plan for the protection of citizens against income risks did not become an *enduring* principle of federal responsibility for welfare until 1935 with the passage of the Social Security Act. Cohen has said: "If the enactment of the Social Security Act in 1935 represents the beginning of

[1] Elizabeth Wickenden and Winifred Bell, *Public Welfare,* The Project on Public Services for Families and Children (New York: The New York School of Social Work, Columbia University, 1961), p. 13.

national acceptance of public welfare as an essential element in modern society, the Public Welfare Amendments of 1962 represent the maturation of that concept." [2]

The newest federal agency represented in the President's Cabinet, the Department of Health, Education, and Welfare, created in 1953, is the outgrowth of a growing conviction that the federal government has a responsibility for the *general welfare.* The creation of a new Welfare Administration, with Dr. Ellen Winston sworn in as the nation's first Commissioner of Welfare on January 28, 1963, and the emergence of social work in the structure of federal government pinpoints a shift in thinking about governmental responsibility and attests to a new philosophy of welfare.

Emerging upon the American scene are some enduring principles and philosophical concepts about welfare and the use of government as an instrument of social policy, such as: the federal government will take responsibility to ensure American workers and their families against the risk of unemployment, old age, death, and disability; the federal government in cooperation with the states will extend protection to all citizens who qualify for assistance under the public welfare provision of the Social Security Act as a statutory right; medical care shall be available to indigent recipients of public assistance and to the aged whose income is too depressed to provide this care; services will be extended to all recipients of public assistance and medical care; the able-bodied who work for what they receive will be credited with *earnings,* and not be stigmatized by having their income called *relief.*

Public welfare is predicated on the assumption that the strength of the individual is the strength of society and that all suffer when someone goes hungry, is afflicted by disease, or fails to use well his educational opportunities. Modern public welfare is opposed to the concept that helping produces weakness. A philosophy that derogates, punishes, and otherwise destroys the individual is intolerable in an affluent and free society.

Modern public welfare subscribes to the view that government is the servant, not the master of the people, and should cooperate at all levels of operation (county, state, federal) in intelligent concert with the many voluntary efforts to protect the citizens against the debilitating vicissitudes of life.

THE SOCIAL SECURITY ACT

The cornerstone of public welfare in the United States is the Social Security Act, passed August 14, 1935. In general, this Act, with its many amendments, is the chief means by which government at the local, state,

---

[2] Wilbur J. Cohen, "The First Decade of the Department of Health, Education, and Welfare," *Public Welfare,* Vol. 21 (April, 1963), p. 7.

and national levels provides income security to citizens. The income maintenance provisions of the Act are chiefly in the form of social insurance and financial aid to individuals in need of such assistance. Other divisions of the Act make grants to states available for various social services. The 1962 Amendments made sweeping changes possible in public welfare, to extend services and emphasize prevention, rehabilitation, and various incentives for greater financial independence.

Discussion in this chapter centers on provisions under Federal Old Age and Retirement Insurance, Unemployment Compensation, Old Age Assistance, Aid to Families with Dependent Children, Aid to the Blind, Aid to the Disabled, and Other Services.

OLD AGE AND SURVIVOR'S DISABILITY INSURANCE

Old Age and Survivor's Disability Insurance (OASDI) is an income maintenance program for retired or disabled workers or for their survivors. A worker must have reached 62 to receive benefits under OASDI. Any worker "insured" under the provisions of this Act, who has an illness or an injury so severe as to be unable to "engage in any substantial gainful activity" is eligible for disability insurance benefits.

Survivors of "covered workers" include the spouse, minor children under 18 years of age, dependent parents at 62, and "a divorced wife, if, before the worker's death she is dependent on him for her support pursuant to a court order or agreement and if she has in her care his child who is also entitled to payments.

"In addition, a lump-sum death payment may be made to the widow or widower who was living in the same household with the worker at death; otherwise, it can go to pay the worker's burial expenses. The lump sum is 3 times the amount of his monthly retirement benefits, but cannot exceed $255." [3]

OASDI, the most popular provision of the Social Security Act, has been extended to include nine out of ten gainfully employed workers in the country. OASDI enjoys wide public approval, because it is a "contributory" system; citizens pay for their retirement. Payments are based on previous earnings; equity can be claimed for the system. Beneficiaries of OASDI are not subject to investigation and a "test of means." Records are accurately maintained and "claims" processed and paid with dispatch. The administration of the system is handled efficiently, economically, and with a view toward safeguarding the rights of the beneficiary. Bank savings, income from security, from rental property, and annuities, regardless of the amount, do not limit payments. On the other hand, limits *are* placed upon the amount of income which retired workers can

[3] *Your Social Security,* Federal Old Age Survivor's and Disability Insurance (Washington, D.C.: Department of Health, Education and Welfare (May, 1963), p. 7.

earn from employment while still receiving retirement insurance, as indicated below: [4]

Your total earnings and the number of months you work are the two things which determine how much of your yearly benefits can be paid to you.

If your earnings do not exceed $1,200 for the year, you will get all your benefits.

Even if your earnings are considerably more than $1,200, you may still be eligible for some social security benefits. If you earn between $1,200 and $1,700, only $1 in benefits will be withheld for each $2 you earn over $1,200.

An additional $1 in benefits is withheld for each dollar that is over $1,700.

But no matter how much you would earn in a year, you will get your social security benefits for any month you neither earn over $100 as an employee, nor render substantial services as a self-employed person.

You will also receive your benefits for all months beginning with the month of your 72nd birthday—no matter how much you earn.

When the Social Security Act was passed in 1935, the country was experiencing its worst depression. Many workers were without employment. Retirement was written into the law to encourage men 65 and older to retire and to make way on the labor market for younger unemployed men and women. In times of high employment and labor shortages, the Act might well have to be changed to give inducement not to retirement, but to an ongoing attachment to the labor force. The forced retirement features of OASDI are probably the most objectionable.

Taxes, under the provision of the Federal Insurance Contribution Act (FICA), are collected from the employee and the employer during the productive working life of the worker to pay for OASDI. Self-employed workers pay the full amount of the tax. The following table shows the present and projected tax rates for employed workers and their employees, and for the self-employed:

PAST AND FUTURE FINANCING PROVISIONS

Period	Maximum Table Earning Base	Employee Tax Rate	Employer Tax Rate	Self-Employed Tax Rate
1937–39	$3,000	1 %	1 %	*
1950	3,000	1½%	1½%	*
1951–53	3,600	1½%	1½%	2¼%
1954	3,600	2 %	2 %	3 %
1955–56	4,200	2 %	2 %	3 %
1957–58	4,200	2¼%	2¼%	3⅜%
1959	4,800	2½%	2½%	3¾%
1960–61	4,800	3 %	3 %	4½%
1962	4,800	3⅛%	3⅛%	4⁷⁄₁₀%
1963–65	4,800	3⅝%	3⅝%	5⁴⁄₁₀%
1966–67	4,800	4⅛%	4⅛%	6²⁄₁₀%
1968 and after	4,800	4⅝%	4⅝%	6⁹⁄₁₀%

* Self-employed not covered in this period.

[4] If You Work While You Get Social Security Payments (Washington, D.C.: Social Security Administration, 1963), pp. 5–6.

In adopting OASDI the United States radically departed from reliance on the family, the church, private philanthropy, government at the local level, and unending emergency measures, to provide a bulwark against want and income need. Thinking men agree that such a departure was warranted and that for the retired, the disabled, and survivors of insured workers, OASDI offers greater security and financial independence than they previously knew. Five and one-half million persons were receiving social security in 1953; in 1963 over 18.5 million men, women, and children were receiving social security checks amounting to more than $1.2 billion dollars a month. Aged people numbering 12.7 million now receive close to a billion dollars a month in regular social security benefits.

Certainly, no president or congress before 1935 had undertaken so bold and far-reaching a move to secure the citizens against the dread and fear of poverty.

UNEMPLOYMENT INSURANCE

OASDI and Unemployment Insurance are the two insurance provisions of the Social Security Act. Unemployment insurance serves to cushion workers whose income is interrupted by work stoppages and layoffs. Most states will pay Unemployment Compensation for a maximum of twenty-six weeks. Unemployment Insurance is no protection of income against strikes or prolonged periods of unemployment resulting from economic recession and depression. The American system makes no income provisions for prolonged unemployment except to a few workers who can qualify for Aid to Families with Dependent Children or residual general assistance, which in most states contains many features of the "poor laws."

Unemployment Compensation is a form of *insurance* rather than a public assistance program. It is a *nondeterrent* system.[5] Eligibility for a person to receive unemployment insurance in most states is described as follows:[6]

1. He must register for work at a public employment office and file his claim for benefits.
2. He must have worked previously on a job covered by the State law. This usually includes jobs in factories, shops, mines, mills, stores, offices, or other places of private industry and commerce. In more than half the States

[5] Nondeterrent systems, as opposed to deterrent *means test* programs, eliminate tests of need. Beneficiaries are not "investigated," they do not have to be indigent to be eligible for benefits, and it is presumed that benefits are earned by the workers' own productive efforts. Furthermore, repressive measures are not employed as in *means test* systems to discourage claims. To the contrary, under OASDI, for example, the administration actively tries to locate men and women eligible for benefits who, for some reason, have never filed claims.

[6] Wayne Vasey, *Government and Social Welfare* (New York: Holt, Rinehart & Winston, Inc., 1958), p. 97.

the law applies only to employment in concerns that have four or more persons on the payroll during twenty weeks of the year. In other States it applies also to jobs in smaller establishments.

3. He must have a certain amount of "wage credits"—which means he must have had a certain amount of pay for work in covered jobs in a specified "base period" during the year or two before he lost his job or was laid off.

4. He must be able to work. In general unemployment insurance benefits are not payable to workers who are sick or *unable* to work for any other reason, although a few states pay benefits to workers who become ill after they are unemployed and continue paying the benefits within the legal limits, if there are not suitable jobs to offer the individual. . . .

5. He must be available for work and must be ready and willing to take a suitable job if one is offered.

Unemployment Insurance is financed by a tax on employers; only three states have a provision under which the employee participates in paying for unemployment insurance. The employer pays the tax but to show a profit he may pass this tax on to the consumer in higher costs of goods and services, or to the employee in lower wages, or both. Workers pay for unemployment insurance in lower salaries and higher costs of consumer goods and services.

One of the most serious economic problems of our day is that of almost continual unemployment for millions of American workers. The loss to the country because of their lack of productivity and their personal loss due to lack of income for themselves and their families is very great. Personality disorganization and the damage to the self-image of the worker is sometimes incalculable.

PUBLIC ASSISTANCE

Public assistance is an income maintenance system but should not be confused with the insurance provisions of the Social Security Act. Four main categories of clients are classified under this system: the aged, the blind, the disabled, and the families of dependent children. Public assistance is administered at the state and local levels of government in contrast to the OASDI, which is a federal program, and unemployment insurance which is essentially state financed with the federal government paying only the cost of administration.

The states are approved for federal matching funds under grant-in-aid programs for the support of local public assistance programs when the state plan provides for the following: [7]

1. Statewide operation.
2. State financial participation.
3. A single State agency to administer the plan or supervise its administra-

[7] *Characteristics of State Public Assistance Plans Under the Social Security Act* (Washington, D.C.: U.S. Department of Health, Education, and Welfare, 1962), p. 2.

tion by local agencies upon which State rules, regulations, and standards are mandatory.

4. Methods of administration necessary for proper and efficient operation of the plan, including the establishment and maintenance of personnel standards on a merit basis.

5. Restriction of information about applicants for and recipients of assistance to purposes directly connected with the administration of the program. . . .

6. Opportunity for anyone wishing to do so to apply for old-age assistance, aid to dependent children, aid to the blind, or aid to the permanently and totally disabled and to have his application acted upon with reasonable promptness.

7. Opportunity for a fair hearing before the State agency for any claimant for assistance whose claim is denied or is not acted upon with reasonable promptness.

8. Submittal to the Social Security Administration of such reports as it requires.

9. Consideration, in determination of the need of a claimant of assistance, of any income and resources that he may have (with exemption, in aid to the blind, of $85 a month of earned income plus one-half of that in excess of $85).

10. Designation of a State authority or authorities responsible for establishing and maintaining standards for all the types of public and private institutions in the State in which, under the State plan, a needy person may receive assistance (applicable to all programs except aid to dependent children).

11. Prompt notice to law enforcement officials of the furnishing of aid to dependent children in respect of a child deserted or abandoned by a parent.

12. The prohibition of the concurrent receipt of more than one form of public assistance under the State plan.

13. An examination by a physician skilled in diseases of the eye or by an optometrist, whichever the individual may select, in determining blindness.

The State plan may not include:

1. Any residence requirement more restrictive than the maximums in the acts; namely, 5 years in the last 9 and 1 year immediately preceding application in old-age assistance, aid to the blind, and aid to the permanently and totally disabled; and 1 year in the case of aid to dependent children.

2. Any age requirement of more than 65 years in the old-age assistance program.

3. Any citizenship requirement barring a citizen of the United States who is otherwise eligible for aid.

Old Age Assistance

Under the provisions of Old Age Assistance (OAA) 2,226,000 citizens received financial aid in 1962. Dollars paid for OAA in 1962 were $4,296,000,000 compared with $1,039,000,000 in 1940. Amendments to the Social Security Act, which have enlarged payments, have been largely responsible for this increase. The number of aged persons receiving public assistance has declined with the extension of OASDI to larger numbers and more categories of job holders. Some residual program will be likely to continue as a need to protect the aged not covered by OASDI.

Each state has its own program for Old Age Assistance. Typically, factors of eligibility for old age assistance include age, need, value of property, and residence. As an illustration, the aged person in California generally meets the following requirements: [8]

1. Is 65 years of age or older.

2. Non-citizens must not have been convicted of an overt act against the government of the United States.

3. Must have had residence five of the last nine years, with one year immediately preceding the application.

4. Payments can be made to persons in public institutions, except where they would be excluded under the federal act. Payments are made to persons in private institutions, including those where there is no federal matching. Payments are not made in behalf of patients in a general medical institution for any period after a diagnosis of tuberculosis or psychosis, as permitted under the federal act.

5. The statutory amount for minimum need is $101 per month. Needs exceeding $101 are considered in determining the amount of payment but total assistance, plus other income cannot exceed $166, except for certain voluntary contributions.

6. The recipient can own his own home, but other property of the recipient, or of the recipient and spouse, may not exceed an assessed value of $5,000. The personal property of a recipient is limited to $1,200 net value (if the spouse is also a recipient, $2,000 net value), excluding value of personal effects and car, which is needed for transportation. The applicant must have signed or transferred property in order to qualify for assistance.

7. Medical care by vendor payment is provided for practitioners' services, dental care, prescribed drugs, sick room supplies, special duty nursing in the hospital, visiting nurse at home, x-ray, restorative services, prosthetic appliances and transportation by ambulance.

Aid to Families with Dependent Children

Income to Families with Dependent Children (AFDC) is available to eligible recipients who apply and qualify under provisions of the Social Security Act under the various state plans. In Colorado, for example, to qualify for assistance AFDC families must satisfy such requirements as: [9]

1. The child is under 16 years of age, or under 18 if regularly attending school.

2. The child must have lived within the state one year immediately preceding application, or born within one year immediately preceding application if parent or other relative with whom the child is living has resided in the state for one year immediately preceding the birth of the child.

3. Deprivation of parental support or care by reason of death, or the continued absence from the home of parent, or physical or mental incapacity of the parent, and if living with relatives as listed in the federal act.

[8] *Ibid.*, n.p.g.
[9] *Ibid.*, n.p.g.

4. The income is insufficient and other resources inadequate to provide care and income maintenance without public assistance.

5. Ownership of home is permitted; all other real and personal property must be limited to $1,000 for parent(s) and one child. For each additional child $250 is allowed up to a maximum of $2,000 for any family.

6. The amount of payment to a recipient has no maximum to it. Medical care is provided children in hospitals and practitioners' services where needed, in addition to prescribed drugs.

7. The provision in Colorado on financing is for the state to pay not less than 80 percent of the non-federal share and the county not more than 20 percent of the cost.

AFDC represents the largest numbers of recipients under the public assistance program; recipients of OAA rank first in amounts of payments made. Assistance payments were made to 3,823,000 AFDC clients in 1962, totalling $1,347,000,000. While assistance to the blind, the disabled, and the aged has remained more or less constant, assistance to children under the AFDC program has risen rapidly.

None of the public assistance programs has been more consistently under attack than AFDC. Charges are made that this aid encourages large families, illegitimacy, idleness, and dependency. These charges persist although studies show that only a small percentage of families to which illegitimate children are born receive AFDC assistance and although the amount of assistance is too little in some areas to meet the minimal health and welfare needs of children.

Many Americans are strongly opposed to aid to able-bodied citizens, and mothers and fathers of AFDC recipients, for the most part, are able-bodied. The fury of the attacks is apparently undiminished by the argument that mothers should be at home with their children, particularly in their early years; and the acrimony is not softened even in view of the demonstrated fact that many AFDC clients would strongly prefer employment to public assistance. Furthermore, money amounts, which are in some instances too small to provide a decent standard of living, could not possibly offer an inducement to idleness or illegitimacy as sometimes charged. In June, 1961, the average amount paid to recipients per child on ADC (called AFDC since 1962) was $30.30, and the range was from $9.32 in Alabama to $51.61 in Connecticut.

Aid to the Blind

In June, 1962, there were 100,000 recipients of public assistance who were blind, and aid-to-the-blind payments to them averaged $93 per month. In 1961, ninety-three million dollars were paid to the blind, with 47.8 percent coming from federal funds and 52.2 percent from state and local funds.

In determining need for the blind, state programs are required to exempt the first $85 of earned income plus one-half of that in excess of

$85. Secure in the knowledge that he will not lose his assistance, the blind person is *free* to risk seeking earnings from employment.

Most recipients are totally blind or have very limited vision. States usually provide aid to the blind only to persons whose vision with correcting glasses is not better than 20/200 in the better eye. The average recipient has been blind about twenty years.

Since 1958 there has been a gradual decrease in the caseload. The most frequent reason for the closing of an AB case was death of recipient, accounting for about one-third of the closings. Other important reasons were that the recipient was no longer eligible from the standpoint of need—with 30 percent transferring to the OAA program, and an additional 15 percent losing eligibility because of receipt of, or increase in, OASDI benefits.

Aid to the Permanently and Totally Disabled

Aid to the disabled (APTD), one of the newer public assistance programs, was created by an amendment to the Social Security Act in 1950. Those eligible for assistance under this category, as in the case of other assistance programs, subject themselves to a test of need. They must satisfy eligibility requirements related to the degree of disability, the nature of their work, and meet such other qualifications as age, residence, and citizenship which generally obtain in the other assistance programs.

Most states acted quickly after the law was amended and availed themselves of the matching provisions of the Act. By 1952, thirty-nine states had passed legislation supporting aid to the disabled. The trend in the number of recipients has been consistently upward with fifty states making payments in June, 1962.

The number of recipients in June, 1962 under this program totaled 417,000, with an average payment of $72. During the year 1961 total payments amounted to 316 million dollars, with 54.9 percent coming from federal funds and 45.1 percent from state and local funds.

Based on a 1951 study the most frequently diagnosed impairment is heart disease, but most recipients have more than one impairment. About one out of five is housebound, and only one-third have a spouse or children.

Among all recipient-beneficiaries in APTD, 65 percent are 50–64 years of age; 29 percent are 18–49, and over 6 percent are 65 or older.[10]

Aid to the disabled, and to their survivors, is also available to all "covered" workers under the provision of OASDI. This is an important development in American social security, for prior to these two provi-

---

[10] "Special Types of Public Assistance: Program Facts," U.S. Department of Health, Education, and Welfare (February, 1963), pp. 1–2; mimeographed.

sions for the disabled—the one under public assistance and the other under the insurance system—disabled workers, particularly those who were the victims of industrial accidents and disease, were at the mercy of antiquated and inefficient workman's compensation programs.

NUMBER OF PUBLIC ASSISTANCE RECIPIENTS BY PROGRAM, JUNE AND DECEMBER OF EACH YEAR, 1936 TO DATE

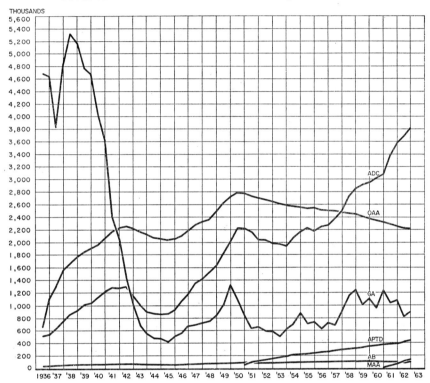

SOURCE: *Trend Report*, Graphic Presentation of Public Assistance and Related Data, December, 1962 (Washington, D.C.: Bureau of Family Services, Social Security Administration, 1963), p. 13.

General Assistance

General Assistance (GA), residual to OASDI and to the categories, AFDC, OAA, AB, and AD, is intended to aid those who cannot qualify under one of the federal-state programs, or who are not covered by social insurance.

General assistance is not a popular program, either from the standpoint of administration, or the beneficiary. Since it is not a federal-state program and taxes for it must be raised at the state and local level, the program is usually poorly funded. Payments tend to be minimal and degrading. Executives are always fighting the budget. Subject to such un-popular practices as voucher payments and giving economic assistance in kind, this form of aid carries with it the presumption that those who receive it are incapable of managing their own affairs or prudently handling money. The GA program in some parts of the country is de-moralizing, a disgrace to a civilized community, and has much in com-mon in the twentieth century with the poor relief of the Elizabethan period three and one-half centuries earlier.

Able-bodied employable men and women are sometimes found in the ranks of General Assistance and there exists a strong aversion in this country to their receiving public "handouts." Also on GA are those whom Gladwin, an anthropologist, has labeled the "undeserving poor." These are the poor who, for reasons we do not fully understand, appear to lack the motivation or the will to help themselves.

It is not that these people are dirty, or dishonest, or unfaithful in marriage. We have no trouble in respecting the natives of other lands who never bathe, and at least some crooks, and the majority of movie stars. The real reason, in my opinion, is that they are unwilling to undertake responsibility on their own behalf. We like to help people who are trying to help themselves. However pitiful the individual, or unsavory his circumstances, if he is really trying to improve his lot we will help him, and we will respect him for trying.

The people with whom we are here concerned do not try. Some of us, cer-tainly most social workers, may be able rationally to understand that in their unhappy environment these people have never learned to try; or, perhaps, even learned that it is better *not* to try. Nevertheless, our objective judgment that their apathy is not their fault seems to help even us professionals very little to persuade our subjective selves that we should accord them real respect. These are, in the immortal phrase of Alfred P. Doolittle in George Bernard Shaw's *Pygmalion,* the undeserving poor. [11]

Mencher [12] identifies several of the classic opinions which opponents of welfare appear to hold, with particular reference to both general and categorical assistance:

1. Assistance should be made as unpleasant as possible as a deterrent to its use. This is to be accomplished by giving relief in kind, rather than money, by threatening prosecution, by continuous re-evaluation of need, by making it only temporary, stopping it if illegitimacy is involved, and removing children from their own homes when these homes do not come up to standard.

2. Relief should be made unpleasant by requiring recipients to work for it re-gardless of the nature of the work, or how depressed the wage, or whether the requirement would be used as means for securing cheap labor, and notwith-standing income from this work is still labeled relief.

3. Assistance should be discouraged by making payments too low for anyone to really want it. It is argued by advocates of this approach that assistance in

11 Thomas Gladwin, "The Anthropologist's View of Poverty," *The Social Welfare Forum, 1961* (New York: National Conference on Social Welfare, 1961), pp. 76–77.

12 Samuel Mencher, "Newburgh: The Recurrent Crisis in Public Assistance," *Social Work,* Vol. 7 (January, 1962), pp. 3–4.

amounts greater than would be received by the lowest paid most menial worker, would encourage individuals to seek assistance in lieu of employment.

4. Outsiders should be prevented from seeking help by extending emergency aid for only short periods of time.

5. People should be forced to remain on their jobs or to return to employment, by denying assistance to anyone who is guilty of a "voluntary quit."

The above proposals have one thing in common. They all aim at making relief unacceptable to the recipient. Social work as a profession identifies with those in society who favor more constructive measures and interpretations, which include:

1. Providing an income floor for all citizens and the elimination of hunger and destitution, or their threat, as an instrument of social policy.

2. Extending relief to applicants who can qualify under eligibility requirements; that is, remove it from subjective, biased, and capricious considerations. Relief should be based on need as it is determined to exist by objective, rather than subjective criteria, and as a legally determined right.

3. It is assumed that workers, generally, prefer income from employment to public welfare and that motivations to work are built into the economy in the form of social, cultural, and economic advantages to the employed man or woman.

4. Psychological and social barriers sometimes stand in the way of rehabilitation and employment. Counseling and other services may be needed to restore certain individuals to economic and social self-sufficiency.

5. Preservation of the independence and self-respect of the applicant for assistance is a prime consideration in the administration of programs of relief.

6. A punitive approach defeats the purpose for which assistance is used, namely, the restoration of the individual to normal functioning; it deepens feelings of inadequacy and dependency, causes embarrassment and humiliation, and brings destructive psychological defenses into play.

7. There are many pulls in society which tend to make work more appealing than public welfare—a higher standard of living, the prestige and sense of importance one receives from work, tenure, the emoluments of society, and others.

Medical Care

Medical care is not at present one of the insurance provisions of the Social Security Act although insurance legislation that would provide medical care for the aged has been strongly advocated by some members of Congress, the Kennedy Administration, and many social workers.

The Social Security Act does, however, provide for medical care to the indigent and to the aged under the Medical Assistance to the Aged program (MAA). Indigent children and adults, regardless of age, may receive care under state-federal programs. This provision typically authorizes vendor payments for hospital care, nursing home care, practitioners' services, dental care, prescribed drugs, sick room supplies, X-ray, prosthetic appliances, transportation, and equipment.

Medical Assistance to the Aged resulted from legislation passed by

Congress in November, 1961; this act provides for medical and remedial care and services as follows: [13]

1. In-patient Hospital Services
2. Skilled Nursing Home Services
3. Physicians' Services
4. Out-Patient Hospital or Clinic Services
5. Home Health Care Services.
6. Private Duty Nursing Services
7. Physical Therapy and Related Services
8. Dental Services
9. Laboratory and X-ray Services
10. Prescribed Drugs, Eyeglasses, Dentures, and Prosthetic Devices
11. Diagnostic, Screening, and Preventive Services
12. Any Other Medical Care or Remedial Care Recognized Under State Law

Eligibility, as in all public assistance programs, is determined at the state and local level of government. For example, the following requirements were in effect in 1962 for MAA in Utah:[14]

a. Each applicant must be at least 65 years of age.
b. Each applicant must be a resident of the State of Utah on the date of application.
c. The net value of liquid assets may not exceed $1,000 for a single applicant, or $2,000 for a couple or family.
d. The net value of other personal and real property must not exceed $10,000 (a home owned and occupied and one necessary automobile are exempt).
e. The amount of net income may not exceed $110 if the applicant is single or $170 for married couples.
f. Individuals who are receiving old age assistance are not eligible for medical assistance for the aged.

The programs of financial aid and income under social security are basic underpinnings of public welfare. Food, shelter, clothing, and medical care are imperatives of all citizens in a healthy and sound community. The income provisions of social security represent a long step forward toward removing the specter of economic want from the population; nevertheless, these provisions are minimum, pitifully inadequate for health and decency in some instances, and may actually result in greater dependency because of restrictive and repressive eligibility requirements, negative attitudes, and policies.

Welfare recipients often need counseling, special education, vocational guidance, social interest, protection against discrimination, and protection of their legal rights. *Services* have been stressed from the beginning but, notwithstanding, little headway has been made in converting ideas to program in the field of practice; and with a few notable and isolated

[13] *Handbook Supplement,* **Medical Assistance for the Aged,** State Letter 531 (Washington, D.C.: U.S. Department of Health, Education, and Welfare, November 17, 1961), n.p.g.

[14] "Medical Assistance for the Aged," Utah State Department of Public Welfare, n.d.g., n.p.g.

exceptions, services have not accompanied *assistance*, although the need for these has been clear. For example, the partly disabled worker who doubts his ability to hold a job which requires the use of new knowledge and skills, without casework or other help may not be willing to risk the loss of income from public welfare entailed in accepting employment. Many mothers on AFDC, left widows in middle age, or who are divorced and have continuing responsibility for children, will hesitate to strike out in a competitive market without counseling or special training, or both, along with the assurance of personal and economic gains. Parents launch employment careers and/or enroll for retraining if, while at work, their interests at home are protected by homemaking and day care services, good schools, and other programs serving and protecting their families.

SOCIAL SERVICES

Services, as distinguished from income maintenance systems, are available under certain provisions of the Social Security Act and include such child welfare programs as those listed in Chapter 8, in addition to Crippled Children's Services, Maternal and Child Health Services, and others.

Federal funds for Crippled Children are appropriated,

For the purpose of enabling each State to extend and improve (especially in rural areas and in areas suffering from severe economic distress), as far as practicable under the conditions in such State, services for locating crippled children, and for providing medical, surgical, corrective, and other services and care, and facilities for diagnosis, hospitalization, and aftercare, for children who are crippled or who are suffering from conditions which lead to crippling.[15]

The Maternal and Child Health Services are designed

to provide or strengthen such services for mothers and children as pre-natal care clinics, well child clinics, health services for school children, dental hygiene and dental care, licensing and inspection of maternity homes, assistance to hospitals through advice on care of the maternity patient or the newborn child, education in nutrition for the mother and child, and related services. The purpose is primarily to prevent natal and neonatal difficulty.

In addition to prevention of pre- and postnatal problems, some states provide medical care facilities. This may include medical and hospital care for premature infants, treatment and hospital care for mothers whose pregnancies have complications, and dental care.[16]

The importance of certain services—foster care, crippled children, mental health, the handicapped, and veterans—have long been recognized. Recent provisions of the Social Security Act broaden services as an essential element of *all assistance* programs as a means of prevention, for

---

[15] *Compilation of the Social Security Laws* (Washington, D.C.: United States Government Printing Office, 1961), p. 138.

[16] Vasey, *op. cit.*, p. 205.

greater efficiency of administration, and to conserve human and other resources. Marin County, California, has reported a study which dramatically attests to the importance of service in public assistance.

The Marin County Welfare Department[17] decided that improvements could be made by a shift in emphasis from *eligibility* and *assistance,* to *service.* This shift was made in the Family Care Unit which handles all General Assistance cases of families with children and all other Aid to Needy Children cases aside from children in foster care.

By hiring only qualified staff (the importance of competence and professional qualifications was emphasized from the beginning) and by reducing caseloads, Marin County demonstrated convincingly that:

Caseloads declined markedly with the extension of *services.* In February, 1954 (before the shift was made),

Marin County had 5.35 Aid to Needy Children family cases per 1000 population, while the San Francisco Metropolitan area as a whole had 8.69 such cases per 1000 population. By February 1957 the Marin rate had fallen to 3.46 while that for the total area had risen to 12.09. Marin was the only county in this group showing such a marked decrease in Aid to Needy Children caseload in relation to population.

When the rate of change in the actual caseload is compared for Marin and the San Francisco area marked differences in trend are noted. The monthly average number of Aid to Needy Children cases in Marin County decreased 8.8 per cent in 1954–55 as compared with 1953–54 and 23.6 per cent in 1955–56 as compared with 1954–55.[18]

It is further indicated that

Marin's practice of tackling family problems at intake may pay off in terms of fewer "requests" becoming assistance cases. In 1953–54 the ratio of applications granted to total applications disposed of was approximately the same in Marin and the San Francisco area (69.7 and 70.3). By 1955–56 the Marin ratio had dropped to 55.9, while the ratio in the total area was 66.6.[19]

Assistance costs

decreased in Marin in 1954–55 as compared to 1953–54 (−17.5 percent), and in 1955–56 as compared to 1945–55 (−22.3 percent) while the six counties' total increased during the same period . . . .

Thus, it can be seen that during the period of increasing investment in salaries there was an overall decrease in assistance costs of such size that total costs were significantly reduced.[20]

An analysis was made of the results of the work of the newest employee social worker in the Family Care Unit, covering an eight-month period. She started with a caseload of forty Aid to Needy Children and General Relief, four of whom had been on assistance five years and one,

[17] *Building Services Into a Public Assistance Program Can Pay Off* (State of California Department of Social Welfare, n.d.g.).
[18] *Ibid.,* p. 18.
[19] *Ibid.,* p. 19.
[20] *Ibid.,* pp. 20–21.

seven. After eight months, sixteen had been discontinued, three of whom in the judgment of the agency were due to the recipients' initiative and thirteen resulted primarily from the efforts of the agency. Total aid to the thirteen cases prior to discontinuance amounted to $38,035.

The question was asked, "Did families and their situations improve when these families received more social services from the Family Care Unit?" The ratings on 100 families are conclusively affirmative and indicate that seventy-five of the families changed for the better in their over-all functioning or situation during the period rated.

That three-fourths showed varying degrees of improvement during the period rated seemed remarkable in view of the long assistance history of most of these cases and of the many serious problems they presented. The problems included personality disturbances or even diagnosed psychosis, alcoholism, illegitimacy and promiscuity, desertion, serious illness, limited intelligence, inadequate vocational skills or experience, and lifelong deprivation.[21]

The Marin County assessment is one of several now being made in different parts of the country. The evidence is not complete but evaluations of this kind lend support to the commonly held view of many, including social workers, that *service* to clients will result in the conservation of resources and improved efficiency.

PUBLIC WELFARE AMENDMENTS, PUBLIC LAW 87–543

There has been a recurring crisis in public welfare as strong criticism is leveled at programs of assistance. It has been forcefully contended, for example, that far too little has been done to prevent economic and social breakdown, or to rehabilitate dysfunctioning individuals and families on public assistance roles. Advocates of reform have urged various measures to improve practices which include: (1) provisions for the recruitment and training of staff to work in public welfare; (2) protective services for children; (3) exemption of certain income in determining assistance as an incentive to youth to save for an education and to adults in seeking employment; (4) safeguarding children in homes of unmarried mothers where fathers have deserted, through provisions of specialized services; (5) services to families and to individuals, for example, the aged, which will assist them to retain existing strengths; and (6) more effective coordination of services.

The 1962 Amendments to the public welfare provision of the Social Security Act, Public Law 87–543, have opened the door to these and other reforms. Among the most significant of the amendments are the following listed by Wilbur J. Cohen and Robert M. Ball: [22]

21 *Ibid.*, pp. 26–27.
22 Wilbur J. Cohen and Robert M. Ball, "Public Welfare Amendments of 1962," *Social Security Bulletin*, Vol. 25 (October, 1962), p. 3.

1. Seventy-five per cent Federal matching is provided for State expenditures for defined social services and training activities in the Federal-State public assistance programs.

2. Federal sharing in State assistance expenditures for the needy aged, the blind, and the disabled is increased. Federal sharing is also extended to expenditures to meet the needs of the second parent when he is unemployed or incapacitated and is living in the home with needy children.

3. The provision for aiding the dependent children of unemployed parents is extended 5 years.

4. The provision for aid to certain children receiving foster-home care is made permanent. . . .

5. Protective payments in behalf of dependent children are authorized.

6. Provision is made for demonstration projects.

7. Funds are authorized for the use of the Secretary of Health, Education, and Welfare in providing for the training of personnel, directly or by arrangements with institutions.

Major child welfare provisions of the 1962 amendments include:

1. Liberalizing authorizations for annual appropriations from $25,000,000 to $30,000,000 for the fiscal year 1962–63 and in steps of five million to fifty million for 1968–1969 and thereafter.

2. Better coordination and extension of services to all children who need them.

3. Provisions for day care services.

4. Authorization of grants to colleges and universities for special training projects beginning in 1962–63.[23]

Under Public Law 87–543, the states are aided and encouraged to improve, and where needed, to establish services, by changes in provisions of federal matching. It is the purpose of the federal government, in stressing services:

to help applicants and recipients attain or retain capability for self-care or self-support or to help them maintain and strengthen family life. These services are to be provided under State plans for old age assistance, aid to families with dependent children, aid to the blind, and aid to the permanently and totally disabled. Services are authorized in the program of medical assistance for the aged, with no minimum prescribed. The Secretary is also to specify additional services to applicants and recipients that prevent and reduce dependency, which would be entirely optional with the States.[24]

Incentives are offered for employment and financial independence and

the new law requires that the State consider all expenses attributable to employment in determining the need of a recipient of public assistance; formerly such consideration was optional and not always provided. In addition, in their programs of aid to families with dependent children, the States may permit earned or other income to be set aside for the dependent child's future identifiable needs, such as his education.[25]

23 *Ibid.*
24 *Ibid.*, p. 10.
25 *Ibid.*, pp. 11–12.

The amendments authorize states to make payments to AFDC families in which children are living with one or both parents. Anyone knows that deprivation may be heightened, not diminished, when, for instance, a father living at home is without work. In the past, it has been charged that divorce, desertion, and abandonment of children by fathers was encouraged by the assistance law, because families whose fathers were living at home were ineligible for assistance.

Only 5 percent of public assistance and 25 percent of child welfare personnel are trained professional workers. Competent workers are badly needed in such a demanding field and under the new amendments funds will be allocated to "provide directly through grants to and contracts with public or nonprofit institutions of higher learning with respect to personnel employed by or preparing for employment with public assistance agencies for (1) training, (2) establishment and maintenance of fellowships and traineeships, and (3) special short courses of study (to last not more than one year)." [26]

Also effective October 1, 1962, the law gave the states the option of combining their programs of assistance to the aged, the blind, the disabled, and medical care to the aged. States which combine these programs will eliminate problems inherent in separate programs for different classifications of people, and allow for experimentation of meeting need where it exists.

The 1962 law represents "the most important changes in the public welfare provision of the Social Security Act in the act's history. The amendments emphasize rehabilitation services and the training of staff, liberalize payments, and provide States with significant new tools for making welfare programs more effective." [27]

How the tools will be used is largely left to the states to decide. Based upon the experiences of the past, considerable unevenness in the adoption of the new provisions can be expected. In many places, however, public welfare will make notable gains, and the emphasis on service, prevention, and rehabilitation is a most exciting and promising new look at the ever-present problem of poverty and want.

The President, in announcing changes in the Social Security Act, highlighted the significance of these changes. On February 1, 1962, in a message to Congress, he said:

Public welfare, in short, must be more than a salvage operation, picking up the debris from the wreckage of human lives. Its emphasis must be directed increasingly toward prevention and rehabilitation—on reducing not only the long-range cost in budgetary terms but the long-range cost in human terms as well. Poverty weakens individuals and nations. Sounder public welfare

26 *Ibid.,* p. 13.
27 *Ibid.,* p. 3.

policies will benefit the Nation, its economy, its morale, and most importantly, its people. [28]

SUMMARY

The Social Security Act of 1935, together with provisions in the amendments to the Act, is the chief government tool for the prevention and relief of economic need, and for the restoration and retaining of capacities of those whose social functioning has been impaired or is in danger of so being.

The Old Age and Survivor's Disability Insurance is an income maintenance system based upon the contributory system. Beneficiaries are presumed to have *earned* benefits by payments to the system during the working period of their lives.

Unemployment insurance eases the economic burden of involuntary unemployment. It is supported by a tax levied against employers on a wage base of $3,000.

Payments to the aged, the disabled, the blind, and to dependent children are based upon need which is determined to exist, followed by an investigation of the applicant's circumstances. These programs are residual to OASDI, and provide income for categories of individuals not protected by other means. Medical care is available to indigent recipients of categorical assistance and to the aged under public assistance and MAA programs.

Public assistance is a Federal-State program, financed by state and federal matching funds and administered by the states within the legal and policy frameworks established for these purposes. In general, the federal law includes eligibility features which cover such factors as age, citizenship, residence; definitions as to blindness, a dependent child, and the disabled; the institutional status, need, property income and limitation, and assistance provided.

General assistance carries much opprobrium, and in general, is inadequate to meet need. It is a residual program to public assistance.

The 1962 amendments to the Social Security Act are among the most significant and far-reaching ever made. These amendments go beyond the program of income maintenance and include services aimed at rehabilitation, the prevention of social dysfunctioning, and restoration of individuals to a place in society where they are free to make the maximum use of their potentials.

The Social Security Act is the basic governmental provision at the state and federal level for relieving distress and providing income to people with growing emphasis on service.

28 *Ibid.*, p. 5.

QUESTIONS FOR DISCUSSION

1. What is meant by a *means test,* a *deterrent system?*
2. Differentiate between a means test program and an insurance program.
3. Who is taxed to pay the cost of the OASDI program and in what amounts?
4. Evaluate the measures frequently employed to discourage the use of public assistance by the public.
5. What are the main objections to a public assistance program, and why is an insurance program more acceptable to the citizens?
6. What are advantages of the program of public assistance? Justify having such a program when strong objection is raised against it.
7. Compare and contrast the funding of public assistance with that of social security.
8. Why is assistance to able-bodied workers less acceptable as an income maintenance system than assistance to the aged, the blind, and the disabled?
9. What are the advantages to the public of *services* to recipients of public assistance?

SPECIAL ACTIVITIES

1. Visit your local public welfare office with the specific purpose of determining which parts of the social security program are under its jurisdiction; the extent to which the local office has implemented the 1962 amendments to the Social Security Act.
2. Based upon your own library study and research, prepare a statement which embraces the essential elements of the controversy over medicare under the provisions of OASDI.

SELECTED REFERENCES

Annual Report, U.S. Department of Health, Education, and Welfare, 1961 (Washington, D.C.: U.S. Government Printing Office, 1962).

Basic Readings in Social Security (Washington, D.C.: U.S. Department of Health, Education, and Welfare, 1960).

BISNO, HERBERT, *The Philosophy of Social Work* (Washington, D.C.: Public Affairs Press, 1952).

BURNS, EVELINE, *Social Security and Public Policy* (New York: McGraw-Hill Book Co., Inc., 1956).

Compilation of Social Security Laws (Washington, D.C.: U.S. Government Printing Office, 1960).

Public Health Concepts in Social Work Education, Proceedings of Seminar held at Princeton University, March 4–9, 1962 (New York: Council on Social Work Education in cooperation with Public Health Service, Department of Health, Education, and Welfare, 1962).

PUMPHREY, MURIEL W., *The Teaching of Values and Ethics in Social Work Education,* Curriculum Study, Vol. XIII (New York: Council on Social Work Education, 1959).

Training for Service in Public Assistance, Selected papers presented at the 1960 Seminars for Field Representatives (Washington, D.C.: U.S. Department of Health, Education, and Welfare, 1961).

VASEY, WAYNE, *Government and Social Services* (New York: Holt, Rinehart & Winston, Inc., 1958).

WEISSMAN, IRVING, and BAKER, MARY R., *Education for Social Workers in the Public Social Services*, Curriculum Study, Vol. VII (New York: Council on Social Work Education, 1959).

WICKENDEN, ELIZABETH and BELL, WINIFRED, *Public Welfare Report*, the Project on Public Services for Families and Children (New York: The New York School of Social Work, Columbia University, 1961).

CHAPTER **8**

Child Welfare

In a sense, child welfare consists of all efforts to benefit children. The Children's Bureau states that a comprehensive program of child welfare should seek to promote the physical, mental, and social well-being of all the nation's youth and specifically those,

who are dependent, neglected, or delinquent, or in danger of becoming so; who have social, economic or behavior problems arising out of disturbance, incapacities or conflicts in family and social relationships, birth out of wedlock, or need for custody, guardianship or adoption; and who have similar problems resulting from community conditions, such as agricultural or industrial migration, prejudice and discrimination with respect to minority groups, socially and economically depressed neighborhoods, child labor and inadequate educational or employment facilities.[1]

For the purpose of this chapter, the definition of child welfare includes those functions which are normally a part of social work practice in the child welfare field—aid to families with dependent children, adoption services, services to unmarried mothers, foster home care, protective services, and homemaker and day care services. This chapter identifies some of the elements of the philosophy which shapes and directs child welfare practice, and describes various services developed in response to existing conditions and needs.

CHILDREN

Children are individuals. No two are alike. They are not endowed with the same qualities and each has his own rate of maturation, growth, and

1 *Child Welfare as a Field of Social Work Practice* (New York: Child Welfare League of America, 1959), p. 4.

developmental pattern. Children differ in their capacities to achieve in the classroom or on the playground. Some are outgoing and friendly, some retiring and quiet. They differ one from another in a wide range of physical, emotional, social, and spiritual characteristics as well as in their interests and goals. Services aimed at benefiting children must be constantly in a state of adaptation to the requirements of the individual child.

Child welfare as a field values children and childhood. It stresses the importance of children, their uniqueness, and the great significance of the various stages in their lives—each to be experienced and, hopefully, enjoyed by the child and those with whom he is shared. Impatience with childhood, often expressed by irate adults as "Why don't you grow up," or more charitably, "My, you're getting big" (as if being little is "too bad" and "big" is good), is out of step with the view that childhood is wonderful. The successive, dynamic periods of life, each in turn, should be lived and enjoyed.

Many children, sensing an inferior status, try to compensate by acting like adults. One nine-year-old girl, it was said, behaved "just like her mother." At school she avoided classmates whose play she regarded as "childish" and sought the attention of teachers exclusively. She became ill when a smudge appeared on her immaculate dress. Her hair always had to be neatly combed. So important to her were adult standards that she could not afford childhood.

Childhood is something which people remember with excitement if its natural joy is shared and appreciated by significant adults. Adults sometimes impose their values and patterns of behavior on children and unwisely stress the importance of "adult" behavior. They force their children to sacrifice experiences appropriate to childhood and lay the groundwork for later rebellion.

Preston [2] said children are special possessions.

If you care for children properly, you lose them. If you paint your house and fertilize your fields, you keep your property and it continues to serve you. When it is at its peak of value, it never walks off and starts working for itself. If you *lose* your property, you fail. If you *keep* your son or daughter, you fail. Children grow up in families but they must also grow out of them.

Social work helps children to become individuals, to mature, and to grow independent.

SERVICES FOR CHILDREN

Services for children have been established under various auspices, some public and tax supported, some through voluntary efforts of federated funding groups, and others by churches and religious bodies. Not

---

[2] George H. Preston, *The Substance of Mental Health* (New York: Holt, Rinehart & Winston, Inc., 1943), p. 27.

infrequently these services represent the combination of public and voluntary planning. Tax supported services for children, which account for almost all financial assistance to families with dependent children, are largely federal-state programs. The Federal Government participates by paying costs up to 75 percent and by exercising leadership needed to accomplish the purpose of the program. The administration of services is left largely to the states whose financial structure must be adequate to absorb costs not defrayed by the Federal Government.

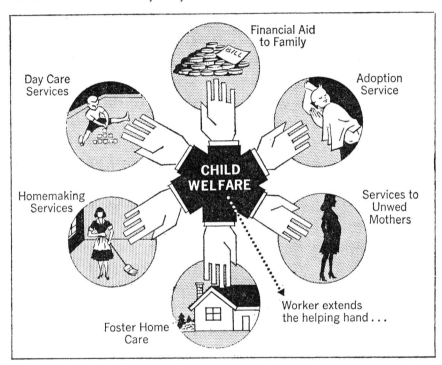

AID TO FAMILIES WITH DEPENDENT CHILDREN

Home life has been widely acclaimed as the finest product of civilization. One tenet of child welfare is that except for the most compelling reasons, a child should not be deprived of a home or of the opportunity to be nurtured by his own parents. A keynote of the first White House Conference, 1909, was that poverty alone did not justify the separation of a child from his parents, and that ways should be found to eliminate economic dependency and to preserve the integrity of the family unit.

Legislation at the state level variously known as *mothers' pensions, mothers' assistance,* and *widows' pensions,* adopted first in Illinois in 1911 and which rapidly spread to other states, was passed to permit mothers to remain at home to rear their children. With the passage of the Social Security Act in 1935 the principle of using tax funds for family support was extended to the federal-state level of government under Aid-to-Dependent Children. With a few notable exceptions, *relief,* or *assistance* has keynoted the Aid-to-Dependent Children program.

Many caseworkers have lacked the necessary training to handle less concrete needs. The large caseloads have been unwieldy, not lending themselves to refinements of practice with a hope or promise of greater rewards in human functioning and dignity. The public has been misled into believing that good welfare could be secured with a saving of money and resources when the opposite is more likely the truth. Good social services, like good medicine, good legal counsel, or a good education, is not purchased cheaply and the measure of value is not the cost, but the gain in richness of living for the citizens. Too often the low cost of a welfare program has been used as the yardstick of its success while human values have been sacrificed.

Social security legislation since 1935, particularly the 1962 Amendments to the Social Security Act, has broadened financial assistance to include a new emphasis on protection, the individualizing of need, prevention, education, and casework services. Some details of the 1962 amendments to the act are indicated below: [3]

The new legislation sets forth a plan requirement effective July 1, 1963, in relation to State agency responsibilities for each dependent child. . . . In meeting the requirement of a plan for each child, the agency is responsible for maintaining current knowledge as to the conditions under which each family lives, the adequacy of and problems, if any, in child care and rearing, and as to the specific needs of each child. Through considering each child individually and planning with the family, children who require special planning by the agency are usually identified. Under this plan requirement, State agencies must provide services to children whose care and supervision are inadequate and to those with special problems. . . .

Where there are serious threats to the welfare of children and they are in need of special protection, the agency is responsible for developing and carrying out an adequate plan for care and protection of the children within the home or substitute arrangements. It is preferable that substitute arrangements be made voluntarily by the parents, but when this is not possible, court action becomes necessary in order to protect the children. The basic purpose is the provision of services related to strengthening family life and improvement in family functioning. The emphasis is upon individualizing the children and knowing any particular needs or problems which should have agency attention. . . .

To assure sufficient time and attention to each family and child under this requirement, provision must be made for visits as frequently as the situation indicates, but not less frequently than once in each three months; for caseload standards of not more than sixty cases per worker; and for case supervisory standards of not more than five workers per case supervisor. States that are unable to meet these caseload and supervisory standards as of July 1, 1963, must present justification and propose different standards. The proposed standards may be accepted temporarily, provided they are such as to assure that ade-

[3] State Letter No. 606 (Washington, D.C.: Social Security Administration, Department of Health, Education, and Welfare, November 10, 1962), Part IV, 400D–4999.

quate time and case supervision will be available for the services to be provided. For such States, planning must be undertaken to assure progression in meeting the defined standards as quickly as possible, but not later than July 1, 1967. . . .

Agency responsibility includes providing leadership to and working with the community and with the family to assure that preventive health measures, educational opportunities and other community resources which are generally available to other children are equally available to dependent children.

In developing and carrying agency responsibility within the meaning of this requirement, the following scope of services are appropriate to the public assistance program: Casework services to children in their own home; complementary services; services to children in foster care under Title IV; helping parents in voluntary placement of children with relatives; and community planning to strengthen family, neighborhood and community life for all children and to deal with the problems of special concern to parents and children receiving public assistance.

ADOPTION SERVICES

Adoption is the legal means by which the child of one set of parents becomes the child of another set of parents. For the adopted child it is the means of acquiring substitute parents. Provision of substitute parents for children appears to have been made as far back as the earliest recorded histories. The Babylonian Code of Hammurabi definitely establishes the existence of adoption practices more than 4,000 years ago. The Bible refers to adoption; the ancient Romans practiced it as a part of their civil law; adoption law is found among the remains of the early Spaniards; and the practice was known among Anglo-Saxon tribes but later disappeared.

The first legislation on adoption in the United States was enacted in 1851 in Massachusetts. Other states followed and by 1867 Pennsylvania, Wisconsin, and Illinois had statutes on adoption. Today all states have legislation regarding adoption.[4]

The number of children placed for adoption in the United States increased from 16,000 to 17,000 in 1937, to 113,000 in 1961.

In general, the first state laws on adoption required only a simple petition on the part of those wishing to adopt to the court of local jurisdiction. If the parents were living, their consent was acquired. If the court were satisfied, the adoption was granted. Later, the laws were tightened, and today a careful investigation of the suitability of the proposed adoption home is required together with provisions for a probationary period in the home of the applicants, safeguards of confidentiality of records, and other such measures as will best protect the welfare of the child.

The Children's Bureau's figures, based on estimates, show that ap-

[4] Hazel Fredericksen, *The Child and His Welfare* (San Francisco: W. H. Freeman and Co., Publishers, 1948), pp. 200–201.

proximately half of the adoptions in the United States are filed with the court by a relative, most frequently a stepparent. Other petitions are filed by couples, mostly childless, who are unrelated.

Children are placed in adoptive homes by one of two methods, either by social agencies licensed to place children or by interested parties independently of social agencies. The latter is called *independent placement* and ranges all the way from so-called "gray" to "black" market placements. "Selling" infants is a black market practice. Gray market transactions are those in which the intermediary is not motivated by commercial interest. Placements made independently lack the safeguards to the child provided by the social agencies and offer no organized services to either the natural or adoptive parents.

Licensed agencies which place children for adoption maintain files of families wishing to adopt children. Applicants are interviewed at the office of the agency and home visits made by professionally trained social workers as a part of the process of determining the suitability of the applicants. A medical history is secured to ascertain the general state of physical and mental health of applicants and to determine whether they are free of communicable disease and debilitating illnesses. Character references are used to help screen applicants and reports are secured on their ability to love, nurture, rear, and educate a child. The age of the applicant, motivation, and interest are all evaluated. Applicants considered for a particular child must, in addition, be examined for their suitability for the child under consideration. Matching the child with the adoptive parents across such factors as race or ethnic characteristics, native endowment, physique, intellect, and religion is a part of this process.

Thus screened, some applicants do not qualify and their applications are rejected. It has been estimated that, in some localities, as few as one out of ten white applicants who apply to agencies can expect to receive a child; in other communities there is a more even balance between the number of applicants and available children. The agency is guided in its decision first by the needs of the child for a home and what will best serve his interests.

The interests of the adoptive applicants are protected by a thorough investigation into the background of a child, by safeguards established to assure confidentiality, and by sound legal procedures.

In no particular is the adoptive applicant protected more than by what is done for the natural mother. If the agency takes the release when the mother is ready to give it; if the mother's fear, doubt, and guilt have been brought into the open and her many questions answered to her satisfaction; if she has good reason to believe that her baby will go into a home where it will be nurtured and loved and her religious wishes and other cultural preferences respected, then the mother will be able to accept and live with the decision to give up her child. She will believe that she has done what is best. On the other hand, if the release is taken when the mother is under pressure, if practices are followed which do not fully recognize her rights and wishes as the mother, or if she lacks assurance of the outcome of her decision, she will remain dissatisfied, unhappy, in doubt, and later may attempt to have the adoption set aside and regain her parental rights and controls.

Applicants Approved by the Agency

Adoption service is society's answer to the problem of finding suitable substitute families for homeless children. Having heard about the function of the local child-placing and adopting agency, the Zufelts applied to the agency to adopt.

After fifteen years of marriage, Mr. and Mrs. Zufelt were childless. Tests and medical procedures made at the local College of Medicine had failed either to disclose the reason for the infertility or to induce pregnancy.

At the time they applied for a baby, Mrs. Zufelt worked on the faculty of a university in the nursery school, where she had the reputation of "real understanding and warmth" in her work with preschool children. Mr. Zufelt, local manager of a large insurance firm, served as a troop committeeman for the Boy Scouts. They owned their own home in a neighborhood that boasted of three churches and good schools. In their mid-thirties they enjoyed good health and upper middle-class living standards. Each was eager to adopt a baby and had been planning for months to file an application if and when obstetrical procedures ruled out the possibility of their having children of their own.

Upon recommendation of their gynecologist the Zufelts applied to one of the four statewide adoption societies for a baby. After a nine-month period of waiting, during which time they were investigated and became well acquainted with the society, a three-week-old baby boy was placed in their home. They were told of the possibility that a second child could be placed with them later.

Applicants Not Approved

The Seidenbergs had filed an application with the Children's Aid Society to adopt a child. Although Mr. Seidenberg was strongly interested in adopting, and was a civic-minded community worker who served on the board of the United Fund, Mrs. Seidenberg was poorly motivated to adopt and extremely ambivalent. She had consented to the application only because of her husband's years of persistent pleading with her. Her true feelings about adoption and her many doubts appeared in the application process when she specified the kind of a child she would take. It had to be a blue-eyed, blond girl whose parents were college graduates and who would be perfectly symmetrical in form and feature. There could not be any question about the child's intelligence, hereditary background, or potential. Mrs. Seidenberg finally admitted she did not wish to share a child with her husband or to be burdened with its care. The application of the Seidenbergs was rejected.

The Adopted Child

Social workers not only facilitate the total process of adoption, placing the right child with the right parents, but they also help adoptive parents to better understand themselves, their child, and adoption procedures and processes. An example which illustrates the results of a social worker who helped a set of parents to accept their adopted child, and to tell him about his adoption, follows:

> Tommy, age eight, an adopted boy who had been told by his parents that he was wanted and adopted—and most important of all had been loved across the years—was playing with his pals one morning. A tense situation arose and he was soon in an argument with Fred, who, in "the heat of battle," turned on Tommy and yelled, "You aren't any good, anyway! You're adopted!"
>
> Tommy calmly replied, "Your mother and father didn't have any choice when you were born. *My* mother and father chose me 'cause they loved and wanted me."

SERVICES TO UNMARRIED MOTHERS

The young woman, faced with an out-of-wedlock child, is an object of great community concern and soul searching. She is received with feeling that mixes maudlin sentimentality, sympathy, protection, hostile rejection, ostracism, and condemnation. Not the least of her problems is her own guilt, shame, and sense of failure to live up to her own and societal expectations. She is called upon to make decisions of the most far-reaching consequences for herself, her unborn infant, and her kinship group, often long before she has the maturity to do so. She is also expected overnight to take on frightening new responsibilities. With variation, these are the problems of every woman, regardless of age, who bears an out-of-wedlock child. What provision in the child welfare field has the community made for her?

Many girls remain at home and continue to live with their parents throughout their pregnancy. For these the family provides food, clothing, shelter, medical care, and hospitalization. The financial burden in these instances is carried largely by the parents or family group. Others, for various reasons, either cannot or prefer not to remain at home. Some would be disgraced and unable to tolerate the shame and embarrassment of confronting relatives and friends. The anonymity of the city and more distant parts beckons them. Not all girls are able to confide in their parents, and some do not have family ties or support. Many, probably most American girls, confide in their parents and seek their counsel and advice on community services. For these, and others who elect not to live at home, many services have been developed. Among these are living arrangements which, in the main, involve foster family care and

SOCIAL AGENCIES PROTECT CHILDREN WHO ARE BEING ADOPTED IN THE UNITED STATES, IN 1958

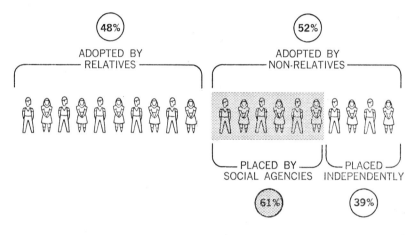

SOURCE: Interdepartmental Committee on Children and Youth, *Children in a Changing World*, Chart Book (Washington, D.C.: Golden Anniversary White House Conference on Children and Youth, 1960), p. 46.

maternity homes. In addition, medical care, hospitalization, planning with the mother for the care of the baby, or for relinquishment if this is desired, and other casework and counseling services are given as needed. The following case is illustrative of child welfare services to unmarried mothers.

Unwed Mother Keeps Baby

A thirty-year-old woman, a trained anesthesiologist from out of the state, applied to an all-purpose child care and placement agency, with the intention of giving up her baby for adoption. She planned to return to her job and her home after the baby was born, but developed symptoms, including headaches, making medical care necessary and forcing a delay in her plans.

She stated that she wanted to place her child, but the child welfare worker delayed taking a permanent release, as it was apparent that the woman had not actually made the final decision to give up her baby. Her headaches and compulsivity were indications of this. She had been under severe pressures for several months; the birth of the baby had been a factor producing low morale. Little by little, with help she was able to reassess her situation, noting her assets and capabilities of earning her own living with the result that she decided she wanted the baby and returned to the agency for it several weeks later.

It is almost axiomatic in child welfare that, unless the natural mother has accepted relinquishment (and acceptance in this sense is more than signing papers), adoptive parents cannot have the assurance that at some future date when ties have been formed, the natural mother will not try to regain her parental rights. Many a suit has been successfully filed to recover a child, based on parental rights following questionable procedures of relinquishment.

Mother Accepts Adoption Plan for Her Baby

A more typical case is that of a seventeen-year-old girl from a small town and a good religious background. She was young, naive, and misled by the promises of an older man into accepting his affection. She had asked such questions, "What will it do to me, to my parents, my brothers and sisters, if I remain home? What will it do to the baby to grow up unwanted because of the stigma and the problems which its arrival will bring?"

She and her parents decided to seek the aid of an agency. She was helped to understand her mistake, to get vocational training and a job, and to handle the business with the least amount of publicity. The agency placed the girl in a home in a good neighborhood, where she received proper diet, good medical care, and had the interest of people who understood and accepted her, a home in which she was free from embarrassing questions. This home also provided anonymity, an important consideration where matters of such delicacy are concerned.

When the baby was born, it was placed and supervised in a foster home approved for this purpose by the agency. The foster mother who cared for the baby was a trained, practical nurse and mother of several children, capable of providing the physical care the baby needed. This arrangement allowed time for the mother to make a decision to keep or not keep the baby. Furthermore, it allowed time for plans involving placement and ultimate adoption.

Later this young woman married and became the mother of three children of her own. She was satisfied with the earlier decision to place the out-of-wedlock baby. She had been assured by the agency worker that the baby would receive intelligent, excellent treatment, and have the opportunity to be well reared and educated, and that her religious faith and wishes concerning the welfare of the baby would be respected. Excerpts from a letter written by the mother to the executive of the agency attest to her feelings in the matter.

Dear Mrs. R.,

So often my thoughts still turn to you and Celia (the name she gave to her baby).

I expect you are as busy and helpful as always. You seem to love your work so. Not one of the many you have helped could repay you a fraction of what you deserve.

I assume Celia is a third-grader now. I wonder how she does in school, at play and at home. . . .

Young John was five this month. He is so interesting and interested in so much. Nancy is two now and very capable. She is still a peanut, and I think she will always be dainty in stature, but very much a tomboy. Johnny and Nancy are willing and helpful with their new sister, Janet.

Janet was born in June and a big one from the start. She weighed two pounds more than my other three babies, a good and healthy baby as John and Nancy were. This time, however, I think I have a baby who looks like me.

I am indeed lucky to have such wonderful children. I can remember the day I left the agency and Celia, and the empty feeling that was with me for so long. I shall always long for and miss what I didn't have, but don't ponder on this as I know I made the correct decision for Celia—and for me. I just thank God there was a person like you for me to trust.

With love,
Mary

FOSTER CARE OF CHILDREN

Foster homes and institutions are often used for dependent, neglected, and homeless children. The selection and use of these homes is made by the child welfare worker who evaluates the family across standards within the field.

The social worker assesses the ability of the family to provide adequate physical care—food, clothing, shelter—and of the community to provide schooling, recreation, and religious training. Also considered are such things as family harmony, the emotional climate of the home and interaction among family members, interest, and motivation in the caring for a homeless child.

Some homes for various reasons do not meet adequate standards. Some families apply to take children to augment meager family incomes. Children would be deprived in the homes of families where income is this depressed. Seldom are children recommended for care in the home of a relief client, for the income of the relief family is substandard, and too often, wholly inadequate for minimum health and decency.

The capacity of prospective foster parents to tolerate the continuing interest of natural parents must be taken into consideration. Not infrequently the natural parent will make intolerable demands upon foster parents and upset their children. Competition is too painful for some natural parents to accept. It is not easy for parents to enjoy the success of substitute parents when they have failed.

It is recognized that not all children can be helped through foster home care. The foster home is a treatment of choice for the infant and for the small child where the emotional tie to an adult is the main dynamic of growth. Foster care is good for the child who is able to accept substitute parents. Children whose home experiences have made healthy relationships to adults possible can more readily accept the foster family.

In each instance the child welfare worker makes an effort to place the child in a home suitable for him. This is done with clear recognition that separation from the natural parent can be a disturbing and traumatic experience; perhaps few experiences result in greater trauma. Using a medical analogy, placement represents major surgery. It should be undertaken when the child's own home is no longer capable of functioning in his best interest. There are many reasons for substitute care of children. Parents may become ill or die. Sometimes they are too immature or inferior to assume the responsibilities of parenthood. Children born to such parents are in great need of care, and foster home care is one of society's provisions for them.

Foster Care Pending Termination of Parental Rights

The Larkins were appealing children, three girls age 9, 7, and 4. They had been taken from their divorced parents through action of the juvenile court. The parents had each remarried and failed several times in the care of their children. A complaint was filed by neighbors who, seeing their neglect and abuse, were aroused by the poor living arrangements. Study showed that the parents were unable and unwilling to provide for them. They were placed in a foster home with the recommendation that a permanent plan for their care be made through adoption. Months elapsed before the children could be placed for adoption because the parents refused to give their consent and court proceedings had to be instituted to terminate parental rights. Foster home care was provided for the children pending court action.

In child welfare practice mothers are not deprived of custody of their children unless neglect is severe and constitutes a hazard to the welfare, and even to the life of the child.

Babies born to unwed mothers are sometimes kept in foster homes until a decision is made by the mother to make the baby available for adoption.

If a baby whose mother has made arrangements for it to be adopted is born with a defect, foster home care for this child is often indicated until such time as corrective medical procedures can be instituted. One such infant was born with malformed feet and legs. While in a foster home this child received extensive surgical and orthopedic care which corrected the defects and made way for a permanent arrangement in an adoptive home. Not all children can be placed for adoption, and long-term foster home care for some is frequently indicated.

INSTITUTIONAL CARE

Foster home care is not suitable for some children. Group living arrangements may be a treatment of choice for them. Children who act out excessively, who have serious conduct and behavior disorders, impulse-ridden children who steal, set fires, or who are sexually promiscuous ordinarily are not candidates for foster home care. Furthermore, some children who have experienced prolonged emotional deprivations resulting in emotional stunting and who are unable to form close and satisfying relationships may not accept foster home care. Foster parents themselves, because of their needs and expectations, may be sorely disappointed when these children are unable to share affection.

Children are often candidates for group living where the demands for personal response are not great. Some children benefit from the professional services which can be provided only in a group setting. Some find it impossible to tolerate the demands of making attachments to new sets of parents and are relieved in the group where such demands are minimized. For these and other children, group living experiences can, and often do, provide a healing experience.

A child living in a group home or institution can direct his aggressive feelings against many more people safely. He is not under the same necessity to form close emotional ties and attachments. He can move into the group at his own pace and is not traumatized by pressures to give or accept the affection of others. The routine of the institution provides tangible security—meals at regular intervals, a place to sleep, medical and nursing care. With planning on the part of administration it can offer privacy and even a place for the child's personal belongings. Child-centered group living is a treatment resource for the emotionally disturbed and socially disorganized child.

The social worker in the child welfare field is knowledgeable in the use of services developed by the community for children. He knows of their existence, their legal structure, and something about their organization and function. Perhaps most important, the social worker is trained to bring the need together with the provision in the interest of rehabilitation, protection, and prevention of social breakdown and disorganization. Child welfare services are illustrative of the community's attempt to provide for children, and to help them to find suitable expression of their legitimate interests and rights. The shift in the care of the child from the almshouse and indenture to foster home care and modern group living is one of great significance.

PROTECTIVE SERVICES

In one sense, all child welfare work is protective work. Children in day care centers, while their mothers work, are being protected from the neglect to which they would otherwise be subjected. Children who go into foster homes receive care which they are unable to find in their own homes. Physical and mental abuse is often a stark alternative.

Courts and the law enforcing agencies give protection to children and to the community. Modern juvenile court philosophy stresses protection, treatment, and restoration. Punishment is minimized.

Some children do not fit any of the types of services mentioned above. Children who can remain at home and receive love and care, should never be removed because of poverty or minor family disturbances. Only when they are abused and exploited or when there exists some serious violation of the law, can such radical treatment be justified. Protective services are for those who can benefit from services to themselves and their families, preferably in their own homes. The court intervenes when custody and control is removed from the parents. Under protective services the custody remains with the parents. Unaided, these parents are unable to take steps on their own to get help. Usually they come to agencies upon referral of neighbors or of individuals who know that something within the home is harmful or not conducive to the welfare of the child.

As people in agencies become more aware that there is a group of children for whom many communities have no resources, efforts are being made to meet this need. These children are those found in the twilight zone, between the authoritative role of the law enforcement office and the function of the family or the public welfare agency. They are called the "neglected ones." They have been neglected physically, emotionally, or have been abused. If the neglect or abuse does not fall within the legally defined limits of the law enforcement agency, that agency cannot work on the case. Public and private welfare agencies have traditionally been set up to counsel with parents who come to them with problems about their children, but have not accepted the function of reaching out to parents and families, a necessary part of the protective service program.

According to many authorities protective services are defined as specialized services to neglected, abused, exploited, or rejected children. The focus of the service is preventive and nonpunitive, and is geared toward a rehabilitation through identification and treatment of the motivating factors which underly the neglect.

The following circumstances are usually present in a protective service referral: [5]

1. A complaint is made by someone outside the immediate family that a child or children are in danger of neglect, abuse, exploitation, or rejection.

2. The agency takes the initiative to reach out to aid the family by helping them realize when neglect exists and of the resources which are available for help.

3. The agency reserves the right to use authority, if necessary, to protect the welfare of children.

Physical Neglect

The Mandel case illustrates protective services in handling physical neglect.

Mrs. Mandel, middle-aged and the mother of eight children, ranging in age from 5 to 23, was referred for protective services by the local constable and neighbors. Mrs. M. had been married twice; the first time ended tragically when her husband crashed in a plane in World War II. The second husband, the father of seven of her eight children, died in a mental hospital.

Mrs. M. was reared in an orphanage. She experienced extreme deprivation as a child. Her parents were unable to provide for her and she was strongly rejected by her mother. At the death of her second husband, she received insurance and social security for the oldest child, and a widow's pension from the war department until the first girl was 18 years of age. The social security and insurance, in addition to supplemental help from her local church group, provided food and part of the clothing for the family. She had sufficient means for the payment of her utilities; she paid the mortgage and upkeep on the house with insurance left by her husband.

The neighbors and school authorities had observed neglect over a rather long period of time, but reluctantly reported it only when the children began to steal and appear at school disheveled, dirty, and infested with vermin.

Upon investigation, protective services confirmed all of the above. The social worker also recognized some limitations in Mrs. M. and

[5] "A Study of Protective Service Needs in Ventura County with Analysis and Evaluation of Cases Handled over a One-year Period" (Denver: Children's Division, American Humane Association, n.d.g.), p. 4.

her own serious deprivation, and that she was operating at a low level of efficiency. Although she deeply loved her children she was limited in her ability to discipline them effectively. A daughter was becoming delinquent at 17. The possibility of school failure loomed. The fifteen-year-old son had refused repeatedly to accept his mother's control within the home. When the worker called on her, she pleaded with her not to take the children. However, she accepted the placement of the seventeen-year-old girl in a group living home provided by the community. The fifteen-year-old son went to live with a married sister, and Mrs. M. was helped to accept day care for two of the children, as well as homemaking services. A marginal person, she could not handle the responsibilities of rearing and caring for children without community support. With support she was able to do an adequate job and the integrity of the home was maintained. Without protective services, she might have lost all of her children to substitute family care.

Physical Abuse

Physical abuse is illustrated by a teacher and his wife who were first reported when neighbors observed that the former beat his two adopted daughters.

Examinations by the school nurse disclosed ugly open sores on the scalps of the two girls and black and blue marks covered their bodies. The adoptive father, a teacher in the public schools, held status in the community which shielded his sadistic treatment of the girls from friends and neighbors. When the beatings were brought to the attention of the school nurse, she determined that no medical care had been provided for these girls, although the scalp wounds were deep and infected. The nurse brought the matter to the attention of the protective service center whose investigation disclosed gross neglect and abuse. The parents were mentally sick. The father was referred for treatment and determined unfit to have the children who were finally ordered by the courts into foster homes.

DAY CARE SERVICES

Eight million mothers of children under 18 years of age are in the labor force. Three million of these have children under 6, five million have children 6 to 17 years of age.

The mothers of fifteen million children under 18 years (one-fourth of all children under 18) of age are employed. Children living with their mothers only are twice as likely to have employed mothers as children living in families with both parents. There are 177,000 children under 6 living in father-only families.

Economic factors bear a clear relationship to working mothers. Forty-four percent of the children living with their mothers only have mothers whose income is less than $2,000 a year, and an additional 39 percent have mothers whose income is between $2,000 and $4,000 annually. In households with both parents, the lower the father's income the greater proportion of children whose mothers are employed. Twenty-seven percent of all children under 18 in husband-wife families whose fathers earn less than $2,000 per year have an employed mother. By contrast, the figure is 18 percent for children whose fathers earn between $6,000 and $10,000. Only 7 percent of women whose husbands make over $10,000 a year are in the labor force.

What provision is made for the care of children of working mothers?

About six out of ten children of mothers who are employed full-time are cared for in their own homes while their mothers work, usually by fathers or other relatives. About four out of ten are cared for away from home, by relatives, neighbors, in group care, or under other arrangements. According to a 1958 survey, about 400,000 children under 12 were expected to take care of themselves while their mothers worked full-time.[6]

It is estimated that in the United States, all day care facilities combined can serve about 185,000 children. Thirty-three states require licensing of all day care facilities, but there are eight states which make no such provision. The estimated cost for the care of children in day care centers is $20 per week or about $1,000 per year. The estimated cost for care in family day care homes is $12.50 a week or $650 per year. This is for full-time care, five days a week throughout the entire year. These estimates do not represent the full cost, since they do not include care for services and administration.[7]

Mrs. Katherine B. Oettinger, Chief of the Children's Bureau, has reported that day care services for children of working mothers add up to a "national disgrace." She says: [8]

The supply of good day care programs is inadequate to meet the need. On a national basis, the quality of day care now being offered is frequently so poor that children who receive it may suffer serious personality damage—if not physical harm. . . .
There is urgent need for action. We can see the tangible results of the physical abuses suffered by children in day care. We will be coping for years to come with the intangible results of the damage they are suffering in their most formative years.

The 1962 Amendments to the Social Security Act should help to shore

[6] "Working Mothers and Day Care Services in the United States" (Washington, D.C.: Social Security Administration, U.S. Department of Health, Education, and Welfare, 1962).
[7] Ibid.
[8] News Release (Washington, D.C.: U.S. Department of Health, Education, and Welfare, July 28 1962), p. 1.

up day care services. At present, the capacity of facilities is seriously limited. New legislation will probably provide for additional facilities and the improvement of existing ones. Under the law, up to five million dollars of child welfare funds can be earmarked for day care facilities in 1963, and ten million for each succeeding year. Authorizations under these Amendments are: [9]

1. Establish more public day care centers, making full use of health, education, and welfare agencies in States and communities.

2. Stimulate increased cooperation with voluntary agencies, so that all well-qualified resources may be used for needed day care of children. Many voluntary agencies stand ready to modify their programs, to obviate full-time placement of children away from home and to meet the tremendous needs for more flexible child-care arrangements.

3. Facilitate continued close collaboration and coordination between the Children's Bureau and the Bureau of Family Services in child welfare and public assistance programs—Federal, State, and local—so that day care, provided when it serves the best interest of the child and the mother, may take its proper place in strengthening family life. Expanded counseling services are needed to make this possible.

4. Help the States make effective use of the important tools of licensing and consultation to improve both the quantity and quality of care in these centers.

5. Help develop and maintain the standards for meeting needs of groups of infants under 3 years in foster family day care, groups of 3 to 7-year-olds in creative group or foster family day care, and the neglected group of older youngsters in protective opportunities that offer enriched experience.

6. Recruit and train the broad range of needed day care workers through the section of the new amendments that authorize grants for special projects for training personnel in the field of child welfare.

7. Encourage research in day care practices and scientific aspects of child development in group or foster family care through the 1960 amendments authorizing research and demonstration grants in the field of child welfare.

HOMEMAKING SERVICES

Homemaking services are a much needed aid to children, but have never been adequately developed. It is the function of a homemaker to keep the family together during periods when the mother is unable to function with adequate effectiveness in the home, or when she is absent.

A lingering illness which results in incapacity of the mother, or hospitalization forcing absence from the home when children are too young to care for themselves, illustrate the need for homemakers. They are generally needed for relatively short periods of time.

Homemaking is not housekeeping. The homemaker may "keep house" as part of her job, but this is only one of her functions, and a minor one, when compared with the broader responsibility for disciplining and caring for the children and managing the household.

9 *Ibid.*, p. 3.

A homemaker must have household management skills, and, above all, the ability to get along with people. She needs to know how to handle children, to manage their interests, win their acceptance and approval, yet not alienate them from their natural parents in the process.

Homemaking service cannot be expected to relieve stress and hold the family together unless and until it is recognized by the community as a basic service and compensated for accordingly. Basic to sound homemaking services is the recruitment and training of the homemaker.

Before World War II, and the great influx of women on the labor market, homemaking service was being rather widely developed in family agencies throughout the country. Since the War, however, not many homemakers have been available. If homemaking services are provided as a measure to strengthen the family, it will be necessary to recognize the importance of the homemaker's position, to give it status, and to compensate adequately for it. Homemaking service is one means of preventing family disorganization, which, when used properly, results in substantial benefits to the family and to the community.

OTHER SERVICES

Establishing and maintaining adequate standards of practice is basic to child welfare. Service exists for this purpose and for licensing and regulating social agencies, foster homes, day care centers, and children's institutions. There are also organizations which coordinate services, plan cooperation among agencies, offer consultation, and publish articles, journals, and other literature in the field.

Two national organizations whose influence in the child welfare field is monumental are the Child Welfare League of America and the United States Children's Bureau. The Child Welfare League, established in 1915, sponsors regional and national conferences on child welfare practice and maintains a directory of member agencies. It publishes *Child Welfare,* many books, pamphlets, and other materials in the field of child welfare, and makes various kinds of teaching material available to children's agencies and schools of social work. The League is but one of "many national agencies whose functions include the development of standards for services, large-scale research, publication of technical journals, consultation to state and local services, creation of a professional literature, recruitment of personnel, the further development of public understanding, and cooperation with governmental agencies." [10]

The United States Children's Bureau was established in 1912. Its purpose was to "have a central office where facts of child life may be collected, reviewed, and interpreted to individuals and organized groups,

---

[10] Wayne Vasey, *Government and Social Welfare* (New York: Holt, Rinehart & Winston, Inc., 1958), p. 54.

thus making possible intelligent action and reducing needless experimentation." [11]

The Children's Bureau functions in the following ways: [12]

(1) Continuing responsibility for study and for the publication of reports concerning child welfare and child life; (2) The collection and distribution of information regarding research studies being developed in such facilities as universities, hospitals and clinics, public schools, child welfare agencies, and many other types of public and private health and welfare organizations; (3) The provision of technical assistance in various fields of child life designed to improve the level of services in such areas as juvenile delinquency, health services, mental retardation, and others; (4) The administration of grants-in-aid to the states for programs of crippled children's services, maternal and child health services, and child welfare services; (5) The promotion of better standards of personnel in services to children through the provision of research grants, teaching materials, and educational consultation.

UNMET NEEDS IN CHILD WELFARE

The need for qualified child welfare personnel is urgent and critical in all states. Shortage of personnel at every level of operation is resulting in an inferior quality of service and inestimable damage to children.

Foster care facilities show another critical inadequacy, especially for children with physical handicaps, of minority groups, the mentally retarded, and children being released from correctional institutions. Detention facilities and group homes for adolescents and for children who cannot use foster home care are also badly needed.

Most states need specialized psychiatric and psychological services, remedial therapy of various kinds, dental and medical services, residential treatment centers for the emotionally disturbed, vocational guidance, and individual or family counseling. The 1962 Amendments to the Social Security Act open the door to the states for extensive development and improvement of services in the child welfare field.

If the trend of mothers entering the labor market continues, the need for day care services will expand greatly. Services to unmarried mothers have become critical because of the increasing number bearing children out-of-wedlock. This is particularly true of mothers in minority groups.

Other sorely needed services in many parts of the country include protective services, various kinds of preventive services, counseling help to families and children who are particularly vulnerable to mental illness and delinquency, adoption services, research, and the upgrading of standards.

[11] Hazel Fredericksen, *The Child and His Welfare* (San Francisco: W. H. Freeman, & Co., Publishers, 1948), p. 23.
[12] Vasey, *op. cit.* pp. 351–352.

SUMMARY

Child welfare is a widely diversified program of services for children and their families who require the help of the community. These services have the underpinning of community interest, concern, and substantial financial support. When professionally staffed, they are the means of preventing social breakdown or restoring the usefulness of individuals and families who have known disorganizing experiences.

Financial assistance for keeping children in their own homes is available to families under AFDC. Adoption services and services to unwed mothers are providing much needed service to large numbers of Americans who wish to adopt children, or who need help with difficult social and personal problems.

Foster care is used for children who require substitute families on a less permanent basis than adoption. Protective service is one means by which family strength and organization are maintained and children are helped to adjust in their own homes. Day care services are set up for children whose mothers work outside the home. Homemaker services are available in some urban communities for families whose need is for someone to manage the home while the mother is sick or incapacitated.

The Children's Bureau is an arm of the Health, Education, and Welfare Department which promotes the welfare of children and, through financial and other aid to states, upgrades and extends services to all the political subdivisions in the United States. The Child Welfare League is a voluntary organization with many affiliated agencies in the United States. It establishes standards of practice and gives consultation to public and private agencies.

QUESTIONS FOR DISCUSSION

1. What in your experience or training would suggest that the need for services for children as outlined in this chapter might be conservative? Exaggerated?

2. In your judgment why would training and skill be required for child welfare practice?

3. Evaluate the importance to children of the Child Welfare League of America and the Children's Bureau.

4. What is the meaning to you of a child welfare service?

5. What are a few of the advantages and disadvantages of group living for children?

6. What ways do the 1962 Amendments to the Social Security Act offer hope of improvement in the practice of child welfare?

7. What are the advantages of placing children for adoption through licensed child welfare agencies?

8. Explain why it is important in the interest of the adoption procedure for the natural mother to be able to "live with her decision."

9. When, and under what circumstances, is foster home care indicated?

10. Give examples of families you know, or have heard about, who could benefit from protective services.

SPECIAL ACTIVITIES

1. Make a survey of all the child welfare services in your community. Note whether the services provided are for day care only or for twenty-four hour care. Include in your survey a list of training centers, community chests and councils, and similar organizations serving children. Make a similar list of services which you feel might still be needed.

2. On the basis of the projected child population for 1970, and the need for trained personnel, formulate a statement of training and recruitment designed to fill the manpower shortages in child welfare.

3. Make a list of priorities of services assuming that it is not possible for your community to provide a well-rounded program for all children. What services in your estimation should come first? Which are more basic and which could be deferred or postponed with the least disorganization?

SELECTED REFERENCES

BURMEISTER, EVA, *Forty-Five in a Family* (New York: Columbia University Press, 1949).

CHARNLEY, JEAN, *The Art of Child Placement* (Minneapolis: University of Minnesota Press, 1955).

FREDERICKSEN, HAZEL, *The Child and His Welfare* (San Francisco: W. H. Freeman & Co., Publishers, 1948).

FREUD, ANNA, and BURLINGHAM, DOROTHY, *Infants Without Families* (New York: International Universities Press, Inc., 1944).

GLICKMAN, ESTHER, *Child Placement Through Clinically Oriented Casework* (New York: Columbia University Press, 1957).

HUTCHINSON, DOROTHY, *In Quest of Foster Parents* (New York: Columbia University Press, 1943).

Report of the Advisory Council on Child Welfare Services (Washington, D.C.: Children's Bureau, U.S. Department of Health, Education, and Welfare, 1954).

YOUNG, LEONTINE, *Out of Wedlock* (New York: McGraw-Hill Book Co., Inc., 1954).

ZIETZ, DOROTHY, *Child Welfare, Principles and Methods* (New York: John Wiley & Sons, Inc., 1959).

CHAPTER 9

Correctional Services

An eighteen-year-old senior stole a Cadillac from a wealthy family and was sentenced to thirty days in jail. During his first three years in high school he had worked well and had received excellent grades; then he began to fail his classes. His father had given him a car, money, everything he wanted; in fact, too much, and he had finally been arrested by the police for theft. A social worker, attached to the Youth Bureau, talked with the judge who agreed to have the boy spend each night in jail, but have his father pick him up and take him to and from school each day. Prior to completion of the sentence, the social worker checked with the boy's teachers and found that he was doing very well. They could not figure out what had happened to him. The answer was, apparently, that the father and boy had had a chance to talk with each other, to share their inner feelings, problems, and hopes for the first time in their lives. The social worker had opened the door for rehabilitation through strengthening the father-son relationship.

THE SOCIAL PROBLEMS OF DELINQUENCY AND CRIME

Delinquency and crime are major social problems of modern society. They are of concern not only to persons who are involved directly as victims and otherwise, but to those who consider present and future implications of the increasing amount of antisocial behavior. In 1961, serious offenses amounted to 1,926,090 in the United States and crime continued its upward surge, 3 percent over 1960, the previous all-time recorded high. The first year of the sixties recorded a new all-time high, with 98 percent more crime than in 1950. According to FBI reports, the crime clock ticks off four serious crimes per minute, and crime has outstripped population growth over five to one in the past five years.[1]

Economic-wise it is estimated that delinquency and crime cost the people of the United States from fifteen to twenty-five billions of dollars annually.

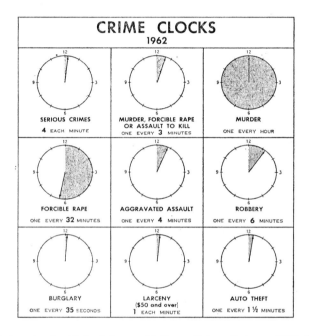

CRIME CLOCKS
1962

SERIOUS CRIMES 4 EACH MINUTE	**MURDER, FORCIBLE RAPE OR ASSAULT TO KILL** ONE EVERY 3 MINUTES	**MURDER** ONE EVERY HOUR
FORCIBLE RAPE ONE EVERY 32 MINUTES	**AGGRAVATED ASSAULT** ONE EVERY 4 MINUTES	**ROBBERY** ONE EVERY 6 MINUTES
BURGLARY ONE EVERY 35 SECONDS	**LARCENY** ($50 and over) 1 EACH MINUTE	**AUTO THEFT** ONE EVERY 1½ MINUTES

SOURCE: *Crime in the United States, Uniform Crime Reports, 1962* (Washington, D.C.: Federal Bureau of Investigation, 1963), p. 14.

At present more than 200,000 persons are confined in some 230 penitentiaries, reformatories, and correctional institutions in the United States. In addition, there are some 3,000 local and county jails and lockups, many of which handle both sentenced and unsentenced prisoners. In 1958, between one and one-half and two million youngsters under 18 were dealt with by the police for misconduct. More than 600,000 children came before juvenile courts for alleged delinquent behavior, and some 100,000 were held in jail awaiting court trial. In common language, this means that about one boy in five appears in court during adolescence on delinquency charges.[2]

1 *Uniform Crime Reports for the United States—1961* (Washington, D.C.: FBI, U.S. Department of Justice, 1962), p. 1.

2 *Report to the Congress on Juvenile Delinquency* (Washington, D.C.: U.S. Department of Health, Education, and Welfare, 1960), pp. 3, 8, 20, 43.

It also means that in an average twenty-four hour period about 5,000 boys and girls are handled by law enforcement officers, about 2,000 appear before one of the juvenile courts, and approximately 300 spend the night in one of our jails or lockups, most of which are deplorable places for keeping children or youth.

In addition to the dollars and statistics, antisocial behavior rends the heartstrings of thousands of parents and loved ones. A single act of delinquency or crime may change the whole existence of a particular family; and as families are weakened and filled with tension, society is injured and threatened.

What is being done to offset these startling developments? What has been done in the past? What might be done in the present, and in the future? The profession of social work offers one answer to these questions.

SOCIAL WORK AND CORRECTIONS [3]

Throughout the history of man, punishments, especially corporal and capital, have often been offered in answer to antisocial behavior. Public hangings, floggings, mutilation, branding, banishment, the stocks and pillory, and many other physical penalties have been utilized to "punish the culprit and be a lesson to others." It was only toward the end of the eighteenth century, at the Walnut Street Prison in Philadelphia, in the shadows of Independence Hall, that the beginning of a new method—the use of a time sentence in an institution—came into general usage. Enlightened humanitarians claimed that it was inhumane and unwise to torture offenders or put them to death. Instead the *penitentiary system* was developed, devised to give the offender a chance to think, have a "change of heart," and "mend his ways" through meditation in solitary confinement. Subsequently various kinds of penal institutions evolved to allow for incarceration. Eventually the use of probation came into being as a substitute for imprisonment through the efforts of John Augustus, a Boston shoemaker, and other benevolent reformers.

As offenders were sentenced to institutions and were placed on probation and parole, various professional groups became interested in making these efforts as effective as possible. Social work was one of these.

During the nineteenth century the roots of the emerging profession of social work were growing rapidly and a major area of focus involved

[3] Parts of this discussion are adapted from Rex A. Skidmore, "The Social Worker Uses Time in Rehabilitation of the Offender," *The Prison Journal*, Vol. 41 (Autumn, 1961), pp. 53–60.

the offender. For example, the *Proceedings of the National Conference of Charities and Correction* indicate that at the conference which met in 1885 a portion of the program was devoted to consideration of employment in reformatories, prison reforms, jails and police, and even to discussion of prevention of related social problems. During the past two decades, in particular, there has been a revived interest in the field of corrections by social workers. This is epitomized in the Curriculum Study of the Council on Social Work Education: [4]

> The modification of the penalty system did more than require a different kind of administrative structure and personnel. It made possible the idea of treatment. . . . With the increasing knowledge about the dynamics of human behavior and how it is modified, which has become available in the 20th century, it has become possible to give attention to the rehabilitation of the offender.

Corrections is one of four social processes utilized in the administration of criminal justice. They include "(1) law enforcement, which is concerned with the collection of evidence about reported offenses and with the detection and arrest of suspected offenders; (2) prosecution and defense, or the preparation and presentation of criminal cases before the court; (3) judicial process, which is concerned with the legal determination of guilt and the assignment of penalties; (4) corrections, which is responsible for administering the assigned penalties." [5]

Corrections, in one sense at least, is the total process of helping persons who have violated the law to be rehabilitated. The social worker plays a very important role in this total process. His basic goal is summarized in the Curriculum Study: "The correctional process has come to mean the administration of the penalty in such a way that the offender is 'corrected,' i.e., his current behavior is kept within acceptable limits at the same time that his general life adjustment is modified." [6]

The aim of the social worker in assisting boys and girls who are in trouble with the law is basically to rehabilitate rather than to punish them. The goal is to help them to understand themselves, their relationships with others, and what is expected of them as members of the society in which they live. Corporal and physical punishment have been pushed aside, relegated to history, and the emphasis is upon trying to bring about positive change in behavior patterns. Reformation and rehabilitation are the key words today.

The specific tasks of social workers in corrections are summarized by the Curriculum Study as follows: [7]

4 Elliot Studt, *Education for Social Workers in the Correctional Field,* Curriculum Study, Vol. V (New York: Council on Social Work Education, 1959), p. 7.

5 *Ibid.,* p. 6.

6 *Ibid.,* p. 7.

7 *Ibid.,* pp. 15–16.

1. *Act as the officer of the court or other quasi-judicial body to investigate and report on the offender and his social situation, contributing the results of such social studies in an appropriate and meaningful way to the making of legal decisions.*

2. *Supervise the client's social activities in such a way that:*

Violations of the conditions of his status and his success in meeting conditions are perceived and can be reported.

The general control plan provided in the status is individualized according to the client's need for constructive social control.

Controls are provided by the worker in such a way that the client is supported in viably conforming behavior and inner growth toward self-control is stimulated.

3. *Help the involuntary client to:*

Handle the stresses produced by the law enforcement and correctional process constructively.

Become motivated to ask for and use help in problem solving.

Modify his behavior in the direction of increasingly viable conformity with social expectations.

4. *As the formal authority person in the client's life, work with other authorities associated with the client (parents, teachers, employers, social agencies, institutional personnel) in such a way that:*

The problems of these authorities with the client are alleviated.

The activities of the authorities support the client's efforts toward satisfactory behavior.

The client is more soundly linked with the resources of his groups and his community.

5. *Administer a caseload or group load in such a way that:*

The worker's decisions are appropriate and responsible.

The decisions of other personnel in the administration of criminal justice are respected, implemented, and appropriately influenced by the social worker's knowledge.

The necessities of legal and administrative deadlines are observed.

The emergencies in the lives of clients are met with full attention to their significance for change.

6. *Enact a role in a multidiscipline agency involving shared decisions and teamwork obligations in partnership with:*

Personnel from other professions.

Personnel in the same role as his but with other educational backgrounds.

Personnel with sub-professional assignments and backgrounds.

Personnel from other agencies in the administration of criminal justice.

Personnel in other correctional agencies who have served the client or will in the future.

7. *Take a responsible part in the social change of his agency and in the development of the field of service to which his agency belongs, contributing from his professional knowledge and experience to the determination of policy.*

8. *Contribute to the developing professional knowledge of social work in corrections.*

According to the Curriculum Study, the tasks of the social worker in corrections include four in particular: (1) Investigation and surveillance for the purpose of securing information about the client's failures or successes in meeting the obligations of his legal status; (2) The use of controls to modify client behavior; (3) Acting as a legal authority in the client's life with responsibility for value change; and (4) Correctional decision making. These are all important in working with persons in trouble, and, in particular, in attempting to help them adjust better to society.

The social worker's aim is to help the offender, not to retaliate or to punish him. The goal is to utilize the knowledge and skills of the profession in a corrective manner, to rehabilitate the individual, to help him to help himself so that he can return to and become a part of his society, and to guide him toward becoming comfortable with himself and his associates. "More than in any other social service, the correctional social worker's task is defined in terms of changing the values of the client so that they become congruent in action with the values of the community." [8]

The social worker aims to help the offender to change his patterns of behavior so that he can relate constructively to others and become socially acceptable. This is done through two avenues: (1) working with the individual to help him to change through better understanding of himself and by tapping his own strengths and resources; and (2) modification of his environment to bring about a more healthy social climate in which to live. Newman observes that the "redirection and re-education of persons who have demonstrated anti-social and illegal behavior are complex matters requiring both time and skill." [9]

Examples of individual problems of offenders with which the social worker helps are: serious feelings of inferiority and inadequacy, inability to socialize, lack of status, negative feelings toward relatives, sibling rivalries, and family disorganization. The worker encourages the offender to talk about his problems, to feel about them, and to come to an insightful understanding of himself, accompanied by socially constructive behavior.

In regard to environmental problems, the worker may help the offender to bolster his abilities to accept and withstand the pressures and/or assist in bringing about changes which alleviate such conditions as: inadequate housing or diet, a family where no one cares, inadequate vocational training or job placement, and economic stresses.

[8] *Ibid.*, p. 47. For an interesting analysis of some of the dilemmas, problems, and challenges for social workers in corrections see Lloyd E. Ohlin, Herman Piven, and Donnell M. Pappenfort, "Major Dilemmas of the Social Worker in Probation and Parole," *NPPA Journal*, Vol. 2 (July, 1956), pp. 211–225; Eileen L. Younghusband, "Report on a Survey of Social Work in the Field of Corrections," *Social Work Education*, Supplement, Vol. VIII (August, 1960), pp. 1–24; and Swithun Bowers, "The Application of Social Work in the Correctional Field," *NPPA Journal*, Vol. 5 (January, 1959), p. 16.

[9] Charles L. Newman, "Concepts of Treatment in Probation and Parole Supervision," *Federal Probation*, Vol. 25 (March, 1961), p. 11.

In working with both individual and environmental situations, the social worker keeps close to the family unit; in fact, social work is family-centered.

SOCIAL WORK PRACTICE IN CORRECTIONS

"Social Work practice," according to the Code of Ethics, National Association of Social Workers, "is a public trust that requires of its practitioners integrity, compassion, belief in the dignity and worth of human beings, respect for individual differences, a commitment to service, and a dedication to truth."

In working with offenders the social worker attempts to achieve socially desirable objectives within two kinds of settings: institutional, and noninstitutional—probation or parole. Time is a reality factor; for example, the average length of probation for delinquents is about ten months, and juvenile delinquents average about nine to ten months in training schools before being released. During this time, the social worker endeavors to establish a meaningful relationship with the individual and to help him alter his behavior patterns so as to prepare his return to society as a contributing member. Although inmates of reformatories and prisons receive longer sentences, most offenders return to society sooner than is generally supposed. Barnes, for example, states that "at the most, prisons only offer a modicum of social security, and even this is slight in light of the fact that the average convicted felon only serves some $2\frac{1}{3}$ years within prison walls, and the 'lifer' only 9 years." [10]

For inmates in reformatories or prisons the social worker attempts to establish a relationship which, over a period of time, frees the individual to express his feelings in a cathartic manner, muster his ego strengths, change some of his values, and become a law-abiding citizen. This relationship is the essence of the social worker's contribution—along with the use of community resources. It means that the worker accepts the client, understands, and respects him, and that the client develops feelings toward the worker, and shares his ideas, emotions, and problems. Then, through a bond of warmth and support, changes are effected. The social worker is nonjudgmental, warm, sensitive to his needs, and conveys a feeling of respect for the integrity and individuality of the client regardless of his questionable conduct.

Kenneth Pray [11] states that the helping process depends "upon a relationship between worker and client within which the client may, if

[10] Harry Elmer Barnes, "Shall We Get Tough or Be Sensible in Facing the Increase of Crime?" *Federal Probation*, Vol. 23 (June, 1959), p. 30.
[11] Kenneth L. M. Pray, "The Place of Social Case Work in the Treatment of Delinquency," *Social Service Review*, Vol. 19 (June, 1945), p. 236.

he is able and willing, ask, receive, and use help in clarifying his own wants and purposes, in relation to the resources available to him, and in mustering his own powers to achieve his chosen ends."

Robison [12] describes five basic assumptions underlying casework which are applicable in helping the offender:

(1) Every individual must be seen as a person of dignity and worth; (2) behavior, whether acceptable or unacceptable to the community, expresses a need of the individual; (3) an individual can and will change his behavior if the right help is given at the right time and in the right amount; (4) if the offer of help is given before the problem becomes seriously aggravated the response is likely to be better; and (5) the family is the most influential force in the development of personality in the crucial early years.

In institutions, the social worker ordinarily meets weekly or even more often with the client for about an hour and, through interviewing, helps him to achieve his goals. The pattern outside institutions is fundamentally the same and includes periodic interviews which give support and assistance to the offender, focusing on treatment rather than punishment, reform rather than punitiveness. Reinemann [13] observes that the length of probation is dependent upon the needs and requirements of each individual case and that short-term probation is of little value. Several months are usually needed to accomplish the goals desired. Cases show that meaningful interviews inside and outside of institutions can be most helpful in the rehabilitation of the offender—especially if continued over a period of time.

The social work process consists of three parts: *social study* (finding the facts), *diagnosis,* (defining and evaluating the problems), and *treatment* (solving the problems). These three ordinarily proceed simultaneously from the beginning, although in emphasis there is usually sequential order. Often the first interview, or two or three, is utilized for social study and diagnosis; then treatment entails varying numbers of interviews, depending upon individual problems and environmental situations.

The number of interviews is significant. Many social workers leave the number open to the worker and client to ascertain as they move along together; others stipulate a specific number of interviews, so that termination goals and dynamics may be anticipated. Although a common pattern is for interviews to take place weekly, the number can be increased or decreased depending on the needs of the client in the rehabilitative process. During emergencies the social worker may be needed at once.

12 Sophia M. Robison, *Juvenile Delinquency, Its Nature and Control* (New York: Holt, Rinehart & Winston, Inc., 1960), p. 275.

13 John Otto Reinemann, "Probation and the Juvenile Delinquent," *Annals of the American Academy of Political and Social Science,* Vol. 261 (January, 1949), p. 118.

The social worker acts as a catalytic agent who makes it possible for an offender to understand himself better, feel about himself, and in particular, to strengthen his ability to interact with others constructively. The worker helps him to tap his own strengths, bringing about better harmony within himself and in his associations with others. Studies show that offenders often need help in learning to function adequately in interaction with others, particularly in close, personal relationships.

Pray describes the place of social casework in the treatment of delinquency by indicating: [14]

It is a means of individualizing the impact of the social forces that bear down upon him, of helping him to discover their meaning to him, their effect upon him, and of helping him to choose a course of action that sustains his own individuality and integrity, while yielding enough of his old self to accept the limits these social forces represent.

Ohlin and Lawrence stress the importance of the offender's peers in exerting a profound control over his responses to social interactions, particularly "in the closed social systems of correctional institutions." [15]

They also indicate that inmates are acutely aware of their deficiency in the social skills and will "respond positively to the establishment of clearly defined routes out of the status of failure to which they have been assigned, if these pathways to opportunity are broad enough and clear enough to win support of the inmate system." [16]

Although some problems may be eased by the social worker in an interview or two, most persons who are in legal trouble need assistance over a period of time [17] in a series of interviews, and require guidance in making effective use of community services and resources.

Timing is also important in the social worker's role. There are certain periods when he can be particularly effective, such as: during intake, when emergencies occur, in preparing for release, and in aftercare treatment. A meaningful relationship between worker and client can lubricate these time-bound experiences, resulting in desired change.

A major problem is the shortage of trained workers. The *Report to Congress on Juvenile Delinquency* reflects that better results are obtained when probation officers are well trained, and then concluded that eighty-five percent of more than 2,000 probation officers polled said that they were college graduates but only 10 percent had "a master's degree in social work, the training called for by agreed-upon stand-

14 Kenneth L. M. Pray, *op. cit.*, p. 241.

15 Lloyd E. Ohlin and William C. Lawrence, "Social Interaction Among Clients as a Treatment Problem," *Social Work*, Vol. 4 (April, 1959), p. 5.

16 *Ibid.*, p. 13.

17 For interesting analyses regarding short-term contacts see Jacob Chwast, "Casework Treatment in a Police Setting," *Federal Probation*, Vol. 18 (December, 1954), pp. 35–40; also, Joseph R. Silver, "Social Casework in Jail," *The Prison Journal*, Vol. 39 (October, 1959), pp. 51–55.

ards." [18] The *Report* also indicates that 3 out of 10 state training schools have no social workers on their staff and that staff turnover is high.

PROCESSES AND PRINCIPLES [19]

What are the methods [20] utilized by the social worker in assisting with antisocial behavior? There are three in particular: *casework, group work,* and *community organization.* Research and administration also bolster social work services both directly and indirectly. Casework is the process of assisting an individual or family on a personal face-to-face basis to consider and solve their problems. Traditionally, casework has been the essence of social work. Group work utilizes the group as the main tool in the helping process, assisting youth to face their problems and do something about them. In industrial schools and among groups of probationers, many groups meet together advantageously to consider their problems and solutions. Some fascinating experimentation is being sponsored in New York and other localities, using this method to reach and influence the "tough corner gangs."

Community organization is the intergroup method in which an attempt is made to tap community resources for solving and helping with social problems that affect a large number of people. This includes family life education, community welfare councils, and many specific programs.

A few of the key principles which the social worker keeps in mind as he works with offenders and their families are: (1) He utilizes a *relationship* to help clients to help themselves; (2) He never condemns or moralizes. He accepts the clients as they are and also their behavior, regardless of what has been in the past; (3) He respects their right of self-determination; that is, he assists them to think and feel through their problems and situations, but does not make basic decisions for them. He helps to provide an emotional climate in which they can face their problems and work out appropriate solutions; (4) The probation

[18] *Report to the Congress on Juvenile Delinquency, op. cit.,* pp. 26–27; also, for a discussion of training of social workers for corrections, see Edmund G. Burbank, "What the Schools of Social Work Can Do to Increase the Pool of Trained Correctional Personnel," *Education for Social Work Proceedings,* Ninth Annual Program Meeting, Council on Social Work Education (New York: Council on Social Work Education, 1961), pp. 163–177.

[19] Adapted in part from Rex A. Skidmore, "The Philosophy and Function of the Social Worker in the Prevention and Control of Juvenile Delinquency," in *The Role and Responsibility of the Juvenile Judge, Peace Officer and Social Worker in the Prevention and Treatment of Delinquency* (Boise: Idaho Department of Health, 1963), pp. 62–81.

[20] See Ben S. Meeker, "Social Work and the Correctional Field," *Federal Probation,* Vol. 21 (September, 1957), pp. 32–42; and Gisela Konopka, "The Social Group Work Method: Its Use in the Correctional Field," *Federal Probation,* Vol. 20 (March, 1956), pp. 25–30.

officer recognizes that he has to study and understand normal behavior as well as antisocial behavior in order to comprehend the *why* of delinquency and criminality and what should be done about them; (5) Contrary to what some people believe, the probation social worker ordinarily provides a security-giving firmness, not physical punishment, but not "coddling," as some maintain. He recognizes that in many ways a child is like a coil spring, and that the harder one pushes on him, the farther he will be likely to spring back when an opportunity arises; (6) Authority is used in a positive manner to help offenders to help themselves face their problems and readjust their thinking and behavior.

What are the specific functions of a social worker in relation to juvenile delinquency and crime? Some of his main functions are:

Helping to strengthen motivation. Many boys and girls, or adults, do not care much about what they do in life or what they do not do. The social worker, through talking with them sympathetically and understandingly, can usually be of aid. For a person to know that someone is interested in him and will accept him as he is, is a tremendous motivating factor. One delinquent, for example, who talked to a probation officer over a period of many weeks, said: "He was just like a hypnotist. I couldn't say no to him. To know that someone cared enough about me to spend time with me, to try to understand and help me, led me to where I am today." His desire to become a law-abiding citizen had been increased and supported.

Allowing for ventilation of feelings is a second service of the social worker. Most youth and adults who come to a probation officer need to share with someone, in confidence, their inner feelings, their fears and frustrations, as well as their hopes and aspirations. The importance of this is illustrated by the man who talked to a worker for more than sixty minutes, giving the listener only an opportunity to nod his head and acquiesce. At the end he stood up, greatly relieved, and said, "I feel much better. Thanks for all your wonderful advice!" Youth and adults have feelings well up within and social workers provide a safe emotional climate in which they can express and verbalize them.

The giving of information is another important function of the social worker in the field of corrections. Many youth and adults need help in understanding who they are, where they are going, and where they should go. Many times they do not comprehend the society to which they belong and the social worker can help them to develop such an understanding, and to acquire insights into their proper roles.

The probation officer *helps offenders to make decisions.* They do not make them for them, but help them to consider, rationally, their problems and the alternatives which face them. Should they obtain employment? Should they stay with their own family or move out? Should they continue to associate with their old friends? Should they return to school? How can they alter their behavior patterns? These are some of the typical questions which arise.

The social worker helps the client to *define the situation*. He assists him not only in *thinking* about a problem or a situation, but also in *feeling* about the situation. An illustration would be the young boy who has serious feelings of inferiority and, as a result, is in legal trouble on a compensatory, acting-out basis. The social worker helps him to think and feel about himself and his behavior, and thereby to realize that his feelings of inferiority are not based on facts. This new understanding and insight can alter his whole pattern of living.

Assisting in modification of the environment is another major function. With his knowledge of community resources, the social worker is able to help persons and families to tap various financial and social resources to meet their individual needs. The social worker may help a boy who is on probation to get a part-time job. He may assist him in finding a place to live; he may help him become enrolled in a vocational training program to prepare him for worthwhile citizenship for the rest of his life.

Reorganizing behavior patterns is one of the most difficult functions of the social worker. This includes help for the homosexual, the chronic alcoholic, the person who uses drugs excessively, and those with other deep personality problems. The social worker may refer such a person to another expert or talk to him himself, depending on his background, training, and experience. These kinds of cases usually require long periods of treatment.

Another major function is in *facilitating referral*. Sometimes his job is "helping Susie to get to the clinic." Often it is difficult for a person to take his personal problems to another, and he needs support in so doing. Referral may be made to a psychiatrist, minister, internist, geneticist, or other person who may help with a particular situation. The social worker's comprehensive knowledge of community resources is used to advantage in making referrals.

One of the main contributions of social work today is in relation to prevention of delinquency and crime through the school setting. In 1919 Dr. Jan Don Ball, psychiatrist, examined clinically 220 children in the Hawthorne Grade School in Berkeley, California, and discovered that twenty-two children (10 percent) presented problems involving mental, moral, physical, or social abnormalities. He recommended that each be given specialized treatment and consideration—neither of which was ever done. Fourteen years later, a follow-up study confirmed the idea that "society's effort to combat crime must begin at the high chair level, rather than that of the electric chair." [21] It was found that 90 percent of these

---

[21] Reported in V. A. Leonard, "Crime Control: A Police Officer's Attempt to State the Problem," *Journal of Criminal Law and Criminology*, Vol. 37 (May–June, 1946), p. 96.

former problem children were in institutions, had been, or were community problems of one kind or another. The school social worker, of course, works effectively with such boys and girls with problems, and also with their parents and teachers.

Nathan Bodin [22] made a study in the spring of 1934 to ascertain what had become of 116 adults who were considered by their teachers in California public schools as definitely unadjusted in the primary grades, as problem children. Bodin secured information on 93 of the 116 and ascertained that 92.5 percent were in jail or had acquired delinquency or criminal records.

Social workers in general are becoming more interested in the field of corrections. In 1959 the Ford Foundation allocated $149,000 for a five-year grant to develop a corrections project with the Council on Social Work Education. Illustrative of the several priorities set up for this project are the following:

1. That the resources of the project be concentrated to the greatest extent possible on using a variety of ways of getting social work educators and correctional administrators together at the local level to look at correctional training programs, and to determine means of working together toward improving the situation.

2. That the efforts of the project be directed toward helping the schools of social work increase their contribution to a larger pool of trained correctional personnel.

3. That the consultant enlist the cooperation of appropriate national agencies, schools of social work, and correctional services to develop institutes significant for training in the correctional field.

SOCIAL SERVICES AND CASE EXAMPLES

POLICE DEPARTMENTS AND YOUTH BUREAUS

Social workers are just beginning to be utilized in working with the police, particularly in their youth bureaus. In many larger cities professionally trained social workers are integral parts of these police departments. They help the law enforcement officers to better understand the boys and girls whom they apprehend. They also help the total department to develop a rehabilitative attitude rather than a punitive one, and in particular, to facilitate the rehabilitative processes. In addition, they play an important role in trying to prevent antisocial behavior among children, youth, and adults. The social worker is in a strategic position to utilize existing community resources and to draw upon whatever may be most needed to assist a particular offender to change his hostile attitudes and behavior to those within societal standards.

22 Nathan Bodin, "Do Problem Children Become Delinquents and Criminals?" *Journal of the American Institute of Criminal Law and Criminology*, Vol. 27 (November–December, 1936), pp. 545–59.

To illustrate, young Rebecca who was picked up on the street at
2 A.M. one morning with an older married man, was interviewed by a
social worker, who found that her family was "psychologically broken"
and disorganized. The social worker, in cooperation with the police,
accompanied the girl to her home. In the next several days, the worker
interviewed the mother, father, and some of the neighbors. After several
weeks, the mother and father, through the help of the social worker, began to realize for the first time in their lives that they needed to provide
more love, care, and attention for their children. Within a few months,
the family constellation changed from one of constant bickering, trouble,
and hostility to one on the pathway to becoming a solid, loving family.
The daughter who had been in trouble with the police several times
prior to her escapade, settled down, and began to do well in school and
otherwise.

COURTS

Social workers are attached to juvenile courts, district courts, federal
courts, and to some municipal courts, performing the role of probation
officer. In this connection, they have several functions. The first is conducting investigations to find out the facts and the feelings involved
in a particular violation of law. With the training that he has, a social
worker can usually be objective yet sympathetic, and can secure a picture of the total situation that is most helpful to the court. More and
more often judges are making decisions regarding disposition of cases
based on facts and understandings supplied through the investigation
of the social worker. Investigations are primarily related to the offender
but nearly always involve the family, close relatives, and other key persons in the lives of the accused.

An example of this function is the case of a young man, who during
World War II was brought before a California judge on a charge of
"stealing state property." The judge was a most understanding, capable
person. The young man was handsome and appeared to be intelligent
but was a person who had been "kicked around from place to place."
He had been born into a family where he was not wanted. He had
run away from home many times, had been placed in foster care on
several occasions, and for years had been a "knight of the road." The
judge took a personal interest in him and asked his social worker to
make a careful investigation. The social worker reported the significant
facts and feelings. On the basis of this investigation, the judge be-
friended the boy as no one had ever done before. The boy felt the sincere interest—even love—of this judge and social worker. The disposition was that the boy was given an opportunity to go into the service
to perform his military obligation. When he filled in his papers, he asked

the judge if he could put his name down as the person "closest to him, who would always know his whereabouts." The judge said he would be complimented to be so designated. The boy was accepted into military service and within a year was "lost in action." Some of his personal belongings, including a wristwatch, were returned to the judge. They were clear evidence of the need of one young man for understanding, love, and interest from judges, social workers, and others who might supply these when they have not come through a regular channel.

Another major function of the social worker is to represent the court after the judge has made a decision. Probation involves regular interviews and contacts between the probation officer and the offender. Again, the social worker attempts to use his best knowledge and skills to help bring about desired changes in the thinking, feeling, and behavior of those with whom he works. Many offenders for the first time in their lives have someone, the social worker, who really cares about them and is trying to help them to understand themselves and their relationships with others. The essence of this service is illustrated by the statement of young Joe, age 17, who said, "For the first time in my life I was receiving love, not personal love, but the kind that made me feel someone cared, that I was important to someone, and that I was wanted."

Not only is probation carried out on a one-to-one relationship, but today there are experiments and activities involving groups of probationers who are trying to help each other. An interesting example of this, is the Pinehills' experiment in Provo, Utah, made possible by a grant from the Ford Foundation. Here groups of boys who have been before the juvenile court and placed on probation meet daily for group therapy sessions under the guidance and direction of a social worker. The youth are allowed to discuss whatever they wish. Observations, from those who have evaluated this development, are that the boys, through this group process, help each other to think and feel about their problems, and in particular to consider solutions to them. In many ways, these youth can tell each other what should be done and are often more effective than adults.

SOCIAL WORK IN INSTITUTIONS

Although many industrial schools, detention homes, reformatories, and prisons do not have trained social workers on their staffs, it is encouraging to note that the number of such persons is constantly growing. Within such institutions the social worker can play an extremely important role. He is usually assigned several inmates with whom to work on a face-to-face, individualized basis. He ordinarily meets with them weekly, giving them an opportunity to talk over their problems in relation to society and life, especially in relation to their families. All kinds of cases exist which indicate that thousands of boys and girls, youth, and adults are being helped by social workers who open the door for rehabilitation. Not only is casework used advantageously within these institutions but group work is also more common.

That youth and adults need help in institutions is illustrated by the example of two seventeen-year-old boys who had been placed in a state prison for robbery. They were "ideal" prisoners. When they had served their time and were about to leave, the warden cautioned them to be truthful and law-abiding. They walked out of the prison gates with about $15 in their pockets. They located some stores, bought a few things which they had not had for some time, and then began to look for jobs. When the applications were handed to them, they were faced with the question, "Have you ever been in prison?" They answered truthfully. No one would give them a job. Three nights later, about midnight, the two boys returned to the prison, rang the bell at the gate, and asked if the warden would give them a place to sleep. He, of course, granted their request. The next morning the guards passed a hat around, making a collection for the boys. More important than this, a social worker called employers and arranged for a job for each of them. Several years later it was ascertained that these two young men had followed the warden's instructions, had lived law-abiding lives, and were respected citizens in their communities.

PAROLE ACTIVITIES

Most youth and adults who spend time in a correctional institution leave on parole. This means that they are released to a person who meets with them periodically, and endeavors to help them. Social workers are used in this challenging position. Again, a social worker in such a position can be a most valuable anchor to a person who has a very inadequate place to go or a family which really does not want him. A parole officer can not only support and sustain a person but can work with his family, helping to bring about changes in the total constellation which are helpful to all concerned.

PREVENTION

Social workers are becoming very interested in preventive aspects of delinquency and crime. Philosophically, they believe that if more time and talent can be put into preventing antisocial behavior in the first place, society, as well as individuals and families, will be much better off. Prevention has many sides to it and involves all of the helping disciplines. Education is particularly important. Several studies show that there are many boys and girls in school who are near-delinquent and who will get into trouble if something is not done to help them solve their problems and adjust better to school, their families, and life in general. Marriage and family counseling, particularly premarital counseling, is another avenue which seems to be promising in preventing social ills.

Recreational activities and clubs can be utilized for prevention where there is proper leadership. An example was in the city of Battle Creek, Michigan, where in one dilapidated area the police arrested each year an average of 135 of the 450 boys and girls who called it home. Through the efforts of an energetic, enthusiastic police chief and other community leaders, a clubhouse was built in 1938 in this area. Within the next twenty-two months not a single boy or girl from this shabby neighborhood landed behind bars.[23] There are many other kinds of challenging activities open to those who would like to work toward reducing and preventing antisocial behavior.

SUMMARY

The key ideas of this chapter are:

1. Juvenile delinquency and crime are major problems in modern society.

2. Four social processes utilized in modern administration of criminal justice are: law enforcement, prosecution and defense, judicial process, and corrections.

3. Social work has a major contribution to make in the control and prevention of juvenile delinquency and crime.

4. Social work attempts to help the individual, his family, and the community to face and solve delinquency and crime problems through utilization of individual, family, and community resources.

5. Casework, group work, and community organization are the basic processes utilized by the social worker in corrections.

6. The social worker helps particularly with police departments, courts, probation, institutions, parole, and prevention.

7. The social worker is really just beginning to tap individual and community resources in the control and prevention of delinquency and crime.

QUESTIONS FOR DISCUSSION

1. What is delinquency? What is crime?

2. Have delinquency and crime actually been increasing in recent years in the United States?

[23] Karl Detzer, "Bad Boy + $25 = Good Boy," *Reader's Digest,* Vol. 39 (December, 1941), p. 119.

3. What causes crime?

4. What are the main contributions which the social worker can make toward the control and prevention of delinquency?

5. Give an example of a boy or girl who has violated the law who has been helped by a social worker or some other professionally trained person.

6. Should we try to rehabilitate rather than punish youth who violate the law?

7. How important is the family in relation to antisocial behavior?

8. What are two or three valid suggestions for preventing juvenile delinquency?

SPECIAL ACTIVITIES

1. Invite a local member of the police department or FBI to talk to the class on "The Nature and Extent of Juvenile Delinquency and Crime."

2. If feasible, visit a juvenile detention home or a state industrial school, and find out about its social services or lack of them.

3. Sponsor a panel in class on "Reaching the hard-to-reach delinquent."

SELECTED REFERENCES

BLOCK, HERBERT A. and FLYNN, FRANK T., *Delinquency, The Juvenile Offender in America Today* (New York: Random House, Inc., 1956).

Juvenile Delinquency References (Washington, D.C.: U.S. Department of Health, Education, and Welfare, 1961).

KVARACEUS, WILLIAM C., *The Community and The Delinquent* (New York: Harcourt, Brace & World, Inc., 1954).

Perspectives and Guides in the Expansion of Social Work Education for the Correctional Field (New York: Council on Social Work Education, 1958).

Report to the Congress on Juvenile Delinquency (Washington, D.C.: U.S. Department of Health, Education, and Welfare, 1960).

ROBISON, SOPHIA M., *Juvenile Delinquency, Its Nature and Control* (New York: Holt, Rinehart & Winston, Inc., 1960).

STUDT, ELLIOT, *Education for Social Workers in the Correctional Field,* Curriculum Study, Vol. V (New York: Council on Social Work Education, 1959).

The Educational Needs of Personnel in the Field of Corrections (New York: Council on Social Work Education, 1956).

YOUNG, PAULINE V., *Social Treatment in Probation and Delinquency,* 2nd ed. (New York: McGraw-Hill Book Co., Inc., 1952).

YOUNGHUSBAND, EILEEN L., "Report on a Survey of Social Work in the Field of Corrections," *Social Work Education,* Vol. 8 (August, 1960).

CHAPTER 10

International Social Work

In the presidential campaign in 1940, Wendell Wilkie emphasized "one world" as a basic theme of his political thought. In recent years the globe has shrunk in size, due to improved means of communication and transportation. A person may board a jet liner at O'Hare field in Chicago and be in London, Paris, or Frankfurt about six hours later. It is possible to eat breakfast in Europe, lunch in New York, and dinner in Los Angeles. The Atlantic and Pacific oceans today are bridged by jets which travel at speeds in excess of 600 miles an hour. On the drawing boards are airliners which will carry more than 400 passengers and which will take only an hour's time from San Francisco to New York City.

Telstar and shortwave radios allow radio and TV broadcasts to be beamed around the world. Modern inventions make it possible for representatives of different nations to listen to a speech in Russian at the United Nations and, with the use of earphones, to hear the speech in a variety of different languages almost instantaneously as the speaker proceeds with his message and discussion of pertinent issues and questions.

With the speed and communication miracles of the present day, the needs and problems of the peoples of the world are altered. There is a blending and fusion of cultures, subcultures, and nationalities. Social problems and needs of one people become of interest and concern to other peoples. A human being who is starving to death on the other side of the earth may become of vital concern to his "brother" thousands of miles away.

Social work is developing an international flavor. Not only are social problems and needs shared on a global basis as never before, but numerous leaders and educators in various countries are doing what they can to help train their people to become professionally capable of assisting individuals, families, and communities with problems of social functioning within their own boundaries. Schools of social work have been established and social work leaders have joined forces on an international basis to improve training programs and practice. World organizations have developed which invite representatives of all countries to join hands, to meet together periodically, to help each other in improving total services. This chapter includes a brief description of the main international social work organizations, historical developments, their programs, and issues.

INTERNATIONAL SOCIAL WORK ORGANIZATIONS

Three international social work organizations are most active and prominent in social work affairs. These are the International Association of Schools of Social Work, the International Conference of Social Work, and the International Federation of Social Workers.

INTERNATIONAL ASSOCIATION OF SCHOOLS OF SOCIAL WORK

The International Association of Schools of Social Work, formerly the International Committee of Schools of Social Work, was established in 1929. From a small nucleus of schools located mainly in Western Europe, its membership has grown to include twelve associations of schools of social work and 282 different schools in forty countries in all parts of the world.[1] Numerous key individuals have contributed much toward making the Association an effective means of providing a channel of communication across national frontiers.

It was Dr. Alice Salomon, founder of social work training courses in Germany, who, with Dr. M.J.A. Moltzer, Director of the Amsterdam School of Social Work in the Netherlands, established the International Committee of Schools of Social Work in 1929. Dr. Salomon also served as its first president. Many other names known to social workers in all parts of the world could be mentioned among the early leaders, but none stands out so clearly as that of Dr. René Sand of Belgium, who served as president from 1946 until his death in 1953. Under his inspired leadership, the International Committee of Schools of Social Work expanded its membership, strengthened its program and became associated with the work of the United Nations and other international organizations.[2]

Across the years, the Association has achieved its purposes primarily through international congresses, seminars, and other types of study

---

[1] "Directory of Members and Constitution," International Association of Schools of Social Work (November, 1962).

[2] *Ibid.*, p. 3.

groups. Historically, it is of interest to note that meetings have been held in Frankfurt (1932), in Brussels (1934), Bentveld, Holland (1935), London (1936), Geneva (1938), Paris (1947), New York (1948), Paris (1950), Stockholm (1952), Madras (1952), Toronto (1954), Oxford (1955), Munich (1956), Zurich (1957), Tokyo (1958), Strasbourg (1959), Rome (1961), Belo Horizonte, Brazil (1962), and Edinburgh (1962). The Twelfth International Congress of Schools of Social Work is scheduled for Athens in 1964.

At the General Assembly of member schools of the Association, held in Munich in 1956, the name of the Association was changed to the International Association of Schools of Social Work. "The change in name reflects its steadily increasing membership and the growing influence of the Association as the international spokesman for schools of social work in every part of the world. A new constitution was adopted, an expanded program was initiated, and cooperative relationships with other international organizations were strengthened." [3]

A significant development took place in 1958 when the Association, in cooperation with the International Conference of Social Work, initiated publication of a new journal, entitled *International Social Work*. Published in English, this periodical appears quarterly and carries articles on social work education and social welfare and practice, along with significant notes which are of interest to social welfare and social workers on an international plane. Subsequently, the International Federation of Social Workers joined with these two organizations in sponsoring this journal.

The International Association holds a nongovernmental consultative status with the United Nations, UNICEF, and UNESCO, and has working agreements with the International Conference of Social Work and the Pan American Union. It maintains working relationships with numerous other international organizations and associations and has as its basic aim, when working on its own program or cooperatively with other organizations, "to promote social work education of high standard in order that the quality of personnel in social welfare programs may be constantly improved." [4]

The present constitution, which is a complete revision of the original one adopted in 1929 and amended in later years, includes the following preamble: "The International Association of Schools of Social Work is concerned with the promotion and development of sound programs of professional social work education designed to prepare well-qualified professional social workers." Its purposes are specified as follows: [5]

[3] *Ibid.*, p. 4.
[4] *Ibid.*
[5] *Ibid.*, p. 7.

I. To provide international leadership and encourage good standards in social work education by such means as the following, and in such other ways as the Executive Board may deem appropriate.
   A. Provision of an international forum on social work education and related matters.
   B. Collection and dissemination of information.
   C. Initiation of international study-courses, including regional meetings.
   D. Representation of the interests of social work education in connection with the activities of other international bodies, governmental or nongovernmental.
   E. Encouragement of the exchange of teachers and students.

There are two categories of members, full and associate. Full membership is open to schools which provide instruction for professional workers and which offer full-time courses of at least two years' duration, including theoretical teaching and supervised field experience. Associate membership is available to individuals with a demonstrated interest in professional training, to agencies which are concerned with the promotion of good standards of training for professional social work other than the associations of schools, and social work training institutions not yet eligible for full membership.

The constitution specifies that a General Assembly of the Association shall be held every two years to handle business and to provide for consideration of matters of mutual interest and concern.

As examples of the activities of the Association and of the issues considered and decisions made, there follows a brief review of the activities of the International Congresses held at Munich in 1956 and in Brazil in 1962.

In Munich, in 1956, representatives from more than 200 schools of social work attended and participated in the General Assembly. The delegates adopted a revised constitution, approved a modest operating budget, and put into effect a new scale of annual dues. Plans were made for a regional seminar on teaching materials and teaching methods to be held in Switzerland in 1957. A working group on teaching materials was organized and work was started on the formulation of international criteria for the selective use of casework and group work teaching records. Preliminary plans were made for the Ninth International Congress of Schools of Social Work to be held in 1958 in Tokyo and for the Tenth Congress scheduled for Rome in the summer of 1960. Twenty-five new schools were admitted to membership from the following countries: Germany, Greece, Iraq, Italy, Japan, the Netherlands, and Yugoslavia. A very positive feeling existed in regard to the Association and international social work and the secretary, Katherine Kendall, reported to the member schools, "It was evident that the International Association is on the threshold of an expanded and increasingly effective international effort."

The Eleventh International Congress of Schools of Social Work, with more than 300 delegates from some forty countries, met in Brazil, August 14–18, 1962. The papers given by social workers from various countries provided excellent topics for discussion in small groups; but general sessions were also conducted. The central theme of the Congress was "Education for Professional Service to Communities." Two major papers were presented. One, "Social Work and Social Development of the Community," was given by Dr. Mario Reis, Director, Social Service for Industry, Porto Alegre, Brazil, and the second one, "Common Elements in Education for Social Work Practice with Individuals, Groups and Communities," was presented by Dr. Virginia A. Paraiso, United Nations Social Welfare Advisor, Honduras. Questions and issues were considered in discussion groups with commentaries offered by the following speakers: Dr. Herman D. Stein, Professor, New York School of Social Work, Columbia University, United States; Sra. Leonor Mardones de Martinez, Director, Escuela de Servicio Social, "Alejandro del Rio," Santiago, Chile; Miss Jean Robertson, Director, Department of Social Studies, University of Singapore, Singapore; and Mlle. M. L. Ginet, President, International Federation of Social Workers, Montrouge (Seine), France.[6]

European member schools of the Association, which were unable to participate in the Congress in Brazil, were given an opportunity to send representatives to a European Regional Seminar, which was held in Edinburgh, Scotland, in September, 1962. Registration reached the upper limit of fifty participants and nearly every European country was represented at this seminar which gave attention to the subject of "The Teaching of Social Work with Individuals, Groups, and Communities."

At the meeting it was reported that the membership of the Association had increased at a more rapid rate than in any previous period and that IASSW had included in its membership 280 schools in forty-one different countries and twelve national associations of schools of social work with representatives from all of the continents. The Congress in Brazil considered constitutional amendments, membership classifications, and noted that increased cooperation with all related international organizations had been taking place. It was announced that the IASSW had been accepted by UNESCO as a nongovernmental organization with which it maintains a relationship of mutual information (Category C status). The delegates were reminded of the Seminar on the Contribution of the Social Sciences to Social Work Education, which was cosponsored by the United Nations and UNESCO. It was announced that special training projects were under way, or under consideration by UNICEF, which were of particular interest to IASSW and that close cooperation was being developed with UNICEF in many ways. It was observed that there is a growing unity of interest among the three major inter-

6 *International Social Work,* Vol. 5 (October, 1962), p. 11.

national social work organizations. The secretary described IASSW representation as a nongovernmental organization with consultative status at meetings of the Social Commission of the United Nations. The delegates were invited to respond expeditiously to the request of the United Nations for information to be used in the preparation of the *Fourth International Survey of Training for Social Work.* Interest was shown in seminars which had been held and in those which were being planned, including the European Seminar for Edinburgh, Scotland, in September, 1962. A report was made regarding the plan to make a survey of the curriculum studies conducted in different countries and to publish a series of reports on these studies in *International Social Work.* There was considerable interest shown in developing a teaching materials project in South America. Plans were presented for the Twelfth International Congress, to be held in Athens in 1964.

INTERNATIONAL CONFERENCE OF SOCIAL WORK

In 1923, Dr. René Sand of Belgium proposed the establishment of "the world's forum of social work" during the fiftieth meeting of the National Conference of Social Work which met in the United States. The first such meeting was held in Paris in 1928 and was attended by 2,500 people from forty-two countries. Since that time the Conference has met eleven times in the following places: Paris, Frankfurt, London, Atlantic City, Paris, Madras, Toronto, Munich, Tokyo, Rome, and Petropolis, Brazil.

Membership is open to individuals and organizations recruited through national committees. The purpose of the Conference is to "provide an international forum for the discussion of social work, social welfare, and related issues, and to promote the exchange of information and experience among social workers, social agencies, and others interested in social welfare throughout the world." [7]

In an attractive brochure the ICSW explains to readers that this Conference is "one more link between nations," "one more army raised against war," and "one new account on the credit of peace." ICSW has consultative status with the United Nations' Economic and Social Council and works closely with UNESCO, WHO, UNICEF, and the Pan American Union.

The reasons for the existence of the ICSW are explained as follows: [8]

Concern for human well-being has become . . . the pivotal point upon which swing the world's hopes for peace and progress. With organization of the

[7] *Social Work Yearbook, 1960* (New York: National Association of Social Workers, 1960), p. 627.
[8] "International Conference of Social Work" (New York: Secretariat, ICSW, 345 East 46th Street).

United Nations, governments began to pool resources for improved health, education and welfare services. Agencies of many countries, both voluntary and statutory, have become deeply involved in international social welfare.

Serving as a rallying-point to which all these efforts and activities may relate, the ICSW is the only international forum of its kind. It is autonomous and independent of government or voluntary agencies of any country. Yet it is out of wide experience in these very agencies that the thousands of lay and professional members speak freely for themselves.

World-minded people working in social welfare in over half the 100 countries of the globe support the Conference through their contributions and participation. Many share the unforgettable experience of the biennial meetings through the Proceedings or first-hand reports of delegates; but all are share-holders in the greatest investment of our times: the health and welfare of the peoples of the world.

Another brochure, printed especially for United States consumption, indicates that this Conference provides a world forum of people working in the health, education, and welfare fields. It is a spokesman for social welfare on international social questions. It is a source of stimulation, encouragement, and practical assistance to countries with social services in early stages of development—and a challenge to countries with more highly organized services. The Conference is a medium of learning and exchange in technical knowledge, program planning, and social philosophies, as well as a significant bond among peoples of many different countries who cherish a happy, healthy, and productive life for all people.

World forum meetings are sponsored by this organization and are held biennially, focusing on a central theme of current global interest. Special preparation is made by national committees of member countries, including written papers on national social experiences. The committees also disseminate Conference findings and materials through articles, newspapers, and speeches by delegates. Speakers from all parts of the world are invited to the forum platform. Commissions composed of people from the various member countries work together to develop recommendations regarding major issues related to the Conference theme.

The Conference helps to plan and facilitate study tours for delegates attending the biennial meetings, acts on a consultative status with the United Nations regarding worldwide social issues and plans, helps with publications of the proceedings and the quarterly journal, *International Social Work,* provides organizational assistance, and acts as an information and referral service on an international level.

Approximately 2,100 delegates from fifty-four countries and territories attended the Eleventh International Conference of Social Work which was held in Petropolis near Rio de Janeiro, Brazil, from August 19–24, 1962. Many international and regional organizations, both governmental and nongovernmental, were also represented. The Brazilian delegation, numbering more than 600, was the largest from one country; the United States group was second with 420 members.[9]

The Conference consisted of Plenary Sessions, five Commissions on major aspects of the Conference theme, "Rural and Urban Community Developments," seven Study Groups, and a number of special consultation conferences. Several films were shown each day.

The René Sand Award, in memory of the founder of ICSW, was given to the Most Reverend Dom Helder Camara, Auxiliary Archbishop of Rio de Janeiro, who delivered a major talk on "Spiritual Values in Community Development." The proceedings of the conference were approved for publication in full in three separate editions—in English, Portuguese, and Spanish. Before the Conference concluded, it was agreed and announced by the Executive Committee that the Twelfth International Conference of Social Work would be held in Athens, Greece, in 1964.

INTERNATIONAL FEDERATION OF SOCIAL WORKERS

For many years social workers in different countries of the world have been interested in creating an international organization of professional workers. The International Federation of Social Workers is a successor to the International Permanent Secretariat of Social Workers which was founded in 1928 in Paris and was active until the outbreak of World War II.[10]

In 1950, at the International Conference of Social Work held in Paris, definite action was taken and a decision made to create the International Federation of Social Workers. The original action was that IFSW would come into existence when seven national organizations from different countries agreed to become members. After considerable preliminary work, the Federation was finally founded in 1956 at the meeting of the International Conference of Social Work held in Munich, Germany. By 1961 there were twenty-two national associations or organizations belonging to the Federation. The Constitution of the IFSW states that the aims shall be:

To promote social work as a profession through cooperation and action on an international basis, especially as regards professional standards, training, ethics and working conditions, and to promote the establishment of national associations of social workers.

To encourage and facilitate contacts between social workers of all countries and to provide media for discussion and the exchange of ideas, through meetings, study visits, research projects, exchange of publications and other means of communication.

9 *International Social Work,* Vol. 5 (October, 1962), p. 28.
10 International Federation of Social Workers (New York: Secretariat, IFSW, 2 Park Avenue, December, 1961).

To present the point of view of the profession on an international level by establishing relations with international organizations operating in, or interested in, the social welfare field, and to assist in the carrying out of welfare programs sponsored by such international organizations.

Provisions specify that one professional national organization of social workers in each country may become a member of the Federation. Such an organization may be a national association or a coordinating agency representing two or more such associations.

The governing body of the Federation is the Council which consists of representatives of the member associations on the basis of three from each country. The IFSW publishes a quarterly newsletter entitled "The Social Worker," which is sent to all member organizations and furnishes a means for exchanging information concerning the work of the member groups. The Federation also cosponsors the publication of *International Social Work*. Meetings of the Council are held at the same time as the meetings of the International Conference of Social Work. Consultative status has been granted to the Federation by the Economic and Social Council of the United Nations and by the United Nations Children's Fund (UNICEF).

At its business meeting in August, 1962, in Brazil, the Federation elected Miss Litsa Alexandraki of Greece as President, and continued Miss Margaret Adams of the United States of America as Secretary-General.

Descriptive of some of the activities of the Federation is the report published in *International Social Work* [11] on the theme of "Function and Working Methods of the Personnel Social Worker." This report summarizes the work of study groups sponsored by the International Federation of Social Workers and United Nations, which took place in September, 1957, at Zurich, Switzerland, and in March, 1959, at Dortmund, Germany. Members of the study groups were experienced personnel social workers representing nine countries. Indicative of their conclusions were the following general principles which they observed are common to social workers in the various countries.

a) General basic principles
1. Social work offers specialized help to people with social problems.
2. Social work is performed by means of a professional relationship between the social worker and his client.
3. Social work requires confidentiality and therefore professional secrecy.
4. Social work requires a non-judgmental attitude from the social worker.
5. Social work demands respect for the client's right of self-determination, for his own responsibility and individual integrity.
6. Social work requires understanding of the client in his total situation (including past, present and future experiences, family, work environment, etc.).

[11] *International Social Work*, Vol. 3 (April, 1960), pp. 1–5.

7. Social work requires the social worker's psychological independence from all people and parties involved.
8. Social work requires the social worker to be aware of the possibilities and limitations:
   a) of the client
   b) of the social work profession
   c) within the social worker himself.
9. Social work requires the social worker to be conscious of his own appearance, attitudes and development.

b) Basic principles specifically related to personnel social work
10. Personnel social work does not allow the social worker to have functional authority, except towards direct subordinates.
11. Personnel social work requires the social worker to be a consultant; he should not make decisions.
12. Personnel social work requires the social worker to recognize the limits of his functional relationships.
13. Personnel social work demands that the social worker promotes communication along the line of authority.
14. Personnel social work requires the social worker to be at the disposal of individuals and groups at any level of the organization.

OTHER INTERNATIONAL SOCIAL WORK ORGANIZATIONS

The United Nations is playing an important role in regard to social work on an international basis. During the 1950's the United Nations sponsored three significant international surveys on training for social work. These surveys, proposed by the Social Commission and in accordance with a resolution of the Economic and Social Council, provide evidence of the evolving international dimension of the profession of social work. The first survey, in 1950, described the patterns of training, country by country, in use at that time. The second survey, in 1954, provided a useful directory of the schools of social work and printed information on faculty and student composition in various countries throughout the world. The third survey, published in 1958, unlike the two earlier ones, was concerned with the content of training in social work, particularly as it was beginning to emerge internationally. The primary focus was upon subject matter rather than a description of existing situations. It was related to both the range of subject matter and educational methods for teaching.

The content was developed from biennial reports on new developments in social work, from three regional seminars held in Uruguay, Pakistan, and Greece; from reports of the regional social affairs officers of the United Nations and specialized agencies; from consultation with experts from many countries; and from the literature in the field from various parts of the world. It was the first study of its kind at an international level.

The volume which appeared as a result of the Third International

Survey is most interesting and helpful in relation to social work on an international basis. Its importance was explained in the following: [12]

The Social Commission in considering the Second Survey at its tenth session, reaffirmed its position regarding the continuing emphasis that should be given to the establishment and extension of social work training programmes. The Commission's attention was also drawn to the importance of a more thorough study of the basic content of and methods used in the training of social workers. After taking into account the report and recommendation of the Social Commission, the Economic and Social Council at its twentieth session adopted resolution 585 D (XX) regarding the training of welfare personnel which included a request to the Secretary-General:

"(d) To promote regional seminars and conferences for the development of the content and techniques of training of social workers at all levels;

"(e) To focus attention on selected problems of social training in the preparation of the next survey on social work training."

The United Nations has assisted in sponsoring many conferences as well as publications. Indicative of this activity was the meeting held at Munich in 1956. It was attended by experienced social work educators from various regions of the world, and was convened by the United Nations, to discuss training for social work. Here it was agreed that: [13]

Social workers can only be effectively trained through courses which are based on an integration of theory and practice. The three-fold aim of such courses should be to impart the necessary knowledge, to develop skill in the practice of social work, and to help students to incorporate the philosophy, attitudes and self-understanding essential to their function as professional workers.

Another service of the United Nations is to call to the attention of social workers everywhere job openings which are available in various countries throughout the world. For example, an announcement dated February 5, 1963, was distributed under the auspices of the United Nations, Technical Assistance Recruitment Services, which briefly described openings in social service in family and child welfare in Columbia, in social welfare training in Bolivia, and in social work training in Pakistan. This same document described several openings in community development and related activities in various other countries.

Another example of an international attempt to utilize the abilities and services of social workers is related to the meetings and activities of the International Society for Rehabilitation of the Disabled. This organization held its Eighth World Congress in New York City in 1960 and invited participants from all over the world, many of whom were social workers. At the Seventh World Congress, held in London, there were 1,200 people from fifty-three countries in attendance. In New York City, approximately 3,000 people participated from more than seventy coun-

[12] United Nations, *Training for Social Work, Third International Survey* (New York: United Nations, 1958), p. 1.

[13] *Ibid.*, p. 9.

tries. The Secretary-General explained that the two aims of the world meetings of the International Society were indicated by the themes of the Eighth World Congress: "Rehabilitation and World Peace" and "Helping Disabled People—Basis for International Cooperation." It was the opinion of the leaders that communication is of utmost importance and such world congresses help to strengthen training and services to assist the disabled throughout the globe. The Ninth World Congress was scheduled for Denmark in 1963.

TRAINING ON AN INTERNATIONAL LEVEL

The United States has provided considerable training facilities for students from foreign countries and has been valued by these students because of its large public welfare program and its resources in schools of social work and in agencies related to professional training. The total number of countries now accepting exchange students can only be estimated, but in 1959 the United Nations Fellows alone found forty countries offering training facilities. "University contracts, third-country training projects administered by the International Cooperation Administration, and other plans have increased enormously the number of countries involved in the education of other nationals." [14]

Further facts regarding exchange scholarships and training of students from different countries were summarized by Whalen: [15]

The number of consultants and of exchange scholarships to date has been wholly inadequate to meet the known demand for manpower in this profession; the number of students coming to the United States has been small; the number of social workers from the United States who study abroad has been infinitesimal. The funds available at the United Nations for advisory social welfare services in 1959 totaled $1.2 million, with 50 countries sharing in the services available, but unmet requests would have cost an additional $400,000. The International Cooperation Administration reported 6,789 participants in training during the Fiscal Year 1960, of which only 67 were in the field of community development and social welfare. The stream of inquiries from other countries regarding scholarships for study in the United States attest to the awareness within other countries, as well as in the United States, of the present shortage of manpower in social work. A greatly expanded number of consultants and of exchanges would do much to alleviate this problem.

Murase indicates that well over 2,000 international students registered for full-time study in schools of social work in the United States and Canada during the period from the end of World War II through the 1959–60 academic year.[16]

[14] Cecile M. Whalen, "International Training for Manpower to Meet the Needs of Nations in Social Work," (San Francisco: Workshop on Social Work, Institute of International Education, Nov. 30–Dec. 3, 1960), p. 7.

[15] *Ibid.*, p. 10.

[16] Kenneth Murase, "International Students in Education for Social Work—An Assessment by International Graduates of Schools of Social Work in North America, 1948–57," *The Social Service Review*, Vol. 35 (June, 1961), p. 171.

Data available since 1950 reflect that international students annually have comprised about 2 to 6 percent of the total full-time student bodies of accredited schools of social work. This means that schools of social work in North America have a considerable investment in the education of students from other countries.

Murase describes the educational problems and programs for students from abroad and makes the following significant conclusion: [17]

What is suggested is that there is an increasing convergence of the educational goals of both domestic and foreign students. This trend in turn reflects the emergence of a truly universal profession, with common values, a unified body of knowledge, and generic methods. The trend also signifies social and economic advances in the underdeveloped areas of the world to which social workers trained in the United States and Canada have made important contributions.

The Committee on International Social Welfare Education, a standing committee of the Council on Social Work Education, since its inception, has provided leadership in the preparation of students from other countries, preparation of American students in the field of international social welfare, identification of international social welfare content in the social work curriculum with emphasis on community organization and community development, cooperation with other organizations and promotion of international cooperation among schools of social work with organizations interested in social work education, and advice to the Council in respect to promotion of research in any part of the program of education for international social welfare. At a meeting in New York in March, 1961, the Committee took action as follows, indicative of its philosophy and activities. They agreed to:

1. Complete work on a pamphlet, *Opportunities for Study of Social Work in North America,* which would be available to help foreign students to prepare for and get the most from training in this country.

2. Consider and make suggestions regarding the proposal for a second Interprofessional Conference to be held in 1961.

3. Recommend to the Board of the Council on Social Work Education that it take steps to develop interprofessional activity involving both educational and professional organizations. It was suggested that a beginning might be made by learning whether the National Association of Social Workers and the Canadian Association of Social Workers would be interested in joining with the Council on Social Work Education in the development of an interprofessional committee to deal with matters of mutual interest in the profession.

4. Recommend that the Committee on International Social Welfare Education be authorized to stimulate several campuswide one-day conferences in universities with professional schools to discuss educationally

17 *Ibid.,* p. 183.

oriented questions and issues which have been identified through the experience of technical assistance personnel serving abroad.

5. Send a memorandum to the Curriculum Committee encouraging them to incorporate a view that students are responsible members of a worldwide profession and that they should understand social work in their country as it relates to the social needs, resources, and developments of the rest of the world. They should be expected to develop an international perspective of social work.

6. Continue to explore means whereby materials regarding curricula of schools of social work in other countries might be made available to schools of social work in North America.

7. Propose to the Board of the Council on Social Work Education that a National Workshop be devoted to consideration of international social work.

8. Suggest that the Council on Social Work Education call together a small *ad hoc* committee of deans and directors of schools of social work to discuss possible responsibilities of the schools with respect to the Peace Corps being developed by the United States government.

9. Recommend that a "sub-committee be charged with preparation of (1) a statement to be circulated to schools of social work in other countries providing information about various means available to them for securing professional social work books and periodicals from North America; (2) a statement outlining the kinds of material noted by schools of social work in other countries as being most needed; and (3) a suggested plan for the coordination, centralization, and distribution to libraries of schools of social work in other countries of social work books, periodicals, and so on, which are needed and are available by donation." [18]

Kendall,[19] a key advocate and participant in international social work, summarized some of the current trends in social work education, internationally. She observed that there has been an almost universal shift in emphasis in the direction of systematic teaching of social work methodology. There is a lessening of stress on content and special areas of interest. There is considerable emphasis on field instruction as an educational experience involving teaching principles and methods. Recently, in European countries there has been an increase in the preparation of case records for teaching purposes. A worldwide move away from the specialization is taking place, and the number of university-sponsored schools of social work is definitely on the increase.

18 "Committee on International Social Welfare Education," *Social Work Education,* Vol. 9 (June, 1961), p. 3.

19 Katherine A. Kendall, "Social Work Training Around the World," *Social Service Review,* Vol. 34 (June, 1960), pp. 210–212.

PROBLEMS AND ISSUES INVOLVED IN INTERNATIONAL
SOCIAL WORK AND TRAINING

Several problems and issues come to the fore as one contemplates international social work training and practice.

One of the basic principles in social work education and practice in North America is stress on the democratic process. Considerable emphasis is given to the idea that a client, whether a person, family, or community, be given the right of self-determination. In regard to social work on an international level, this basic principle becomes the core of controversy, particularly in countries where democracy is not in operation as it is in the United States and in Europe. What does a social worker do in working with clients when there is an authoritative, dictatorial direction in government as well as in the cultural plane of living? Can a social worker trained in the United States, for example, who has been indoctrinated with the importance of self-determination and the democratic process, function adequately if he is employed in a country where dictatorship or culturally-enforced mores and customs result in authoritarianism at every turn? To explain further, Witte, who visited several countries abroad, described the problem as follows: [20]

Another question for social workers in the United States relates to the Egyptian project. Given our deepest commitment to nonmanipulative methods working with people, can we function effectively in situations where manipulation is a culturally determined and universally accepted mode of operation? Even further, does the social work we know and the social work that may be found in countries not committed to democracy belong to the same professional species?

Witte observes further that there are other matters relating to social work that are implicit in certain of these observations on the nature, philosophy, and process of community development. He mentions that group work and community organization, in particular, could be used advantageously in relation to community development in foreign countries. Yet, he observes "these are the areas of practice that have been called on least to contribute their know-how in the technical aid program and have shown little initiative in this direction."

Another issue which imposes a challenge for social work on an international level has to do with the different ways of life found around the globe. Culturally, nations differ from one another to a great extent and even considerably within their own geographical boundaries. How well, then, can students who are trained in the United States and who return to their own countries understand and put into practice the principles and skills acquired in America in relation to their own homeland

[20] Ernest F. Witte, "Community Development in Selected Countries,"*Community Development Review*, Vol. 7 (June, 1962), p. 9.

and way of life? There apparently is considerable need for enriching the social work training curriculum, especially for foreign students, to teach them how to utilize social work principles, skills, and concepts in their native lands and cultures. Murase, after quoting an Australian educator who deplored the failure of many workers trained overseas to meet adequately the challenge of the jobs to which they return, concluded "that the central issue thus appears to be one of a lack of congruence between the specialized functions for which international students are trained in North America and the generalized functions they perform upon return to their own countries." [21]

The opinion of some Asian educators was summarized as follows: [22]

> There was some skepticism in the groups as to whether study abroad was ever helpful. Asian students trained in the West often learn a great deal about technical social work but cannot apply what they have learned abroad, when they return to their own countries.

Another difficulty facing schools of social work is related to financial costs for establishing such schools and for supportive money to keep them in operation.

The first United Nations Survey of Training for Social Work reported that: [23]

> Schools in all parts of the world—old and new, large and small, independent and university-sponsored—report the same needs and the same preoccupations. They are all hindered, though to varying degrees, by lack of funds and resources (particularly with respect to teaching staff and practical training facilities) for the preparation of fully qualified practitioners, by inadequate community understanding of the role of the social worker and of the need for professional training for the performance of social work functions, and by the inadequate prospects that they can hold out to their graduates as regards compensation and professional status.

The second United Nations Survey of Training for Social Work further described some of the pertinent problems: [24]

> In spite of the efforts in many countries to interpret social work and the action by the Social Commission and Economic and Social Council recognizing, in principle, the distinctive contribution professional social work should make to programmes for social development, the extent to which this is generally accepted or understood continues to vary widely from country to country irrespective of the stage of economic development. This fact is emphasized in all the reports received which call attention to the importance of social work training leaders and institutions assuming a more dynamic role in the interpretation of the practical application of social work concepts and principles. . . .

[21] Murase, *op. cit.*, p. 173.
[22] *Ibid.*
[23] *Training for Social Work: An International Survey* (New York: United Nations, 1950), p. 99.
[24] *Training for Social Work: Second International Survey* (New York: United Nations, 1955), p. 6.

In most countries funds now available are grossly inadequate to provide either the required training facilities or to permit the employment of sufficient trained workers to expand or improve welfare programmes as rapidly as desired, and as is necessary in some cases to provide suitable field work instruction.

The third International Survey sponsored by the United Nations on Training for Social Work concluded that the basic situations in schools of social work in different parts of the world are, to a greater or lesser extent, about the same and are related to the following: [25]

1. There is an inadequate number of candidates from whom to select, resulting in some "bad risks" having to be accepted.
2. A heavy preponderance of women candidates exists, when men are also urgently needed in social work.
3. There is general ignorance about or failure to recognize the profession of social work, which results in difficulty in recruitment, low salaries, long hours of work, limited promotion prospects, and high turn-over rates after training.
4. Admission in many countries to training is on the basis of secondary school education only.
5. Many small full-time faculties are in operation, which means a high student-staff ratio, which becomes costly.
6. The large number of part-time lecturers means that too often many short courses are given by too many different people and continuity and integration are often lacking.
7. The small full-time faculty in many schools also results in insufficient individual work with students through small seminars and on a tutorial basis.
8. A large number of the part-time lecturers are neither trained social workers nor have had experience in working with them. This means some of the materials presented are not related or integrated into the total social work process.
9. There is a lack of social workers with adequate educational and professional qualifications to teach the basic methods courses.
10. There is a scarcity of adequate field work facilities and insufficient contact between school staff and supervisors in the agencies.
11. There is a lack of teaching materials.
12. Many schools have very small student enrollments.
13. Some schools seem to scatter their energies too widely by running small specialized courses, as well as courses which are not part of a professional training for social work.
14. It is recommended that schools of social work review the total structure and content of their curricula in the light of the educational criteria and basic curriculum content proposed in this study.
15. In any country where it would not be possible for a school of social work to take the initiative regarding recommendation #14, such a comprehensive review might be instituted on a national scale by an appropriate public authority.

Although there are numerous issues and problems in social work on an international plane, nevertheless the overall picture is encouraging.

[25] *Training for Social Work: Third International Survey, op. cit.,* pp. 31–34.

Dedicated and capable leaders in most countries are devoting time and energies to improving the health, education, and welfare of their citizens. Social work is forging ahead around the world, steadily and forthrightly, with significant results in dealing with welfare issues and solving social problems.

SUMMARY

International social work is gaining considerable recognition in the world today. Social workers are practicing in various countries on all continents. Schools of social work in many lands are training men and women for positions in social service. In particular, students from many foreign countries come to the United States to receive training in social work and then return to their homelands for practice.

The three major social work international organizations are the International Association of Schools of Social Work, which aims to improve and facilitate social work training throughout the world; the International Conference of Social Work, with its purpose of enhancing knowledge and skills about social welfare problems and issues and abilities to meet them; and the International Federation of Social Workers, which aims to bring professionally qualified people together from various countries to help strengthen professional standards, training, research, and related activities. These three associations join forces to publish *International Social Work*, a periodical regarding social work practice and training in the various parts of the world.

Some of the more significant problems and issues in international social work are: (1) emphasizing social work as a democratic process and the importance of self-determination in countries which politically and culturally are not democratic; (2) understanding of and working with training and practice in relation to varying nationalities and cultures; and (3) developing training programs, both quantitatively and qualitatively, to meet the needs and demands of social work on an international basis.

QUESTIONS FOR DISCUSSION

1. What is the meaning of *international social work?*
2. Trace briefly the historical development of social work on an international basis.
3. What is the significance of the shrinkage of the globe, transportation-wise, in relation to social work services and training?
4. Describe the purposes and some of the activities of the International Association of Schools of Social Work.
5. Describe the purposes and functions of the International Conference of Social Work.

6. What is your evaluation of the International Federation of Social Workers?

7. Give examples of the role which the United Nations has played in international social work.

8. How can schools of social work in the United States be made more effective in training students from foreign countries?

9. Can social work be practiced in a country which is administered by a dictator? Discuss.

10. What parts do varying cultures play in social work practice?

11. Why is it that the United States does not hire more social workers in its international program of technical assistance and community development?

SPECIAL ACTIVITIES

1. Read a current article from *International Social Work* and give an oral report on it to the class.

2. Try to find someone in your community who has either been trained or practiced social work in a country other than your own, and interview this person for comparisons and contrasts with local training and social work services.

3. Make a library study of the development of social work in some foreign country.

SELECTED REFERENCES

CHETKOW, B. H., "Some Thoughts on the Participation of American Social Workers in International Welfare Programs," *International Social Work,* Vol. 6 (January, 1963), pp. 39–45.

GOLDMAN, BENJAMIN W., "International Social Work as a Professional Function," *International Social Work,* Vol. 5 (July, 1962), pp. 1–8.

KENDALL, KATHERINE A., "Social Work Training Around the World," *Social Service Review,* Vol. 34 (June, 1960), pp. 203–212.

LALLY, DOROTHY, "International Social Welfare," *Social Work Yearbook, 1960* (New York: National Association of Social Workers, 1960), pp. 318–338.

MURASE, KENNETH, "International Students in Education for Social Work," *Social Service Review,* Vol. 35 (June, 1961), pp. 171–183.

The Professional Education of Students from Other Lands (New York: Council on Social Work Education, 1963).

Training for Social Work: Third International Survey (New York: United Nations, 1958).

YOUNGHUSBAND, EILEEN L., "The Challenge of Social Change to Education for Social Work," *International Social Work,* Vol. 6 (April, 1963), pp. 1–4.

CHAPTER 11

Group Work Services

One sunny spring afternoon in 1936, in a mid-western city, report cards and promotions were distributed. Most of the boys and girls in the elementary school received promotions. In a particular class, one of the girls was given a promotion to skip a grade. Two boys in this same unit were informed that they were to be retained in the same grade during the next year.

When the bell sounded for the ending of school and the boys and girls started to wend their way homeward, the two boys began to talk about the situation. They, of course, were disappointed and upset. Someone mentioned that one girl had received a promotion to "skip a grade." This stirred up their feelings. They began to discuss this girl and call her names. Coincidentally, the girl walked by at that moment. The boys made disparaging remarks about her and soon their classmates gathered around. Someone picked up a rock and threw it at the girl. One of the crowd blurted out, "This is not fair. Let's get even with her." Another yelled, "Let's beat her up." By this time the influence of group interaction was predominating and there was an intensification of suggestions and responses. As the reactions heightened, someone wildly suggested, "Let's kill her." Another said, "Let's get a rope and hang her to death." One of the group said he knew where a rope was.

One of the crowd obtained a rope, the "mob" of "typical" elementary boys and girls grabbed the girl, dragged her to a nearby garage just off the school grounds, put the rope around her neck, and were about to hang her when the commotion aroused the attention of adults who came to the rescue. Why such behavior? Analysis of this incident portrays the power inherent in group interaction and group behavior.

Groups may be used either positively or negatively in regard to human feelings and behavior. Many delinquencies and crimes are committed because gangs of boys and girls, or mixed groups, get together and supportively encourage each other in antisocial behavior. On the other hand, all kinds of positive activities take place through the support, love, and encouragement of groups. Alcoholics Anonymous and Divorcees Anonymous are two examples of organizations which have evolved because of the power of the group in influencing men and women for good. Thousands of alcoholics have been rehabilitated through the helping arm, physically and psychologically, of a group of other alcoholics who have shared similar experiences. Thousands of persons with their marriages shattered resulting in separation, have joined together to talk, feel, and act positively in relation to problems resulting from marriage failure.

The primary group, described by Charles H. Cooley, is particularly powerful in influencing the thinking, feeling, and other behavior of youth and adults. This is the kind of group which is characterized by intimate face-to-face association and cooperation. Such small group association is fundamental in forming the social nature and ideals of the individual. Franklin H. Giddings described the influence of group behavior and identification when he talked about the *consciousness of kind,* descriptive of individuals developing a feeling of belonging and allegiance to others which molds their characters and their behavior patterns. He emphasized that the in-group can be a most powerful factor in influencing the behavior of its members. The important social-psychological processes of imitation, suggestion, and summation are inherent in group interaction and play important roles in the resultant behavior.

All people have certain basic needs: (1) to love and to be loved, and (2) to belong to a group or groups. Gregariousness seems to be inborn within man or has its beginnings practically from birth. We want to love and be loved, and we want to belong; thus, the power of the group is particularly significant.

Studies indicate that even moral judgments of children are related to the moral judgments of the groups with which they associate. Marital research shows that individuals who come from a happy home, other factors being equal, are most likely to have successful marriages of their own. Ordinarily, performance before or in a group results in a higher level of performance.

Group work is based upon the premise that the group is a most powerful determinant of human behavior. It also recognizes that the group may be utilized to help individuals to solve problems and to enrich their living. Konopka [1] illustrates, by brief presentations of a few verbal pictures, what might be done by the group worker in action:

Since group work as a helping method is still comparatively new, it may be in order to give a brief presentation of the method itself and then move on to the use of groups by practitioners of different backgrounds in our profession. Let us begin by throwing a few verbal pictures against an imaginary screen showing the group worker in action.

In the first picture imagine a group of giggling nine-year-olds surrounding their group worker. Separated from them stands Sue, a shy and fixed smile on her face; the group worker gives the happy youngsters a warm, quick hug, yet slowly moves over to Sue. She does not press her to enter the group. She knows that Sue wants badly to be one of them, but would be frightened if pushed into it. So the worker lets her feel the warm concern of an adult, encouraging her without words by showing that she thinks of her as part of the group. The move over to Sue involves knowledge of individual and group, use of the principle "start where individual and group are," and professional self-discipline. . . .

Another picture: a group of teen-age girls in an institution for emotionally disturbed youngsters, or perhaps one that works with delinquents. Their faces are flushed and you see signs of upset and anger. Yet at this moment they sit in a circle talking about their anger, while the group worker listens and helps them to understand why it is so strong, that it is really directed against the harsh and painful experiences of their past and not just—as they think—at "this horrible place."

Another picture: a group of young couples earnestly discussing the far from easy job of bringing up children in a constantly changing world. The group worker as the skilled discussion leader is not simply giving them a "lecture," but helping them to understand their feelings, prejudices, fears, and strengths.

Finally: teen-age boys and girls, of different races, worrying about a world that does not accept each one as equal. They are helped not only to *discuss* this but to learn to live together, through the understanding guidance of a group worker in a summer camp.

DEFINITIONS

Coyle, in 1939, defined social group work as a "type of educational process carried on in voluntary groups during leisure time and with the assistance of a group leader. It aims at the growth and development of individuals through the group experience, and at the use of the group by its members for social purposes which they consider desirable." [2] Sullivan, in 1945, stated that social group work is a "method of personality development in which the group itself is utilized as a chief tool." [3]

In 1949, a statement of the Executive Board of the American Associa-

---

[1] Gisela Konopka, "Social Group Work: A Social Work Method," *Social Work*, Vol. 5 (October, 1960), p. 54.

[2] Grace L. Coyle, "Social Group Work," *Social Work Year Book, 1939* (New York: Russell Sage Foundation, 1939), p. 413.

[3] Dorothea F. Sullivan, "Social Group Work," *Social Work Year Book, 1945* (New York: Russell Sage Foundation, 1945), p. 421.

tion of Group Workers was issued which explains that: "the group worker enables various types of groups to function in such a way that both group interaction and program activity contribute to the growth of the individual and the achievement of desirable social goals." [4]

The definition given by the Council on Social Work Education Curriculum Study, in 1959, was: "By social group work method is meant the systematic ways in which the worker affects social and group process to achieve specified objectives. Such ways include some which are common to all social work practice and some which characterize social group work practice."

The group work process was explained further: [5]

Group process is one of the social processes; it signifies the totality of the group's interactions, developments and changes which occur in the group's life. *Social group work process* refers to group process when consciously affected by the worker toward specified ends. Interrelationships of member to member, of worker with members and group-as-a-whole, members' and group's reactions to activity and experience, the worker's professional responsibility and judgment are components of the social group work process.

Group work is both a method and a field of social service. As a field of service, it encompasses the Settlement House, the Neighborhood House, the YMCA, YWCA, the Girl Scouts, and, more recently, group activities in hospitals, detention homes, and other host agencies. As a method or process, group work aims to bring about the solution of personal, family, and community problems through the use of the group as the tool, and with the assistance of professionally trained persons to help, directly or indirectly, in guiding and providing an opportunity for the solving of these problems. Group work may be used to prevent problems as well as to provide services and to solve problems. Its basic goal is to utilize the power of interaction of human beings for their own benefit in solving social problems and in enriching living, facilitating interaction and relationships through planned programs or activities.

Group work is recognized as an integral part of social work methodology. In October, 1962, the official curriculum policy statement of the Council on Social Work Education reaffirmed group work as one of the three basic methods of social work.

Coyle describes some of the aims and functions of group work in the total of social work practice by the following assumptions. Group experience can be related to the maturing process since experience in small face-to-face groups affords opportunity for intimate relationships which can play an important role in the process of human maturation. Group

[4] Grace L. Coyle, "Social Group Work," *Social Work Year Book, 1954* (New York: American Association of Social Workers, 1954), p. 480.

[5] Marjorie Murphy, *The Social Group Work Method in Social Work Education,* Curriculum Study, Vol. XI (New York: Council on Social Work Education, 1959), p. 32.

experience can be utilized as a supplement to other relationships. It can be effective not only with children and youth, where its programs have been emphasized traditionally, but also with adults and with parent and youth groups. Group experience can be utilized in preparation for active citizenship in a democracy. This may be accomplished through three ways: first, face-to-face self-governing experience provides opportunities in the development and pursuit of common goals, in the control of implusive behavior, and in the creation and acceptance of self-imposed authority. Second, group experience may be preparation for citizenship through the introduction of social issues and their consideration; and third, the use of planned group experience can be effective in dealing with neighborhood tensions, especially in interracial or interethnic group situations.

Coyle mentions further that group experience may be utilized as a corrective for social disorganization. It may also be used advantageously in the treatment of intrapsychic maladjustments.[6]

HISTORICAL DEVELOPMENTS

Group work began as a form of *social service* with various kinds of activities under the auspices of the church. In the 1855–65 decade, the YMCA and YWCA were organized and became formalized, independent associations which provided group programs, activities, and opportunities.

During the latter part of the nineteenth century the settlement movement developed. The Industrial Revolution had brought considerable social disorganization and the breakdown of the primary group in many situations. Dedicated leaders believed that social improvement could be accomplished by having members of the more fortunate classes live or visit among and with the underprivileged groups, sharing their ideas and ways of life. Certain philanthropists donated money as well as time to help sponsor Settlement Houses in the underprivileged districts, especially in the large cities.

Toynbee Hall was established in London in 1884 in an attempt to help, with a group program, the underprivileged in that huge, mulling city. The Neighborhood Guild was established in 1886 in the United States and was the first settlement house in this country. Hull House, begun in Chicago in 1889, and other settlement houses were not long in developing and have become part of the American tradition. The basic aim of these settlement houses was to provide a place for the underprivileged to go and, through the two-way process of association and interaction, to develop their personalities and enrich their living.

6 Grace L. Coyle, "Some Basic Assumptions About Social Group Work," in Marjorie Murphy, *The Social Group Work Method in Social Work Education*, Curriculum Study, Vol. XI (New York: Council on Social Work Education, 1959), pp. 91–100.

Many group work agencies have developed in the twentieth century, including the Boy Scouts, the Girl Scouts, Campfire Girls, 4H Clubs, and others. Each one of these originated and has acquired many members through its stress on one particular group and activity. Today there are millions of boys and girls, youth, and adults who belong to organizations which operate on a group interactional basis.

In 1935, a group work section of the National Conference on Social Work was established to give additional emphasis and focus to this rapidly developing movement. In 1936, the National Association for the Study of Group Work was organized with a representative coordinating committee of about 100 from all sections of the United States, and an executive committee of ten. The Association was established to further the interest of group work practice and to help in recruiting and getting more people professionally trained. In 1939, its name was changed to the American Association for the Study of Group Work.

In 1955 several different professional associations of social workers joined together to create a single professional organization, the National Association of Social Workers. The American Association of Group Workers, formed in 1946 as the successor to the American Association for the Study of Group Work, joined with the new organization, declaring itself an integral part of the new, unified social work professional organization. The members, however, have maintained a separate section of NASW and have been active within this section in promoting the group work process as well as the profession of social work as a whole.

In addition to the developments in areas of service, there have been several significant developments in regard to training of people interested in group work practice. Apparently it was in the United States that the first major emphasis on training in group work was established. For example, in 1906, the Chicago School of Civics had a course on "children's clubs and outing work." [7] However, the first systematized class in a school of social work came at a considerably later date. Such a course in "group service work" was offered in the School of Applied Social Sciences of Western Reserve University in the 1920's. Grace Coyle, a pioneer social group worker, summarized these developments: [8]

In the 1920's, as group work itself was defined and gradually gained some acceptance in the agencies, the theory available anywhere about the group process was very meager. . . . As group workers began, in the 1920's and 1930's, to define their functions and to examine their practice by a study of group records, there evolved certain agreed upon concepts and at least a rudimentary theory which drew upon the theoretical sources available at that time

[7] *Training for Social Work: Third International Survey* (New York: United Nations, 1958), p. 116.

[8] Grace L. Coyle, *Social Science in the Professional Education of Social Workers* (New York: Council on Social Work Education, 1958), p. 31.

for its understanding of the behavior of groups. When group work began to be taught in the schools of social work (1925–1935), the theory of individual behavior taught was already in its psychoanalytic stage. It therefore became necessary to integrate an advanced and highly developed personality theory already focused on treatment purposes, especially on emotional problems, with a relatively rudimentary small group theory and with agency programs geared to recreation and informal education rather than individualized treatment.

Cogan [9] observes that the first training course in group work was the course entitled "Group Service Training Course," offered in 1923 at the School of Applied Social Sciences, Western Reserve University. By the early 1930's the words *social group work* were used to distinguish it from social casework, the other main social work practice method. The National Conference of Social Work in 1935 included group work as a division at its annual program meeting, and several people joined together in sharing their thinking about this relatively new development. In 1939 a committee concerned with professional education began a study of the courses in group work offered by the schools of social work on both graduate and undergraduate levels. As a result of this study, an official statement, "Professional Education for Group Work Practice," was accepted by the American Association of Group Workers in 1947. "This statement made the distinction between in-service and professional training, the respective functions of school and agency, and the content and method of training for the professional practice of group work." [10]

During the 1940's the American Association of Schools of Social Work encouraged and recommended the inclusion of group work courses in the graduate curriculum of its member schools, of which less than half offered a sequence in group work. Today, all schools of social work offer one or more classes in group work and many of them offer a basic sequence, including class, field instruction, and related experiences in the group work method. To illustrate, in 1962, there were 448 students enrolled in group work sequences in the schools of social work in the United States and Canada.

In 1949 a statement was published by the American Association of Group Workers' Committee on the "Function of the Professional Group Worker," which was a major attempt to define and describe group work. This statement identified three components of method more clearly than had been previously stated, namely: [11]

(1) the use of relationship, interaction between group members and between worker and members; (2) the concomitant use of program as a tool; and (3) the inseparable give and take among individual persons, the group, and the community or larger social body in which persons live and the group operates.

9 Juanita Luck Cogan, "Social Group Work," *Social Work Year Book, 1960* (New York: National Association of Social Workers, 1960), pp. 545–546.

10 *Ibid.*, p. 546.

11 Murphy, *op. cit.*, p. 30.

The Committee on Practice of the Group Work Section of NASW presented the next significant definition statement in 1956. Murphy observes that although there was considerable unanimity regarding certain aspects of definition of purpose, there were also considerable differences regarding these, and she feels the goal of social work as the "enhancement of social functioning and the social work functions of provision, prevention and restoration . . . were thought to provide a more comprehensive and accurate basis for detailing components of the social group work method." [12]

Another way to understand the philosophy and current interpretation of social group work is to consider the objectives mentioned in the Curriculum Study of the Council on Social Work Education, wherein "the enhancement of persons' social functioning through purposeful group experience, the concept proposed to unify the social work goal and characteristics of the group work method, is seen . . . as the central idea to which all the following statements are oriented." [13] The study presents several relevant objectives which are epitomized as follows: [14]

Objective I. Understanding of and commitment to the attainment of social work goals through use of group work method.

Objective II. Familiarity with and appreciation of the bases for establishing ultimate, long range, and proximate goals for service groups and their members.

Objective III. Understanding and acceptance of characteristics and attributes of groups as units of society.

Objective IV. Understanding of and commitment to social work functions as they obtain in the practice of group work.

Objective V. Understanding and appreciation of characteristics and attributes of groups as units of social work service.

Objective VI. Understanding and appreciation of persons as users of social work services.

Objective VII. Awareness and acceptance of the agency as the organ of providing social group work services.

Objective VIII. Familiarity with and acceptance of the community as the matrix of social work services.

Objective IX. Understanding of, commitment to, and ability to execute with moderate skill, the social work activities (assessment, planning, implementation, evaluation) in problem-solving through group work services.

Objective X. Understanding and acceptance of, and ability to observe, interpret, and to share responsibility in performance of, a variety of procedures (such as intake and registration, grouping, referral, termination) which are required in carrying out social work activities through group work services.

Objective XI. Understanding and appreciation of and ability to observe responsibly psycho-dynamics of individual and group behavior.

Objective XII. Understanding and appreciation of the variety of relationships within and peripheral to the service group. Ability to observe responsibly the

12 *Ibid.*, pp. 30–31.
13 *Ibid.*, p. 64.
14 *Ibid.*, pp. 64–68.

nature and qualities of relationships; to respond with both empathy and maintenance of the worker role and to interpret appropriately and communicate the significance of interaction.

Objective XIII. Appreciation of the roles of persons in other positions than the group worker's own which bear upon his goals and performance, with accompanying understanding of and commitment to the social work functions.

Objective XIV. Understanding and appreciation of and ability to participate with a range of communications skills used in providing group work services.

Objective XV. Understanding and acceptance of and ability to participate in personnel processes and procedures (supervision, in-service training, etc.) which are employed in provision of group work services, with appreciation for respective roles of participants.

Objective XVI. Familiarity with resources for program media and understanding of criteria for selection of media and evaluation of program experience.

Objective XVII. Awareness, appreciation, and ability to observe, facilitate, and interpret communication through program activities.

The Practice Committee of the Group Work Section of NASW accepted the responsibility of formulating a framework statement as a guide to group work practice. In 1962 it issued a report which defined social group work as the part of social work in "which the primary medium of practice is the group, served for the purpose of effecting the social functioning of its members." [15]

The Committee also described the range of purposes of social group work which are summarized as follows:[16]

1. To help group members learn to participate actively in group life as experience in developing a sense of responsibility for active citizenship and for improving participation in social action.

2. To provide for personal enhancement of members, bringing fulfillment of the individual's potential and enrichment of life.

3. To allow for normal growth and extension of effective social functioning of the group members.

4. To prevent social breakdown of group members.

5. To provide corrective experiences where there has been social breakdown in group members or in their social situations.

EXAMPLES OF GROUP WORK IN AGENCIES

TRADITIONAL AGENCIES

The social settlement movement harbored developments which provided opportunities for group work activities. This movement began in England with the establishment of Toynbee Hall in 1884. Samuel Barnett, vicar of St. Jude's parish in London, invited some university

15 "Report, Practice Committee, Group Work Section, National Association of Social Workers" (April, 1962), p. 3; mimeographed.
16 *Ibid.*, pp. 3–4.

students to join with him and his wife to move into a deprived, over-crowded area of the city. The aim, of course, was to understand better the living circumstances of the poorer people and to improve conditions for the disadvantaged. The hope was to comprehend the social problems better and then to do something about them.

The first settlement in the United States was begun in its largest city, New York, in 1886, and was called the Neighborhood Guild. The basic goals were the same as those for Toynbee Hall. The famous Hull House was opened in Chicago soon thereafter in 1889, by Jane Addams and her associates.

Settlement houses today, mainly located in disadvantaged areas in the larger cities and metropolitan centers, sponsor and house a variety of kinds of activities, many of which utilize group process as a basis of their operations. Nursery schools, dental clinics, study groups, recreational opportunities, hobby groups, clubs, evening classes for adults, and many other related activities are found within the walls and grounds of these multipurpose agencies. The aim of these centers is to provide services for unfortunate individuals and, particularly, to help them through the use of the group as a tool to develop their personalities and enrich their living.

To illustrate specifically, in a particular settlement house a club was established which offered membership to boys within this area to join together in an organization, have fun, and participate in a variety of recreational activities. A trained group worker was the leader who helped with the organization of this club and supported and guided the boy leaders and the members in their efforts and activities. At the first meeting, which resulted from invitations sent out in writing and from telephone calls, ten teen-agers came. Most of these young men had had little opportunity for club activity and membership. The group worker helped them to understand some possibilities which they might pursue and to begin to think about organizing with their own leaders. Several of the boys had personalities which needed development, particularly in helping them to overcome their shyness and inability to interact and mingle with other young people. Jim, a freckle-faced youngster of 16, in particular, always felt inferior and inadequate around other young men and women.

Soon the club was organized with its own officers and was meeting twice a week. The club worked out recreational programs involving basketball, tetherball, baseball, and soccer. It also sponsored parties and activities, and soon Jim was in the midst of all of these. As he felt wanted and a part of the club, he began to feel more secure within, and after a while his shyness almost disappeared.

The YMCA and the YWCA are current examples of agencies which focus on the use of group process in helping youth. The YMCA, established in 1854, has a membership of 1,848 local associations, representing two and a half million individuals and 379,668 additional non-registered members.[17] The purpose of the organization is to "minister to the needs of boys and young men, by giving them opportunities for greater self-development of body, mind and spirit." A varied, positive program is offered with stress on character-making ideals through the following: health education and physical activity, opportunities for intellectual self-improvement and culture, acquainting boys and young men with the teachings and ideals of Christianity and Jesus, and "providing wholesome social fellowship and economic, vocational and citizenship education." [18] This organization has spread throughout the world and since 1889 has become established in thirty-eight other countries with representatives in the Far East, India, the Near East, Europe, and Latin America. The organization publishes the *National Council Bulletin, Christian Citizenship,* the *Intercollegian,* and the *YMCA Yearbook and Official Roster.*

Many of the YMCA units sponsor housing and dormitory accommodations for young people which become a major effective service in many ways. For example, Ted, a young man who had been reared on a farm in an isolated area, moved to a large city to obtain work. A close friend in his home area had suggested he apply to stay at the YMCA, which he did. Here, almost immediately, he received the hand of fellowship and developed friends rapidly. Instead of being an anonymous, isolated individual in a large, sprawling metropolis, he met people, almost immediately, who cared about him and with whom he could associate in a positive manner. This engendered feelings of security within him. It helped him to maintain his ideals and goals in life and to move ahead as he had wanted to do. The various activities sponsored by the "Y" gave him a well-rounded experience and an opportunity to enjoy life in his new home. His feelings of inadequacy from being a "farm boy" disappeared as he became a part of the different groups within the total framework and activities of the YMCA.

The YWCA, established soon after its brother organization had begun and likewise organized on an international base, has local associations in more than 1,800 communities and in more than 500 colleges and universities. It endeavors to "improve the mental and physical well-being of women and girls and to encourage their spiritual growth in keeping with Christian traditions." [19] Any girl over twelve years of age may become a member, regardless of race, creed, or nationality. Women and girls in business, the professions, industry, agriculture, college students,

[17] "National Agencies—Voluntary," *Social Work Year Book, 1960* (New York: National Association of Social Workers, 1960), p. 729.
[18] *Ibid.*
[19] *Ibid.*

and many others participate in YWCA activities. Programs vary considerably in relation to local community needs and resources and include clubs, forums, classes in homemaking, vocational training, health education, recreational opportunities through arts and crafts, music, and sports, spiritual activities through religious observances, and community services.

Again, housing accommodations are provided for young women who are away from home, particularly in large cities. Recreational opportunities are also offered for youth within the areas served by this organization.

Various kinds of recreational activities are sponsored, including swimming, arts, crafts, basketball, and many others. Girls not only learn to play together and enjoy these activities, but they develop their personalities in a positive manner through association with leaders and other girls who share basic similar goals in life.

Mildred came from a home broken by divorce. She felt alone in the world and left a small village to take a job in the "big city." She fortunately arranged to stay at the YWCA. Here she mingled with other girls her age, some of whom had similar problems. She became an active member in one of the girls clubs sponsored by the "Y." This club, although organized primarily for recreational activities, planned and accomplished many other worthwhile things. Once a week it had meetings of an intellectual and spiritual interest. Guest speakers were invited and there was a group worker who assisted in organizing and supporting the club and its activities. After several lecturers had been asked to make presentations, one evening the members informally decided to have some group discussions limited entirely to themselves and their group worker to discuss some of their own problems and questions about life.

These group sessions were most interesting and effective. Mildred shared with the other girls some of the emotional hurts that had come her way. She discovered that other girls had problems and psychological scars also. As they shared these experiences, and particularly feelings regarding them, many of the emotional hurts were lessened, and Mildred, in particular, changed from a frightened, uncertain girl, bewildered by the perplexities of life and social interaction, to a girl who felt more comfortable in her daily living and more secure in her associations with others. Frank, informal discussions, on an intimate group basis, had unlocked some of the fears, uncertainties, and anxieties that had welled up within her. The group process had opened the door to a new outlook and perspective on life and to new patterns of behavior.

Another well-known organization which utilizes group workers is the Girl Scouts of the United States of America. This organization, established in 1912, has a membership of 2,530,000 girls and 765,000 adults, some of whom are professionally trained group workers. Membership is open with no restrictions regarding race, creed, or color to girls aged 7 through 17 and to adults over 18. The purpose of the organization is to "inspire girls with the highest ideals of character, conduct, patriotism, and service that they may become happy and resourceful citizens." This program provides group activities for girls, planned democratically and carried out in accordance with a code of ethics embodied in the Girl Scout Promise and Laws. It offers a variety of kinds of practical training opportunities for service to others in the fields of agriculture, arts, crafts, community life, health and safety, homemaking, international friendship, literature and dramatics, music, dancing, nature, out-of-doors, sports, and camping.

Mary, a girl of twelve, was not only shy, but did not have the ability to share with others. Through encouragement and support of her parents she joined the Girl Scouts. Gradually, through the various camping and social activities of this organization, she began to think more of others, to share her ideas and personality with friends. With the support and understanding of a group worker, she developed her personality in many ways. After two years' association with the Girl Scout group, she was elected, by vote, as one of the leaders. People who knew her before and after her membership in this organization could hardly believe the changes that had taken place. Group association, with understanding, interested leadership, had offered encouragement and opportunity for her to alter her personality and her ability, in particular, to associate effectively with other girls of her own age—to give as well as to receive.

Numerous other youth organizations exist which also provide group work activities, among which are Boys' Clubs, Campfire Girls, the Catholic Youth Organization, Jewish Community Centers, and Young Men's and Young Women's Hebrew Associations. These agencies, and others, offer various recreational, health, and welfare opportunities, many of which relate to group endeavors.

GROUP WORK IN HOST AGENCIES

One of the more recent developments in the use of group work is rooted in the agencies which are not predominantly geared for social work services. Numerous agencies whose primary services are non-social work, are now introducing group process in the treatment of clients in an attempt to facilitate and improve social functioning. Gifford [20] observed that groups in treatment-focused programs originate in three different ways:

[20] Talk by C. G. Gifford at a Workshop, "Group Work in a Treatment Centered Program" (Brighton, Utah, June 18–20, 1958).

1. *Where everything else fails, a group may be organized.* One of you mentioned to me the formation of a group of relatives who were in everyone's hair. Peck and Bellsmith, in their book on the treatment of delinquent adolescents tell of forming their first group with youngsters who had shown no movement in other forms of treatment. We had a recent example of this at Montreal General Hospital where there were a large number of asthmatic patients who on one hand resisted insight into their condition and on the other hand were very demanding of time and attention. A group was formed to deal with their similarity of behavior.

2. *Groups have been organized to try to handle the large number of individuals assigned to case loads.* We can handle more people faster in groups than we can individually.

3. *In some cases group treatment is the treatment of choice.* It has been found that some people can accept help more readily in a group, particularly where the group members share some mutuality of interests or problems.

Group work is being used considerably in the field of corrections. One interesting example of this approach is the Provo Experiment.[21] The project attempts to study scientifically the influence of the peer group upon those who have been in trouble with the law, specifically, teen-age boys. These boys meet together daily in group sessions with a trained group worker to guide them, mainly indirectly. There are, of course, a variety of interrelated activities which support this group action. To illustrate the influence of the group, one of the authors sat in as an observer and listened to eight of these delinquent teen-agers talk about their activities and feelings. On this particular occasion, a new boy had just been introduced to the group. His peers began to question him and to make comments. He was in legal trouble for stealing. They asked why he stole and he said "to get even with my dad." He had taken a gun and killed a goat belonging to his father. They asked him why he did this, and he again replied, "to get even with my old man." The boys questioned him further, and it was apparent that they were helping him to bring out some of his feelings as well as their own. Through these group discussions the youths share with each other what they have done, why they have done these things, how they feel about their behavior and society, and what they think they should do in the future. Although this experiment is not yet completed, there is enough evidence to indicate that there are beneficial results and that many of the boys are turning away from antisocial behavior as a result of these group sessions and related activities.

Another example of the power of group process is found in the Citizenship Training Group which is related to the Boston Juvenile Court. A recent brochure described its program and included a brief description related to the group discussion: [22]

21 LaMar T. Empey and Jerome Rabow, "The Provo Experiment in Delinquency Rehabilitation," *American Sociological Review*, Vol. 26 (October, 1961), pp. 679–696.
22 "Citizenship Training Group, Inc.," Boston Juvenile Court, n.d.g.

Responsibility, too, is accented in twice-weekly group discussions around a large table and under the guidance of a skilled adult leader. Here the boys face the experience of being asked their opinions, before members of their own age group, about a particular problem in their communities.

How would a boy, arrested a month ago for snatching a woman's handbag, make his community a better place in which to live? "Put more cops on the beat," was his answer. Another might suggest, "Clean up the alleys." The answers aren't profound but these problem boys are unconsciously led, through open talk, into revealing their troubles and steering their confused minds in the right direction.

In various kinds of hospitals and wards in hospitals, group workers are used to help patients to understand and meet some of the medical and emotional problems which they possess. An example involved a group of about fifty elderly cardiac patients in a county general hospital. They were invited to meet together weekly for two-hour sessions in which social workers helped to guide the meetings. These patients talked about their heart conditions, their feelings about these conditions, the reactions of family members to their medical problems, what they were doing about these things, and what they might do. As these elderly individuals shared their medical problems and some of their fears and anxieties, they felt better and their total adjustment medically and psychologically improved.

In psychiatric hospitals groups of patients join together on a group basis under the guidance of a group worker. They meet once or twice a week and discuss themselves, their difficulties, their hopes, their aspirations, and their plans. In one such hospital, the patients were even given the opportunity and responsibility to discuss and help with the planning of group members regarding their leaving the institution. The doctor who reported this experience said that the patients did an effective and fair job in helping people to plan for and to carry out departure from the hospital. In other words, through the use of the group as a tool, many patients were influenced and assisted in planning for release.

Many school districts utilize group process in working with boys and girls who have various kinds of personal and family problems. Under guidance of a qualified social worker, eight to twelve boys and/or girls meet together regularly. They discuss themselves, their problems, adjustments, relationships in school, family situations, and help each other to understand their difficulties and that effective action can be taken regarding them. Many boys and girls today are adjusting well in school because the group has been utilized as a tool to assist them to understand themselves better, to face personal and family problems, and to actively work towards improvement. The group has helped to free them of the problems which have shackled them and kept them from achievement in school.

Even in public welfare settings, group work is being introduced. Trained workers invite persons who are receiving public assistance to meet weekly in groups of eight to sixteen. As these individuals come together, get acquainted, and talk over their problems and hopes, the group process seems to have a therapeutic effect. These people realize that they are not alone in the world in requiring public welfare assistance; they realize also that other individuals are facing similar difficulties and working to alleviate them. They discuss how they feel about receiving such assistance and how they can muster their individual and family resources to move away from public welfare and become independent, functioning members of society.

There are also several uses of group process in the areas of marriage and family relations. John and Mary Smith are having serious marital difficulties which involve lack of affection and the inability to communicate. After having been to a Family Service Society for a series of individual interviews, they are invited to join a group of six couples about their age who have similar and other related marital difficulties. They meet once a week for two hours with a group worker who directs the sessions, and share with the others their problems, hopes, and plans. As they describe their marital difficulties and listen to the problems of the others, they are assisted by the group and its leader to develop understanding of themselves, of each other, and of their marital relationships. After about ten or twelve weeks of these group sessions, Mary and John discover they are talking with each other and communicating as they never have done before. They are also aware that each is more affectionate. Again, the power of the group has been manifest.

Even on a premarital level the group process idea is being utilized. Five or six couples who are contemplating marriage meet periodically for several weeks before "tying the knot." They raise questions and share fears and anxieties about marriage. They learn that all couples anticipating marriage have some problems and questions. They discover also there are answers to most of these. Premarital group counseling helps the participants in many ways, in particular to learn more about marriage and what is involved in husband-wife, parent-child, and family relationships.

NEW APPROACHES

One of the interesting recent developments in the use of group work relates to the "hard to reach" youth and gangs, particularly in large cities and metropolitan areas. Trained group workers now "loaf around" on street corners and, using their best skills and techniques, become acquainted and friendly with these young people who are "tough and unreachable" by traditional approaches. Numerous examples exist of the effectiveness of this approach in getting a qualified worker into close relationships with these youth who, when this has been accomplished, face their problems and work them through just as others do in the more traditional settings.

The use of volunteers is another major development in recent years. Trained group workers act as consultants to volunteers from such organizations as the Junior League and churches whose members give their time and talents to work with clients, patients, and others who are receiving help in various kinds of agencies and/or institutional settings. The trained group worker assists these volunteers to understand what they can do, what their limitations are, and how they can operate most effectively. Again, the group process is most helpful.

SUMMARY

Group work, one of the basic social work methods, is utilized in providing services both in traditional group work agencies and in various host and treatment centers. It is being used effectively to help individuals and families to face their problems and to solve them through utilization of the power of the group and group interaction.

Group work services are relatively new but are increasing rapidly. They first sprang up in the form of settlement houses and within the YMCA, YWCA, YMHA, YWHA, and similar youth organizations. At present group work is being utilized in practically every phase of social work, i.e., in corrections, in marriage and family counseling, and in other settings including hospitals, schools, public welfare, and family service societies. Newer approaches being introduced by group workers involve working with gangs and individuals of the "hard-to-reach" classification in large cities, and consultation with volunteers in many welfare and other agency settings.

QUESTIONS FOR DISCUSSION

1. What is group work?
2. Describe and illustrate the power that is inherent in group interaction.
3. Describe the historical development of group work agencies.
4. What facilities are available at present for the training of group workers?
5. What part has the American Association of Group Workers played in the development of group work?
6. What are the philosophy and aims of the settlement movement?
7. Give an example of how group work might be utilized in a host agency.
8. How are volunteers utilized effectively in relation to the group work method?

SPECIAL ACTIVITIES

1. Visit a traditional group work agency, such as the YMCA or the YWCA, and report to the class on the purposes and program of such an agency.

2. Invite a group worker from a treatment agency to talk to the class on group work in treatment-centered agencies.

3. Divide the class into groups and present skits to depict the role of the group worker on the street corner in a large city as he attempts to reach the "hard-to-reach" boys.

SELECTED REFERENCES

COGAN, JUANITA LUCK, "Social Group Work," *Social Work Year Book, 1960* (New York: National Association of Social Workers, 1960), pp. 540–549.

COYLE, GRACE L., *Group Work With American Youth* (New York: Harper & Row, Publishers, 1948).

FRIEDLANDER, WALTER A., ed., *Concepts and Methods of Social Work* (Englewood Cliffs, N.J.: Prentice-Hall, Inc., 1958).

KONOPKA, GISELA, *Social Group Work: A Helping Process* (Englewood Cliffs, N.J.: Prentice-Hall, Inc., 1963).

MURPHY, MARJORIE, *The Social Group Work Method in Social Work Education,* Curriculum Study, Vol. XI (New York: Council on Social Work Education, 1959).

TRECKER, HARLEIGH B., *Social Group Work,* rev. ed. (New York: Association Press, 1955).

WILSON, GERTRUDE, and RYLAND, GLADYS, *Social Group Work Practice* (Boston: Houghton Mifflin Company, 1949).

CHAPTER 12

Community Organization Services

In a Western city juvenile delinquency was rampant. Boys and girls in their early years were getting into trouble with the law, and both youth and adults were becoming apprehensive about being out on the streets at night. Newspaper accounts reported robberies, burglaries, moral offenses, even occasional murders. What should be done? Could the citizens band together to do something?

Various citizens and community leaders began to think seriously about their local situation. Leaders in the Community Welfare Council met and discussed this perplexing social problem. A committee was appointed in the Council to make a study and recommendations.

From several months of study the committee ascertained that juvenile delinquency and youth violations had definitely been on the increase in this locality during the previous decade and warranted concerted action by citizens and community leaders. Another committee was appointed by the Council to formulate plans and recommendations for alleviating this problem. This committee met twice a week for several weeks and finally devised an overall plan with many recommendations for action. They invited some of their youth to serve on the planning and action committees. The teen-agers presented many ideas which the adults had never even thought about. Together they formulated sound plans and began to put them into operation. These plans called for informing the public about juvenile delinquency on a local level and inviting their cooperation in facing this problem. Professionally trained social workers were hired to work with the street-gang groups and to use their abilities in other ways. Local clubs and organizations, after discussing the problem of delinquency and the plans of action, gave support to the positive program for reducing antisocial behavior. Two recreational centers were established in temporary quarters to provide more opportunities for youth in their leisure-time hours.

What was the outcome? Within two years the amount of delinquency in this community had been reduced by one-half. Violence and moral depredations had almost disappeared. Parents and youth were communicating with each other and helping each other as never before.

Why had the change come about? Simply because people within a given community faced a given community problem and worked together, helping each other to confront and reduce it.

The Philadelphia Association for Youth reported on a "pilot project" initiated in January, 1961, in an attempt to reduce youth group violence in an area which for many years prior to that time had had the highest incidence of murders and depredations in Philadelphia.[1]

Staffs of settlement houses in South Philadelphia and other leaders and individuals worked together to meet the problems and do something about them. Three full-time workers were employed to operate in the areas where the youth problems were the greatest. Three strategically located school gymnasiums were made available by the Board of Education for special youth programs. Periodic meetings were held with school superintendents, attendance and guidance personnel, and school principals to acquaint them with the program. The department of recreation increased its planning and services for youth in this area. The help of the juvenile aid officers was enlisted and they were made aware of the intensified youth programs. A committee on intergroup tensions provided for increased cooperation between the Crime Prevention Association and the Commission on Human Relations. As the program developed, need for a worker-at-large became apparent. He should be a person fully oriented to area-youth work, but without responsibility to any particular group so that he is free to move about the area, take inventory of situations, troubleshoot, and help in a variety of ways. As the project progressed, two property owners made facilities available in strategic locations. One turned over a small community hall to the "20th Streeters" for a clubhouse; another made available a store at 28th and Ellsworth.

What was the outcome of these united Community efforts? In 1960 within this community there were three homicides; in 1961 there was none. In 1960 there were thirty-four major youth group conflicts recorded by the police; in 1961 the number had been reduced to twenty-one. In 1960 there were thirty-eight major intergroup incidents recorded by the Commission on Human Relatons; in 1961 there were twenty-one.

Community organization is used not only in metropolitan centers but

1 Stephan H. Kneisel, "A Report on the First Year of the 17th District Pilot Project, January Through December" (Philadelphia: Crime Prevention Association, Philadelphia Association for Youth, January 15, 1962); mimeographed.

also in small communities. A fascinating example is "the Lebanon story." [2]

Lebanon, a town of 10,412 population in Wilson County, Tennessee, is helping footloose youngsters to become productive members of the community. In less than a year, through community organization efforts, the community developed programs to provide many job opportunities for boys and girls, to help them with vocational decisions, to keep the youth from being exposed to pornographic or obscene literature, and to strengthen total community services.

Wherever communities exist and wherever there are social problems, there are opportunities for community organization to be developed, to find out and face community problems and needs, and to take action regarding them.

WHAT IS COMMUNITY ORGANIZATION?

Community organization is recognized as one of the three main methods of social work. In fact, the Curriculum Policy Statement of the Council on Social Work Education, issued in 1962, includes community organization, along with casework and group work, as the three major methods of direct service in social work. Dunham says that community organization for social welfare, or community welfare organization, is "the process of bringing about and maintaining adjustment between social welfare needs and social welfare resources in a geographical area or a special field of service." [3]

McNeil states that community organization "is the process by which people of communities, as individual citizens or as representatives of groups, join together to determine social welfare needs, plan ways of meeting them, and mobilize the necessary resources." [4]

In the Curriculum Study, of the Council on Social Work Education, community organization is described as being commonly used in three different ways: [5]

(1) as referring to a structure or stage of development as in the "organized" and the "unorganized" community, (2) as a field of practice such as "planning social welfare services," "federated fund raising," "national service agencies," and (3) as a method, "a way of working on an orderly conscious basis to effect defined and desired objectives and goals."

[2] U.S. Children's Bureau, *The Lebanon Story* (Washington D.C.: U.S. Government Printing Office, 1961).

[3] Arthur Dunham, *Community Welfare Organization: Principles and Practice* (New York: Thomas Y. Crowell Company, 1958), p. 23.

[4] C. F. McNeil, "Community Organization for Social Welfare," *Social Work Year Book, 1954* (New York: American Association of Social Workers, 1954), p. 121.

[5] Harry L. Lurie, *The Community Organization Method in Social Work Education,* Curriculum Study, Vol. IV (New York: Council on Social Work Education, 1959), p. 19.

Murphy defines community organization in the following manner: [6]

In determining what community organization is, as a concept, and what it accomplishes, as a practice, it is essential to synthesize the dual view of it as a process and as a field. Seen as a process, community organization for social welfare consists in the skills that are used to coordinate, promote, and interpret the social services in any setting. As a field, it is viewed as itself a kind of superstructure made up of agencies whose primary responsibility is to coordinate and promote the work of the various service organizations and agencies.

From these and other definitions it is apparent there are three major meanings of community organization. The one that is most commonly acknowledged is the designation as a *field* of service. This is illustrated by community welfare councils, united funds, coordinating councils, and other agencies which operate to coordinate and integrate total community needs and resources. A second meaning refers to a *stage* of development, related to the degree or extent to which a given community is organized or disorganized. A minimum of social problems characterizes good community organization; a maximum of social problems and difficulties reflects community disorganization. The third definition of community organization is that it is a *method*. A method, or process, is a way in which change takes place. Community organization in this sense is a way or manner in which social action can be taken for facing, solving, or reducing social problems. A later chapter will define, describe, and illustrate the method of community organization and the processes that are incorporated in it.

Certain basic factors underpin a definition of community organization. The community is the client. The needs of the community are paramount. These needs are spelled out in problems that affect large numbers of people. The resources of the community are taken into consideration and are tapped. Casework stresses the individual to individual relationship. Group work uses the group as the tool to help bring about personality development and to solve personal and family problems. Community organization is the intergroup process which utilizes community agencies and resources to ferret out its social sores and take appropriate action to remove them.

COMMUNITY ORGANIZATION AGENCIES

COMMUNITY WELFARE COUNCILS

The first attempts to coordinate community activities and actions stemmed from the London Charity Organization Society, begun in 1869, which tried to eliminate duplication and fraud in relief administration. Its aim was to improve total services in the community through better

[6] Campbell G. Murphy, *Community Organization Practice* (Boston: Houghton Mifflin Company, 1954), p. 29.

cooperation and coordination. The first organized attempt to coordinate and systematize social services in the United States was made in 1877 with the establishment of the Buffalo Charity Organization Society. The need for the Society was great because many private agencies had been established and this brought about much duplication, with many gaps in total services, as well as unnecessary competition.

In 1909 in Pittsburgh and Milwaukee, the first Community Welfare Councils in the United States were established. They were called Councils of Social Agencies. They have since spread and been extended so that most of the larger population centers now have a community welfare council. There are some 700 of them in the U.S. and Canada today. A few have developed to the extent that they have as many as ten persons on their staffs who spend full-time in research, helping to locate and interpret information which will be of value to the community.

These councils, organization-wise, generally focus on three main areas: health, welfare, and recreation. Most of them have a council delegate body which is representative of all of the agencies in the community which join the council. This membership body is the basic authority for carrying out the council's activities. Usually a board of directors, elected by the delegate body, is the operating authority. The board of directors appoints various administrative committees which consider such matters as membership, personnel, and budgets. It also sponsors project committees which deal with particular problems; for example, a committee to work on the problem of transients, services to the aged, or school dropouts. Social policy and action committees often play important roles.

The actual work of the council is, of course, carried out in the main by the professional staff, with the help and support of the committee members. The staff varies in size depending on the composition of the council; but there is usually a minimum of a director and an assistant who is in charge of fact-finding or research. In large councils, staffs amount to fifteen or twenty and divide their responsibilities, working with the various committees, helping with research, acting as consultants, furthering public relations, and supporting and aiding the council projects. Secretaries and other office staff play significant roles in backing and facilitating council programs and activities.

The council helps with many services and functions among which are the following:

1. To collect facts and information regarding community problems and plans of action.
2. To disseminate information to help the public and citizens in the community increase their understanding of community problems and solutions to them.
3. To formulate plans of action for the elimination of community problems and for supplying community needs.

4. To coordinate community services. The representatives of the various agencies which meet together through council auspices become better acquainted with the total community services and can ordinarily cooperate and help each other to avoid unnecessary duplication and fill gaps in services that exist.
5. To raise standards of community services through various interdisciplinary committees involving both professional and lay people. Councils, as a result of scientific studies and careful deliberations, often give guidelines for improving and raising standards and services within a community.
6. To help facilitate referrals for people who need social services. This is accomplished in a variety of ways. Some communities have Social Service Exchanges attached to the Community Welfare Councils. Other councils provide Community Information Services, operating mainly on a telephonic basis, for answering inquiries and making referrals to proper agencies.
7. To help provide training services for both professional and lay leaders in the community. Welfare councils often sponsor institutes and workshops for this very purpose. A popular example is the sponsoring of institutes for volunteer workers who come together with professionally trained leaders to help them better understand the jobs they are to perform and how best to carry them out.

FEDERATED FINANCIAL DRIVES

The pages of history reflect that private agencies have conducted individual drives for money to maintain themselves and their services. As additional agencies came into being, various leaders suggested it might be best to join hands to collect money and divide the amount among the several agencies. In 1873 in Liverpool, England, the first such federated drive took place. In 1887 the first federated drive in the United States originated under the auspices of the Associated Charities in Denver.[7] Twenty-three agencies joined together and raised a total budget of about $20,000. After World War I the name Community Chest became popular in designating federated fund driving. Expansion has taken place in these drives to the extent that in 1958 united funds and community chests in 2,100 American communities raised $427,262,622 for the support of services of the 27,700 participating agencies during 1959. "These united campaigns enlisted the efforts of 3,300,000 volunteers and secured 26,700,000 contributions."[8]

In the past decade United Funds have superseded Community Chests in many communities in the United States. Attempts have been made to include private agencies which had not joined the Community Chest as members of the United Fund. Theoretically this was an effort to get all welfare and health agencies to join together in one huge budget-raising drive. In practice, some local and national social service agencies

[7] Arthur P. Miles, *American Social Work Theory* (New York: Harper & Row, Publishers, 1954), p. 191.
[8] Russell W. Leedy, "United Funds and Community Chests," *Social Work Year Book, 1960* (New York: National Association of Social Workers, 1960), p. 586.

TRENDS IN GIVING IN THE UNITED STATES

AMOUNTS RAISED BY FEDERATED CAMPAIGNS AND
DISPOSABLE PERSONAL INCOME, 1947-1962
(1947-1949 = 100.0)

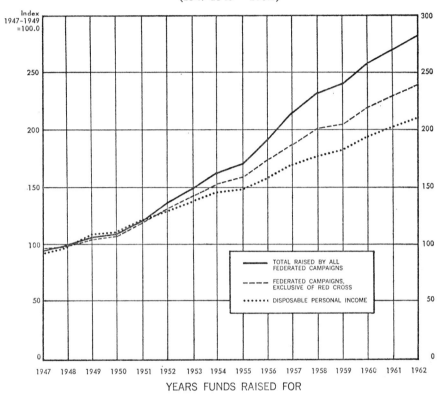

YEARS FUNDS RAISED FOR

SOURCE: *Trends in Giving, 1962* (New York: United Community Funds and Councils of America, Inc., June, 1962), p. 2.

have preferred to carry out their own drives and have not joined with United Funds. A considerable amount of additional discussion is currently taking place in regard to federated drives. Many leaders hope that agencies may be encouraged to join together into two basic federated drives, one for health services and the other for welfare services. Others maintain that it would not be best, or generally advantageous, for all agencies to belong to federated drives since they tend to obliterate identification with specific illnesses, services, and causes. For example, a person may be more willing to give to a drive which, through realistic posters, portrays a crippled or dying child than to a cause which somewhat abstractly focuses on "social services."

United funds have organizational structures somewhat similar to community welfare councils. They are usually incorporated legally within the community and are governed by a board of directors, elected from citizens who are humanitarian-minded and particularly interested in community affairs. Officers are elected within the boards, and committees, including budget, personnel, public relations, and others, carry out the major part of the work. A staff is hired to administer the fund and to sponsor an annual drive to collect money, or to hire professionally trained people to conduct such a drive. The money that is collected is then allocated to the community agencies which belong to the fund. If the drive reaches or exceeds expectation, the agencies receive the money which has been tentatively budgeted for them. If the drives fall short—as they sometimes do—revisions in budgets are made, and the agencies have to operate on more limited financial allocations.

SOCIAL SERVICE EXCHANGES

The Social Service Exchange is another example of community organization. The Exchange originated in the Charity Organization Movement of the 1870's. The basic idea was to provide a central registration place and clearing house where people who were receiving assistance would be listed, thus avoiding unnecessary duplication and making more efficient services available in a given community at a given time.

Here was a cooperative service for health and welfare agencies with the purpose of sharing knowledge of a person or family and aiding in careful planning and in giving of services. It provided for a central index. Of course, the procedure was to keep this information strictly confidential among professional people within agencies.

In the last decade there has been considerable discussion regarding this kind of agency. Some communities are initiating such services while others are abolishing them. Those who are establishing them believe they will help to make the total community services more efficient and effective. Those who oppose them maintain they are not necessary in the total scheme of services at present, and that, particularly in large communities, it is impractical and impossible to maintain an up-to-date, accurate, central register. The question is also raised about the propriety of registering a person's name in such a central index, making it available to other agencies and people without his consent.

The practice today in many agencies is for the intake worker to simply ask the client if he or she has been to other agencies or received help elsewhere. Experience has shown that answers to such inquiries are generally truthful.

The number of exchanges in operation in the United States and

Canada declined from 320 in 1946 to 168 in May, 1959. Williams [9] suggests that the most frequently mentioned reasons for closing the exchanges have been "(a) decline in use due to selective registration by voluntary agencies, (b) changes in casework philosophy, (c) widespread knowledge of the increased specialization of agency program, (d) increasing costs, (e) discovery after study that communication among agencies upon receipt of registration effected an insignificant proportion of total cases served, and (f) decline or cessation of use by public agencies."

Community Information Services are supplanting Social Service Exchanges in some communities at present. A community information service is mainly a telephone and office service, manned by qualified persons who have comprehensive knowledge regarding community agencies and resources. The staff advises people as to whom to call and where to go in relation to particular problems. This service is increasing in popularity and seems to be much needed in most larger communities. It is important because so many people with problems do not know where to go for help.

COMMUNITY COORDINATING COUNCILS

In populated centers, coordinating councils are often established in relation to specific social problems and needs. For example, such councils have been established in Chicago, San Diego, and many other large cities to consider the problem of juvenile delinquency. Such a council usually includes representation from various clubs, PTA groups, schools, churches, and other organizations which band together to learn more about a social problem in their community and to do something about it. These councils are often particularly effective because they involve people who live in the same neighborhood, contiguous to each other, and who have many social and psychological interests and goals in common.

OTHER PROGRAMS

Community organization is not limited to the aforementioned, well-known agencies. A variety of kinds of activities and projects fit into this field. For example, a state commission on youth or a state commission on aging may well be an effective community organization for coordination of total state agency services. The PTA organization with its local, district, state, and national affiliations harbors many characteristics, projects, and other aspects of community organization. In fact,

9 Kenneth I. Williams, "Social Service Exchanges," *Social Work Year Book, 1960* (New York: National Association of Social Workers, 1960), p. 560.

the extent to which community organization may be utilized advantageously is almost unlimited. It can involve volunteers and lay people as well as professional experts.

KINDS OF COMMUNITIES

MacIver defined the community as follows: [10]

By a community I mean any area of common life, village or town, or district, or country, or even wider area. To deserve the name community, the area must be somehow distinguished from further areas, the common life may have some characteristics of its own. . . . All the laws of the cosmos, physical, biological, and psychological, conspire to bring it about that beings who live together shall resemble one another. Wherever men live together they develop in some kind and degree distinctive common characteristics—manner, traditions, modes of speech, and so on. These are the signs and consequences of an effective common life.

Other definitions of the community stress that there is not only a geographical entity and oneness, but there is a sharing of many social and psychological factors. There is a belongingness which exists within the geographical area.

The Committee on Community Organization of the National Association of Social Workers explained the social work interpretation of the word *community* as follows: [11]

The word "community" is used to refer to people and the pattern of social relationships among them when these relationships may be characterized by (1) a common system of values, (2) normatively defined relations, (3) interdependence, (4) a recognition of belonging, (5) a system of stratification, and (6) locality. Sometimes the term is used to describe people and the patterns of relationships among them when these are ordered by a special interest, such as the church, school, or welfare community. The "geographic" community is composed of many "special interest" communities. In addition, smaller segments of the geographic community may be referred to as communities in microcosm, i.e., an area, district, neighborhood, block. When the C.O. practitioner works with a community, he is working with the members and representatives of one or more of the "special interest" and "geographical" sub-communities. These different (although related) smaller systems are increasingly referred to in communication among professionals as the "client system."

Community problems exist in all kinds and sizes of communities, including local, state, national, and international. Brief examples are presented to illustrate each.

[10] R. I. MacIver, *Community: A Sociological Study* (London: Macmillan and Co., Ltd., 1917), pp. 23–24, quoted in Arthur P. Miles, *American Social Work Theory* (New York: Harper & Row, Publishers, 1954), p. 177.

[11] *Defining Community Organization Practice* (New York: National Association of Social Workers, December, 1962), p. 13.

LOCAL COMMUNITIES

In neighborhoods, towns, villages, cities, and in metropolitan centers various kinds of social ills arise which upset and confront the citizenry. Problems of juvenile delinquency, family disorganization, transients, older persons, and many others call for some kind of concerted action.

Community welfare councils, united funds, social service exchanges, and coordinating councils are examples of community organization agencies which are established and operated on a local level. These can be very effective, depending upon the interest, motivation, and efforts provided by lay and professional people.

STATE LEVEL

Most of the local social problems can be considered and attacked from a state as well as a local vantage point. In fact, some of the most effective community organization in action today is at this level.

On a state level there are many examples of community organization. State Conferences on Social Welfare illustrate this kind of coordinated, cooperative effort. At State Conferences on Social Welfare, lay and professional people meet together to think and feel about community problems and solutions. Other state associations have similar goals. A state council on family relations aims to coordinate services and facilities involving training, research, and practice for the betterment of families within the state. The Pennsylvania Citizens Association is another example. This group attempts to find the facts regarding social problems and propose legislation in the state which will benefit the citizens as a whole.

NATIONAL LEVEL

Many national organizations exist which function on a community organizational level. They attempt to consider community needs and problems nationally and to make proposals and plans for action to solve these. The National Conference on Social Welfare, which has been meeting since 1874, with a current membership of some 5,500 is an excellent example of this kind of organization. Although its main effort is an annual discussion forum, it supports and sponsors many activities which help to bring national social problems to the forefront so that they will be considered and appropriate action taken. At the annual forum meeting lay and professional people from the United States and many parts of the world join forces to consider social problems, current issues, and plans of action.

The United Community Funds and Councils of America, established in 1918 and formerly called Community Chests and Councils of America, is another major national organization in the field of community welfare in the United States. Membership is open to community chests, united funds, and community welfare councils, and there are presently more than 1,500 memberships in the United States and Canada. Its purposes are (1) to assist in developing community organization for health and welfare; (2) to give service and leadership to local community organization agencies in joint financing, joint planning, and interpretation of social work; (3) to sponsor appropriate conferences, institutes, workshops; and (4) to sponsor jointly with the National Social Welfare Assembly, the National Budget and Quota Committee which reviews programs and budgets of more than thirty national agencies, and recommends quota data to achieve equitable patterns of local support for national services.

The National Social Welfare Assembly, originated in 1945, has a membership of 133 individuals (nominated by fifty-five affiliate national voluntary organizations, fourteen federal agencies, and four associate groups) and 88 members-at-large who are elected. This organization was established on the premise that social welfare means the well-being of all the people and that all parts of social welfare are interrelated. The Assembly aims to achieve its function as the national planning body for social welfare through a partnership involving government and voluntary lay and professional interests. In addition to working cooperatively with the United Community Funds and Councils of America in relation to budgets and quotas for national agencies, it also does the following: studies and defines problems of broad social policy and plans action for meeting these; provides guidance and appropriate materials for national organizations and local communities regarding social welfare programs, operations, and administration; keeps social welfare agencies informed on major social issues; helps to bring understanding and agreement among government and voluntary agencies; and takes action when appropriate in behalf of social welfare on national and international issues.

There are various other kinds of national associations and organizations which do what they can to further coordination and cooperation in regard to social problems and their solutions. The Family Service Association of America, with its 284 constituent members, is an example of this kind of association. The White House Conferences on Children and Youth which have been held every decade since 1909 illustrate this type of effort. The one in 1960, for example, brought together some 7,500 men, women, and youth from villages, towns, and cities. They represented the states, territories, almost 600 national organizations, and came from eighty-six foreign countries. They were a token representation of more than 6,000,000 persons who had participated in the preparatory activities for more than a year prior to the Washington meetings. They joined their ideas and recommendations, focusing particularly on the problems of children and youth in the space age, what might be done to help meet some of these problems, and how to expand "their creative potentials."

INTERNATIONAL COMMUNITIES

With increased speed in transportation and communication the globe has "shrunk" in size and numerous social problems in one part of the world become of vital concern to people elsewhere. Poverty, disease, and war are three of the social problems which are of concern to peoples all over the world.

Community organization has been extended to the international level. The International Conference of Social Work, holding its first meeting in Paris in 1928, has been meeting periodically every two years. At the first such conference, 2,500 people attended from forty-two countries. They focused on international social problems and plans of action for alleviating the same.

UNESCO of the United Nations in another example of a community organization agency which is operating on an international level. It attempts to find out facts and supports various programs for reducing social problems on a worldwide basis.

COMMUNITY ORGANIZATION IN SOCIAL WORK

Community organization has been the last basic social work method to emerge. Casework gained status and recognition in the 1920's, as group work did in the 1930's. In 1909 the first section meeting of a national conference, The National Conference of Charities and Corrections, was held on the theme "Neighborhoods and Civic Improvement." This appears to be a beginning of specific interest in community organization in social work. In 1939 significant discussions on community organization as a field and method were held at the National Conference of Social Work. In 1944 the curriculum for the schools of social work included community organization as one of the "basic eight." By 1946 enough interest had developed in community organization so that, at the annual meeting of the National Conference of Social Work, held in Buffalo, the Association for the Study of Community Organization was founded. Its purpose was "to increase understanding and improve professional practice of community organization for social welfare." From its beginning until it merged with six other associations in 1955 to form the National Association of Social Workers, it had a membership which varied from about 500 to 1,000 individuals.

In 1950 representatives at the National Conference of Social Work at Atlantic City presented several papers on community organization topics and agreed that community organization was one of the basic processes in social work. In 1950 there were about 100 field work placements in community organization in some sixteen of the accredited schools of social work. As of November 1, 1962, there were 116 students in training in community planning services in the United States and Canada. Thus, it is apparent that community organization, particularly as a method, is relatively new and is evolving and changing rapidly. Current studies by the National Association of Social Workers and the Council on Social Work Education are attempting to define practice in the field of community organization. The 1962 Curriculum Statement of the Council on Social Work Education reaffirms the importance of community organization today in both training and practice by specifying it as one of the basic methods of social work.

CASE SUMMARIES

Following are two case summaries [12] of community projects of the Community Services Council, Salt Lake Area, which are illustrative of activities on a community organization level:

The Transient Problem

Changes in communities evolve slowly out of (1) identification of problems, (2) the gathering of facts about the problems, (3) deliberations in which a variety of viewpoints are brought to bear, (4) the selection of the best solutions, and (5) the action required to resolve the problems. The educational process is often slow and painful since change in attitudes is not a simple matter.

Dealing with the transient problem in the Salt Lake area was a case in point dating back to the 1930's when the federal government stepped in to help and then withdrew with the necessity for states to move into action. Some assistance was provided to help families through State legislation which offered some relief but left many needs untouched. Churches and various state and local agencies were overburdened by the problem through the years with no concerted effort to alleviate the situation.

After a number of stop-gap measures, the Community Services Council decided a coordinated effort was required to meet the problem. As a result, representatives of the several involved agencies and

[12] Prepared by Miss Eva Hancock, Executive Director, Community Services Council, Salt Lake Area.

churches in Salt Lake County were called together to explore the existing programs and determine how overlapping services and haphazard methods could be reduced and gaps in services identified. The Council formed a Transient Services Committee representative of the agencies and the community. It was out of the discussions of the Committee that agreements were reached among the agencies regarding the responsibilities each would carry and a referral system was devised.

As the Committee work progressed and inter-agency relationships were strengthened, gaps in present services became apparent.

The single, unattached male transient appeared to be the "forgotten man." Churches and agencies complained of numerous requests for help and the police were booking an increasing number of men for vagrancy. Tickets issued the men by churches and agencies for lodging and food were being cashed in for money and the taverns were the recipients of increased trade.

After considerable discussion and numerous contacts, it was recommended that a mission type facility was needed. The Salvation Army with its long experience in this type of service was contacted and encouraged to sponsor a program which would include over-night lodging, food, showers, washing facilities, and a means of referral for employment and rehabilitation services. A study of the program of the Salvation Army was completed to determine how the transient service might fit in with the agency's existing activities.

The Committee found a location to house the services, and the Council worked out an agreement with the agency to undertake the program. Contacts were made with the City and County Commissions and the United Fund with financial support forthcoming. The churches gave funds the first year to get the program underway. A referral system was worked out with other agencies and institutions, and in 1959 the Hospitality House became a reality. In 1949, 2,157 individuals had been given meals and lodging. In four months after Hospitality House was set up, 670 men were given jobs, 2,623 were served meals and 964 were given lodging, and a more orderly plan had been developed. The program continues to the present and has support from the Police, City and County, as well as the other agencies. It has proved itself as a product of cooperative community planning.

Protective Services

At a meeting of the Community Services Council, Salt Lake Area, representatives of several community agencies expressed concern over the large number of child neglect complaints which regularly came to them. It was reported that many children involved were being taken from their homes and lodged in the Salt Lake County Detention Home, to await possible placement in foster homes, which was considered unsatisfactory and undesirable from the standpoint of both child and agency.

In discussing the situation, several questions were raised: How many complaints of child neglect were received by the agencies? What was the nature and source of such complaints? How many agencies were offering protective services? How adequate were the services? What constitutes a sound protective service program? As a result of the discussions which were carried on over a period of time, a Committee was formed to find answers to these questions based on an agreed upon definition of protective services.

Questionnaires were distributed to agencies to gather information concerning agency protective service activities during 1958 and protective service complaints. During the year the Committee studied the responses and deliberated on a proposed plan of procedure. It was finally recommended by the Committee and approved by the Council's Board of Directors that a unit of Protective Services be established in the Salt Lake County Department of Public Welfare's Child Welfare Division. Negotiations with the State and local departments culminated in the unit being established with the provision that the Council cooperate in appointing an Advisory Committee to aid in getting the program underway, and in helping set up a plan of procedure and referral system with the other agencies. As a result, the State Conference on Social Welfare adopted Protective Services as the theme of its annual conference a year after the program was started, and other counties have requested assistance of the Council in organizing such a service.

SUMMARY

Community organization is a state or stage of development, a field, and a process. As a state it is related to the degree of organization or disorganization of a particular community. As a field, it encompasses various agencies such as welfare councils, united funds, and coordinating councils which are actively engaged in studying community problems and using community resources to meet them. As a process, community organization is a method, the intergroup method, of bringing people together and effecting desired changes, particularly in relation to community needs and problems. It is one of the three basic social work methods which considers community human needs and problems.

Community organization is relatively new, particularly as a field and a process. Yet there are many professional leaders today who believe it has great potential in benefiting communities and society as a whole.

Community organization is particularly important, and its potential is almost unlimited, because it can affect large numbers of people. The community is the patient. Prevention can play an important role through this rapidly developing process.

Community organization can operate on a local, state, national, and even international level. In fact, at present there are numerous community agencies carrying out effective, worthwhile programs on all these fronts.

QUESTIONS FOR DISCUSSION

1. What is community organization? Define, describe, and illustrate.

2. Explain how community organization may be a field as well as a process.

3. Give the history and functions of the Community Welfare Council movement.

4. What are the purposes and functions of a United Fund?

5. Present arguments for and against a Social Service Exchange.

6. Describe a neighborhood Coordinating Council, giving its functions, and evaluating its services.

7. Give an example of community organization on an international level.

8. How may prevention be related to community organization?

9. What is meant by the statement, "In community organization the community is the patient?"

SPECIAL ACTIVITIES

1. Visit a community organization agency in your community and give a report on it to your class.

2. If there is a social service exchange in your community, invite a representative to appear before the class to describe its activities.

3. Sponsor a debate in class on the subject, "Resolved that all health and welfare agencies should join together in one federated financial drive."

SELECTED REFERENCES

DUNHAM, ARTHUR, Community Welfare Organization: Principles and Practice (New York: Thomas Y. Crowell Company, 1958).

LURIE, HARRY L., The Community Organization Method in Social Work Education, Curriculum Study, Vol. IV (New York: Council on Social Work Education, 1959).

McNEIL, C. F., "Community Organization for Social Welfare," Social Work Year Book, 1954 (New York: American Association of Social Workers, 1954), pp. 121–128.

MURPHY, CAMPBELL G., Community Organization Practice (Boston: Houghton Mifflin Company, 1954).

OGG, ELIZABETH, Good Neighbors—the Rise of Community Welfare Councils (New York: Public Affairs Committee, 1959).

United Community Funds and Councils of America, Catalog of Publications (New York: United Community Funds and Councils of America, 1963).

U.S. Children's Bureau, The Lebanon Story (Washington, D.C.: U.S. Government Printing Office, 1961).

CHAPTER 13

Services for the Aged

Grow old along with me!
The best is yet to be,
The last of life, for which the first was made:
Our times are in His hand
Who saith, "A whole I planned,
Youth shows but half; trust God: see all, nor be afraid!"[1]

The bright future painted by Browning of the later years of life makes youth dream of growing old when they will have a gift of time to do the things they have always been too busy to do, when they will be free from economic worries, when responsibilities will be lessened; in short, when they will really enjoy life. But what are the actual conditions that senior citizens find when they reach the "golden years?" Do all their dreams come true? Is the last of life really that for which the first was made? Can they trust God, see all, and be unafraid?

The optimism with which Browning viewed old age is not shared by many of the eighteen million Americans who have arrived at that time of life when "The best is yet to be."

To find out the conditions of older Americans governmental agencies, universities, and private organizations have been studying the older citizen to learn everything about him—where he lives, how many hours he works a week, what he does with his leisure, how much money he has, his mental attitudes, and his physical capacities. Few groups have ever been so thoroughly studied before; and the research continues.

[1] Robert Browning, "Rabbi Ben Ezra," quoted in *Complete Poetic and Dramatic Works of Robert Browning,* Cambridge ed. (Boston: Houghton Mifflin Company, 1895), p. 383.

Results of these studies show that science has added twenty-one years to life expectancy since 1900, but at the same time society has not developed enough ways for making the additional years useful and meaningful.

The number of Americans 65 years of age or older has increased from three million, representing 4 percent of the population in 1900, to 12.3 million, or 8 percent of the population in 1950. There are now nearly eighteen million Americans over 65, 10 percent; and it is estimated that by 1970 there will be twenty million, and more than thirty million by the year 2000.[2]

From a greater awareness on the part of many Americans of the important national problem created by the needs of this segment of the population evolved the White House Conference on Aging, held in January, 1961. This Conference was a nationwide citizens' forum designed to focus public attention on problems and potentials of older Americans, and to consolidate the opinions and recommendations agreed upon at State Aging Conferences held prior to this time. More than 2,500 delegates participated in the meetings, representing fifty-three states and territories and more than 300 national voluntary organizations interested in the field of aging. The basic objectives were to define the circumstances, needs, and opportunities of the older citizens, and to recommend actions by governmental and private groups which would enable older people to achieve maximum satisfaction in their later lives.[3]

President Kennedy in a message to Congress stated national goals for the future in making it possible for older citizens to lead fuller lives:

Our national record in providing for our aged is a proud and hopeful one. But it can and must improve. We can continue to move forward by building needed Federal programs, by developing means for comprehensive action in our communities, and by doing all we can, as a Nation and as individuals, to enable our senior citizens to achieve both a better standard of life and a more active, useful and meaningful role in a society that owes them much and can still learn much from them.[4]

The legislation that is being enacted and put into practice concerning the financial needs, better housing facilities, tax reductions, medical assistance to an increasing number of older people, encouragement to private agencies in the building of nursing homes, and other group housing all attest to the fact there is a growing awareness of the needs of this large group in this nation. All these activities will pave the way for general betterment and should improve conditions that have made old age a time of trial and worry instead of peaceful retirement.

2 The Older American, President's Council on Aging (Washington, D.C.: United States Printing Office, 1962), p. 6.

3 The Nation and Its Older People, Report of White House Conference on Aging (Washington, D.C.: U.S. Government Printing Office, 1961), p. v.

4 The Older American, op. cit., p. 6.

Regardless of how comfortable and convenient the material aspects of life become for the senior citizens, there will still be turmoil and dissatisfaction with their lot unless they can maintain a high degree of independence with resulting self-respect and dignity. Better housing alone cannot guarantee the occupants a tranquil, trouble-free life. As stated by Vasey, "The heritage of a long life should be a secure place in the world, a place that is occupied with dignity and self-respect. The older person should have a serene sense of belonging somewhere and of being significant to the society in which he has spent his years." [5]

INCOME FOR THE AGED

Although the economic standard of living is generally much improved over those of even a dozen years ago, incomes for older citizens are usually inadequate for even a modest level of living.

In 1950, 74 percent of persons over 65 had incomes of less than $1,000 per year; by 1961, 50 percent had incomes of less than $1,000. Those who received more than $3,000 rose from 7 percent in 1950 to 14 percent in 1961. The median money income in 1960 of two-person families where the head was past 65 was $2,530, and of those persons living alone over 65, the median income was only $1,055. The older male resident living alone had an average income of $1,315 while the older woman living alone had $960. This is considerably higher income than that received by such persons who live with relatives. In this group, the average was $895 for men and $350 for women.

In 1950 the 12.3 million Americans 65 and over had a total income of about $15 billion; while in 1961 the seventeen million people had a total income of $35 billion. About three-fifths of the increase—$12 billion —came from Government programs with nearly $9 billion deriving from Old Age, Survivors, and Disability Insurance (OASDI), commonly known as Social Security. The remaining $3 billion increase came from employee retirement programs, veterans' payments, and public assistance. In 1950 public OAA was about half of all the money paid to the aged under government programs, while in 1961 it represented only about one-eighth.

With the governmental retirement programs constantly expanding, it is almost certain that those retiring in the future will be better off financially than those today. Eventually 95 percent of the population[6] will qualify for social security retirement payments, and many will also receive higher payments from private pension plans; notwithstanding this

[5] Wayne Vasey, "The Aging Population: A Challenge to Social Work," *Social Casework*, Vol. 42 (May-June, 1961), p. 227.

[6] It is estimated that nine out of ten workers are covered by Social Security today (1964).

increase, there is still the real possibility that a gap between the income and needs of the older people will continue and additional efforts will be needed to bridge it.

Americans can be secure in the knowledge that government income programs will protect the elderly against income loss. Nevertheless, for many, public assistance is a humiliating and demoralizing experience. According to Lazarus, "To maintain one's sense of dignity when receiving assistance is an achievement. For the aged, more than any other group, it can be called a great achievement." [7]

Casework services focused on helping the aged retain self-respect and dignity are concomitant needs to assistance, and financial help, without these services, may actually cause more harm than good. Fortunately, governmental assistance programs have experienced a dramatic shift from a philosophy that emphasized assistance to one making service a prime consideration.

HEALTH AND MEDICAL FACTORS

Almost invariably, aging results in physical changes in the individual. Frequently the older person suffers from a disabling condition such as cardiac disease, arthritis, loss of hearing, impaired eyesight, or a combination of several disabilities. Grim evidence testifies that the causes and cures for diseases that come with age are still to be found.

Statistically, here is the health report of today's older Americans:
More than 12 million have at least one chronic condition such as high blood pressure, arthritis, diabetes, heart disease, or mental disorder.
More than half of those with a chronic ailment have some limitation on their activities.
More than 800,000 older people are in institutions.
About 1,250,000 elderly people are invalids who, though not in institutions, are unable to get along without help from others.[8]

If we consider the rising costs of doctors' fees and hospital costs, it is readily apparent that the elderly citizens with their low incomes are unable to meet the financial costs of their medical care. There are many reasons for the enormous number of elderly people who need medical care, and the first reason, of course, is that sickness, disease, and disability are common to the process of aging. But there are also other considerations.

Early detection and prompt treatment would result in better health for many of those suffering with serious conditions. In this area the problem lies with the older person himself, who often neglects to seek

[7] Esther Lazarus, "The Influence of the Social Structure on Casework Practice with the Aging," *Social Casework*, Vol. 42 (May-June, 1961), p. 232.
[8] *The Older American, op. cit.,* p. 12.

medical help until it is too late. Many of these people have not been educated in the need for regular check-ups, the dangers of self-doctoring, or methods of accident prevention. Furthermore, families are often indifferent to the ailments of an aging parent and dismiss early symptoms as a part of growing old.

Another basic reason for insufficient medical care is often lack of finances to pay for this service, coupled with the individual's resistance to taking charity either from agencies or their families. Also, some individuals are afraid of treatment and hospitals because they have lived during a time when these services were not as widely used as now.

Many are victims of poor nutrition because they are caught by food fads, poor food habits, or lack of interest in eating when they have to eat alone.

Older people are also victims of accidents—many preventable—having nearly twice as many home accidents as the average adult, and three times as many fatal accidents.

Many social workers are employed by medical institutions and in county departments of welfare who are responsible for Old-Age Assistance and Medical Assistance to the Aged programs. They provide counseling, psychological support, referral, and information services, helping the aged to use services and retain their social and occupational skills and effectiveness as citizens. Open-ended federal-state matching features of services to recipients of Medical Assistance to the Aged programs encourage the widespread use of medical, legal, and psychological services for purposes of keeping the aged healthy and functioning independently, in their various social roles.

During the first half of the twentieth century science has made great strides in controlling infectious disease and in improving nutrition and sanitation. Now the main spotlight of research has been trained on the diseases of the later years. Hundreds of millions of dollars have been spent since 1950 by government agencies and by voluntary groups for research on diseases of older people. Much has been accomplished in new techniques in surgery, new drugs, and methods of easing pain and suffering. But these marvels of science have made the treatment of illness for everyone more costly and complex.

Because of the physical condition of older people, their illnesses last longer and if hospitalization occurs, their stay is, on the average, twice as long as for young people. As a result, the hospital bill is apt to be twice as large. In 1961 the average medical care expenses for an older person were $228 compared with $103 for a younger person.[9]

Although the cost of living, resulting in higher salaries, has gone up 26 percent, it has not nearly kept pace with rising medical costs, which

9 *Ibid.,* p. 14.

have jumped 56 percent. The fees of doctors have risen 47 percent while hospital daily charges have risen 125 percent.

Of the one in six aged persons hospitalized in a year, the hospital bill alone averages about $525. Some have money to pay their expenses, others seek help from relatives or public assistance programs. Some borrow money, while others seek free care under other public programs or private charity.

But, as can be expected, there are many who suffer and receive no care. Just how many this includes is not known, but it is known that nearly half of the older citizens with arthritis, rheumatism, hernias, or who have trouble seeing or hearing are not now under care. One out of seven with a heart condition is not receiving medical attention.[10]

Arising from the tremendous need, federal and state governments working together have developed two important programs of public medical assistance through the old-age assistance (OAA) and medical assistance for the aged (MAA).

In 1962, for example, about $635 million was spent by the States and Federal Government, on a matching formula, to provide public assistance medical care under OAA and MAA.

About 390 million of the total was spent for medical care for people receiving old-age assistance. They received the help because they had little or no other income than their old-age assistance, which averaged about $60 per month.

Approximately $245 million was paid out under medical assistance for the aged—the program commonly referred to as the Kerr-Mills program. The aged who received help under MAA are the "medically indigent"—by definition, those who are not so needy that they are eligible for cash payments through old-age assistance but who do not have money to pay medical bills.[11]

EMPLOYMENT—RETIREMENT

One of the significant changes that has come into the labor picture in the past few decades is compulsory retirement of the workers in many industries and professions. Although the age limit varies, the idea is the same; at a certain age all workers must retire regardless of their position, capacity or desire for continued work, or financial need. Even before workers reach retirement age, they are often pushed into do-nothing positions so that younger men can take their places.

This forced idleness presents a problem for many men and women, not only because of the financial loss, but also because of the physical and psychological need to continue working. Another problem often faced by persons forty years old or more is that it is extremely difficult in many fields to find employment because they are "too old."

Until comparatively recently the term *retirement* meant a dream come

10 *Ibid.,* p. 15.
11 *Ibid.,* p. 19.

true for the small minority of upper-income men who were financially able to give up their work to travel, work with hobbies, or pursue activities which they had heretofore been too busy to enjoy. The idea of complete retirement had great appeal to those who could afford it, and doctors often recommended it as a preventive measure to heart disease and hypertension, two of the greatest killers among chronic diseases. But it was not long before both the older people and the doctors realized that having nothing to do, even in comfort, was not an ideal situation. The loneliness, the feeling of uselessness, made them miserable. When people had these feelings, coupled with financial worries, then retirement brought frustration, not dream fulfillment.

Because of the great advances in medical science in the past half century, men in their sixties are not old. Although aging is a highly individual matter, dependent upon a whole life history and experience, large numbers of people are forced to retire at a time when they are most valuable to their company or organization. Wisdom that accompanies years of experience cannot be replaced by younger workers who possibly move just a little faster.

Recent surveys of firms with pension plans show that nine out of ten companies employing 1,000 or more workers have compulsory retirement and most employers show little inclination to discontinue these policies. In fact, evidence points to an increasing number of employers who are joining the ranks of retirement at a fixed age. In December, 1958, only one person in five past age 65 was reported in a paying job. Many workers cannot find work because of these restrictions; and if their jobs are discontinued because of automation and other advances in industry, they are not considered for retraining for other work.

On the other side of the picture, many people desire to retire because of physical disabilities and declining health. Some have only limited skills and insufficient education for advancement to better jobs. Others raise barriers to their employment by putting their own limitations on the wages, hours, or willingness to move to another location where work may be available.

Two factors must be considered in planning for the employment of older people. First, it is necessary to know which elderly persons want to earn money, and then to concentrate the efforts in job development for them. Second, there is a need to provide opportunities to satisfy the psychological needs of those who want activity through use of community, public service, and other kinds of noncompensatory activities.

Before employment opportunities for older people are increased, it will be necessary for employers to accept the principle of employment on the basis of ability rather than age, and to be willing to look for qualifications in older workers who are available for employment. Some of the big hurdles to be overcome are the adoption of flexible retirement policies based on the individual's capabilities, needs, and desires rather than his age and the development of part-time opportunities for those who do not wish to work full time.[12]

PART-TIME WORK FOR A RETIRED MAN

Employment, even for just a few hours a day or week, is important to an elderly person as a means of keeping him in touch with the world so that he does not become isolated or develop feelings of loneliness and rejection. For many people, a little extra income from such work is more than welcome to make them comfortable, add zest to life, and pay for a few luxuries. An example follows:

> Mr. Starr was a pharmacist who for more than fifty years had worked in a small-town drug store owned by his brother. His salary had never been high, but he had maintained an adequate standard of living. He had continued to work long past the usual retirement age, and was eighty-one years old when his brother died. The family sold the business, and Mr. Starr wondered what would happen to him. He was active both physically and mentally and had planned to continue working for a few more years. He was pleased when the new owner asked him to stay on as an "extra," just to work two hours a day— from 5 till 7 P.M. While these hours were not the most desirable and he would have preferred to work several hours two or three days a week, he accepted these conditions because it gave him something definite to do, he felt he was useful and wanted, it offered diversion from sitting at home, and provided him with extra income.

In addition to providing gainful employment for older people, there is a great need for finding rewarding activity for those who just want to have something to do and someplace to go. Voluntary work in hospitals and health and welfare agencies, service on community boards, work as consultants for business, and other needed services can be done by older people to the advantage of all. For example, seven million service hours were given by volunteers in 1960 in the Veterans Administration's 170 hospitals, and a significant number of these workers were over 65. The Red Cross is another organization which attracts large numbers of volunteers. Growing in interest is the successful volunteer groups known as the *friendly visiting program*. The volunteer visitors bring friendship and stimulation to lonely people in their homes and in hospitals. Volunteers who reap their satisfaction from knowing there is a job to be done, and that they can do it, have found that this work gives new meaning to life for many retired men and women.

The volunteer work in welfare and social agencies is largely under the direction of social workers who, in many of these services, maintain ac-

[12] *Ibid.,* p. 21.

tive recruiting and training programs for volunteers. Social agencies use volunteers for a wide variety of agency functions which include reception work, transportation for clients, entertainment of patients in hospitals and other institutions, shopping for the homebound, tutoring, maintenance work, and various professional and semiprofessional services. Social workers interpret the need for volunteer services to the public, develop programs, and direct the activities of the volunteers.

While most older volunteers find outlets for their services in their own communities, there are a few opportunities for those with unusual stamina, a sense of adventure, and good health in serving with the Peace Corps in foreign lands.

In the planning stage is the National Service Corps designed to provide opportunities for volunteers to be of service to underprivileged persons including mentally retarded children, the mentally ill, and migrant farm workers.

Other opportunities for service are found in citizens committees, commissions, and boards where older citizens can serve as conscientious, wise members.

Emphasizing the worth of the mature minds of older citizens, English and Pearson state: [13]

> Studies of intellectual functioning disclose that significant contributions in chemistry, physics, biology, and medicine are made less frequently after age 60, but leaders in the fields of legislation, jurisprudence, diplomacy, military and naval strategy, religion, and education are significantly older. In a study of 2,607 scientists it was found that most made their major contributions between the ages of 30 and 70. It is not unimportant that more than 20 of these savants realized their major achievement after the age of 70.

Many older persons have discovered that education just for the sake of learning is rewarding. Many who were unable to attend college during their early years have the time and drive to enroll after they have retired, and learn language, art, music, and other cultural subjects. Basic education classes taught by high schools have also become popular with those who did not have the opportunity in their youth. Nevertheless, a powerful deterrent to educational courses, particularly at the college level, is the high cost of tuition.

HOUSING

Adequate housing facilities are a necessity for everyone; however, the basic needs in housing for older people are somewhat different from the needs of a growing family. With smaller incomes and poorer health, older people require less room in their homes, particularly the one in four who lives alone. Smaller size and efficient arrangement are im-

---

[13] Spurgeon English and Gerald H. J. Pearson, *Emotional Problems of Living*, rev. ed. (New York: W. W. Norton and Company, Inc., 1955), p. 439.

portant; and considerations should also include proximity to public transportation and access to shopping facilities and recreational, church, and cultural centers so that the individual can be active in the community.

It is estimated that one-third of those over 65 live in dilapidated housing, or deteriorated housing which may or may not contain all plumbing facilities. Forty-five percent of all aged are in need of better housing accommodations. An interesting fact is that those poorest in health, generally occupy the poorest housing.

Despite the unpleasant picture, the outlook for the future is much brighter. The federal housing program has made progress in housing for the elderly through the cooperation of private groups and governmental agencies. The federal finance programs for those who want to buy their own homes, or for privately owned and operated nursing homes, are expanding and encourage better facilities.

Large rental housing projects are being built in many parts of the country which include in addition to small apartments, recreation and commercial facilities, beauty parlors, auditoriums, hobby and craft shops, libraries, and laundry facilities; some even include a small infirmary. These units are being administered by the Public Housing Administration which provides not only funds but also technical planning knowledge. In addition, considerable private capital is used to build housing for older citizens.

While progress is being made in providing more units of adequate housing, the number of available units is small in comparison to the need, and the program will undoubtedly be expanded in the future.

For those elderly people who are well enough to stay at home, but need some help, a variety of services are available. Unfortunately these services are not found in all parts of the country, and some are extremely limited. However, as the value of these services becomes more apparent it is hoped that they will multiply.

These services include homemaker services, meals on wheels, visiting nurses, shopping, counseling, and other social services. All these are of great help in making life easier and more comfortable for those whose physical conditions make it difficult, or impossible, to care completely for themselves.

In some communities there are coordinated home-care programs to extend hospital services into the home. Nurses, doctors, social workers, nutritionists, and physical or occupational therapists work as a team to meet individual needs.

SERVICES TO THE AGED IN THEIR OWN HOME

Elderly individuals can continue to live in their own homes, although somewhat physically handicapped and incapacitated, if nursing, homemaking, and other services such as are illustrated in the following case, are available to them.

Two sisters who never married had lived together in a modest home; Helen had taught school, Josephine had been a nurse. They enjoyed good health, owned a car so they were independent when they wanted to move about, and utilized their incomes so that they had been able to save and invest for their "old age."

For many years after they retired from active work, they were able to participate in church and community activities, to travel in Europe, Hawaii, as well as to various sections of the United States and Canada. They found old age (before they reached eighty) as pleasant as they had dreamed.

As the years went by, the physical disabilities common to aging gradually began taking their toll. Josephine's eyesight and hearing both began to fail and it became increasingly difficult for her to see to do the cooking and housekeeping which had always been her responsibility. After Helen had a laryngectomy when she was 73, she persevered until she learned to speak again, and for many years she was able to communicate almost normally. But after she reached 84 she suffered a series of strokes which not only made her quite helpless, but also made it extremely difficult for her to speak. At the same time her mental capacities began to fail, until she was unable to make decisions for herself.

This put the entire burden of responsibility upon Josephine, who at 89 was unable to accept it. Nieces and nephews were of some help but could not be depended upon for daily care. Part-time nursing care and later twenty-four hour nursing care was necessary. In addition, homemaker service was instituted.

Josephine and Helen were not indigent, but they did need professional help, which for them was coordinated by the Family Service Society, a United Fund agency. The caseworker at the Family Service assisted with arrangements for part-time nursing services, and later full-time nursing care and for the services of a homemaker.

Guardianship was needed and after investigating Josephine's feelings about this, one of the nieces was appointed to manage the family estate. Typical of the casework problems was that of persuading Josephine to agree to nursing services. It was difficult to keep a nurse because she was so critical that the nurse would quit. Having been a nurse herself, she felt competitive and it was difficult for her to grasp the reality of the wage scale for a modern practical nurse. "When I worked," she would say, "I never made that much money, and I was a registered nurse."

Preserving the independence of older men and women, along with care in their own homes where this is possible and their desire, is an object of social services to the aged. But for those who become so disabled that they are unable to care for themselves or to be cared for in their own homes or homes of relatives, special types of accommodations are needed. These include foster homes, nursing homes, group-care residences, boarding homes, and homes for the aged.

HOMES FOR THE ILL AND DEPENDENT

More than half a million older citizens lived in 23,000 nursing or other types of homes providing nursing or supportive services in 1961.

Some of these were well-designed units featuring special construction which make life more comfortable, with adequate facilities, cheerful atmosphere, and special program activity planned for the patients. At the other end of the scale were nursing homes in large, old residences which had been converted into rooms for elderly people, providing custodial care. The number of "acceptable" nursing-home beds is far short of the need. Even though all states have laws requiring nursing homes to be licensed and to maintain standards, these standards are often minimal.

Most people's attitude toward nursing homes is that they are the point of no return, the last stopping place. For this reason there is very little being done in them to provide restorative and rehabilitation services even though there is evidence that physical rehabilitation could restore many bed patients to ambulation and partial self-care.

More than 300 million dollars was spent by the federal and state governments in 1962 for nursing home care for the aged under the public assistance programs, MAA, and OAA.

MEDICAL AND NURSING HOME CARE

Nursing home care may become a necessity for even the most independent of aged persons. Mrs. Mayer was taken to a nursing home following hospital treatment after an accident.

Mrs. Mayer had developed a way of life eminently successful for herself. The objectives of services to her beginning with medical and nursing care were not only to make her comfortable, but to preserve for her in the remaining years of her life the qualities of independence, self-management, and enjoyment exemplified in her earlier life. The social worker accomplished this by casework services which preserved for her the right to choose among alternatives, plans for physical care, her church affiliations, and social contacts which made life rich and meaningful for her.

Ruth Mayer, aged 92, was living in her small home where she had lived all her married life. She had resided alone since her only daughter had married and her husband had died. Her income came from a private pension and was limited, but her wants were few. In the northern climate where most homes accepted automatic heat as a necessity, she still burned wood and coal both for heating and cooking.

She lived near the bus line and often rode downtown and to the grocery store. She was diabetic, but had learned how to control this condition, and was careful of her diet. Otherwise she was well physically. Her mental condition was good and she was alert and bright with a delightful sense of humor. Neighbors and friends were good to her both because of her need for them, and because she was always so pleasant and appreciative of what they did for her. She attended church regularly; and even though her hearing was impaired and she could not always hear what was being said, she enjoyed being with people and the feeling of peace in the church.

Among the activities she enjoyed was a regular activity day each month with the women of her church. While others engaged in arts, crafts, and sewing work, she sat and tore old clothing into strips which she sewed together to make carpet rags. These were later woven into rugs and sold. This was about the extent of her handiwork ability, since her eyesight had deteriorated and her hands were stiff. It offered her an activity that was useful, she shared the companionship of other women, and she enjoyed a hot lunch with friends.

All was well with her until she fell and broke her hip. Then different arrangements had to be made. After her stay in the hospital, which was financed under the Medical Care for the Aged program, she was in a foster home for several months. When she was able to accept the change, she moved into a nursing home. A friend who visited her on her ninety-third birthday, after she had been in bed five months asked, "When are you going to start walking again?" and was surprised to hear her say, "The doctor says in about another month I'll be able to be up." Her friend was even more surprised to see her walking, with help, a month later.

At a time in life when many would have given up and been willing to be waited upon for the rest of their days, she was learning to walk again, and during the spring days she would go outside and walk up and down the sidewalk.

The social worker accomplished two major services for Mrs. Mayer. First, she eased her into accepting the necessity for nursing home care; and second, she arranged for financial assistance to pay for both the hospital and doctors' fees, and later for care in foster and nursing homes.

In addition to the retirement problems of inertia, boredom, and inactivity of retired people, communities are building creative activity and recreational centers for older citizens. It is at these centers that many learn a wide range of arts and crafts, such as home repair, maintenance, beautification, as well as participate in recreational programs. They have opportunities to make new friends and find new interests, to find accept-ance, companionship, and interest of their peers, which is all some need to find satisfaction.

There are more than 700 senior citizens activity centers in the country in addition to approximately 3,000 clubs sponsored by welfare and rec-reational departments, religious groups, and labor organizations.

PROTECTIVE SERVICES

Because of chronic and progressive mental deterioration, workers serv-ing aged clients often see persons who are in need of guardianship or protective services.

When once a guardian is appointed, there is little hope that the aged person will regain control of his affairs. The irreversible loss of ability to manage financial affairs makes it difficult for the client and those closely associated with him to face the situation comfortably and realistically. Everything possible should be done at the time of the appointment to have the client accept the decision and feel satisfied with the choice of guardian. A caseworker may need to initiate proceedings if there is no one else who is sufficiently interested in the client to do this, and may be called upon to give unlimited support at this time.

It is estimated that between 5 and 10 percent of the urban aged not in institutions may be in need of protective services of some kind.[14] This percentage represents between one and two million persons, many of whom are cared for by relatives.

Elderly persons with benign symptoms often remain in the community, and many others could do so if some protective services were available to them.

THE AGED ARE INDIVIDUALS, TOO

The National Council on the Aging has given high priority to semi-nars designed to deepen the knowledge and skills of practitioners in working with the aging and to help them overcome negative attitudes toward older persons. The Arden House Seminar held at Columbia Uni-versity in November, 1960, brought together about eighty outstanding social workers, educators, and resource persons from related fields who discussed the many aspects of aging from the point of view of the indi-vidual. Zaki, who summarized the seminar workshop discussions, stated that:

"The goal of casework with the aging client is the enhancement of his social functioning to the end that he may lead as full and creative a life

14 Edna Wasser, "Responsibility, Self-Determination, and Authority in Casework Protection of Older Persons," *Social Casework*, Vol. 42 (May-June, 1961), p. 258.

as possible." [15] This can be accomplished by helping the older person to adjust to current reality and by giving him hope and a sense of purpose.

Although growing old is a highly individual matter, there are typical crises that are faced by a majority of people in their later years. During the preretirement age, people usually have a psychological adjustment to make concerning the degree of success they have achieved and the satisfaction or sense of failure resulting from their early life. When retirement actually takes place the problems of aging that have to be faced are reduced income, dependence on savings or insurance, precarious physical or mental health, death of marital partner and friends, loss of employment, and perhaps a change in living arrangements.

After one reaches age 75 there is often a marked decline in physical capacities, sight, hearing, locomotion, and mental powers resulting in greater need for care as well as causing some degree of isolation from the familiar world. At this age the chief emotional problem might well be maintaining the right to make decisions for oneself.

With a general background in the problems of aging, the caseworker has an obligation to see that the generalities do not obscure the individual problems of each client. It is well to remember that the later years of life can be years of opportunity and challenge as well as years of crises, and social workers are alert to provide opportunities for growth and self-fulfillment.

Unlike other age groups, the older American seldom goes to a welfare agency except at a time when he is in need of financial help. Relatives of the older client, too, seek help for him only at a time of crisis. As a result, public welfare agencies are the main source of help, and in many communities, the only source of help for the aged. Considering the large caseloads of most workers in public welfare agencies, it easy to understand why the elderly person has been neglected so far as casework services are concerned. Until recently there has been little effort made to do more than alleviate financial distress, provide housing facilities, or arrange for medical care. Because of the neglect of emotional needs with this age group, there are no clear diagnostic guides to help in the enabling process, and many workers have a tendency to rush into treatment without adequate knowledge of the client or his particular problems.

Since clients usually come to an agency at a time of crisis, the pressing need is to alleviate the stress. This involves an accurate preliminary diagnosis. The complete psycho-social diagnosis requires investment of time, patience, and genuine concern on the part of the worker. This often takes several interviews because older people may move and think slowly, and have difficulty remembering specific information. For this reason it is imperative that caseworkers helping this age group have a positive attitude toward aging as well as considerable personal maturity.

[15] Elinor P. Zaki, "Summary of Workshop Discussions," *Social Casework*, Vol. 42 (May-June, 1961), p. 268.

Older clients typically have feelings of rejection, anxiety, suspicion, and uselessness making it doubly important that the caseworker establish a good relationship with them and explore fully their current functioning. To keep them buoyed up in spirit, frequent contacts are often necessary. In the past many agencies have had a policy of contacting aging clients just once a year to keep the agency apprised of financial needs. It is apparent that this situation adds practically nothing to the client's emotional needs. It is well to recognize that working with older people requires service over a long period of time.

Three areas of inquiry essential to make a proper diagnosis are the client's physical condition, his financial status, and his familial and other interpersonal relationships. To effectively plan for treatment it is often necessary to involve doctors, nurses, and therapists to decide whether or not the patient can safely remain at home, or if it is necessary to transfer him to a nursing home.

Many older Americans are more anxious about money than they are about their health. With the ever-increasing costs of living many find that their savings for their "old age" are not sufficient for their needs, and they become concerned about being dependent upon their children or charity. Even for the older people who have sufficient money for their needs, often their habits of spending do not allow them to part with their money, even for necessities. Most of them were at their prime earning capacity during the bleak years of the depression. Memories of the hard times and low wages keep them careful of their spending.

The White House Conference on Aging in 1961 stressed the importance of the family in providing help to older persons. The Conference recognized changes in our present society which create difficulties for three-generation families trying to live in harmony together. Social services are extremely helpful to such families when difficulties arise, especially when physical or mental illness is involved. High priority is or should be given to services which will enable persons to live in their own homes or with their families, or those which make it possible for them to return to their families when feasible if care outside the home has been instituted. In planning for elderly clients, relatives and close friends are utilized as an essential part of the plans.

As in all casework, *client's choice* should not be overlooked. The available choices may be limited with older people, but the caseworker has an obligation to encourage the client to choose the course of action which most nearly represents his wishes. If a genuine choice is not possible (as in the case of severe disablement or terminal illness), the worker must help the client to accept the inevitable, and to live as comfortably as possible with the situation. The goal with some aged persons can only be to help them accept unavoidable dependency with an extremely limited degree of self-direction. The worker also has an obligation to other adult family members in working through their interpersonal relationships with the older member.

SUMMARY

Growing numbers of old people and the problems which appear to accompany aging are forcing nationwide awareness of old age and action aimed at making the role of the aged useful and meaningful. Legislation to this end features income, medical care, housing, and various services, including social work and social services. Income maintenance is increasingly secured by OASDI, improved programs of medical care, and liberalized public assistance.

Research in the field of health and services which will help the aged to utilize existing medical care, to observe the rules of nutrition, to control infection, and to take preventive measures against avoidable accidents and disease are among the measures now being widely instituted to make longevity rich and meaningful.

Compulsory retirement and the forced idleness which it brings is a damaging and destructive experience for many of the aged, both psychologically and in terms of income. Retirement should be made more flexible and opportunities for useful activity provided for the aged who wish to remain active and continue to earn and be self-supporting.

Housing needs are inadequately provided for the aged, and while progress in the field has been made through private groups and governmental agencies much remains to be done.

Many of the aged prefer to remain at home and with the expansion and improvement of various home care services this can often be realized. Alternatives to care in their own homes are such special types of homes as group care residences, nursing homes, boarding homes, and other homes for the aged. These should be improved and such services provided as needed to lend enrichment and importance to their occupants.

The social worker individualizes problems of the aged, and addresses his efforts to the prevention of breakdown and to the solution of problems of social functioning. Social workers who administer the services provided for the aged of society are strategically placed to administer these services in ways that will preserve the respect and dignity of those who receive them.

QUESTIONS FOR DISCUSSION

1. What are the facts and factors of aging which are focusing the problems of the aged upon the American conscience at present?

2. What legislation enacted by Congress in the past thirty years is basic to the income needs of the aged?

3. Securing good medical care for aged citizens often poses serious personal, family, and community problems. Discuss some of the factors to which these problems are referrable.

4. Problems of employment and retirement are among the most serious faced by the aged population. Discuss economic, psychological, and social aspects of these problems.

5. What services are especially needed for the retired and elderly citizens?

6. Indicate the role of the social worker and the social work profession in program planning for the aged.

7. What specialized knowledge is needed by those who work with and administer services for the aged?

8. How can the independence and self-respect of the aged be preserved and enhanced?

9. List the constructive and creative work which the elderly can most capably perform.

SPECIAL ACTIVITIES

1. Make arrangements to visit your local community services council for a firsthand report on community work being done in the interest of the aging population. Note particularly the philosophy and principal method actuating these efforts.

2. Visit one of the senior citizens' centers in your community, interview several of the men and women who use the center, and report their description and evaluation of the center's program and activities.

SELECTED REFERENCES

ANDERSON, JOHN E., ed., *Psychological Aspects of Aging* (Washington, D.C.: American Psychological Association, Inc., 1956).

"Casework with the Aging," *Social Casework,* Vol. 42 (May–June, 1961).

HOUWINK, EDA, coordinator, *Toward Better Social Work Services for the Aging,* An Institute on Social and Health Needs (Syracuse, N.Y.: School of Social Work, Syracuse University, 1960).

How the Government Works for Older People, Federal Council on Aging Report (Washington, D.C.: U.S. Government Printing Office, 1962).

The Nation and Its Older People, Report of White House Conference on Aging (Washington, D.C.: U.S. Government Printing Office, 1961).

The Older American, President's Council on Aging Report (Washington, D.C.: U.S. Government Printing Office, 1963).

TIBBITTS, CLARK, compiler, *Aging in the Modern World,* A Book of Readings (Ann Arbor: University of Michigan, 1957).

TIBBITTS, CLARK, and DONAHUE, WILMA, *Aging in the Modern World,* A Handbook for Group Members (Ann Arbor: University of Michigan, 1957).

part **III**

Social Work Processes

CHAPTER 14

Casework

The term *social casework* appeared rarely in the literature before 1920, and the practice of casework was at such a low ebb near the turn of the century as to prompt Mary K. Sinkovitch to declare at the conference on Charities and Corrections in 1909, "I believe that this paper will interest nobody, for I think that the modern emphasis is so strongly on preventative work of a social character, that casework is secretly, if not openly, despised. . . . The general feeling is that casework is a small affair, unimportant, a necessary evil, a depressing piece of business, a practically hopeless job."

In 1964, social casework is practically a household phrase, and as a method of social work widely employed by thousands of trained social workers in scores of agencies. Social casework, far from being despised is more generally known and practiced than any other method of the social work profession, and some social workers say that casework receives too much emphasis, that preventive work is given far too little prominence.

Be that as it may, social casework has become a respected and highly refined method of social work practice. What is social casework?

DEFINITIONS OF SOCIAL CASEWORK

Mary Richmond, who pioneered scientific social casework, states that, "Social casework consists of those processes which develop personality through adjustments consciously effected, individual by individual, between men and their social environment." [1]

[1] Mary Richmond, *What Is Social Casework?* (New York: Russell Sage Foundation, 1922), pp. 98–99.

Regensburg declares that social casework is a method of "measuring against reality the client's capacity to deal with his problem, or pieces of it, while the worker helps him to clarify what the problem is and enables him to think of different ways to solve it."[2]

The art and science of casework are elements of Bower's definition as he affirms that, "Social casework is an art in which knowledge of the science of human relations and skills in relationship are used to mobilize capacities in the individual and resources in the community appropriate for better adjustment between the client and all or any part of his total environment."[3]

In Hamilton's voluminous and incisive writings appears the definition, "Casework is characterized by the objective to administer practical services and offer counseling in such a way as to arouse and conserve the psychological energies of the client—actively to involve him in the use of the service toward the solution of his dilemma."[4]

The thirteen volume curriculum study of the Council on Social Work Education states that:[5]

Social casework is a method of social work which intervenes in the psychological aspects of a person's life to improve, restore, maintain, or enhance his social functioning by improving his role performance. Intervention occurs when the person, or members of his group or his community, realize that his role performance is hampered or threatened. The intervention takes place through a professional relationship between the worker and the person, and also between the worker and other individuals whose interaction with the person affects his role performance. Since social functioning is a product of interaction among intrapsychic, somatic and social forces, social casework involves assessing the internal and social factors which impair or threaten the person's role performance in helping him to find and use the somatic, psychic and social resources at his disposal, to eliminate or reduce malfunction and to enhance functioning in social role.

Several elements emerge from the various definitions of social casework. It is a method of helping people based on knowledge, understanding, and the use of techniques skillfully applied to helping people to solve problems. It is individualized and although it is scientific, that is, it derives its understanding from the disciplines of science, its method also includes artistic effort. It helps individuals with matters which are external and environmental, and with those within the individual himself. It focuses upon the individual and makes him the center of the stage. It is neither environmental manipulation nor preoccupation with

[2] Jeannette Regensburg, "An Attempt to See Casework Apart from the Related Professions," *A.A.P.S.W. Newsletter*, Vol. 7 (1938), p. 4.

[3] Swithun Bowers, "The Nature and Definition of Social Casework," *Social Casework*, Vol. 30 (December, 1949), p. 417.

[4] Gordon Hamilton, *Theory and Practice of Social Casework*, 2nd ed. (New York: Columbia University Press, 1951), p. 24.

[5] Werner Boehm, *The Social Casework Method in Social Work Education*, Curriculum Study, Vol. X (New York: Council on Social Work Education, 1959), pp. 44–45.

wholly subjective considerations; it combines psychological and social elements and is psycho-social.

HISTORY OF SOCIAL CASEWORK

Stereotyping, making broad generalizations about individuals and situations, not an uncommon practice, is the antithesis of social casework; yet the past has been punctuated with efforts to lump categories of individuals together for convenient classification, if not for study and favorable attention. The "workhouse test" and the "less eligibility" clauses of the infamous English Poor Laws are based, in part, on naive and unfounded general assumptions, namely that *all* the poor are poor because of ignorance, willful refusal to work, shiftlessness, and depravity; that assistance to all of them should be made noxious, given in small amounts, extended for short periods of time, and only for emergencies. For only in this way can *poor* people be made to work, sense their responsibility, and be protected from the evils of relief.

The Association for Improving the Conditions of the Poor (AICP), founded in America in 1843, approached the problem of poverty more individually than had been previously the case. The aims of the AICP were to "visit the poor at their homes, to give them counsel, to assist them when practicable in obtaining employment, to inspire them with self-respect and self-reliance, to inculcate habits of economy, industry and temperance, and whenever absolutely necessary, to provide such relief as should be suitable to their wants."[6]

The Charity Organization Society (COS) established in the United States in 1877 gave additional impetus to individualization and casework. The main plan of this organization included an investigation of applicants to determine need, central registration, recording, relief-giving, and the use of the volunteer family visitor.

It was probably through the efforts of the family visitor that the concept of *scientific charity* evolved, and the seeds of social casework were sown. The visitors discovered that all poor people are not alike and that they should not be treated in the same manner. Various papers presented at the National Conference of Charities and Corrections during this period enunciated the principle of individualization. They affirmed that the aim of the COS was to reach the individual, and that its broad purpose was restoration of function, not detection of imposters on relief. "The poor, and those in trouble worse than poverty, have not in common any type of physical, intellectual or moral development, which would warrant an attempt to group them as a class."[7]

6 Quoted from Memorial of Robert M. Hartley in Virginia P. Robinson, *Changing Psychology in Social Casework* (Chapel Hill: University of North Carolina Press, 1930), p. 4.

7 *Proceedings of the National Conference on Charities and Corrections* (Boston: George H. Ellis, 1886), p. 187.

With the development of schools of social work at the turn of the century, *visitors in training* received instruction in methods of investigation, diagnosis, and treatment from experienced social workers. Developing out of the COS movement the first family welfare association was organized in 1905. Pioneered by Mary Richmond and Frances H. Mc-Klean, family service societies, numbering nearly 300 today, offer specialized casework services to thousands of clients. *Social Casework,* journal of the Family Service Association, grew out of the efforts of this great pioneer movement.

Preoccupation with social conditions external to the individual was characteristic of casework during the early part of the twentieth century. Finding work for families in distress, getting all children to school, placing children in institutions when abused, neglected, and abandoned were natural products of this type of *manipulative* therapy. "The ready answer was to change environment or remove the individual from the environment, even if that meant breaking up the home or lifting it bodily from one place to another."[8]

A shift in emphasis from external *sociological* factors to the individual's conscious social attitudes marked an important step in the development of social casework. Problems were considered as the outgrowth of real life experiences, such as neglect and rejection, and dealt with at the conscious level. This shifting of emphasis posed a need for new knowledge about the individual, and it was at this time that the impact of psychoanalysis was felt. Psychoanalysis shed new light on the importance of instinctual drives as part of psycho-biological growth, as opposed to life experiences and the part played by repression and the unconscious in personality makeup and problems.

G. Stanley Hall, who invited Freud to this country in 1910, and William White, who later brilliantly presented Freud's work, paved the way for the introduction of psychoanalytic theory and *depth* psychology into the casework movement. This was the mental hygiene and psychiatric era of social work. In the decade following World War I, the psycho-social component of the problem-solving method in social casework was clearly focused. There had been a decided shift in interest from sociological improvements to those in which psychology predominated, placing the individual squarely in the center of the stage. It may be truly stated that, "after playing upon scenery, and chorus, the audience, and the orchestra finally caused the spotlight to rest upon the individual actor."[9]

Deluged with psychoanalysis and *depth psychology,* caseworkers strug-

[8] Arthur E. Fink, *The Field of Social Work* (New York: Holt, Rinehart & Winston, Inc., 1942), p. 30.

[9] Virginia P. Robinson, *Changing Psychology in Social Casework* (Chapel Hill: University of North Carolina Press, 1930), p. 61.

gled to retain their social work identity in the twenties; nevertheless, it was during this period that individual therapy came into its own. Whereas the friendly visitor of the prepsychoanalytic era more or less intuitively relieved the patient's feelings in the last five or ten minutes of the interview, by "dwelling upon hopeful and cheerful things," the caseworker consciously handled anxiety, helped the client to help himself, and used relief as a tool of treatment. Feelings, emotions, attitudes, repressed conflicts, and the struggle within the unconscious, became an integral part of social casework understanding and method.

The social and economic needs of the Great Depression refocused sociological and reality considerations for social work and compelled action on the part of the federal government. This was the period of the many work programs such as the Federal Emergency Relief Act, the Works Progress Administration, the Public Works Administration, and the Civilian Conservation Corp, culminating in the Social Security Act of 1935. One social worker has argued that the depression resulted in a "healthy turn about face not to a new but to a renewed study of economics, budgets, environmental resources, legislation—a concern for the real and present world of the client. The interesting thing is the way in which the pendulum, having swung from one extreme to the other, seems to be bringing those two extremes together."[10]

According to Perlman,[11] since World War II:

A growing rapproachment between the social sciences and dynamic psychiatry has yielded a number of ideas of potential usefulness for caseworkers. Consonant with casework's focus upon the social environment are concepts such as these: role performance, as index of social functioning and as cause as well as effect of personality disturbances; culture identifications as affecting personality, behavior, interpersonal conflicts, case-worker-client relationships; class differences in behavior standards and values, as determinants of responses to given situations; social stability in its relation to personal stability; and so on. Practice has yet to test the actual value and import of these ideas for casework.

There has also developed a renewed interest in the family, family dynamics, and the interaction of family members with the result that families are "better understood today and therefore potentially better dealt with. . . . Thus 'family diagnosis' and 'family treatment' are theoretical and methodological problems in casework today"[12] and there is a greater interest than ever before in the "hard-to-reach" individual and family, in efforts to conceptualize practice, in research and evaluation.

Casework is practiced today in a wide range of services and agencies.

[10] Florence R. Day, "Changing Practices in Casework Treatment," *The Family*, Vol. 18 (March, 1937), p. 4.

[11] Helen Perlman, "Social Casework," *Social Work Year Book, 1960* (New York: National Association of Social Workers, 1960), p. 538.

[12] *Ibid.*

A few of the better known are public relief agencies, family and children societies, correctional institutions, hospitals, clinics, rehabilitation centers, and offices of the American Red Cross. World War II and the cataclysmic social changes since then have resulted in a greatly expanded demand for casework services. For the first time in our nation's history, social work in World War II was classified and given a "military spec" number. Social work personnel were assigned to induction centers, consultation clinics, base hospitals, and other military installations as caseworkers. The number of caseworkers in schools of learning is on the increase. With our present social security legislation and a new emphasis on services, caseworkers are likely to be in greater demand than ever before to fill positions in state and county departments of public welfare, and to organize and offer services.

KNOWLEDGE, ATTITUDES, AND SKILLS OF SOCIAL CASEWORK

The basic preparation and professional equipment of the social caseworker consists of knowledge, attitudes, and skills.

KNOWLEDGE

Knowledge of the individual is a major component to the understanding required in social casework practice. The caseworker must know what it takes to motivate clients and the *whys* of his behavior. It is not enough to know, for example, that Tommy will not eat. The caseworker must know *why* he will not eat, if this can be determined; and *what,* if anything, can be done about it.

Casework interest in classification is suggested by scientific training but uppermost in casework practice is knowing how an individual functions socially, as a parent, on the job, and in the marital relationship. Employees who cannot hold jobs will return to work, employment stability, and to the breadwinning role when problems of role relationship, stress situations, intrapsychic disturbances, or whatever, are removed or modified by casework help.

Knowledge for casework is derived basically from social work practice and such disciplines as physical medicine, economics, psychology, sociology, psychiatry, psychoanalysis, and anthropology. The profession of social work orders, arranges, adapts, and aligns "borrowed" knowledge to its purpose of knowing physical maturation, body systems and their laws, nutrition, physiology, anatomy, human behavior, interpersonal relationships, the dependency needs of children and adults, and what can be done to promote good health. For example, caseworkers know that infants languish if not loved and may be retarded mentally and physically unless the causes of the failure of the mother-child relationship can be ascertained and eliminated. The caseworker uses knowledge of stress in assessing role performance and for purposes of intervention to improve a stressful situation.

The caseworker applies knowledge of social role to casework practice and in his armamentarium lies an understanding that most people who use the services of social agencies believe they have failed in one or more of their social roles. They believe they have failed themselves and others, in part or in whole, and regardless of their objectivity, or lack of it, their self-image has been damaged. The casework philosophy of acceptance along with casework techniques and skills are addressed to the repair of this damage.

Caseworkers understand that social roles are culturally determined and controlled. For instance, it is inconceivable for a physician to refuse medical care to an indigent, critically ill patient. The physician is expected to "take care of sick people" and this is what he does to the best of his ability. It is likewise inconceivable for a person whose role is that of idler to seek employment, or to do anything other than draw his monthly relief check. Everyone is assigned one or many roles by the group and the culture to which he belongs. The performance of the individual in these roles, with some leeway, can be fairly accurately predicted. Social role becomes a determinant of behavior and cuts across a wide variety of situations in which individuals find themselves. Knowledge about these forces and their culturally determined influences is a part of the equipment of the social caseworker.

A third body of knowledge has to do with stress and its influence upon personal performance. Stress-producing conditions are economic, social, or emotional, and can come from within the individual, as in the event of unresolved intrapsychic conflicts, or result from external influences.

The caseworker must understand the psychodynamics of human behavior and both conscious and unconscious motivations. He studies and learns about such affective states as love, sympathy, jealousy, and hate, and the interrelationship of hostility, guilt, and anxiety. The theory of psycho-social stages of development of the individual from infancy to maturity, the psychological defense mechanisms, and self-knowledge, insights, and understanding, are all part of the psychological accoutrements of the caseworker.

Not the least stress-producing situations are those resulting from various failures in life, and the social caseworker is confronted daily by clients who are humiliated and embarrassed because they have been forced to accept charity, to seek guidance, or to discuss their marital and family problems. In American society initiative, judgment, industry, and self-management are esteemed, and their opposites condemned.

Knowledge about the various services of the community is basic to the practice of social casework, and caseworkers help people to solve their problems because they know the community and the functions and purposes of its various agencies. In a complex society, many services have been developed, some of which are highly specialized; some, such as hospitals, clinics, and health services, have been established to provide medical care; some are character building in purpose, including the scouts, boys' and girls' clubs, and recreational agencies.

Society's provisions within the scope of the Social Security Act have been largely those of income maintenance; and the function of many agencies developed under the provisions of the Act is seen as that of keeping the level of income from falling below a certain subsistence level. The function of unemployment agencies is to dispense unemployment compensation and to make job information available to workers and employers alike. Children's agencies provide substitute family or institutional care for children whose parents are dead, or who cannot or will not provide for their children; and family agencies offer counseling.

The function and purpose of agencies along with proper referral procedures constitute knowledge which the caseworker uses to relieve stress, remove want, and help solve personal, family, and community problems. The caseworker may assist others to develop services. One social worker who had led the fight for reform in the treatment of the mentally ill, jubilantly declared, when word was received that the governor had signed the desired legislation, "At last we now have a tool with which to combat this malignant social cancer—mental illness."

Services require community sanction and support, and knowledge of this fact is related by the caseworker to his work. He must know, for example, that public welfare is a legally determined right to clients who are eligible for it, and authorized by the Social Security Act; it is the law of the land and the mandate of the people. Similar structuring is given to various programs of mental health, vocational rehabilitation, child welfare, and many others; laws, when implemented by administrative policy, become the framework out of which a particular program operates. Constitutions and bylaws of voluntary organizations and agency policy statements serve a similar purpose for these organizations and are binding upon the directors and administrative officers.

ATTITUDES

The caseworker has conviction about the soundness of what he does and its effectiveness, and a commitment about the worth and value of people. His conviction stems from his own belief in the democratic process and from his experience in using the method of casework and seeing the improvement in individual lives resulting from it. He knows that the client who is devalued, or whose self-regard has been badly shaken, can reappraise himself through the professional relationship of the caseworker who believes in his worth, and whose attitude is one of approval, not condemnation.

The caseworker identifies with the social work profession, its aims, and its purposes, and derives benefits from his professional activities. He finds satisfaction in the work done by his professional associates through their writings and conferences. He shares his knowledge and research with others by means of publications in professional journals and he works for improvement in living conditions of all people through his efforts on social action committees, welfare councils, and policy-making boards. Indignant upon learning that a commissioner of welfare was using public assistance rolls illegally for campaign purposes, a caseworker, through his professional organization, exposed and thus ended this practice.

The caseworker strives for objectivity, uses the scientific method, and handles need on the basis of data collected and analyzed scientifically. Assistance, for example, is given when a need is realistically determined, and not because of patronage or political considerations.

Personal biases and prejudice are eliminated as far as possible, or disciplined to prevent their harm to the casework relationship. Objectivity in casework is enhanced by learning which emphasizes self-awareness and professional self-control. Individual workers learn about themselves through study and as they work with clients who mirror their thoughts and feelings. Supervisors play a major role in assisting staff to achieve objectivity, and remain affectively neutral. "I never realized," confessed one student social worker, "until my supervisor pointed it out that I was failing with Susan by planning her schooling for her, when I should have been helping her make her own plans." The public expects physicians to prescribe *for* their patients and lawyers to prepare briefs *for* and defend their clients; social workers help clients to *help themselves*. Caseworkers render service not solely because they *like* someone but because of their professional obligations and commitments.

Healing, supportive attitudes create the climate for the client's use of help and free him from crippling emotions. "Whenever I talked to Mother," one teenage girl complained to her caseworker, "she told me I was acting like an adolescent! Until I came to you I was always on the defensive, feeling I had to justify and explain everything I believed and did." The client is free to move ahead, to try, and to risk himself, if he knows he is not going to be censored. He sloughs off destructive approaches to his own life because the worker, as a model, accepts him uncritically, although not condoning antisocial acts.

SKILLS

Casework practice is based on knowledge and involves attitudes, but it is also action-oriented; it is thinking, wishing, willing, feeling, and *doing*. The primary responsibility of the caseworker is to apply his knowledge to cases and case situations. The *how* of the practice of social casework, when artfully and scientifically applied, makes an effective helping tool combined with disciplined attitudes and rounded knowledge.

Casework method is systematic and orderly and includes the processes of (1) social study, (2) diagnosis, and (3) treatment. Casework begins with the premise that problems involving social functioning are due to multiple factors within the individual and his social environment, and that a scientific approach to casework treatment calls for the gathering of relevant data pertaining to the individual or family, and the interpretation of these data in the light of knowledge of societal norms, values, and goals for the individual. Treatment is based on understanding of the psycho-social components of the individual's problem.

For instance, a social study revealed that the Martel family was besieged with problems and overwhelmed by them. Johnny, who was twelve, was stealing at school and setting fires in the neighborhood. At the birth of the last child three months previously, Mr. Martel disappeared and with him the family income. The Martels had run out of groceries and were threatened with eviction for nonpayment of rent. The phone had already been taken out, the lights and power disconnected, and the family given notice that the gas would be turned off. The children were ill and Mrs. Martel was frantic. The social study revealed many aspects to the problem and suggested a psycho-social assessment and definition of it.

The social study begins with a statement of the problem by the client. It is guided by what is indicated by the client to be the major problem, and may penetrate a range of somatic, psychological, social, cultural, spiritual, and environmental forces. Diagnosis results in an understanding of the problem. It includes initial impressions which are confirmed, modified, or even rejected in the light of additional information as the case moves from moment to moment. Casework diagnosis includes the assessment of strengths and limitations and the defining of the situation based on this assessment.

Treatment begins with the first contact with the client. The study process *is* treatment when it helps the client to clarify the problem for himself, and to make changes in his life situation resulting from this understanding. Treatment goals are determined by the client and the worker together, relevant to what they see the problem to be. Treatment is determined by the client's need and when the agency does not provide the service indicated, the worker has a responsibility to help the client to find and tap other resources.

Treatment in the Martel case involved referral to a health service for medical care for the children, psychiatric help for Johnny, casework for Mrs. Martel, and income maintenance for the family from a public source until Mr. Martel could be located and restored to his former role of supporting the family.

The caseworker's activity includes interviewing, recording, letter writing, referrals to other agencies and services, and helping the client to use personal and other resources. He supports and strengthens the client's ego through emotional catharsis, reassurance, clarification of the problem, and sympathetic listening. The professional activity of the worker is always geared to the worker-client relationship and guided by such basic principles as:

1. The client's right to determine his own course of action within the limits of his capacity and to make sound choices. This right carries with it some assumptions of social responsibility. The caseworker also has a responsibiliy to help the client to develop his capacity for self-determination through assisting him to consider alternative choices and their possible consequences.

2. Acceptance of a client as he is, which implies acceptance of his capacity to change, and expectation that he can and will utilize his resources to improve his social functioning. It does not condone antisocial behavior, but seeks to understand the individual or family and the reasons for the behavior, and to help the individual and family develop their potential for more satisfying social and personal adjustments.

3. Social work traditionally relates to and works with strengths rather than pathology. Limitations should be recognized and handled realistically, but the worker seeks to assess and develop strengths and resources within the client and community.

4. The caseworker does not seek to determine guilt or fix blame, but to understand the person and to help him plan for constructive change. The caseworker makes diagnostic and goal-setting judgments and supports the values of society.

5. Knowledge about the client's family and its situation is used responsibly for the welfare of the family and society. This permits sharing pertinent information in a collaborative or team relationship wherever possible and appropriate, and with the knowledge of the client.

6. The caseworker has a professional responsibility for the welfare of the total family and is constantly evaluating the effect of treatment of one member of the family upon other members. A family-centered focus is maintained where the treatment is carried out through work with one or several family members, or through individual or joint interviews.

7. The caseworker is responsible not only to the client, but also to himself, his agency, and to the community, as well as to the profession.

8. Innovations to those professional activities which are determined for the worker by various principles and concepts must be consistent with casework goals.

9. As a *mobilizer* of material, environmental, and psychological resources, casework arrays itself with efforts to develop, improve, change, and strengthen services, and facilitates their constructive use by the client in need.

PROBLEMS IN SOCIAL CASEWORK

Social casework addresses itself to the solution of problems which block or minimize the effectiveness of the individual in various roles. Problems within the family which interfere with or prevent the discharge of the family's social and economic obligations are of paramount concern to the caseworker, as are those which block communication and the free expression of the affective states.

Problems preventing the maximum use of the opportunities offered by the school are pinpointed by the school social worker. In the clinic or hospital, of concern to caseworkers are those problems which militate against the effectiveness of treatment, the relationship of patients to their families and their physicians, their feelings about treatment and employment, and income maintenance.

Difficulties in classification of problems are immediately apparent when viewed in relation to the discrete needs of individuals. Nevertheless, some grouping appears desirable and can be justified. Obviously, problems related to income need and to social change are basically external to, and may be ouside, the control of the individual. Problems of interpersonal relationships can be identified and clearly recognized. Typically, for example, are stressful and disturbed marital relationship problems which center in the marriage itself. Intrapsychic conflicts, trait disturbances, and other personality disorders are still another broad classification of problems with which casework is concerned. Some problems are environmental and sociological; some interpersonal and familial; some strictly personal and intrapsychic; and most contain both social and psychological elements.

Caseworkers are frequently confronted with situations in which the casework objective may be that of helping a client to use a service. Problems related to attitudes toward accepting and using social services are often among the most difficult, although, paradoxically, these problems only exist for clients in relation to their decisions to do something about their problems.

Beck,[13] in a research-oriented statement, contends that "an adequate

[13] Dorothy Fahs Beck, "Research Relevant to Casework Treatment of Children," *Social Casework,* Vol. 39 (February-March, 1958), p. 107.

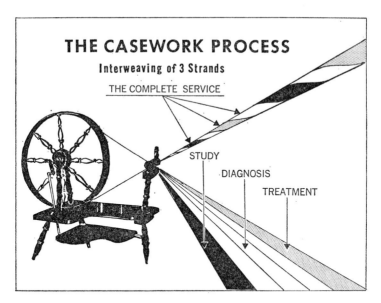

THE CASEWORK PROCESS
Interweaving of 3 Strands

THE COMPLETE SERVICE

STUDY

DIAGNOSIS

TREATMENT

diagnostic classification will have to provide three independently usable components: (1) a personality classification, (2) a family or environmental classification, and (3) a crisis-problem classification. Common combinations of these three components should together provide us with typologies useful for research analysis."

Boehm says: [14]

In the light of this analysis, the following can be said about problems: (1) problems to which casework is addressed are conceived in terms of both the psychic and the social factors which affect a person's social functioning; (2) casework problem categories which are needed for effective diagnosis have not been developed to any large extent but the field of practice seems to be moving in this direction; (3) conceptualization of the phenomena of practice will facilitate the research needed to establish problem categories; (4) the term problem is not clearly defined and is frequently used synonymously with stress. Distinction between these terms should lead to identification of either. Stress is a pressure which may manifest itself in malfunctioning. Malfunctioning is the problem.

THE CASEWORK PROCESS

The steps in the process of the casework method—study, diagnosis, and treatment—are illustrated in the Flandro case, which follows. During the time the case was active, Mrs. Flandro was seen by a school social worker, a family service caseworker, and by social workers in the hospital, in a child guidance clinic, and at Neighborhood House. How-

[14] Boehm, *op. cit.*, pp. 22–23.

ever, primary responsibility for the case was carried by a family agency, the Family Service Society.

Defining the situation, getting to know the problem in its several dimensions, was a primary first phase emphasis. This step was followed by case formulation where the worker did some "hunching" about what was needed and tentatively mapped a plan of action. Study and diagnostic thinking remained fluid and open throughout treatment, although their *emphasis* was early in the contact with the client.

Treatment started with the initial interview, but was emphasized in later contacts after the stage for it had been set and the outlines of the problems were clearly brought into focus. In the Flandro case, treatment was extended over a period of months, and involved several agencies —both public and private—and provision of casework, medical day care, and income-augmenting services.

Social Study

At the invitation of the school social worker, Mrs. Barbara Flandro visited the school to discuss her oldest boy, Gary, age 8 and in the third grade. When she was told that Gary had been stealing at school, Mrs. Flandro replied angrily, "Not my Gary!" He had been caught with the teacher's wallet, and had confessed so there was no mistake. The social worker also told her that Gary had been bringing money to school the past few weeks, spending lavishly, and treating other children in the class, possibly in an effort to buy friends. When he was not the center of attention he was sullen and disinterested and really did not have many friends. She admitted having missed money at home, but did not know the extent of it, and had never suspected that Gary was the culprit.

The social worker told her that her other boy, Michael, in the first grade, was also having some difficulty, though not so serious as Gary. He could not make an adjustment to the school, his attention span was much shorter than other children in the class, and he was having difficulty, particularly with reading. The worker noted also that he had been absent repeatedly which made it difficult for him to keep up with the class.

After her first anger and resentment subsided, it was readily apparent that Mrs. Flandro had a genuine interest in her children and wanted them to make the best possible use of their experience in school.

Before the interview was concluded the social worker knew that Mrs. Flandro had serious personal problems and that it would be impossible to help her children with the school situation until their mother received help for herself. However, it was only after much persuasion and encouragement from the school social worker that Mrs. Flandro went to the Family Service Society for assistance. She protested strongly and vehemently that it was useless for her to visit a "counseling agency." During her first interview there she was tearful, badly shaken, and angry. At age 28 she looked much older, and had an anxious worried look which was not concealed from the observing eye of the caseworker. The worker listened quietly, making comments and asking questions only when these were needed to clarify her story, for elaboration and more information, and to keep the interview focused on the "problem."

Mrs. Flandro was bitter and disillusioned about her recent divorce, the problems of her children at home and at school had been thrust upon her consciousness, and finances were a great worry to her. Her family doctor had been telling her for several months that Michael must have his tonsils removed to keep from having repeated throat and ear infections. This had been the reason for his absences from school. But since her divorce she was not covered by medical insurance and "a doctor's fee of $75 and $100 for the hospital" was more money than she had.

Her total resources were $200 a month alimony and support money, and she was running behind every month with unexpected expenses. All the children needed dental care, she knew it was important, but there was no money to have it done.

She became resentful when the credit manager of the furniture store called to ask for another payment on her account. She found herself turning a deaf ear to the telephone, and making up excuses when bill collectors called. This was contrary to what she had always been taught and to her way of life. All through her marriage finances had been something of a problem, and she was completely worn out trying to cope with money problems.

She was full of hate and frustration, centered on her marriage. She said that Mr. Flandro was childish and immature and that he had never been cut loose from his mother's apron strings. She had been taught by her parents and in Sunday School that marriage was the finest expression of companionship and love, but the memories of her marriage held none of this.

In later interviews she was able to tell the story of her marriage and learned to view it objectively. She had grown up in a small town and her dating in high school had been limited. When she went away to the University she met Roger the first week and went out with him occasionally for several months. She was flattered by his attentions because he was handsome, had a sports car, and always a host of girl friends. She, as well as her girl friends, thought she was so lucky when, during the spring quarter, he settled down to dating her exclusively, and she was "swept off her feet" by his "smooth line." His family was prominent in the community, and she was sure this was really love, and that marriage to him would be wonderful.

Against the advice of her parents they were married during the summer when they were both just 19. They decided he should continue at the University and she would quit school to work. She found a job as a saleslady in a department store and managed their little apartment after work. They dreamed of the time he would be through school, earning the living, and she could stay at home. When she became pregnant and her job and housekeeping drained all her energy, he began casually mentioning his old girl friends whom he saw at school, how attractive they were, and how clever their conversations.

She tried desperately to keep his interest focused on her, but the worries of how to meet their household expenses, keep Roger in school, pay medical expenses, and provide necessities for the baby began to show in her disposition and appearance. Gary, a husky baby, was an angel to care for and peace returned to their home. Roger was delighted with him and became a good husband and father for a while.

Still in school, he took a part-time job selling silverware and china and his principal contacts were young girls who were engaged, and young working girls. He was a good salesman and his commissions kept them solvent; however, domestic relations suffered because of his attraction to his clients. As a psychology student, he offered free "counseling" to the girls, just for "good practical experience." Since he had no office, this was done in the privacy of his car or the girls' apartments.

When Gary was 2 years old, Michael was born; and two years later their twin girls, Karen and Sharon. The twins were tiny, premature, and cross. They demanded all the time and attention that Mrs. Flandro could give them. Coupled with two active preschoolers, they were more than she could handle.

In the meantime, Roger had received his Bachelor's degree from the University, but decided that in order to get a good job, he would have to continue his studies. Mrs. Flandro urged him to find other part-time work, but he "liked" the selling job and could make more money at it than anything else he could find, and with their growing family, they did need the money. When he finally finished school and took a job in a clinic, she was relieved thinking that her problems would be over, but he did not change; he insisted that, "every man should have an adolescence, if not before marriage then after; and I was married before I was through this period of my life." His romances, which he began to boast to her about, continued. He left her alone night after night, found fault with her housekeeping, with her response to his affection, and criticized her handling of the children. Finally, she knew they would never have a successful marriage, and filed for divorce.

This had not been an easy decision even after her years of frustrating experiences because she had a deep religious conviction against divorce, and she knew her children needed the father's love and attention.

As she found acceptance and understanding from the caseworker, she was able to consider her part in the failure of her marriage. She asked, "Do you suppose that I am partly to blame? Did I mother Roger too much? I remember I nagged him and would tell him he was going to be late for school or an appointment if he did not hurry. It was so important to me for him to finish school that I was only trying to protect him from failure."

She recognized that her housekeeping had not always been the best, that she had not always had attractive clothes, but blamed her limited budget and the fact that four children in a little more than four years drained her energy. She had felt justified in expecting more help and consideration from her husband; instead, he had accused her of being more interested in the children than in him. With their many demands on her, it had been imperative that she respond to their needs, and she felt he should have been willing to understand. With Roger working and going to school, she had done many things for the children that fathers ordinarily do. She realized, too, that she had married young and had been immature and unskilled in housekeeping and management. As the interviews continued she accepted more and more blame for the marital failure.

Mrs. Flandro was not satisfied to rear her children on a marginal income, but she felt trapped. When she was in college she had wanted to be a teacher, for she had always loved children. But when Roger had come along she had willingly given up this ambition as she was so sure he would always provide well for their family. Roger never had any question about his ability. As she recalled, it seemed that even before their marriage she had thought him a little grandiose, but not enough to make her hesitate.

She was an intelligent woman, and as her personal problems were resolved through contacts with the family caseworker, it became apparent that it would be possible for her to make a career for herself. She had won a scholarship to the University upon her graduation from high school which would have continued throughout the four years if she had continued her study. All of these points were noted by the social worker, who got to know her situation as completely as possible during the first several interviews.

Psycho-social Diagnosis

Gary's stealing is symptomatic, suggesting psychological disturbances within the child and, possibly, serious difficulties within the home and family situation. Treating Gary without involving the family would in all probability have little value. The total situation must be considered. Michael's trouble, too, further attests to the problems and difficulties which these children are experiencing.

Mrs. Flandro obviously is in need of services. It is difficult for her to function appropriately in the mothering role at the same time that she is beseiged with worry about light, heat, and other utilities, the loss of income, and the failures of her marriage. Obviously, too, she is full of hate, which will have to be ventilated before she can think constructively.

Mrs. Flandro lacks preparation for a vocation or a profession and although apparently a person of good intelligence and superior ability, without training she will be unable to compete successsfully in an age which places so much value on education and training. Overprotected as a child she is ill-equipped to face her present realities and is disillusioned about marriage because of her idealism and unrealistic expectations.

Apparently Mr. Flandro was somewhat immature and unready for the responsibilities of marriage, children with whom he was in competition, and a job. When the pressures mounted as they did with the birth of additional children and increasing demands for income, he collapsed.

Mrs. Flandro needs casework which will help her to clarify her thinking, to ventilate her hostile, angry feelings, and drain off her resentment. She needs medical assistance for Michael whose tonsils are infected and need to be removed. The family income is too inadequate for long periods. On $200 a month they can get by until the clothing is gone and the food supply on hand is exhausted; but after that they will need more income.

Mrs. Flandro has known middle class standards and is not satisfied when she has to live from hand to mouth as they did while her husband was in school.

Additional schooling for Mrs. Flandro, possibly for one of the professions, will need to be considered. She has mentioned that she wanted to be a schoolteacher before her marriage and this will need to be explored along with such practical matters as augmenting the family income and care of the children in the event that she goes to school.

Treatment

In treatment which continued for approximately one year, Mrs. Flandro saw several social workers and used the services of different agencies. However, the caseworker at the Family Service Society carried primary treatment responsibility. It was the Family Service Society which provided emergency funds and coordinated her use of other community services as these were needed.

After the emergency was over Mrs. Flandro spent several hours talking about her disappointments, about being "trapped" at age 28, with a family of four children, and no father for them. Angrily she said, "But I guess they never had a father anyway." Her resentments, her frustrations, and disappointments spilled freely and the anger toward her husband and her plight poured out. She was bursting with negative, destructive emotions. She berated herself for not divorcing Mr. Flandro when she first learned he was going with other girls. She was a "fool" to trust him. Her friends and family had warned her that his "counseling" was not a good arrangement.

Over a period of several interviews she moved from the disappointments of her marriage to her feelings of not being able to get the medical care she needed. Her anger toward society poured forth: "When we pay taxes, why can't we get the medical care our children need? Why is it necessary for a child to be sick and miss important schooling which is so essential for him all his life?" At the same time she stressed the importance of an education, she attacked the school for Gary's trouble. At first she denied that he could be guilty of stealing, then as the evidence forced the truth upon her she blamed Mr. Flandro and the home situation. She was critical of the neighbors who would not permit their children to play with her children because she was divorced.

Greeted with understanding, encouraged to express herself, warmed by the acceptance of the worker, Mrs. Flandro's negative, hurtful feelings began to subside and she was able to *hear* when the worker referred her to the county hospital for medical care for her children. Although she had a strong aversion to going to the county hospital which she had always believed was for "poor people," she remembered that this hospital was used by the medical school, and patients were given excellent medical care. As she was able to dispel her doubts, and to plan intelligently, she arranged for Michael to have his tonsils removed and other medical and dental care for the family as needed.

In a relationship of trust and confidence Mrs. Flandro discussed the perplexing problems she faced with the family welfare worker and gained confidence in herself as she learned to manage her affairs. She became less needful as a person, freer in relationships, and more giving in the role of mother. When she began to feel that her situation was not hopeless and that she could still remain in control, she took heart. She said later, "For the first time I saw what was happening to my family—that we were disintegrating because the only problem I could see was my own."

Little by little Mrs. Flandro had more of herself to give to her family. She helped the children with their school work, read to them, planned and had picnics, and for the first time in years, made a special occasion of Gary's birthday. Michael and Gary, who had responded not only to their father's desertion, but also to psychological abandonment by their mother, showed improvement.

Getting Gary into the local Child Guidance Clinic was more of a problem than having Michael's tonsils removed. The social worker at the Family Service Society told her it would be several months before they could take him, which seemed a long time to wait with more incidents of stealing being reported by the school, and one of the neighbors calling to tell her that her boy had missed his savings bank. She did not accuse Gary, but strongly implied her suspicions. However, eventually Gary was treated at the Child Guidance Clinic and his symptoms disappeared.

Mrs. Flandro had always been interested in her church and its activity program for women and children. She began to attend Sunday School and meetings for the women's auxiliary and discovered that the women were interested in her and welcomed her. She felt she belonged to the group; she enjoyed meeting with them as her own social and cultural background was the same as these women, and she quickly fit into the group. Taking an active part gave her enjoyment and the "spiritual" influence was uplifting. When the ladies learned more about her and her needs, they began to ask if there were things that they could do for her and one of them made dresses for the twins. This was the start of many activities which the group found enjoyment in doing to help her. They made clothes, gave her clothing which their children had outgrown, and baby sat when she went to the clinic for she was so "appreciative and grateful" for their help.

When she told her caseworker about the women of her church she said, "I did not realize there were so many good people in the world. I had felt that no one took time out for anyone else and I am finding out that this is not true. The women are wonderful and the social workers at the County Hospital and Child Guidance Clinic have been most helpful."

She became a Cub Scout den mother which gave an opportunity for her to work with Gary and the other boys of the pack.

After three months when the situation looked more hopeful, Mrs.

Flandro began to seriously talk about further schooling and two sessions were spent considering a plan for her return to the University. As the plan took shape, and after she had made up her mind, Mrs. Flandro was helped to make arrangements for the care of the children while she was in school. Fortunately, she lived close to the University and not far from a day care center. She chose Neighborhood House because she felt the facilities and personnel there were superior to those found in smaller, private, day care centers near her home.

Her schedule of classes made it possible to attend school while her boys were in school and to be home when they returned home. When it was necessary for her to study at the library in the evenings, the ladies from the church took over. Her church also provided her family with milk, other dairy products, and commodities from their welfare program. They gave her furniture, an automatic washer, and in other ways supplemented her income.

Finally, she was able to go to college and to become a school teacher. Three years seemed a long time and after it was over she wondered how she had done it, but she was bright, made good use of her instruction, and graduated with honors. It gave her a great deal of pleasure to see her caseworker at Commencement for, except on one or two emergencies, it had been more than two years since she had seen the worker.

SUMMARY

Social casework is the process of helping individuals to make adjustments to each other and to their social environments. It is a well-organized, clearly defined method of helping people to help themselves, aimed at the improvement, restoration, and enhancement of social functioning.

Social casework developed from society's efforts to improve methods of helping people, with its origin in such movements as the Association for Improving the Conditions of the Poor, and the Charity Organization Society. The efforts of these organizations were sociological, manipulative, and concerned with social improvement and reform. Focusing the spotlight on the individual and on the family are relatively recent developments.

The knowledge base of social casework includes understanding of the individual and draws heavily on the philosophy of social work practice and the sciences of man. Knowledge includes understanding of the family, culture, society, the community, and those health and welfare services provided to reduce stress and to relieve poverty, destitution, and other kinds of suffering.

Casework is a process which features (1) social study, (2) diagnosis, and (3) treatment. It embraces organized, systematic thinking; responsive, sensitive, and disciplined feeling; and the scientific application of theory to practice.

Principles of assistance predicated on human values, constructive attitudes, and the democratic process are the guidelines for the direction and control of the casework process.

Casework is widely employed in a large number of social agencies and institutions and covers many types of problems of concern to the social worker and the community alike.

QUESTIONS FOR DISCUSSION

1. What significant events and factors mark the shift from sociological and environmental to individual considerations in social work?

2. What are the main elements of social casework found in definitions appearing in this chapter?

3. What distinguishes modern social casework from charity as you understand it?

4. Illustrate the application to casework of knowledge about the individual, the family, and the community.

5. Name several areas of knowledge upon which scientific social casework is based.

6. What activities are performed and what processes distinguish social casework in its applications?

7. In what ways are attitudes germane to the casework process?

8. What are some of the problems to which the casework method is appropriately addressed?

9. How are skills in casework related to knowledge of values, social work philosophy, and human behavior and the social environment?

SPECIAL ACTIVITIES

1. Consult your local community welfare council for a list of the social work agencies in your community. Determine which, if any, employ social caseworkers. Delineate specialized features of practice in a juvenile court or other correctional institution, a child-placing agency, and in your local department of public welfare.

2. Compare and contrast social casework with psychotherapy, marriage counseling, and guidance in the schools.

SELECTED REFERENCES

BELLSMITH, VIRGINIA, GABELL, MARCENE P., KNEE, RUTH I., and SCHROEDER, DOROTHY, eds., *The Case Method in Teaching Social Work,* Proceedings of the Institute on the Use of the Case Method in Teaching Psychiatric Social Work (New York: National Association of Social Workers, 1957).

BOEHM, WERNER W., *The Social Casework Method in Social Work Education,* Curriculum Study, Vol. X (New York: Council on Social Work Education, 1959).

BOWERS, SWITHUN, "The Nature and Definition of Social Casework," *Social Casework*, Vol. 30 (December, 1949), pp. 412–417.

FENLASON, ANNE F., *Essentials in Interviewing* (New York: Harper and Row, Publishers, 1952).

HAMILTON, GORDON, *Theory and Practice of Social Casework*, 2nd ed. (New York: Columbia University Press, 1951).

HOLLIS, FLORENCE, *Social Casework in Practice* (New York: Family Welfare Association of America, 1957).

PARAD, HOWARD J., *Ego Psychology and Dynamic Casework* (New York: Family Service Association of America, 1958).

PERLMAN, HELEN HARRIS, *Social Casework* (Chicago: University of Chicago Press, 1957).

RICHMOND, MARY E., *What Is Social Casework?* (New York: Russell Sage Foundation, 1922).

CHAPTER 15

Group Work

Man is gregarious and the more he discovers himself, the more he discovers society. He does not live by himself; he is not an island. His welfare and happiness, in fact, his very existence is tied to the success and failure of other human beings.

There was a time when man's interests were mainly self- and family-centered; the clan, the tribe, and then the nation, in succession, received the spotlight of concern. But today the world is the stage and man is the center of it. Man's existence on this globe can be secured depending upon how well the lesson is learned that human beings are social and must learn to live in society regardless of ethnic origins, national ties and loyalties, or even personal preferences.

To his daughter, Thomas Jefferson wrote:[1]

I am convinced our own happiness requires that we should continue to mix with the world, and to keep pace with it as it goes; and that every person who retires from free communication with it is severely punished afterwards by the state of mind into which he gets, and which can only be prevented from feeding our sociable principles. . . . From 1793 to 1797 I remained closely at home, saw none but those who came there, and at length became very sensible of the ill effect it had upon my own mind, and of its direct and irresistible tendency to render me unfit for society and uneasy when necessarily engaged in it. I felt enough of the effect of withdrawing from the world then, to see that it led to an anti-social and misanthropic state of mind, which severely punishes him who gives into it; and it will be the lesson I shall never forget.

Science has made the startling discovery that infants who are isolated from other human beings, however, well cared for otherwise,

[1] John Day, *Jefferson Profile* (New York: John Day Company, Inc., 1956), pp. 136–137.

succumb to inattention. Children find loneliness intolerable, and psychologists have observed that learning can actually be enhanced by association with others. A parent can tell whether his teen-age son or daughter has been driving the family car—the radio begins to play the moment the key is turned on; for youth is impatient with solitude, and the human voice, albeit on radio, is a welcome intrusion to loneliness.

It is a well-documented fact that many of the physical and mental illnesses of people are caused by social and emotional viruses and that social hungers bring clients to the office of marriage counselors and social workers. A key idea presented at the Conference on Educational Problems of Special Culture Groups, held at Teachers College, Columbia University, in September, 1949, was that "the human hunger to give and to receive love is insatiable. No one ever feels that he can love or be loved enough. Yet this root fact of human nature is seldom acknowledged or studied by psychologists." [2]

People not only need to be loved, they need to know that they are wanted and understood. A patient, about to be discharged from a mental hospital, voiced anxiety about leaving because the hospital had become "my home" and she was not sure that the future she faced in the community would be hospitable. In talking to the social worker, she found courage as she remembered that, "Mrs. Jones will be my neighbor. I can talk to her and she will understand." Anne Frank wrote in her diary, "A person can be lonely even if he is loved by many people, because he is still not the 'One and Only' to anyone." [3]

A patient who was a registered nurse living in a mental hospital, when greeted perfunctorily, "How are you?" stated with indignation, "I was invited to come to this hospital to head the nursing service!" This person, like any human being, had the need to feel important and the right to be indignant at so casual a greeting. The fear of being unloved and devalued exists in the mind of the psychotic and the neurotic along with yearning for intimacy and friendship. The behavior of delinquents, the handicapped, shut-ins, and many others is marked by social dysfunctioning, and failure.

Isolation may not be physical. Everyone knows he can be lonely in the midst of a crowd. Members of families, living under the same roof, sometimes become isolated one from another. No sense of loneliness is more painful than that which exists between friends and loved ones because they are unable to communicate. The poet, Matthew Arnold, captured this universal dilemma with the words: [4]

[2] Quoted in Gordon W. Allport, *Personality and Social Encounter* (Boston: Beacon Press, 1960), p. 199.

[3] Anne Frank, *Diary of a Young Girl* (Garden City, N.Y.: Doubleday and Company, Inc., 1952), p. 139.

[4] Frederick William Roe, ed., *Essays and Poems of Arnold* (New York, Harcourt, Brace & World, Inc., 1934), p. 411.

> Alas, is even Love too weak
> To unlock the heart and let it speak?
> Are even lovers powerless to reveal
> To one another what indeed they feel?
> I knew the mass of men conceal'd
> Their thoughts, for fear that if reveal'd
> They would by other men be met
> With blank indifference, or with blame reproved:
> I knew they lived and moved
> Trick'd in disguises, alien to the rest
> Of men, and alien to themselves—and yet
> There beats one heart in every human breast.

Human relations are blocked by many influences—physical disability, illness, racial prejudice and discrimination, religious intolerance, class superiority and preference, and others.

WHAT IS SOCIAL GROUP WORK?

Social group work is a method of working with people in groups (two or more people) for the enhancement of social functioning and for the achievement of socially desirable goals. Group work is based on the knowledge of people's needs for each other and their interdependence. Group work is a method of reducing or eliminating road blocks to social interaction and for accomplishing socially desirable purposes. Social group work, according to Konopka,[5]

is the method in social work which relates its helping function specifically to individuals in groups. Its goal is the creation of qualitative group life, differentiated according to the needs of the group it serves. The group worker always works in the actual, realistic context of interpersonal relations, whether he works with community groups or with clinical ones.

The group approach places strong emphasis on individualization in the group. The group worker realizes that a group frequently presents a total organism and that he has to work with this, but he also never loses—or he is not allowed to lose—focus on the importance of the individual.

Group work early recognized that there is not a dichotomy between individual and group, that individuals can reach their highest potential and feeling of self-worth by participation. Also that they can achieve security by a feeling of belonging to a meaningful group, and they take on responsibility toward others in and through those relationships. Group workers have realized the power of group associations, and they know that this power can also be disastrous; it can destroy and harm a person.

Konopka also explains that "group work is an approach consciously directed toward developing the individual's greatest capacity while relating him to the group and learning when he has to contribute and when he has to withdraw." [6]

[5] Gisela Konopka, "A Healthy Group Life—Social Group Work's Contribution to Mental Health," *Mental Hygiene*, Vol. 45 (July, 1961), pp. 330–331.

[6] Gisela Konopka, "Group Work: A Heritage and a Challenge," *Selected Papers in Social Work With Groups* (New York: National Association of Social Welfare, 1960), p. 8.

The social group worker uses his knowledge of group organization and functioning to affect the performance and adjustment of the individual. The individual remains the focus of concern and the group simply the vehicle of growth and change. Enhancement of social functioning through the use of the group is the primary aim of group work. Program and facilities are used as dynamics of interaction and change. Because of the importance of the individual in all group work, the worker equips himself with the knowledge of the individual. Thus, the student who specializes in social group work learns a great deal about the physical, social, mental, and spiritual forces which activate the individual. The group worker, as the caseworker, in preparation for professional practice obtains knowledge and develops scholarship in such sciences of man as physiology, psychology, and sociology as well as group dynamics and sciences which contribute understanding to group and individual behavior.

A generic social work curriculum serves in the preparation of group workers, caseworkers, and community organizers. For instance, the group worker must know individual behavior and be able to assess the capacities of the individual for group participation. It is not possible for every person to use and be helped by a group experience. There are those for whom group work is a disruptive if not a damaging experience, and others who cannot profit by the experience. The group worker, knowing individual behavior, can assess the needs of the group and plan meaningfully for it.

EARLY BEGINNINGS

Programs and services for groups have been in action as long as history has been recorded and before *professional* group work was known. In the United States the first YMCA was founded in Boston in 1851 followed shortly by the organization of the YWCA and the first Jewish Community Center in Baltimore in 1854. Adult education had its beginning in Lake Chautauqua, New York, in 1874, where one of the first organizations to develop group discussion techniques was formed, thus launching what the sociologist Badget called the "age of discussion."

The Settlement House movement began in America in 1886 with the establishment of the Neighborhood Guild, under the aegis of Stanton Coit and Charles Stover, in New York City. Both of these men had worked with Cannon Samuel Barnett and Arnold Toynbee in London where Toynbee Hall was created as the first Settlement House in 1884. Jane Addams established Hull House, the most famous of the Settlement Houses in the United States, in Chicago in 1889. In 1896, Boys Clubs of America had their beginning in Salem, Massachusetts. The turn of the century saw the development of such programs as 4H Clubs, the Boy Scout Movement, Girl Scouting, and Campfire Girls. Future Farmers of America was inaugurated in 1928 and the Catholic Youth Organization had its beginning in 1930.

As organizations were established, the need grew for trained people to administer their programs. The Community Organization Society launched the first program of training for social workers in the summer of 1898. By 1902 a one-year school of social work had been founded, and by 1963 this number had risen to fifty-six schools in the United States, twenty-seven of which offer group work specializations.

Traditionally, the knowledge and skill of group work was used in settlements by professional group workers. In recent years, group method has found its way into casework agencies and some caseworkers are now applying the skills and knowledge of group work to their programs. Moreover, group workers are being employed in treatment-centered agencies, such as hospitals and clinics formerly staffed only by caseworkers.

ACTIVITIES OF GROUP WORKERS [7]

In our society great numbers and varieties of groups exist. Groups are formed as a result of felt needs on the part of individuals for association and creative activities. They form and continue because of socially determined interests, which, when constructive in purpose, add enrichment to the lives of people. The social group worker uses his knowledge of the purposes served by groups in planning programs and in guiding group activities.

Group workers know that the creative power within people and their social interests can be awakened and put to the service of humanity by sound and intelligent use of program media—games, dances, dramatic arts, and crafts. Shy, reticent, withdrawn children may be recognized for the first time by their peer group because of their excellence of self-expression in planned work and play. A physically small or undeveloped youngster who is handicapped in athletics may make a solid impact in dramatics, where his particular size is a valuable asset. The aged learn useful activities to occupy their time in retirement and the group association provides opportunity for the sharing of ideas and social interaction.

Groups sharing a common purpose provide opportunity for intellectual stimulation and learning, recreation, diversion from burdensome tasks, and physical exercise. One such group organized in a YWCA

[7] Several of the following case glimpses and ideas on grouping and the application of group work to administration are adapted from mimeographed papers presented by Mr. Kenneth Griffiths, Assistant Professor of Group Work, University of Utah, at the Northwest Regional Conference, Child Welfare League of America, Spokane, Washington, May, 1962.

called themselves the "Young Mothers." These mothers learned that it was good mental health to bring their children to a well-staffed nursery to be cared for while they joined other young mothers in a morning swim, an hour of "slimnastics," a few hands of bridge, an arts and crafts program, listened to a special lecture on foods, fashions, child-rearing, or simply sat and talked to others who had similar worries, concerns, and problems with their young families. Their program usually included light refreshments or lunch, planned and arranged by their own committee. "Young Mothers" provided an outlet for social contacts and relieved the stress and strain of caring for the children born in rapid succession. One of the young mothers who was receiving Aid to Families with Dependent Children was helped by the group to make an adjustment to divorce. The group assisted her to find new purposes in life, to accept and enjoy her children rather than to see them as a burden. Before joining the group she was beginning to think there was nothing to look forward to but dirty dishes, soiled diapers, and runny noses. By talking to the other young mothers who were going through periods of adjustment not unlike she was experiencing, she drew strength and experience from them, and at the same time contributed her talents and understanding to the program.

Imagine a facility which consists of a workshop, a craft shop, a quilting room, a number of sewing machines, an auditorium for guest speakers, and a small kitchen where refreshments can be prepared. Think of the many possibilities of such a workshop for bringing elder citizens together during morning or afternoon hours, and the opportunities for these citizens to interact, to plan, to build, and to find purpose in the long days ahead. Perhaps it is the opportunity of making a bookcase for the nursing home, a small nightstand, a piece of leather work, or some soft toy to be donated to the children's hospital or orphanage. Maybe it is a chance to reminisce with someone with similar interests. But whatever they find to do, enlivens, revives interest, or even gives meaning to longevity.

A group worker, sensitive to the importance of activity, uses both activity and program to bring about improvement in living situations for people. For example, a group worker may use what he knows about group activity to improve a disturbed or difficult child-parent relationship. One mother noticed that her boy took a greater interest in his schoolwork and was much more responsive to the family after he became a member of a Boy Scout troop. What she did not realize fully was that her attitude about her son had changed and that this was a dynamic resulting in the improvement in his behavior. She could recall her tears at a Court of Honor when, recognized along with her boy, she said, "It is wonderful to have my boy do something good for once, rather than something for which he is always getting into trouble." The change in him was brought about because of his activity in the troop, guided and directed by the social group worker, and because for the first time he enjoyed his mother's approval and acceptance.

A group of adolescent girls formed a basketball team. One evening, in a discussion with their leader, they expressed their concern and misconceptions about menstruation, pregnancy, childbirth, and how to be lovable and affectionate in socially acceptable ways. This discussion led to new interests, and in subsequent meetings an hour each evening was set aside for talks by a public health nurse, an obstetrician, and other specialists who discussed their concerns about their maturing sex roles and gave them much needed information about being women. The second hour was still devoted to basketball; that is, on those nights when the girls had run out of questions on the topic of the evening.

Actually, there is much value in information. When individuals become wrapped up in unconscious motivations, insights, and interpretations, they overlook the here and now, the orientation to the present, and search for causes which are apparent and obvious if only they look for them. They search for hidden, unconscious motivations when actually all that is basically involved is sound education at the conscious level. A group of overweight adults wanted to reduce. The approach which proved effective in bringing lasting weight reduction for most members consisted of medical information, diet, and exercise, along with encouragement and support from group members and the leader. Similar results were obtained by an educational approach with cardiac patients in adhering to salt-free diets, exercise, and rest, and in accepting a medical regimen. The group also provided the means for diagnosing more serious emotional problems related to the physical difficulties, which were then approached in individual casework or in treatment groups.

One social work student, who worked in a public welfare department, developed a program for the mothers of dependent children which was primarily educational, and also therapeutic. Nutritionists and dieticians were called upon to help these mothers to make efficient and palatable use of surplus commodities. A home economist assisted them to budget their welfare checks. As the mothers saw value in the program and became free enough to raise questions with which they felt they needed aid, other specialists were invited to discuss fashion and design, child health, child discipline, vocational counseling, and other pertinent topics. Information from these meetings had value in helping these mothers to solve difficult, concrete problems. Such experiences are examples of the educational information-giving and sharing aspect of social group work.

APPLICATIONS OF GROUP WORK PROCESS IN ADMINISTRATION

Much administrative work is group related and oriented, and workers in staff meetings assigned to committees who work on boards of agencies and who engage in other kinds of community work make application of their knowledge of groups and group process. Group work knowledge and skill, democratically applied, provide a safeguard against autocratic control, sometimes exercised by administrative staff and policy-making bodies. Group work can be put to the service of the decision-making process by involving staff and eliminating the "rubber stamp" approach to administration. It can be the means of identifying committee assignments and expediting the work of an agency. Many experiences could be mentioned to describe administrative groups which reflect the use that can be made of group process for purposes of administration. There are both positive and negative activities in making the most effective use of groups.

Below are a few of the elements which are important in considering the development of administrative or task-oriented groups:

Functioning in an administrative group involves human relations. What happens to people determines how they feel about the organization and how they perform on their jobs. All staff must be involved in the administrative process and know how they can most effectively contribute to the decision-making process in administration.

The formation of a task group deserves the utmost consideration. Choices of group members must allow for various individuals to work together, and the choices should be made in such a way as to make maximum use of the capabilities of the staff. The person chosen should also know upon what basis of capability and strength he was chosen. This helps him to clearly perceive agency expectations and to know that the assignment was carefully thought out, not just another job dreamed up for him. Decisions on assignments should consider staff relationships which could be strained or negatively affect the ability of a group to seek and find solutions.

Involving and motivating staff around a certain topic calls for imagination. Recognizing that a problem exists and agreeing that time should be invested in outlining and discussing possible solutions is essential.

After some general consensus has been reached and the appropriate committee set up to approach the task, the group must quickly be brought to a clear goal and purpose.

An effective discussion leader is extremely important to the success or failure of the group in the accomplishment of an administrative task. Good leadership is a skill which few have intuitively, but which can be developed.

While the five areas discussed—human relations in administrative groups, the formation of administrative goals, consensus on problems by staff, appropriateness of goals and solutions, and effective discussion leadership—represent only a part of what could be said about the use of group process in administration, they do reflect important considerations which, if worked on conscientiously, result in greater effectiveness in attempts to translate social policy into services to people through the administrative group.

GUIDELINES FOR SOCIAL GROUP WORK

Kaiser [8] has compiled a list of principles of social group work which can be applied to individuals and to administration which are:

1. The function of the social group worker is a helping or enabling function: This means that his goal is to help the members of the group and the group as a whole to move toward greater independence and capacity for self-help.

2. In determining his way of helping, the group worker uses the scientific method: fact-finding (observation), analyzing, diagnosis in relation to the individual, the group and the social environment.

3. The group work method includes the worker forming purposeful relationships to group members and the group: This includes a conscious focusing on the needs of the members, on the purpose of the group as expressed by the members, as expected by the sponsoring agency and as implied in the members' behavior. It is differentiated from a casual unfocused relationship.

4. One of the main tools in achieving such a relationship is the conscious use of self. This includes self-knowledge and discipline in relationships without the loss of warmth and spontaneity.

5. There should be acceptance of people without accepting all their behavior: This involves the capacity for "empathy" as well as the incorporation of societal demands. It is the part of the method that is most closely intertwined with a high flexibility and abundance of warmth in the social group worker as well as identification with values and knowledge.

6. Starting where the group is: The capacity to let groups develop from their own point of departure, of capacity, without immediately imposing outside demands.

7. The constructive use of limitations: Limitations must be used judiciously in relation to individual and group needs and agency function. The forms will vary greatly. The group worker will mainly use himself, program materials, interaction of the group and awakening of insight in the group members.

8. Individualization: It is one of the specifics of the group work method that the individual is not lost in the whole, but that he is helped to feel as a unique person who can contribute to the whole.

9. Use of the interacting process: The capacity to help balance the group, to allow for conflict when necessary and to prevent it when harmful; the help given to the isolate not only through individual attention by the group worker alone but also by relating him to other members.

8 Clara A. Kaiser, "The Social Group Work Process," in Marjorie Murphy, *The Social Group Work Method in Social Work Education*, Curriculum Study, Vol. XI (New York: Council on Social Work Education, 1959), pp. 125–126.

10. The understanding and conscious use of nonverbal as well as verbal material: I especially put nonverbal material first, since the group worker deals to a large extent with this, especially in work with children. His capacity to use program materials, which do not demand verbal expression and yet are helpful, should be very wide.

SELECTION OF GROUP MEMBERS

How are individuals selected for groups? There has been much written on this subject, some controversial material, and some which has been generally accepted. Common threads run through the writings and in essence the following are a few of the factors and principles which guide group selection.

1. *Age.* Chronological age seems to be less important in the early age group than the maturity of the individual. However, in adolescence where age enjoys greater status and additional freedom privileges, it may be extremely important to strive for homogeneity of age in the group. With young adults and adult groups age seems much less important than other social or economic factors.

2. *Value System.* Some differences in value system can be tolerated and stimulate discussion in interaction. If the differences are too great, however, they may present problems. A group with more or less common values can work together, whereas a group with extremely diverse values can be expected to run into difficulty and to lose cohesion because of the differences. For example, in a group of girls whose members had been placed together to assist each other with an adjustment problem, some very destructive things occurred because the girls were physically attacking each other across a different value system.

3. *Common Problems.* Sometimes children who have common problems are grouped together. Children carry over from family groups to other groups their home relationship patterns which have previously met their needs. A child who has been allowed great freedom in the home in the overt expression of hostile feelings may present a real difficulty to the youngster who has been considerably curtailed in the expression of his feelings.

4. *Enjoyment Patterns.* Common interest, while not always of the greatest importance, can help to bring about groupness among individuals. Groups find a common interest in an activity. The base of interest can always be broadened and used to assist in better social adjustment in peer groups and in proper male and female identification.

5. *Intelligence.* Intellectual differences do not appear to be of prime importance, and yet where the extreme is great, difficulty may be encountered unless this factor is given consideration.

6. *Tolerance of Structure.* Sometimes groups do not congeal simply because the members of the group are not able to accept the structure

or the leader. Treatment does not take place when clients are not interacting or relating to one another. As one colleague expressed it, there
is nothing very therapeutic about sitting and listening to the "gastric
rumbles of the other members of the group." In other words, an important part of skill is to foster therapeutic relationships which will result in integration.

7. *Sex.* The sex of the members is less important in younger age
groups. However, coeducational groups have been quite successful in
working with certain problems of adolescence. Adolescents and adults
have been most successful when some work is done separately with each
sex group and then the groups are brought together to integrate what
has been considered separately. Marriage counselors, social workers in
schools, and those who work with parent groups and alcoholics, have
recognized in single sex groups a greater freedom for intimacy in the
discussion and greater support and encouragement around expression
of common problems.

8. *Ego Strengths.* There is almost unanimous agreement that group
members must have sufficient ego strengths to stand exposure, since
group reactions cannot be controlled in the same way individual work
is controlled.

Other variables might be considered but those touched upon briefly
here seem to be of the greatest importance and are more or less recognized by most workers in the field.

STAGES OF GROUP DEVELOPMENT

A group does not exist simply because it is a collection of individuals.
Actually, group workers in the field recognize four stages of development
into groupness, indicated as follows:

1. *Groping.* Every beginning group goes through a groping stage.
Members do not know what to expect or what is expected of them. The
first interviews tend to be tentative and the group wary, sometimes pro-
vocative, with members assuming relatively passive roles as they assess
possible threats. There may be some appearance of leadership as suggestions are made by more aggressive members of the group. In general,
however, members are somewhat anxious and fearful and are looking
to the leader at this point for reassurance and direction. The leaders
are always more active at this stage than in later stages.

2. *Griping.* We think of this as the role emergence phase, where members seek out roles which will meet their own needs and in which they
will be accepted by the other members. It is also referred to as the testing phase; that is, group members test one another to determine what
behavior is acceptable and yet avoid any serious breaches between other
members and themselves. More important, this is a period of testing

the leader and his acceptance of them as individuals. It is a period during which the leader must be most tolerant and patient, objective, and clear in thinking about his role. If he can anticipate this testing behavior he can help the group to move to the next stage without undue trauma for himself or the other members. The group must be used at this point to begin to control and limit the behavior of members, and the leader should be less active. This is also the stage that often needs interpretation to other agency people if the group's behavior is to be understood and accepted by them.

3. *Grasping*. The grasping stage is the one in which member and leader roles are quite clearly defined, and where close reflections of group identification appear. Members refer to "our club," and "our group," and "we will do this." Members relate to group purpose and assist one another to follow the acceptable patterns of behavior agreed upon by the group. More structure is apparent. There may be concern about designated leadership responsibility. While the leader may still need to assist in group focus and direction from time to time, this can mainly be done through a reflection upon past group decisions with which the group will then be able to deal.

4. *Grouping*. During this stage structure becomes codified and leadership roles more formal. The group spirit is high and the group takes almost complete responsibility for direction. It is at this point that treatment groups tend to become self-perpetuating social groups which serve entirely different purposes for group members from those for which the group was originally organized. This is the stage to which all aspire in working with groups, but one that takes great time, patience, and energy to attain.

SUMMARY

Everyone born into the world soon discovers social needs, interests, and imperatives basic to the individual's effort to survive. Social hungers are the common lot of mankind. People need association with other human beings, to be loved, to be wanted, and to have a sense of importance.

Group work, a primary method of social work, is based on the assumption that individuals have a need for each other. Personality enhancement and social functioning are tied to considerations which are related to the group. Group work is a method of working with the individual, of treating him, of helping him to adjust, of helping him to achieve his potential through the vehicle of the group, and of helping the group as a whole toward achievement of goals approved by society.

The group worker uses the knowledge of the individual and his group association to effect change, and uses program and various media such as crafts, games, and other creative activity to produce change within the individual.

Group work activity can bring about change and improvement in individuals which are conducive to greater self and group realization.

Group work is used advantageously in administration in the democratic tradition to effectuate administrative policy and in the accomplishing of their purposes by boards of directors, committees, agency staff, and other groups. The principles which characterize various kinds of human relationships apply to work with administrative groups. Setting up goals and purposes and using discussion as an effective tool are important considerations in the administrative aspects of social group work.

The principles of social group work include recognition of the fact that it is an enabling function based upon scientific knowledge and understanding. It is guided by such principles as the use of relationship, use of self, use of the agency, acceptance, starting where the group is, individualization, personal involvement and responsibility, and the use of verbal and nonverbal techniques for achieving communication. Principles of group selection lead to more effective results in working with groups.

Individuals who associate in groups progress in *groupness* through various developmental stages including groping, griping, grasping, and grouping.

QUESTIONS FOR DISCUSSION

1. Make a list of the groups with which you are personally identified.
2. What common needs are satisfied through your group association and membership?
3. What is the social group work method?
4. Compare and contrast social group work with social casework and community organization.
5. Describe an activity in which the group was a vehicle for the achievement of your purpose.
6. State a rationale for the use of group work principles as you understand them.
7. In forming a group, what would be the essential factors which you would take into consideration?
8. Explain the stages of group development.
9. What is the best size for a committee?

SPECIAL ACTIVITIES

1. Report on the activities of a group in which you now have membership. In your report indicate the achievement of purposes which required the group as a vehicle.

2. Invite a group worker in practice to sit on a panel which discusses the role and function of the social group worker in a community mental health program.

SELECTED REFERENCES

ABRAHAMSON, ARTHUR C., *Group Methods in Supervision and Staff Development* (New York: Harper & Row, Publishers, 1959).

BIEN, W. R., *Experiences in Groups* (New York: Basic Books, Inc., Publishers, 1961).

CARTWRIGHT, DARWIN and ZANDER, ALVIN, eds., *Group Dynamics: Research and Theory* (New York: Harper & Row, Publishers, 1960).

COYLE, GRACE L., *Group Experience and Democratic Values* (New York: The Woman's Press, 1947).

FRIEDLANDER, WALTER A., ed., *Concepts and Methods of Social Work* (Englewood Cliffs, N.J.: Prentice-Hall, Inc., 1958).

KONOPKA, GISELA, *Group Work in the Institution* (New York: William Morrow and Company, Inc., 1954).

———, *Social Group Work—A Helping Process* (Englewood Cliffs, N.J.: Prentice-Hall, Inc., 1963).

———, *Therapeutic Group Work With Children* (Minneapolis: University of Minnesota Press, 1949).

MURPHY, MARJORIE, *The Social Group Work Method in Social Work Education,* Curriculum Study, Vol. XI (New York: Council on Social Work Education, 1959).

PHILLIPS, HELEN, *Essentials of Social Group Work Skill* (New York: The Association Press, 1957).

TRECKER, HARLEIGH B., *Group Process in Administration* (New York: Woman's Press, 1950).

———, *Social Group Work* (New York: Association Press, 1955).

WILSON, GERTRUDE and RYLAND, GLADYS, *Social Group Work Practice* (Boston: Houghton Mifflin Company, 1959).

CHAPTER 16

Community Organization

Social workers are interested in individuals and families, but also in communities. In fact, many of the problems with which social workers are concerned involve the community as the client. Various sizes and kinds of communities have varying kinds of social ills. The social worker attempts to understand these social situations and to help the people to help themselves face the problems, understand them, and take appropriate action.

How does the social worker help communities? Community organization is one major answer. Casework has to do particularly with the individual-to-individual relationship. Group work utilizes the group as the tool for bringing about changes in personal and group living. Community organization is the method of working with the community as a totality.

Community organization, as mentioned in an earlier chapter, has three different connotations. In one sense it applies to a state or stage, meaning the degree or amount of organization, disorganization, or *unorganization*. Secondly, it is a field of practice, encompassing various agencies which focus on the total needs of the community. A third definition stresses community organization as a basic method or process, a way or manner in which changes can take place in the community constellation. The aim of this chapter is to explain the community organization method and how the social worker performs in facing and solving community problems.

Community organization as a method in social work is relatively new, at least as one of the accepted basic methods. It was only in 1939 that the first significant discussion about community organization as a process was held at a National Conference on Social Work. Since that time there have been many individuals and some committees working to define and describe this basic process. In 1959, the National Committee on Community Organization was asked by the National Association of Social Workers, Commission on Practice, to define community organization practice; and in 1962 it published its findings.[1] This report indicates that community organization as a *field of practice* and as a *method of social work* are different but that both are significant and evolving rapidly in this rapidly changing world.

Several graduate schools of social work now offer a major or sequence in community organization which helps in training capable individuals to accept positions of leadership in the community field. As far as opportunities are concerned, there is now great demand for persons who are educated in the use of the community organization method. Salaries in this field are among the highest in social work.

Community organization as a method is not unique to social work. There are other disciplines and fields—such as political science, education, and business—which utilize this basic approach toward solving problems. Nevertheless, community organization for social welfare is particularly important in the fast developing profession of social work.

UNDERLYING PRINCIPLES IN COMMUNITY ORGANIZATION

It is important to understand some of the underlying principles in community organization before looking at the specific processes involved. McNeil observes that there are several principles which seem universally applicable, as follows: [2]

1. Community organization for social welfare is concerned with people and their needs. Its objective is to enrich human life by bringing about and maintaining a progressively more effective adjustment between social welfare resources and social welfare needs.

2. The Community is the primary client in community organization for social welfare. The community may be a neighborhood, city, county, state or nation. Rapidly, too, there has emerged the international community. The factor of interdependence of people and groups living and working together becomes the source of problems with which community organization concerns itself and the force from which it derives the motivation and power necessary to bring about solutions to the problems.

3. It is an axiom in community organization that the community is to be understood and accepted as it is and where it is. Understanding the climate in

[1] *Defining Community Organization Practice* (New York: National Association of Social Workers, December, 1962).

[2] C. F. McNeil, "Community Organization for Social Welfare," *Social Work Year Book, 1954* (New York: American Association of Social Workers, 1954), p. 123.

which community organization process is taking place is essential if seeds of that process are to bear fruit. The professional worker in community organization for social welfare is no more concerned with changing the community's "personality" than is the social caseworker in altering the individual's basic personality structure. The focus in both areas is toward recognizing the inherent values in the personality and in enabling development to the fullest capacity. The full and constructive use of existing resources is indicated.

4. All of the people of the community are concerned in its health and welfare services. Representation of all interests and elements in the population and their full and meaningful participation are essential objectives in community organization.

5. The fact of ever-changing human needs and the reality of relationships between and among people and groups are the dynamics in the community organization process. Acceptance of the concept of purposeful change and John Dewey's philosophy of the "ever-enduring process of perfecting, maturing, refining" as goals in community organization is basic.

6. Interdependence of all threads in the social welfare fabric of organization is a fundamental truth. No single agency can usefully "live unto itself alone," but is constantly performing its functions in relation to others.

7. Community organization for social welfare as a process is a part of generic social work. Knowledge of its methods and skill in their application will enhance the potentialities for growth and development of any community effort to meet human needs. Professional education for the practice of community organization for social welfare can best be provided through schools of social work.

The Committee on Community Organization, National Association of Social Workers, concluded that the purposes and specific objectives of community organization may be summarized as follows: [3]

1. Providing the community or segments of the community with the opportunity to mobilize its resources to meet social problems or prevent their onset:
   a. Providing a means for *citizens* to mobilize, express, and discharge responsibility for community welfare.
   b. Providing an important means for the *social agencies* to discharge efficiently their responsibility to the community.
   c. Providing an important means for the *social work profession* to meet its community responsibilities.
2. Providing an important means of interaction between segments of the community:
   a. Between a variety of citizens and groups concerned with community welfare.
   b. Between specializations within the profession and between practitioners and community leadership.
   c. Between specializations and institutional forces such as the school system, the medical profession, the legal profession, etc.
   d. Between the political community and the social welfare community.
3. Providing social welfare planning service to the community through:
   a. Development of social welfare plans.
   b. Effecting these plans.

[3] *Defining Community Organization Practice, op. cit.,* pp. 8–9.

c. Influencing social welfare policies and other public policies related or having a potential influence upon the welfare of people.

d. Assisting in the mobilization of adequate financing, governmental and voluntary.

Another presentation which gives the underlying philosophy and approach in community organization is the statement presented in the Curriculum Study of the Council on Social Work Education. The position taken is that there are many underlying principles and attitudes shared in common with casework and group work, which are: [4]

1. The worth and dignity of the individual and faith in democratic processes.

2. The desirability of improving relationships among individuals, groups, organizations of people, neighborhoods and communities.

3. The right of the individuals, groups and communities to differ but still retain a responsibility for the well-being of others.

4. The ability of individuals, groups and communities to change.

5. The processes of interaction as an instrument to effect change.

6. The right of self-determination.

7. That the end result cannot be divorced from the means.

8. That in a democracy, participation of people from all walks of life is essential in reaching appropriate decisions.

9. That a worker's self-awareness is an integral part of his performance and accomplishment.

10. That an orderly process is essential and compatible with desirable change in value systems and social institutions.

These beliefs taken as a whole, we are convinced, extend beyond those held or practiced currently by many professional caseworkers and group workers but still embrace the basic beliefs of the two groups. We recognize the role of casework and group work, but believe it demands a larger perspective on the part of the community organization specialist.

COMMUNITY ORGANIZATION METHOD

Differences of opinion exist among social workers regarding the definition of community organization. In fact, some social workers talk about only one method in all of social work, the problem-solving method. These persons maintain that casework, group work, and community organization are processes which are components of a single basic method. Other social workers suggest that the word *method* and *process* may be used interchangeably, particularly in reference to the three mentioned already, casework, group work, and community organization. The authors approve of this second approach as a more practical one to use, at least in an introduction to social work. This means, then, that community organization is one of the basic methods of social work, one of the ways in which social changes may take place. It is one explanation of

[4] Harry L. Lurie, *The Community Organization Method in Social Work Education*, Curriculum Study, Vol. IV (New York: Council on Social Work Education, 1959), pp. 32–33.

how a social worker helps people to solve problems and enrich human living.

Looking at community organization practice as a whole, Carter has worked out, schematically, some of the identifiable elements in community organization practice, as we commonly observe it, and portrays many of the basic processes that are utilized. Her statement follows: [5]

COMMUNITY ORGANIZATION PRACTICE IN SOCIAL WELFARE

MEANS	ENDS
I. SOCIAL WORK COMMUNITY ORGANIZATION METHOD Generic elements of the three social work methods + Specialized elements of community organization	Change toward meeting health and welfare needs more adequately and more cooperative and effective means of accomplishing these goals
II. OTHER MEANS 1. *Facilitating Processes* Administration — board development, budgeting, policymaking, and so on Supervision—formal and informal Other coordinating techniques	To facilitate communication, coordination, develop appropriate structure, controls, channels, intra-agency, inter-agency, and intercommunity
2. *Educational Methods* Conferences, forums, workshops In-service training Interdisciplinary understandings and coordination Teaching, student field work Committee projects	Change in values, extend knowledge, gain understandings, professional improvement, informed citizen leadership, improved programs and service standards
3. *Research Methods* Research Systematic study Fact-gathering	To provide answers to questions posed, and to provide basis for decision-making and courses of action
4. *Social Action, Social Reform*	To effect changes in legislation, in social policy, and in community structure to meet social welfare needs
5. *Consultation*	Making knowledge, advice, experience available to others under their auspices and responsibility as they choose to use and implement
6. *Fund Raising* Recruiting and training leadership Developing campaign structure, methods, techniques Financial accounting to donor public	To provide money and leadership for health and welfare causes

[5] Genevieve W. Carter, "Social Work Community Organization Methods and Processes," in Walter A. Friedlander, *Concepts and Methods of Social Work*, © 1958. Prentice-Hall, Inc., Englewood Cliffs, N.J., p. 226.

7. *Publicity, Public Relations* Public information media, speeches, press, radio, TV	To develop the climate and under-standing necessary for community sup-port and interest in health and wel-fare programs
8. *Negotiation, Arbitration* Other strategy techniques	To effect strategic changes in com-munity or agency power structure to-ward improved health and welfare programs.

COMMUNITY ORGANIZATION SUBPROCESSES

Although there are various classifications regarding the processes uti-lized in the community organization method, those which are most com-monly discussed and utilized are next presented. These are the sub-processes of the community organization method in social work.

RESEARCH

Social research is the process of obtaining facts regarding social pheno-mena, social problems, and their solutions. Scientific research is regarded as basic to community organization. For example, a community rec-ognizes that it has a problem in juvenile delinquency. The newspa-pers report a sensational account of a young girl being attacked in a dark alley. What can the community do about it? What does it do about it? How much delinquency is there? Where are the areas of greatest delinquency? These and other questions can be answered by capable and properly trained individuals ferreting out the facts, studying the total situation. Scientific investigation is becoming more and more an important aspect of the community organization program. Some com-munity welfare councils, for example, have more than ten staff mem-bers working full-time on research.

Various research methods are utilized in community organization. Statistical studies, surveys, and case studies are used in particular. The underlying idea is that a community, to act wisely and fairly, must know what the realities are and what the facts do show. In one Eastern com-munity the newspapers described, somewhat sensationally, several com-munity problems in relation to dating among teen-agers. What could be done about it? A coordinating council was established with repre-sentation from most of the service clubs, PTA's, churches, schools, law enforcement groups, and other interested groups. After two meetings they decided that they needed to know more of the facts. They em-ployed a research analyst to interview several of the youth, some of the parents, and to find out facts in other ways. He then reported to the coordinating council. The report indicated that the problems were not nearly as severe as the newspapers had portrayed. Nevertheless, the coordinating council did not stop here. On the basis of the facts they had acquired, they organized active subcommittees. They invited teen-agers to become members of these committees, and before long parents and youth together worked out solutions which were acceptable all around. No longer did a serious community problem regarding dating exist.

PLANNING

Planning is purposeful formulation of future action and ways of pro-cedure. In community organization it is used extensively. It is usually carried out by representatives of various community groups meeting together and making decisions regarding social difficulties and their solutions.

In a Southern community a canal in an old dilapidated part of the city was wide open, with no fencing or protection. Several children had wandered to the banks of the canal, fallen in, and had drowned. What happened? Finally, enough parents and irate citizens voiced their opin-ions to the extent that the community welfare council studied this problem and appointed a subcommittee to see what might be done. This committee, composed of representatives from various professions and organizations, met many times and formulated plans for alleviating the problem. Through careful planning and other activities, they pro-posed to the city fathers that an allocation be made for fencing the dangerous areas. With support of the community welfare council, the press, radio, and TV, enough momentum was gathered so that soon the desired action was accomplished.

COORDINATION

Coordination is the process of working together to avoid unnecessary duplication, effort, and conflict. On the positive side, it is the joining of people, agencies, and forces to support and strengthen each other, making possible increased effective services which surpass what could be done unilaterally. This process is easily exemplified by federated drives for financing, such as those accomplished by united funds and com-munity chests. It is also illustrated by activities of community welfare councils which have as one of their basic aims the avoidance of un-necessary duplication of social services in a community as well as alle-viating service deficits.

Coordination is more than cooperation. Cooperation is a working together to accomplish a given end. It may be used either positively or negatively. For example, thieves may band together and cooperate to violate the laws of society. On the other hand, cooperation is usually utilized positively to bring about effective activities. Ordinarily, it involves a specific, single goal. Coordination generally encompasses a combination of goals and affects several people or groups. In community organization it means that various peoples and agencies in the community join hands to support each other, and help each to attain better individual and mutually-shared goals. This process is illustrated by the account of the young boy who came home one day and asked his mother to shorten his trousers. She said she was sorry she could not do it at that time. He then asked his grandmother for her assistance and her answer was about the same. He presented the same request to his sister who was likewise busy.

Shortly thereafter the mother became free, so she shortened the trousers. A little while later the grandmother was able to set aside some time so she shortened the trousers again. About an hour later the sister's "conscience caught up with her." She picked up the trousers and cuffed them for the third time. When the boy put on the pants, of course he was in trouble. They had all cooperated as best they could under the circumstances, but there had not been proper coordination. In community living many groups of people are travelling in several directions at the same time, and yet they wonder why communities are still disorganized and many social problems continue to exist. Coordination is an essential aspect of community organization.

In some communities there are agencies offering duplicate services, or conflicting services. They could provide more effective services if they were to consider themselves in relation to total community needs and then either join together or favor closer coordination of the various services which each performs.

Coordination is the process of letting all groups know what each is doing and dovetailing the services for the benefit of all. It also involves making cross referrals and giving support to other agencies.

ORGANIZATION

Organization is the subprocess of establishing a structure to accomplish certain goals. In community organization it is the method of formulating a structure to consider community needs, community resources, and the utilization of the resources to satisfy the needs. Various kinds of organizations exist in this area. United funds, community welfare councils, coordinating councils, social service exchanges, community information services, state conferences on social welfare, and national and international agencies are established to understand social problems and to help meet them. A formal organization usually gives sub-

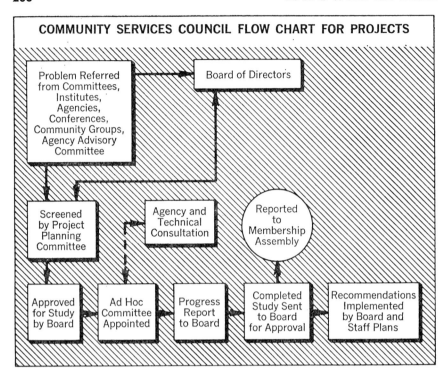

COMMUNITY SERVICES COUNCIL FLOW CHART FOR PROJECTS

Problem Referred from Committees, Institutes, Agencies, Conferences, Community Groups, Agency Advisory Committee

Board of Directors

Screened by Project Planning Committee

Agency and Technical Consultation

Reported to Membership Assembly

Approved for Study by Board

Ad Hoc Committee Appointed

Progress Report to Board

Completed Study Sent to Board for Approval

Recommendations Implemented by Board and Staff Plans

SOURCE: Provided by Community Services Council, Salt Lake Area, Eva Hancock, director, 1963.

stance to a movement. Without it, activities, even though some are significant, often take place on a hit-or-miss basis.

An example of an organization which is effective in relation to community problems is a state-formed association of citizens. It was organized to bring together representative individuals who become well acquainted with social problems in the state, study them, talk about them, and attempt to make specific recommendations to legislative bodies to do something about them. This association was organized as an action group. It has helped to bring about many worthwhile changes in its particular state. The organization has been a tool which has opened one avenue to accomplishing social goals.

FINANCING

Financing is the process of collecting, budgeting, and spending funds in relation to community needs and resources. Collection is usually carried out by a combination of professional persons and volunteers. Current United Fund drives are examples of this kind of activity. Millions of dollars are collected each year. Appeals are made to touch the heartstrings as well as the minds of people.

Most united funds, welfare councils, and other community organization bodies have committees on budgeting. These committees try to study the community needs and make proper allocations so that the total community welfare is best served. This is a most challenging aspect of community organization and requires dedication and careful thought and consideration.

The spending part of this process is done by the specific agencies, most of which have finance committees. These committees prepare budgets prior to fund drives and then work out detailed plans for the best use of the money that is available after the annual allocation has been received. Again, this process is a challenging one which requires careful consideration and planning. Frequently the trained social worker on the staff can be most helpful in assisting the finance committee to work out a fair and appropriate budget, with specific listings of expenditures.

ADMINISTRATION

Kidneigh states that social work administration can be defined as the "process of transforming social policy into social services." [6] It is the process of carrying out plans, implementing the actions upon which decisions have been reached. It is a particularly important process in community organization.

Effective administration includes all the staff, not only the executive, but the janitor, the assistant secretary, and the board. Where all staff members are a part of the total venture and make suggestions and contributions to the total effort, the best results ensue.

CONSULTATION

Consultation is the process of an expert talking with other workers. It is the acquiring of professional information and advice from a person in a particular discipline, whose information can be helpful to qualified persons in other disciplines. A popular example of consultation in many social agencies today involves the psychiatrist who is often invited to meet with staff and to share his opinions and knowledge, particularly regarding the intrapsychic dynamics of particular cases. On the community level consultation often involves sociologists, psychologists, political scientists, public relations experts, and others who have appropriate knowledge and skills related to community problems and their solutions.

[6] Harleigh B. Trecker, Frank Z. Glick, and John C. Kidneigh, *Education for Social Work Administration* (New York: American Association of Social Workers, 1952), p. 8.

Social workers, and community organizers in particular, are frequently asked to act as consultants to other professional persons and groups. In fact, more and more of those with a Master's degree in social work are finding that their daily work involves consultation.

EDUCATIONAL PROCESS

The educational process is one of increasing group and community knowledge about social problems and possible actions regarding them. It involves obtaining unity of thinking among a given group, working out plans for action, hopefully on a democratic basis, and mobilization of community resources in obtaining the desired action.

In thinking of the educational process, it is important to keep in mind that not only facts and knowledge are important, but even more vital in many ways are the feelings which the people involved possess. Community organization workers, in particular, try to help people in the community to understand the problems and to feel toward them in a positive manner. Action results especially when feelings are congruent with the thoughts and rational plans.

COMMITTEE OPERATION

Committee operation is the essence of community organization practice. Through committees most of the planning and action takes place. Through committees decisions are made. Through committees ideas and feelings are brought into the open, making it possible for appropriate action to follow.

The community organization process is effective when committees function on a democratic basis; otherwise complications arise. For adequate committee operation there needs to be adequate representation for all of the groups which may be interested and involved in relation to a particular project. Committees do most of the planning for community action. Ordinarily it is best for committees to be small, otherwise they bog down and become ineffective. Experts in the field recognize that it is difficult for a group of more than ten to fifteen to work together effectively. Usually even smaller groups are better.

Committee members should be selected for their interest in a given problem, for their knowledge and abilities to help with a problem, and for their willingness to use their time and talents in working on the problem to bring about appropriate action. Ordinarily, it is not best to pressure people into accepting committee assignments; rather it is more effective to stress that it is an honor to serve on the committee and that their services are needed for important tasks ahead.

NEGOTIATION

Negotiation is the process of resolving conflicts, often with a neutral, third party acting as an intermediary. As individuals and groups meet together to consider problems, needs, or resources, invariably differences of opinion and feeling arise. This is normal and usually desirable. Negotiation is the process of sharing these differences, talking them over, working them through, and coming to some kind of solution or compromise acceptable to all. Compromise, not in basic principle but in procedure, is an essential element of the community organization process.

RECORDING

Recording is the process of keeping a permanent account of the considerations and actions of committees and other groups concerned with community problems and actions. Most recording is done by writing or by using tapes. If some kind of record is not kept, it becomes almost impossible to maintain continuity across a period of time, bearing in mind that committee members change as well as the situations. A record of committee action can be invaluable as a reminder of thinking and plans of the past and as a tool for opening the door for appropriate action in the present and the future.

COMMUNITY ORGANIZATION TECHNIQUES

The Committee on Community Organization of the National Association of Social Workers observed that, "method in community organization practice is the orderly application of a relevant body of knowledge guided by social work values. The worker applies systematically and sequentially this coherent body of knowledge employing practice-wisdom and learned behavior through characteristic, distinctive and describable procedures to help the community engage in a process of planned change toward community improvement." [7]

The Committee also described the range of professional roles of the community organization worker with examples of the following: [8]

(1) *enabling* the community to engage in establishing goals and setting priorities;
(2) *helping* community groups take effective action;
(3) *guiding* the participants in the process through difficulties;
(4) *initiating* action through education, demonstration, or other similar techniques.

[7] *Defining Community Organization Practice, op. cit.,* p. 15.
[8] *Ibid.*

"Techniques," according to the NASW Committee on Community Organization, "are considered as subparts of method—the specific ways in which the worker applies his method in specific settings. More properly, they may be thought of as ways in which method *has been* applied in practice, since new techniques are constantly being devised or altered to meet new situations under different circumstances and in different locations." [9]

The Committee defined and described briefly several of the specific techniques needed in community organization, as follows: [10]

1. Structuring
2. Social Action
3. Management
4. Formal Study
5. Expert Consultation
6. Education and Promotion
7. Demonstration
8. Preparation for Plans

QUALIFICATIONS OF COMMUNITY ORGANIZATION WORKERS

In addition to a presentation of the principles, subprocesses, and techniques, another way to describe community organization practice and method is to name some of the desirable characteristics of persons who practice in this field.

Barry suggests the following ten *abilities* as a starter for desirable attributes of those engaged in community organization.[11]

1. Ability to relate to people and to facilitate positive relationships among individuals and groups.

2. Ability to analyze a problem and see its potentials (including its difficulties, relation to scheme of things, possibilities of solution).

3. Ability to locate and utilize resources effectively (including human resources, studies, observations, and so on).

4. Ability to organize effective structure, such as a committee, and help it function.

5. Ability to understand and accept the reality of the situation and yet to see the potential for change.

6. Ability to handle oneself professionally, in many different roles, with various types of people, and to handle criticism and praise.

7. Ability to organize one's job, to work under pressures, to establish priorities in terms of time, intensiveness, and so on.

8. Ability to relate and differentiate the various situations within one's own job and, likewise, within the agency and the community.

9. Ability to fulfill and facilitate the agency's purposes and function and thus

9 *Ibid.*, p. 19.
10 *Ibid.*, pp. 19–20.
11 Mildred C. Barry, "Field Work Training in Community Organization," in Harry L. Lurie, *op. cit.*, pp. 82–83.

to perform skills necessary to the task (such as public relations, fact finding, budgeting, administration).

10. Ability and capacity to use knowledge, to apply theory to practice in an integrated way.

CASE GLIMPSE

Current action in community organization is illustrated by the case summary which follows: [12]

OLDER CITIZENS' CENTER

Concern for problems of and services for older citizens prompted the Community Services Council, Salt Lake Area, to appoint a representative committee on aging in 1960 to consider what needed to be done in the community. Based on a study of need made by the Department of Sociology of the University of Utah and information from other communities, the Committee surveyed the community resources and existing programs for senior citizens. These responses indicated that many organizations and agencies were interested and that several had projects underway. However, the survey results revealed that for the most part, these activities were fragmentary in nature and sorely in need of coordination and direction with respect to the overall needs of older persons in the community.

In developing its plan, the Committee agreed that it would be most effective if the various programs were developed one by one, as resources and support became available. Several factors contributed to the selection of leisure-time services as the first area of focus by the Committee. These included, (1) the recognition that leisure-time activities represented a major need of older persons, (2) the need for a focal point around which a number of activities might be supplied, (3) the lack of a coordinated leisure-time program, and, (4) identification of the inadequacies of facilities and program in the largest recreation program in the County, the County Recreation Department.

The Committee involved others in its next steps. Census material was studied. Program experience was sought from other communities. A visit was made to the Los Angeles area to see developments first hand. Out of this investigation came the recommendation for a new facility in a central location. The story of need was presented to the County Commissioners, who agreed to erect the building if the City would supply the land. The City Commission asked the Committee to recommend a location and considerable effort was expended in listing possible spots and an ideal location. Finally, after some disagreement in the community, the location was agreed upon and the building program set into motion. Result is that a new Senior Citizens Center has become a reality.

SUMMARY

Community organization is one of the three basic methods of social work. It is the intergroup process which attempts to help communities

[12] Prepared by Eva Hancock, Executive Director, Community Services Council, Salt Lake Area.

to understand social problems which exist, and to utilize community resources which are available to bring about solutions which will strengthen the total community and enrich the lives of its members.

Community organization is one of the newer methods of social work and one which has great potential for preventing and solving social problems.

Many of the principles basic to community organization are shared with casework and group work, but there are several that are unique.

The basic subprocesses in community organization are research, planning, coordination, organization, financing, administration, consultation, educational process, committee operation, negotiation, and recording.

QUESTIONS FOR DISCUSSION

1. What is meant by community organization as a process?
2. Give an example of the effective use of community organization.
3. Discuss research as an important part of the community organization method. Give an example.
4. Differentiate between cooperation and coordination in relation to community problems.
5. What are the three aspects of financing? Illustrate.
6. How might consultation be used advantageously in community affairs?
7. Give an example of the educational process related to a current community social problem.
8. List ten suggestions for effective committee operation.
9. Evaluate the ten abilities mentioned in your chapter for community organization workers.

SPECIAL ACTIVITIES

1. Arrange for a student panel to discuss the different roles of the community organizer.
2. Invite three practicing social workers (a caseworker, a group worker, and a community organizer) to present a panel on comparisons and contrasts among casework, group work, and community organization.

SELECTED REFERENCES

BARTLETT, HARRIETT M., "Toward Clarification and Improvement of Social Work Practice," Social Work, Vol. 3 (April, 1958), pp. 3–9.

Defining Community Organization Practice (New York: National Association of Social Workers, December, 1962).

DUNHAM, ARTHUR, Community Welfare Organization: Principles and Practice (New York: Thomas Y. Crowell Company, 1958).

FRIEDLANDER, WALTER A., ed., Concepts and Methods of Social Work (Englewood Cliffs, N.J.: Prentice-Hall, Inc., 1958).

LURIE, HARRY L., The Community Organization Method in Social Work Education, Curriculum Study, Vol. IV (New York: Council on Social Work Education, 1959).

MURPHY, CAMPBELL G., *Community Organization Practice* (Boston: Houghton Mifflin Company, 1954).

NEBO, JOHN C., "The School Social Worker As Community Organizer," *Social Work*, Vol. 8 (January, 1963), pp. 99–105.

ROSS, MURRAY G., *Community Organization, Theory and Principles* (New York: Harper & Row, Publishers, 1955).

CHAPTER 17

The Enabling Processes

Methodology in social work encompasses the three main processes of social casework, social group work, and community organization. However, several other processes are utilized often by social workers and are important in the total social work venture. These are administration, supervision, consultation, collaboration, social action, and research. Each will be considered briefly in this chapter.

ADMINISTRATION

Some social work educators advocate that the administrative process is the very heart of social work education and practice. Consequently two graduate schools of social work are named Graduate Schools of Social Service Administration, the University of Chicago, and Arizona State University.

Administration is one of the major aspects of social work practice. Certainly every agency program requires an able administrator in order to be effective.

The demand for trained workers for administrative positions is definitely on the increase. Salary-wise, many extremely attractive opportunities exist for social work administrators.

Historically, administration has been utilized through the centuries, but has not been recognized in a formal way as it is today. More than 2,500 years ago a poem, written by Laotse in the *Book of Tao*, illustrated goals for leaders:

A leader is best
When people barely know that he exists . . .
But of a good leader, who talks little,
When his work is done, his aim fulfilled,
They will say, "We did this ourselves."

At the meeting of the Council on Social Work Education in Detroit in 1958, a study was reported which indicated that only 1 percent of full-time students in graduate schools of social work in 1957 were majoring in administration; yet 54 percent of the men suggested that within ten years they hoped to be in administrative positions. In 1960 about one-third of all social welfare workers in practice in the United State were performing as administrators, either as supervisors or executives.

DEFINITION

A popular definition is the one by Kidneigh which states that social work administration is "the process of transforming social policy into social services . . . a two-way process: (1) . . . transforming policy into concrete social services, and (2) the use of experience in recommending modification of policy." [1] This definition, of course, encompasses the idea that administration is the process of implementation, of translating policies into action programs.

Dunham explains that administration is the process of "supporting or facilitating activities which are necessary and incidental to the giving of direct service by a social agency. Administrative activities range from the determination of function and policies, and executive leadership to routine operations such as keeping records and accounts and carrying on maintenance services." [2]

Kruse, in the 1960 *Social Work Year Book,* states that "the administrative process seeks to mobilize the total resources of the agency to the end that its purposes are translated into efficient and effective service." [3]

The Curriculum Study of the Council on Social Work Education gives the following summary definition: [4]

Administration in social work is the process of transforming community resources into a program of community service, in accordance with goals, policies and standards which have been agreed upon by those involved in the enterprise. It is creative in that it structures roles and relationships in such a way as to alter and enhance the total product. It involves the problem-solving processes

[1] John C. Kidneigh, "Social Work Administration, An Area of Social Work Practice?" *Social Work Journal,* Vol. 31 (April, 1950), p. 58.

[2] Arthur Dunham, *Community Welfare Organization: Principles and Practice* (New York: Thomas Y. Crowell Company, 1958), p. 42.

[3] Arthur Kruse, "Administration of Social Welfare Agencies," *Social Work Year Book, 1960* (New York: National Association of Social Workers, 1960), p. 83.

[4] Sue Spencer, *The Administration Method in Social Work Education,* Curriculum Study, Vol. III (New York: Council on Social Work Education, 1959), p. 32.

of study, diagnosis and treatment (or solution, or action, and evaluation of results).

That administration is relatively new is illustrated by the fact that it was only in 1946 that the National Conference on Social Work sponsored a section on administration, for the first time in its seventy-two years. This program included consideration of the following: process of administration, dynamics of leadership, salaries, job classification, boards, public relations, organized labor, civil service, program development, and retirement planning.

In the early days of social work, administration was not thought of as distinct from direction of services and functions. By 1914 a course in administration was established in at least one school of social work and the content was borrowed mainly from adjoining fields.[5] World War I, the Great Depression, and World War II—with their numerous problems and tensions—gave considerable focus and emphasis to interest in the administrative process. Technical literature began to appear. For a while the Cooperative Committee on Administration was in operation. Further interest in administration was developed through a special department in the magazine, *The Survey,* and through the activities of leaders in the YWCA, YMCA, and Family Welfare Association of America whose organizations were beginning to set standards for their administrators. In 1944 the Curriculum Committee of American Association of Schools of Social Work included social welfare administration as one of the *Basic Eight* for training students.

BASIC ASSUMPTIONS AND PRINCIPLES

One of the basic principles in administration is that all levels of staff participate in the administrative process. This includes executives, sub-executives, supervisors, consultants, caseworkers, group workers, community organizers, secretaries, attendants, and others. Traditionally, people have thought of administration only as involving those at the helm, the directors or the executives. Today, if we are to be realistic, it is essential to recognize that all staff members are involved, directly or indirectly, in the administrative process. It is also apparent that some of the major contributions toward improving administration come from persons in the lesser status categories of staff.

Spencer, in the *Curriculum Study,* suggests there are several underlying assumptions which should be kept in mind in relation to administration. These are summarized as follows: [6]

1. Administration of social agencies is the process of securing and transforming community resources (human and financial) into a program of com-

[5] Arthur Dunham, "Administration of Social Agencies," *Social Work Year Book, 1947* (New York: Russell Sage Foundation, 1947), p. 20.

[6] Spencer, *op. cit.,* pp. 26–32.

munity service. This process involves active participation of the board, executive, staff, and volunteers or constituency in varying degrees.

2. Administration in social work is concerned in a major way with enterprise determination which includes goal formation. This means that the agency itself has the primary responsibility for the creation and control of its own destiny and community planning bodies exercise only a secondary role.

3. Administration in social work is concerned with "provisioning" the service. It has to do with the logistics of the program and activities of the particular agency.

4. The executive is not a neutral agent. This means that creative leadership is needed in all phases of the agency's operation.

5. The executive's functions within the agency combine the following: a. To provide a seeing-the-enterprise-as-a-whole quality. b. To participate in a leadership capacity and policy formulation. c. To delegate, coordinate, and control the work of others to promote and enhance the work of board and staff. d. To provide for board, staff, and community an executive who represents in his personal attitudes, abilities, and activities a person with whom they can identify positively.

6. Administration is involved with the creative use of human resources— board, staff, and volunteer. The social agency is a group enterprise.

7. The parts of the enterprise are interrelated and interacting. This principle is basic to the operation of a social agency and means that a part of the executive function is to establish roles, relationships, rules, and regulations which will produce the optimum of good effects and the minimum of bad effects.

8. What one does not do has effects as well as what one does do.

SUPERVISION

A young agronomist, upon taking his first job in a rural mid-western farming community, scheduled a talk, "New Frontiers for American Agriculture." Puzzled and disappointed when only two farmers came to the lecture, he asked, "Where is every one?" The reply, "The farmers around here know more than they use, they want someone to show them how to use what they already know."

Supervision,[7] one of the main enabling processes, is concerned with helping staff to *use* their knowledge and skill in getting the job done efficiently and well. In the etiological sense the word supervision means "oversight, control, surveillance." In social work it is more commonly used to define the function which one individual, the supervisor, assumes in relation to another, the supervisee. Supervision has been defined by Towle as "an administrative process which has as one of its purposes to contribute to staff development." [8] Towle [9] further explains that staff members responsible for the work of other staff have the obligation of

[7] Some of the ideas on supervision, consultation, and collaboration have been worked out by the authors and Katharin den Bleyker, formerly Assistant Professor of Social Work, University of Utah, and presently at Michigan State University.

[8] Charlotte Towle, *Common Human Needs* (New York: National Association of Social Workers, 1957), p. 95.

[9] *Ibid.*

giving leadership which results in the development of worker competence. The agency will function with the optimum of efficiency, conserving human values in work with clients, when the staff responsible for the operation of the agency is qualified, and when its capacity to render service is aided by effective agency policy and procedures which emphasize the preeminence of the worker in the helping process. Supervision focuses upon the acquisition and use of knowledge and the application of skills to practice. It is a teaching-learning situation, educational as well as administrative.

Supervision has also been described as "a highly specialized practice in which a person of skill and administrative responsibility must accept and carry the standard of practice for the agency, with which she must necessarily be deeply identified, through teaching the workers in her charge the agency's concepts of its place in the community's social structure, and through helping them individually to approximate the standard of practice at the highest level of their ability." [10]

In the public and private welfare agency the position of supervisor enjoys status and respect. The qualified and competent supervisor is a key person in a staff organization who has responsibility for both administration of services and staff development.

Supervision in social work is a response to the needs of clients and the mandate of the community to relieve suffering and to restore people to greater usefulness. Social problems are always a challenge and decisions aimed at relieving stress and rehabilitation are among the most difficult on the spectrum of human experience. The supervisor's role is one of support, encouragement, the imparting of information, and of listening to the worker, particularly to the new and inexperienced staff. Supervisors point out knowledge gaps and deficiencies in skill and assist workers to control their biases. They give psychological support by allaying anxiety and by their interest and understanding; they are professional models for new workers and a bridge to the agency for the experienced worker new to the particular job or agency.

SUPERVISION IS TEACHING

Supervision is essentially a teaching job. It is not casework. It is not psychotherapy. Its fund of knowledge and its techniques are more nearly related to education than to treatment, although the dividing line between the two is not always sharp. Since supervision is teaching, its theory is derived from education as well as social work. Some of the most important educational principles which provide underpinning for supervision are mentioned in the ensuing paragraphs.

[10] Dorothy Bird Daly, "Supervision of the Newly Employed Experienced Worker," *The Family,* Vol. 27 (June, 1946), p. 148.

The supervisee participates actively in his own learning. He is involved in the planning for his function in the agency and not a receptacle of a "ready-made, hand-me-down plan" devised by someone else. He must think through and make decisions relative to clients, which he will implement in his interviews and social study. Supervision is based on the assumption that the worker learns best when he takes responsibility for his learning. Hence, the supervisor resists the temptation, however great, to impose his standards, values, and methods of helping. He encourages, gives information, and even offers advice, but will not preempt the learning role.

The assumption is that the worker learns by doing. The worker must be given the opportunity to carry responsibility for the work performed in the agency, which is service to the public. His mistakes will be stepping-stones to higher levels of achievement, and will be used by the supervisor to call the learner's attention to better ways of doing things.

We learn by doing, in part through identification. A worker, however, may be driven by fear to identify with his supervisor and to accept that which is imposed from without. When this occurs, learning may not be integrated, only falsely imitated, used ambivalently, and later rejected.

The worker learns by using his whole self. Learning is more than an intellectual exercise. It involves the integration of feelings, intellect, and performance. Frequently, learning fails to take place because of a worker's excessive anxiety which often results in stereotyped behavior, excessive dependency, passivity, submission, and intellectualization. A friendly working atmosphere and acceptance of a supporting relationship with one's supervisor are safeguards to performance and a protection against immobilizing anxieties. Feeling and intellect are one in learning in social work.

The worker-supervisor relationship is the main dynamic in learning. It is predicated on the greater knowledge and skill of the supervisor, his regard for the worker, his willingness to share, and on the capacities and desires of the worker. Positive learning takes place through a positive relationship. When the relationship is negative and destructive, learning is resisted or occurs under conditions inimical to good practice. The relationship can be facilitated by the supervisor who has confidence in the worker, who believes in the worker's capacity and worth. He builds on the worker's strengths and emphasizes those qualities which make for competence and efficiency on the job. He freely acknowledges the superiority of the worker in those situations where it is demonstrated. Honesty and integrity must characterize the relationship if the purpose of the agency is to be served.

Learning is inhibited when the supervisor is inaccessible. The supervisor who is overprotective, who has the need to take over and do the work required by the worker, cancels the learner's efforts. Fear of the supervisory authority may also block learning.

TECHNIQUES OF SUPERVISION

Records are kept of supervisory conferences. These are used for teaching purposes and to point up areas of need in the armamentarium of the worker. Evaluations also are used as tools. These are dynamic, continuous, and are discussed freely in worker-supervisory conferences which are regularly scheduled.

Evaluation conferences at times reveal fear on the part of the worker of his ability to control the situation, a loss of self-esteem, a threat to the worker's self-image, and fear of punishment. Evaluations, too, become sources of satisfaction when used to realistically appraise and assess the performance of the worker by his superior.

The supervisor, too, has feelings about evaluations. His lack of self-confidence and a desire to be liked may lead him to cover up the worker's weaknesses and inadequacies. To avoid supervisory conferences too charged with feeling he keeps in mind that the evaluation is a means of promoting the student's learning and self-awareness and a process in which the supervisor and the worker both participate.

The subject matter of evaluation is the worker's feelings about people, his method of handling feelings, understanding of behavior in social situations, as well as his ability to express himself. He will be helped to relate to the client's needs and to the *what* and *how* of resources, and will be taught to participate in the agency's program for staff development—institutes, classes, workshops, and regularly scheduled staff meetings.

Basic to successful supervision are enabling qualities of personality that make it possible for the worker and for the supervisor to be essentially giving persons. Supervisors need to bring to their jobs a readiness to live beyond themselves and a concern for people. Giving and a regard for people combined with a mind trained and disciplined in the science and art of supervision, make supervision a constructive and dynamic force in the life of the learner, enabling him to meet his obligations to the client and the agency.

CONSULTATION

Consultation is the means by which agencies are able to extend and improve their services to clients. One administrator has defined consultation as a "private, confidential interaction between *two professional persons* who *combine* their respective competencies in an attempt to define, explore, and outline solutions to some *job-related problem* so that the consultee can eventually choose and use a solution that fits his personal abilities and his professional role." [11]

11 William G. Hollister, "Some Administrative Aspects of Consultation" (Berkeley: School of Social Welfare, University of California, 1962), p. 2; mimeographed.

As a process, consultation is "rapidly emerging as the major technic for extending caretaker services. This method provides for the conveying of specialized help and technical information that can be applied by a variety of personnel to the handling of social problems. Social workers with training in this method have been successful in aiding nurses, doctors, ministers, lawyers, and other professional persons become more knowledgeable individuals, thus making available a greater volume of service to troubled individuals and families." [12]

Consultation is not the province of any one discipline. The knowledge, skill, and the scientific base it rests upon is that of the professional discipline of the consultant. Social work consultants derive their competence from social work and similarly other professions from their disciplines. Consultation is not ordinarily taught or learned as such. Curricula of schools of social work are limited in their offerings on consultation, and consultation today is about where casework was forty years ago.

Consultation is not supervision or psychotherapy. Supervision carries administrative responsibility for services to clients, to teach, to evaluate, to help the worker grow. Psychotherapy is patient-centered and directly concerned with the needs of clients.

Consultation is predicated on three main assumptions:

1. That the consultant has a greater knowledge than the consultee in the areas of agency and worker needs, which can be communicated to the consultee in usable form.

2. That the consultant can help the consultee to improve upon the use of his skills, or to acquire new ones for the better performance of his job.

3. That the consultee can use the process to enhance his caretaking function by clarifying his thinking, elaborating his own ideas, and defining treatment goals and purposes. Consultation may result in the confirmation of the soundness of what the consultee is doing and identify gaps and weaknesses in his efforts. Psychological support, selective testing of the worker's thinking, and the results of creative interaction of professional people when goal-focused are important products of the consultation process.

PRINCIPLES OF CONSULTATION

The consultant organizes and arranges his knowledge and skill for a specific consultation purpose, namely, that of helping someone else to do the job which he or she is hired to do, and to do it better.

Consultation is a helping process which involves the use of technical knowledge and a professional relationship with one or more persons.

---

[12] Esther C. Spencer, Lecture presented at the Utah Conference on Social Welfare, Salt Lake City, November 1, 1961.

This is a relationship of mutual respect and confidence which the consultant develops, enhances, and maintains by the employment of sound principles of social work. These include beginning where the client is, the use of a nonjudgmental approach, emotional support, acceptance, defining the situation, role clarification, and confidentiality.

Essentially, the consultant has a conviction that the consultee can do the job he is assigned to do. The egocentric person who attaches a magic quality to his own self fails in consultation for the reason that the consultant must be an enabler of others. The consultant does not evaluate or make judgments about the work of the consultee. Promotions, raises in salary, and advancements are administrative matters and are handled in other ways compatible with the job to be done.

The consultant-consultee role is task-oriented and is concerned with only certain aspects of the consultee's function. The consultant helps with problems experienced by the consultee, although he may recognize that the main problem is something other than that for which help is requested. In the process of clarification the consultant may assist the consultee to encompass the broader, more vital elements of the problem. Unless this is done, however, no shift is made in the area identified by the consultee. Again, consultation is not supervision nor is it psychotherapy. "Sometimes insidiously a consultant is lured into supervisory, training, counseling or administrative functions because of the halo of expertness projected upon him. . . .

"The administrator needs to consider carefully how he himself uses the consultant so that he does not surreptitiously begin to employ the consultant in agency decision making, leadership and action roles. The administrator can also prevent some of the bids for the consultant to provide psychotherapy by setting up separate counseling and health programs for his personnel, including opportunities for confidential psychiatric help outside the job setting." [13]

The consultee must be free to accept or reject the services of the consultant. The consultant never carries the force of administration and the consultation role is destroyed when the consultant tries to prescribe the use that will be made by the consultee of the service offered. The confidentiality of communication between the consultant and the consultee is the cornerstone of consultation. Consultation is facilitated when the worker's relationship with the consultant is one of trust, and when he knows that the consultant does not evaluate personnel or report his conversations to administration.

The heavily laden consultee, burdened by the pressures of his job, responds to the emotional support that comes from intelligent listening and understanding of his problems. He will use the consultant's sug-

[13] Hollister, *op. cit.,* p. 5.

gestions as to how to handle the problem and advice, and is free to accept or reject the help offered.

It has been generally observed that a crisis in life can serve as an impetus toward getting things done. Crises may mobilize individuals, families, and even larger groups to more thoughtful, creative behavior, and to action which may lead to constructive change and progress. Thinking behavior can be the product of crises.

Major and minor crises occur in the lives of all people and the staffs of social agencies are often confronted with crises in the lives of their clients. Sometimes workers, unaided, are powerless to give effective help in a crisis; but it is a known fact that a crisis can motivate the worker to seek and use the help of a consultant. Sometimes the inadequacies of the worker result from feelings of helplessness stemming from the magnitude of the task to be accomplished, and sometimes because of gaps in training or lack of preparation and experience. Regardless of the reality, when a need exists the worker who can mobilize himself to array the various forces at his disposal to meet the demands of the situation, according to Caplan, is particularly favorable at that moment for consultation: [14]

. . . the more intense the crisis, the more powerful the force involved, the better chance you have of a satisfactory consultation. . . .

Increasing experience confirms over and over again the importance of a crisis and its consequent emotional disequilibrium in preparing the consultee to benefit from consultation. When his psychic equilibrium has been disturbed by stimulation of unsolved or precariously solved emotional conflicts by having to deal with similar problems in his client, he enters a state in which he can be drastically affected in a short time by apparently minor manipulations of the consultant. Similar techniques applied at other times when his emotional life is in a stable equilibrium have very little effect.

Social agencies and their workers have long recognized the benefits resulting from the contributions of psychiatrists, psychologists, anthropologists, sociologists, and others who have been retained by agencies in consultant capacities. Social workers confronted with difficult and perplexing social and personal situations have been among the first to recognize and to use the knowledge of the specialist. In turn, social workers in increasing numbers serve as consultants to other professions and on staffs in the fields of health and welfare in local, state, regional, and national offices. Services to clients are thus improved and extended.

COLLABORATION

Social work assigns high priority to the task of working with the individual in his *total* environment. The individual's personality—a unique configuration of his many life experiences—is literally a derivation of his

---

[14] Gerald Caplan, *Mental Health Aspects of Social Work in Public Health* (Berkeley: School of Social Welfare, University of California, 1955), pp. 146, 152.

family, neighborhood, school, and church. Walt Whitman depicts this phenomenon in *Leaves of Grass:*

> There was a child went forth everyday,
> And the first object he looked upon and
>   received with wonder, pity, love or dread,
>   that object he became.
> And that object became part of him for the day,
>   or a certain part of the day, or for many years,
>   or stretching cycles of year.

The individual is not an abstraction. He can be known in terms of his present and past experiences, relationships, and intentions. Social services developed to assist individuals to accomplish their aims only as they contemplate man at any one time as a veritable complex of many constantly interacting influences. Social instrumentalities for assisting the needy, mothered by the necessity of invention, include: a wide variety of social agencies usually federated through welfare councils and offering somewhat specialized and unduplicated services; and a division of labor among various professional disciplines—lawyers, doctors, nurses, social workers, and psychologists.

These inventions, designed to make treatment as total as possible, are the outgrowth of society's recognition that no one agency or profession is equipped to offer a comprehensive service to its actual or potential clientele. No professional person, however well-trained, has the knowledge, the training, or experience to understand or provide a total service. Theoretically there should be but one profession dealing with human beings, and this profession would understand, comprehend, and give help to the individual in his totality. "Such a profession doesn't exist, since artificial barriers have, by necessity, law, custom and education subdivided knowledge into various professional disciplines. Fundamentally, then, all the treatment should be *total* treatment, not just medical, social, psychological, vocational or any other sub-division." [15]

Collaboration is a device for making treatment as total and as effective as possible by a wide and discriminating use of resources, and by combining professional competences. At its best, collaboration is an orchestration of agency services, professional talents, and client needs.

Interagency collaboration is achieved formally and informally by cooperation and community planning, communication of information, by case conferences, and referral of clients. Agencies are only loosely federated. Collaboration among them results from their common purpose of relieving suffering and restoring clients to more helpful and satisfying ways of functioning. Thus, a hospital, for example, may, through proper

15 Frederick A. Whitehouse, "Teamwork: Philosophy and Principles" (Pittsburgh, Pa.: American Association of Medical Social Workers, June 21, 1955), p. 7; mimeographed.

use of medication, nursing care, and rest, succeed in relieving a patient of distressing symptoms which are due to severe stress situations in the patient's home environment. Knowing this, the hospital, through its social service department, refers a client to a family agency for counseling, helps with family finances, and aids in the budgeting of the family income. Or again, an adoption agency whose program is to provide food, shelter, clothing, and casework services to unwed mothers, refers these mothers to their own physicians for obstetrical care and uses the hospital services available in the community. If the agency takes relinquishment from the natural mother, and makes plans to adopt the baby, the adopting parents are directed to lawyers who handle the legal technicalities of adoptions.

The clinic team is the best known of the formal arrangements for collaboration. It is a closely knit working group in contrast with the looseness of the organization of a community of agencies. A more rounded service is available to the client when the knowledge, skill, and training of several disciplines are pooled in deciding objectives, building programs, and planning services.

The clinic team functions under one administrator. It has a common budget. It shares the same office and work space with clients whose needs can be subserved by the efforts of the team working individually or in concert. Historically, the team created by the child guidance movement was somewhat proscribed. The social worker did the social study and worked with the parents, generally the mother, with a parent-child focus. Representing other disciplines were the psychiatrist, who treated the child, and the psychologist, who did the testing. These somewhat arbitrary divisions of labor have been relaxed in the child guidance clinic, and team concepts have been modified and adapted to a rather wide variety of clinic settings and agencies.

TEAMWORK CONCEPTS

Teamwork derives its meaning and validity from the democratic tradition; it is incompatible with an authoritarian ideology. The authority is largely that of knowledge and competence which asserts itself at each encounter with the client, or of the work to be done in the agency at that moment when it is needed.

The team has been defined as a

close, cooperative, democratic, multiprofessional union devoted to a common purpose—the best treatment for the fundamental needs of the individual. Its members work through a combined and integrated diagnosis; flexible, dynamic planning; proper timing and sequence of treatment; and balance in action. It is an organismic group distinct in its parts, yet acting as a unit, i.e., no important action is taken by members of one profession without the consent of the group. Just as the individual acts as an interrelated whole and not as a sum of his characteristics, so must the professions act, think, interpret, and contribute toward a diagnosis which is the product of all, and a treatment plan which is dynamic to accommodate the changes which a human organism was constantly making.[16]

The team is a fellowship of men and ideas. The bond which unifies a clinic team is a bond of service; i.e., each member of the team has and shares a common purpose, a common objective, and each is desirous of providing a maximum of service for the individual who comes to the agency for help.

The team is a union of interdependent inquiry. Different team members approach the problem from the standpoint of their particular disciplines and from the framework of their body of knowledge, their philosophy of working with individuals, and their skill; yet at the same time they respect the independence, the skill, and the competence of other team members. Respect and regard for the competences of others is a cornerstone of successful teamwork. The common demoninator of a team is the conception of man as a product of a biological, psychological, social, and spiritual continuum, and the method which pervades the efforts of the team is that of scientific inquiry jointly pursued, or of collaboration.

Teamwork is predicated on the individuality of the participating disciplines. It derives its strength through the preservation of differences. For social work this implies that before one can become a useful clinician he must first have established his identity as a social worker. It is true, however, that individuals on the team surrender some of their independence. Team members are obligated not only to deliver their professional functions, but also to be aware of what is going on in other phases of treatment. In addition, a member must keep others on the team informed about his own progress for other professions depend upon him for the success of the case.

Teamwork does not just happen. It is a process. It develops from the discovery of self and others. It is a dynamic process. It implies a capacity for growth and change.

There must be conviction at the administrative level of the validity of the common purpose. There must be executive conviction that the team purpose is as important as any other. Teamwork cannot exist by administrative decree alone, and structure cannot make a team. The administration should acquaint other services with, and define responsibility for, each service. The chief of the individual service defines his service and explains how it is given. He is responsible for the standards of performance and the quality of services given.

Overall collaboration of team members is a continuous process. Col-

---

[16] *Ibid.*, p. 13.

laboration begins with a group leader, the one who coordinates all services in the setting, who must recognize the positive and negative feelings which he brings to the collaborative process. He must value himself as a professional person and be clear about the way in which the service entrusted to him is to be offered. In social work, stress is placed upon the need for the individual to be clear about his individual responsibility and his relationship to the patient. Unity of purpose within the organization is basic and can be reached best through the planned conference, the formal method by which the team is put together and comes into existence. However, there are informal methods through which team work is enhanced, and the informal methods are often equal in importance to the more formal ones.

SOCIAL ACTION

In this jet-propelled, push-button age with its mass media and modern communication systems, action by individuals, groups, and communities can be rapidly organized to play important roles in many ways. Social workers are recognizing that they not only have the ability to play significant roles in social action but they also have a responsibility. With their knowledge of human behavior and social interaction, they are qualified to understand social issues that confront society and to make recommendations regarding them.

Historically, some of the great leaders of social work have become well known because of their dedication to instigating changes in society and in facing and solving social ills. Dorothea Dix, Jane Addams, and numerous others devoted their time and energies to bring about changes for the betterment of mankind and society, particularly in regard to social functioning. Today, too, there are many social workers who are using their abilities to better understand the social problems of mankind and to do something about them. Action groups are springing up across the country. Most local chapters of the National Association of Social Workers sponsor committees on social action. These committees study local conditions and make recommendations to legislatures and other governing and policy-making bodies.

DEFINITION

Social action is the social work process which includes activities which affect large numbers of people and bring about desired social changes. These changes in particular have to do with social problems and social relationships. Social action is a concerted effort, usually undertaken by both professional and lay people, to face social problems and to bring an alleviation or solution of them.

There are three kinds of problems which become the targets of those interested in social action: personal problems, family welfare, and community problems. Various people band together to help reduce mental illness which affects individuals as well as families. Recently, in a Western state, considerable social action was furthered to bring about a change in the marriage regulatory laws. The law specified that an epileptic could not marry. Through concerted effort of many individuals and groups, the legislature passed a law which abolished this provision and made it possible for persons with epilepsy to marry. The abolition of this provision came about only because many individuals joined hands together for social action.

Various examples exist which illustrate social action regarding problems which affect family living. In one state a group of professional and lay people joined together and, based upon study, proposed recommendations which made it possible for a law to be passed by the legislature which provided for marriage counseling services attached to the district courts. Social action was furthered to strengthen the family, the basic institution of society. This provision came about only through the dedicated interest, enthusiasm, and concerted effort of many people.

In the community area there are all kinds of social problems which confront dedicated lay and professional people. As groups of people join together to study community problems and to make recommendations about them, changes ensue and many of these problems are lessened. In other words, social action is a positive aspect of a democratic society which helps to stimulate social alterations which benefit the welfare of all.

JOINING LAY AND PROFESSIONAL PEOPLE

Numerous problems arise when lay and professional people are brought together to work on common problems. Some of the specific problems are:

1. Different levels of interest often exist.

2. There are differences in language.

3. Different attitudes and feelings towards social problems are usually present.

4. Problems of superiority and inferiority exist.

5. There are often differences in goals.

6. The question arises, "Who will lead?"

7. It is sometimes difficult to get lay people involved.

8. Sometimes the professional person is in competition with other professional persons.

9. What geographical area should be covered?

10. There are often prejudices and commitments which cause some difficulty.

11. Sometimes there is considerable turnover of personnel.

Some of the important principles and suggestions for bringing about a better integration of lay and professional leadership in an attempt to further social action, are:

1. There should be some rotation of leadership and membership.

2. The democratic process should be stressed.

3. A need exists for simple, lucid information.

4. The aim is to involve all the people through planning and co-ordination.

5. There should be sound representation.

6. There must be an effective, efficient, organizational structure.

7. Common language should be used.

8. There should be effective use of committees.

9. Goals should be defined toward the beginning.

10. There should be a reevaluation of goals as the action proceeds.

11. Study and research are imperative to successful social action.

12. Sometimes it is advantageous to formalize an organizational structure through incorporation or other legal activity or procedure.

13. Sessions should be recorded.

14. Premeeting planning and communication are important.

15. Ways should be devised for maintaining interest.

16. There is a need to be sensitive to the community pulse.

RESEARCH

Research is another enabling process in social work, one which is becoming stressed more in practice. Social workers are recognizing the need for scientific answers to numerous questions. They need to know why people behave as they do, particularly in their social functioning, and, also, what happens when various skills and techniques of the social worker are applied in helping disadvantaged people. Social workers recognize that they can ask many more questions than they can answer; thus research is needed as never before.

DEFINITION

What is social research? Webster's *New International Dictionary* states that research is "careful or critical inquiry or examination in seeking facts or principles; diligent investigation in order to ascertain something." The *Encyclopedia of the Social Sciences* explains that research is "the manipulation of things, concepts or symbols for the purpose of generalizing to extend, correct, or verify knowledge, whether that knowl-

edge aids in the construction of a theory or in the practice of an art."
Stated briefly, social research is systematic inquiry regarding social situations and problems, the process of obtaining social facts, or methodical
inquiry into social phenomena.

Social research is related to two or more people, or situations involving
such people, and their interactions. Much social research is focused on
social problems of people who live together.

There is a difference between pure research and applied research.
Social workers are particularly interested in applied research, which is
for utilitarian purposes, contrasted with pure research which is conducted for its own sake. Nevertheless, more social workers today than
ever before are developing an interest and practice related to pure research as well as applied research.

As explained previously, social problems exist in society and cause
pain, unhappiness, and difficulties to millions of people. Crime, for
example, costs the United States at least twenty to twenty-five billions
of dollars each year. Even more important than the financial burdens
are the individual and family heartaches and emotional scars which
result therefrom. What causes crime? How can it be reduced? Can social
work help to prevent it? These and related questions are open challenges
to social workers on the present scene. Such problems as mental illness,
physical handicaps, and many others open the door to similar questions
and the need for research.

People have many false ideas and superstitions regarding the behavior
of others, their social functioning, and their social problems. Millions
of dollars are spent each year on charlatans who give questionable
answers and guidance to people with personal and family difficulties.
Scientific research is sorely needed to help provide data for social planning, improving society, and aiding people on an individual, family,
and community basis.

SOCIAL WORK AND RESEARCH

Many people—and some welfare workers—believe that "Common
sense is enough in working with people." This is not so. Facts are
needed if we are ever going to accomplish the goals of professional
social work.

Many values of research attach to social work. Accurate observation
is basic to both research and other aspects of social work. Students and
practitioners who develop abilities to do research enhance their abilities
to work with people in other ways. A healthy skepticism of statistics is
needed by social workers and is usually acquired by research study.

Social workers need to keep abreast of current investigations and to
obtain access to the new facts, techniques, and skills that are arising

on the horizon of knowledge. Social workers are more and more called upon to participate in social research activities. Many of them are now hired on a full-time basis with their professional energies going into research. Social workers need to utilize the objective techniques of science and research in all that they do. This does not mean that they abolish or eradicate their personal warmth and interest in people, but it does mean that they bring into operation scientific attitudes and techniques which can help them to come closer to the realities of life and to the solutions of problems.

MAJOR STEPS IN RESEARCH

An objective scientific attitude is basic, of course, to any research endeavor. In addition to this attitude, the following steps are important in the scientific method:

1. *A working hypothesis,* which states an idea or assumption, to be proven or disproven.

2. *Observation,* which encompasses objective consideration of social phenomena.

3. *Objective recording,* which involves careful writing down of phenomena observed.

4. *Classification,* which includes defining and grouping of social phenomena.

5. *Organization of data,* which involves the consideration of information obtained in a related integrated fashion.

6. *Generalizations,* which include the basic conclusions.

MAIN KINDS OF RESEARCH FOR SOCIAL WORKERS

Several methods and techniques are utilized in social work research. The *statistical* method is being used considerably and involves study of a number of cases. These cases are generally arranged and classified into two groups, a control group and an experimental group. The control group proceeds in normal fashion, as always, while the experimental group has some new facet or interactional relationship introduced which theoretically will bring about the hypothesized change or alteration. Statistical techniques and procedures are utilized to show relationships and correlations between different sets of data. Most schools of social work now require one or more classes in statistical knowledge and research procedures. They also specify the preparation of a thesis or participation in a research project, either individual or group, which hopefully helps the student to learn about the importance of research for social workers and provides a beginning knowledge regarding research methodology and techniques.

A second approach utilized by social workers is the *case* method. This process is basically an intensive study of one or a few cases, keeping in mind that an understanding of a specific case may be helpful in acquiring knowledge of human behavior and social functioning. Case studies may be accomplished by the social worker through examining records or by interviewing a client or clients. They may be obtained through the *own story* technique which provides an opportunity for a person to write about his experiences and his reactions to them. Not only are the details of a case important, but the feelings and implications are particularly significant to social work practice.

Another method utilized by social workers is the *social survey*. This is an attempt to study on a broad basis a given neighborhood or community and to attempt to understand the underlying foundations and principles related to social problems, the behavior of people within these localities, and the total social milieu. Ordinarily, control groups are not utilized but rather an attempt is made to give an overall descriptive view of a community or other segment of society. This kind of research has been sponsored in particular by community welfare councils and coordinating councils in an attempt to find out the facts of given communities descriptively.

The *human ecological* approach is also used in studying social phenomena. This emphasizes the spatial distribution of human behavior and attempts to explain why there are differentials, geographically speaking, in regard to social conditions and problems. An example of this would be a study in a given community which would result in a geographical map showing the actual distribution by residence of the homes of the delinquents handled by the police or courts. Generally, such a map depicts certain clusterings and concentrations. Using this information, social planners attempt to understand the differentials and to do something to prevent and control delinquency, particularly in the areas of high concentration of antisocial behavior.

Another useful method in social work is the *historical* approach. This attempts to give perspective from the past for understanding present issues, problems, and plans of action, and to help in improving situations. Historical research can be accomplished through library study, interviews, viewing original documents of various kinds, and through objective study, comparison, and contrast of various materials.

SUMMARY

Administration is one of the enabling processes which involves the transformation of social policies into social services. It is a process which is receiving greater recognition in the totality of social work practice.

This process involves many basic principles and skills which are important for adequate agency functioning.

Essentially, *supervision* is a staff development process but it also carries administrative responsibility. Supervision has been the logical outgrowth of the complexity of the job which workers have been asked to do. It is a response to workers' needs to receive help on matters which often are of a difficult nature, and the solution of which have long range consequences for the client.

Supervision is largely a teaching job and makes use of such principles of pedagogy as: learner participation, learning by doing, learning through imitation and identification, a climate conducive to learning, learner feelings, academic freedom, and the dynamics of the worker-supervisor relationship.

Principles of casework and supervision are used in *consultation*. Consultation, however, does not include responsibility for administration. It offers a service to workers which will make them more effective in working with clients. Its primary function is not education, although there may be educative value in what the consultant does. The consultant's job is task-oriented. The consultant must avoid the trap of supervision, training, counseling, or other administrative functions. He must be free to function as a consultant and to permit the consultee freedom in the use he makes of consultation.

The services of an agency can be extended by consultation. They are expanded when the worker is helped to become more skillful and knowledgeable in role performance.

In many instances, the individual is best served when the competences of two or more professions are combined in providing services and when all the resources of a community are available for use as needed by clients.

Collaboration is a social invention for combining skills and knowledge of several helping professions and various community resources in the service of clients. The clinic team is one of the best known arrangements of collaboration among the professions. The team is democratic and guided by an authority of competence. Its strength is the strength of specialization of function and the preservation among team members of differences and individuality, joined with a spirit of sharing, giving, and receiving.

Social action is one of the newer processes emphasized in social work today. It is a method used to attack social problems and to bring about desirable changes in community living. Knowledge and skills are essential with this process as with the other enabling processes.

Research is presently recognized as an important process in social work education and practice. Objective consideration of facts and data is essential for competent practice. Various methods including the statistical, the historical, the social survey, the ecological, and the case method are utilized to gain additional understanding about social functioning and the control and reduction of social problems.

QUESTIONS FOR DISCUSSION

1. Define, compare, and contrast administration and community organization.

2. Discuss the statement, "All levels of staff participate in the administrative process."

3. Justify the investment which an agency makes in supervision from the standpoint of administration.

4. What is the role of the supervisor?

5. What are the competences needed by a consultant in order for him to be effective in the helping professions?

6. Explain why the principles governing relationships are valid when applied to the process of consultation.

7. In what way are the increase of knowledge and the proliferation of skill in the helping professions related to the needs among the disciplines for collaboration?

8. What is meant by social action as a process?

9. Who should be most involved in social action?

10. What is social research? Define; describe; illustrate.

11. Why is social research so important among social workers today?

SPECIAL ACTIVITIES

1. Invite a capable administrator in your community to appear before your class to describe principles and examples of effective administration.

2. Construct a questionnaire and send it to several agencies in your community for purposes of surveying the use now made, if any, of supervision, consultation, and collaboration.

3. Read a current research article in *Social Work* and evaluate it in writing.

4. Sponsor a debate in class on the topic: "Resolved that social workers should be actively engaged in social action."

SELECTED REFERENCES

Administration

REED, ELLA W., ed., *Social Welfare Administration* (New York: Columbia University Press, 1961).

SPENCER, SUE, *The Administration Method in Social Work Education,* Curriculum Study, Vol. III (New York: Council on Social Work Education, 1959).

TRECKER, HARLEIGH B., *New Understandings of Administration* (New York: Association Press, 1961).

Supervision

ABRAHAMSON, ARTHUR C., *Group Methods in Supervision and Staff Development* (New York: Harper & Row, Publishers, 1959).

ROBINSON, VIRGINIA P., *Supervision in Social Casework* (Chapel Hill: University of North Carolina Press, 1936).

TOWLE, CHARLOTTE, *The Learner in Education for the Professions* (Chicago: University of Chicago Press, 1954).

Consultation

NITSBURGH, HAROLD, and KAHN, MARVIN W., "Consultation With Welfare Workers in a Mental Health Clinic," *Social Work*, Vol. 7 (July, 1962), pp. 84–93.

STRINGER, LOREN A., "Consultation: Some Expectations, Principles, and Skills," *Social Work*, Vol. 6 (July, 1961), pp. 85–90.

Collaboration

COCKERILL, ELEANOR, "The Interdependence of the Professions in Helping People," *Social Casework*, Vol. 34 (November, 1953), pp. 371–378.

WHITEHOUSE, FREDERICK A., "Teamwork: Philosophy and Principles" (Pittsburgh, Pa., June 21, 1955), pp. 1–32; mimeographed.

Social Action

KAHN, ALFRED J., ed., *Issues in American Social Work* (New York: Columbia University Press, 1959).

PUMPHREY, MURIEL W., *The Teaching of Values and Ethics in Social Work Education*, Curriculum Study, Vol. XIII (New York: Council on Social Work Education, 1959).

Report of the President's Commission on National Goals, *Goals for Americans: Program for Action in the Sixties* (New York: The American Assembly, Columbia University, 1960).

Research

McMILLEN, WAYNE, *Statistical Methods for Social Workers* (Chicago: The University of Chicago Press, 1952).

POLANSKY, NORMAN A., ed., *Social Work Research* (Chicago: The University of Chicago Press, 1960).

STOUFFER, SAMUEL A., *Social Research to Test Ideas* (Glencoe, N.Y.: The Free Press of Glencoe, 1962).

part IV

Professional Development

CHAPTER 18

Social Work:
an Emerging Profession

Two college students were discussing their goals in life. One turned to his friend and queried, "When I am all through working and about to retire, I wonder what I will have accomplished in life?" He and his friend talked about various professions and jobs and then the first student observed, "I have about decided I want to become a social worker. As I have thought about it, I feel I can make a worthwhile contribution to mankind, as well as obtain real satisfaction within myself through this profession."

Many young men and women today look toward the professions with longing eyes and with plans for the future. Social work is now regarded by most people as one of the professions. Some say it is a regular profession; others believe it is just a beginning or an emerging one. The United States Census Bureau includes, among others, the following as professions: accountant, architect, artist, attorney, clergyman, college professor, dentist, engineer, journalist, judge, librarian, natural scientist, optometrist, pharmacist, physician, social scientist, social worker, surgeon, and teacher. Is social work really a profession? Has it emerged or is it still emerging? What are the characteristics of a profession? These and related questions are considered in this chapter.

CRITERIA OF A PROFESSION

William Wickenden, while President of Case School of Applied Science, gave an address before the Engineering Institute of Canada in which he described the characteristics of the professional man. He mentioned four distinctive marks. The first is a *"type of activity* which carries high individual responsibility and which applies special skill to problems on a distinctly intellectual plane." Second, he said "is a *motive of service,* associated with limited rewards as distinct from profit." The third is "the *motive of self-expression* which implies joy and pride in one's work and a self-imposed standard of excellence." And fourth is "a conscious *recognition of social duty* to be fulfilled among other means by guarding the ideals and standards of one's profession, by advancing it in public understanding and esteem, by sharing advances in technical knowledge, and by rendering gratuitous public service, in addition to that for ordinary compensation, as a return to society for special advantages of education and status."

Wickenden went on to describe the attributes that mark off the corporate life of a group of persons as professional in character: [1]

We may place first a *body of knowledge* (science) and of *art* (skill) held as a common possession and to be extended by united effort. Next is *an educational process* based on this body of knowledge and art, in ordering which the professional group has a recognized responsibility. Third is a *standard* of personal qualifications for admission to the professional group, based on character, training and proved competence. Next follows *a standard of conduct* based on courtesy, honor and ethics, which guides the practitioner in his relations with clients, colleagues and the public. Fifth, we may place a more or less formal *recognition of status,* either by one's colleagues or by the state, as a basis for good standing. And finally, there is usually *an organization* of the professional group, devoted to its common advancement and its social duty, rather than to the maintenance of an economic monopoly.

Boehm, after a study of the literature on professions, concluded that there are five main criteria which distinguish a profession from an occupation: [2]

1. A profession is expected to be responsive to the public interest and to contribute through its services to the advancement of social well-being and to be accountable to the public for the manner and standards with which it conducts its activities.

2. A profession should possess a relatively coherent, systematic, and transmissible body of knowledge rooted in scientific theories which enables the practitioner of the profession to utilize concepts and principles and to apply

[1] William E. Wickenden, "The Second Mile," An Address delivered before the Engineering Institute of Canada, (1941).

[2] Werner W. Boehm, *Objectives of the Social Work Curriculum of the Future,* Curriculum Study, Vol. I (New York: Council on Social Work Education, 1959), pp. 56–57.

them to specific situations rather than to use a rule of thumb. In other words, the professional practitioner must have *know why* as well as *know how*.

3. The professional practitioner must adhere to an identifiable body of values, and display attitudes which stem from these values and which determine the relationship of the professional person with his colleagues, the recipients of his service, and the community. These attitudes must be professional, *i.e.,* different from lay attitudes and characteristic of a professional sub-culture.

4. A profession must have a body of skills which are the result of the fusion of attitudes and knowledge. Skills reflect the application of general concepts and principles which are characteristic of the methods of the profession. These methods are used to attain the goals of the profession. The practice of a method meets the criteria of systematic procedure and seeks to add to the body of theory on which professional practice rests by distilling, from professional practice and related disciplines, concepts which add to professional knowledge and by furthering evaluation of the effectiveness of professional practice.

5. The members of the profession must be organized and consider themselves as members of a group whose knowledge, skills, attitudes, and norms of conduct they share and to whose advancement they are dedicated.

Greenwood [3] canvassed the sociological literature on occupations and came to the conclusion there are five distinguishing attributes of a profession: (1) systematic theory, (2) authority, (3) community sanction, (4) ethical codes, and (5) a culture. He discusses each of these characteristics and then concludes: [4]

Social work is already a profession; it has too many points of congruence with the model to be classifiable otherwise. Social work is, however, seeking to rise within the professional hierarchy, so that it, too, might enjoy maximum prestige, authority, and monopoly which presently belong to a few top professions.

In regard to a systematic body of knowledge or theory, social work is just getting a good start. In comparison to some professions it has a long way to go. Nevertheless, if one studies carefully the research being accomplished and the theories which are now extant in social work, it is clearly evident that there is a beginning systematic body of knowledge which serves as a foundation for this helping profession.

The social worker today possesses a professional authority. He is respected by other disciplines and, in particular, by clients who come for help. Although he honors the freedom of choice and the right of self-determination of the client, he possesses an authoritative demeanor which builds confidence in the client and helps, through the use of a relationship, to bring about desired changes. The client derives a sense of security from this assumption of authority by the professional social worker.

As Greenwood points out, the social worker also has the sanction of the community. It is evident that society approves of social work and respects it—as indicated by the number of social workers who are hired for positions in public and private agencies and the thousands of un-

---

[3] Ernest Greenwood, "Attributes of a Profession," *Social Work,* Vol. 2 (July, 1957), pp. 45–55.
[4] *Ibid.,* p. 54.

filled positions. More and more people are asking, "Where can I find a social worker?" Training centers are provided from public and private funds, again indicating approval of the community of social work.

In 1960 the social work profession developed a code of ethics which was officially approved by the National Association of Social Workers. This replaced the earlier, preliminary codes which were sponsored by local and national groups in social welfare.

The fifth characteristic, that of a professional culture, is certainly existent in social work today. Social work has its own professional organizations such as the National Association of Social Workers and the Council on Social Work Education. It has a characteristic jargon, and has a unique focus on certain values, norms, and symbols. It stresses the importance of social work as a career and the necessity of dedication and interest in mankind and society as personal prerequisites for the individual who plans to go into this field.

If we look at some of the distinguishing characteristics of social work, we find amplification of the uniqueness of social work as a profession. Social work considers the total person in the total social environment, and is usually within an agency which has structure. It sponsors the use of casework, group work, community organization, social research, and welfare administration in a unique combination. It places particular stress upon self-determination and helping the client to help himself, adhering particularly to the democratic process. Social workers are the only persons in the professions who are called *workers*. They use and coordinate agency and community resources. They specialize on the interplay of all relevant knowledge and facts. Money is mainly used by social workers for the agency and its services, not for the personal benefit of the professionals. Social workers have helped to develop and utilize the teamwork approach. Their research has certain distinguishing characteristics. Money is used as a tool in service and training. The social worker stresses the importance of the family. The supervisory process is a unique characteristic of the social work profession. It has a differential educational training program as well as unique literature and professional organizations. All of these factors—and others—set social work apart from the other helping professions.

HISTORICAL BACKGROUND

A profession includes an approved training program, a professional organization, related organizations and activities, and a body of skilled workers. If we turn the pages of history, we find social work has substantial professional underpinning. Several national organizations play significant roles in relation to social work.

NATIONAL CONFERENCE ON SOCIAL WELFARE

The National Conference on Social Welfare is an ongoing, active national association with more than 5,500 members and involving about 1,200 health and welfare organizations. Its origin dates back to 1873. The Conference encompasses more than professional social workers, including lay citizens and organizations which are interested in human health and welfare services. This organization aims to "promote and share in discussion of the problems and methods identified with the field of social welfare and immediately related fields. The Conference is a forum for such discussion. It does not take an official position on controversial issues and it adopts no resolutions except occasional resolutions of courtesy. The Conference conducts an annual national forum as its principal service, also regional meetings on common service subjects in cooperation with selective state conferences." [5]

Other services include providing a list of significant books at discounts to members, supporting state conferences of social welfare, and providing staff who help with public relations and interpretation of issues and factual material regarding social welfare issues, problems, and solutions.

Indicative of the specific activities of the conference was the Eighty-ninth Annual Forum held in New York City, May 27 to June 1, 1962, sponsored by the National Conference on Social Welfare. This conference had several general sessions, numerous sectional meetings, and provided opportunities for associate and special group meetings. The basic theme was "Social Goals in a Free Society." The theme of the 1963 conference held in Cleveland in May was "We the people . . . promote the general welfare," famous quotation from the preamble to the Constitution of the United States of America.

Across the years the Annual Forum sponsored by this conference has been concerned with various issues regarding human welfare including public welfare, correctional matters, mental health, professional social work, and almost unlimited divisions and subdivisions of the total picture of individual, family, and community health and welfare.

SCHOOLS OF SOCIAL WORK

Within the past five or six decades social work has been developing rapidly, and the importance of the training process has come to the fore. Its roots go back into the past particularly in relation to the efforts in England and the United States of more than a century ago when welfare agencies were created to help families and individuals, especially finan-

[5] *Social Work Yearbook, 1960* (New York: National Association of Social Workers, 1960), p. 703.

cially, and also to provide some psychological support. As these services began to increase and become formalized, the need for training became apparent.

By 1898, the New York Charity Organization Society "took the initial steps in the direction of a professional school by holding a six weeks' training course, designed primarily to increase the efficiency of social workers already in the field." [6] This was the beginning of the New York School of Social Work. (The name was changed in 1963 to Columbia University School of Social Work.) Soon other training centers were established in different parts of the the country. Before 1910 there were schools of social work in the five largest cities in the United States.

Professional schools of social work have increased so that in 1963 there were sixty-three such schools in the United States and Canada (seven in Canada). Most of these schools are integral parts of universities and have become recognized as important centers for providing graduate, professional training in higher education.

Enrollments in these schools, involving only a few persons at the turn of the century, have increased so that in 1961–1962 there were 6,666 full-time students enrolled in graduate schools of social work, and in June of 1962, 2,476 students graduated with the Master of Social Work Degree, the basic professional degree.

COUNCIL ON SOCIAL WORK EDUCATION

Established in 1952 through a merger of three organizations with related functions, the Council on Social Work Education gives leadership in the United States, Canada, and throughout the world to the efforts of the "total social work profession and to citizens interested in the welfare of their own families and their communities to increase the number of professionally qualified social workers, and at the same time, to improve the quality of their education for social work." Membership in this association is open to graduate schools of social work, to undergraduate departments offering a concentration in subjects related to social welfare, to the professional membership association of social workers, to public and private national employment agencies, and to organizations and individuals having an interest in social work education. The basic aims of the Council are to support, strengthen, and improve social work education and to increase the number of qualified social workers.

The major services of the Council are epitomized in a current brochure: [7]

[6] Esther Lucile Brown, *Social Work as a Profession* (New York: Russell Sage Foundation, 1942), p. 29.

[7] "Focus and Direction for Social Work" (New York: Council on Social Work Education, June, 1960).

Establishes standards for United States and Canadian graduate schools of social work and accredits schools which meet these standards;

Provides consultation services to accredited schools of social work on curriculum construction and content;

Conducts research for the primary purpose of improving the curriculum, for the improvement of teaching, and for the collection of information which throws light on problems confronting social work education;

Publishes career pamphlets, teaching records, curriculum materials, proceedings of Annual Program Meetings, workshops, institutes, seminars and other educational materials;

Maintains an active file of prospective faculty for use by the educational institutions;

Administers a national roster of interviewers to facilitate a personal interview with an applicant, as a part of the admissions process of a school of social work, irrespective of the applicant's location;

Assists schools in developing ways to measure student's progress;

Plans meetings and forums for the purpose of improving knowledge and in helping those concerned to keep abreast of new developments in social work education;

Cooperates with the International Association of Schools of Social Work in the promotion of educational standards throughout the world;

Participates in appropriate world and national organizations, and when requested, in giving consultation on social work education in other countries.

The Council on Social Work Education sponsors a unique partnership of citizens, social work practitioners, agency executives, and educators who work together. A House of Delegates—an advisory body representing constituent members, the National Association of Social Workers, higher education, and the interested public—meets annually to consider issues and policies of the Council. The general affairs and decisions of the Council are under the direction of a twenty-four member Board of Directors, composed of educators, social work practitioners, and citizens interested in human welfare. A professional staff provides leadership and services within the Council's authority. The Council is particularly helpful in providing consultation visits and publications which offer guidelines for improving and strengthening social work education. A fifteen-member Commission on Accreditation carries responsibility for the formulation and application of educational standards. An annual conference is held each year which focuses on current problems, issues, and activities of educational value to its members including representatives from graduate and undergraduate educational programs and from practice. The Council also sponsors and supports various committees which are concerned with a variety of program activities relating to recruitment and educational development.

The Commission on Accreditation, authorized by the Council, accredits new schools of social work, as well as periodically conducts on-campus reviews of all the graduate schools of social work with the goal of improving social work training and strengthening academic standards.

One of the most valuable services of the Council is to provide publications which help schools of social work, agencies, and individuals to improve educational facilities and social work practice. These publications are now so extensive that the 1961 catalogue included thirty pages of listed cases and other available publications which were related to the social work educational endeavor. These publications encompass a gamut of subjects related to the training of social workers. For example, one was published recently on "Building a Social Work Library," and another on "Social Work Education in North America," a guide for students from foreign countries to help them to learn about and fit into social work training in the United States.

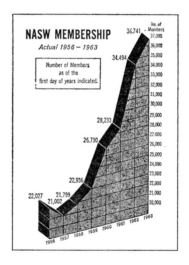

SOURCE: Reprinted from *NASW NEWS*, Vol. 8, No. 3 (May, 1963), p. 9, with permission of the National Association of Social Workers.

NATIONAL ASSOCIATION OF SOCIAL WORKERS

For a discipline to become a profession, it is imperative that a professional organization come into existence. This has happened in social work. The first basic professional organization was the American Association of Social Workers, established in 1921, and which by 1954 had a membership of about 13,500 located in 132 local chapters. Six other professional organizations, built around social work specialties and with memberships totaling more than 7,500, have also furthered the profession. In the 1950's representatives of these seven organizations met together and finally established a single integrated organization, the National Association of Social Workers, which is open to all trained and qualified social workers. This association was officially organized on July 7, 1955, at a special meeting of representatives of the seven predecessor organizations.

This association has grown in numbers and prestige so that by 1964 it has a membership of about 40,000 and is highly respected among professionally trained people in the various helping disciplines. The Association has a Code of Ethics, and has issued policy statements on salaries, on the goals of public social policy, and on standards for social work personnel practices. It has made tremendous strides in helping with the recruitment of qualified personnel for social work training and practice.

The Association has 153 chapters located throughout the United States and Puerto Rico. Each member of the National Association belongs to a local chapter. The Association has its headquarters in New York City.

The seven associations which participated in the formation of the National Association of Social Workers were the American Association of Group Workers, American Association of Medical Social Workers, American Association of Psychiatric Social Workers, American Association of Social Workers, Association for the Study of Community Organization, National Association of School Social Workers, and the Social Work Research Group. Actually, the main activities of most of these groups have been crystallized into functioning sections of the National Association of Social Workers. The various groups have been able to maintain some of their specialized interests, at the same time fusing together into a united organization which is benefiting all social workers, social work education, and social work practice.

The purpose of this association is to: [8]

promote the quality and effectiveness of social work practice in the United States of America through services to the individual, the group, and the community; to further the broad objective of improving conditions of life in our democratic society through utilization of the professional knowledge and skills of social work, and to expand through research the knowledge necessary to define and obtain these goals; to provide opportunity for the social work profession to work in unity toward maintaining and promoting high standards of practice and preparation for practice and toward alleviating or preventing sources of deprivation, distress and strain susceptible of being influenced by social work methods and by social action.

To achieve its aims the Association attempts to do the following: (1) Improve and extend social work practice. (2) Establish principles and procedures for determining and certifying competence to practice. (3) Define and help to bring about the working conditions necessary for the best practice. (4) Define each specialty's area of concern within the practice of social work. (5) Delineate the nature of new, evolving areas of

[8] *Social Work Yearbook, 1960* (New York: National Association of Social Workers, 1960), p. 697.

social work practice. (6) Collaborate with other professional groups to insure cooperative effort between the social work profession and other professions. (7) Interpret to the community the contribution of the professional social worker. (8) Make studies and take action in relation to social conditions. (9) Recruit new workers for the social work profession. [9]

A major development sponsored by NASW has been the establishment of the Academy of Certified Social Workers. Through careful planning and good public relations 18,500 social workers became certified on December 1, 1961, when this program officially began. This is a significant step forward in raising the status of social workers and, in particular, in improving standards of practice in this field. Certification is based upon the qualifications of an MSW degree plus two years of practice under the supervision of a qualified social worker.

An interesting example of common sponsorship and cooperation between the Council on Social Work Education and the National Association of Social Workers is the National Commission for Social Work Careers which is approved and supported jointly by these two organizations. This Commission sponsors plans and activities to provide consultation, publications, a centralized clearinghouse for information and advice about careers in social work, and various other kinds of recruitment activities to increase knowledge and understanding regarding social work as a career.

The National Association of Social Workers has a Delegate Assembly which meets every two years. The 1962 Assembly met in Cleveland. Participants included some 300 official delegates representing 162 NASW chapters and 35,000 professional social workers in the United States and Puerto Rico.

INTERNATIONAL ORGANIZATIONS

There are three main social welfare bodies on an international level which are of particular interest to social workers: the International Conference of Social Work, the International Association of Schools of Social Work, and the International Federation of Social Workers. The International Conference of Social Work was organized in 1926 and has as its aim the bringing together of representatives from various countries of the world to share knowledge, plans, and activities which would strengthen social work on a global basis. Illustrative of the activities of this Conference was the series of meetings held in Munich, Germany, August, 1956. More than 2,600 delegates from fifty-five different countries of all parts of the world participated in this largest and most representa-

[9] *Ibid.*, pp. 697–698.

tive international assembly of social workers ever held until that time. The effect of industrialization on social work was of particular interest and concern at these meetings. More than 750 of the delegates were from the United States, representing every type of agency, public and private.

The International Association of Schools of Social Work has ordinarily met along with the International Conference on Social Work, focusing particularly on educational matters of international importance. An example of the activities of this association was the Congress held in Belo Horizonte, Brazil, in August, 1962, attended by more than 300 delegates from forty countries who profited from the excellent meetings and workshops which were offered. The theme of the Congress was "Professional Education for Social Work with Communities."

The International Federation of Social Workers, begun in 1932, is the third important international organization related to social work. Membership is open to national professional social service organizations. The aims are to "develop a coordinated method for the exchange of ideas, the encouragement and maintenance in every country of high professional standards, and the expression on an international scale of the viewpoint of professional social service." Its activities include: biennial professional meetings in conjunction with the International Conference of Social Work, regional meetings of professional groups on subjects of common concern, exchange of information, advice and assistance to newly forming professional associations, promotion of professional training and standards, and support of exchange social workers.

SOCIAL WORK TODAY

Another way to view the emergence of social work as a profession is to consider some of the major characteristics and activities of social work and social workers in the present era.

CODE OF ETHICS

A major breakthrough in the development of social work as a profession occurred when the Delegate Assembly of the National Association of Social Workers adopted an official Code of Ethics for the Association, October 13, 1960, which stated: [10]

Social work is based on humanitarian, democratic ideals. Professional social workers are dedicated to service for the welfare of mankind; to the disciplined use of a recognized body of knowledge about human beings and their interactions; and to the marshaling of community resources to promote the well-being of all without discrimination.

Social work practice is a public trust that requires of its practitioners in-

[10] *NASW News,* Vol. 6 (February, 1961), p. 14.

tegrity, compassion, belief in the dignity and worth of human beings, respect for individual differences, a commitment to service, and a dedication to truth. It requires mastery of a body of knowledge and skill gained through professional education and experience. It requires also recognition of the limitations of present knowledge and skill and of the services we are now equipped to give. The end sought is the performance of a service with integrity and competence.

Each member of the profession carries responsibility to maintain and improve social work service; constantly to examine, use, and increase the knowledge upon which practice and social policy are based; and to develop further the philosophy and skills of the profession.

This Code of Ethics embodies certain standards of behavior for the social worker in his professional relationships with those he serves, with his colleagues, with his employing agency, with other professions, and with the community. In abiding by the code, the social worker views his obligations in as wide a context as the situation requires, takes all of the principles into consideration, and chooses a course of action consistent with the code's spirit and intent.

As a member of the National Association of Social Workers I commit myself to conduct my professional relationships in accord with the code and subscribe to the following statements:

I regard as my primary obligation the welfare of the individual or group served which includes action for improving social conditions.

I give precedence to my professional responsibility over my personal interests.

I hold myself responsible for the quality and extent of the service I perform.

I respect the privacy of the people I serve.

I use in a responsible manner information gained in professional relationships.

I treat with respect the findings, views, and actions of colleagues, and use appropriate channels to express judgment on these matters.

I practice social work within the recognized knowledge and competence of the profession.

I recognize my professional responsibility to add my ideas and findings to the body of social work knowledge and practice.

I accept responsibility to help protect the community against unethical practice by any individuals or organizations engaged in social welfare activities.

I stand ready to give appropriate professional service in public emergencies.

I distinguish clearly, in public, between my statements and actions as an individual and as a representative of an organization.

I support the principle that professional practice requires professional education.

I accept responsibility for working toward the creation and maintenance of conditions within agencies which enable social workers to conduct themselves in keeping with this code.

I contribute my knowledge, skills, and support to programs of human welfare.

This Code of Ethics gives the social worker a compass to guide him. It helps him realize that he is a person who should have sincere interest and compassion regarding people, their problems, and their relationships with others.

SCHOOLS OF SOCIAL WORK

Social work education is provided on both undergraduate and graduate levels. The Council on Social Work Education has more than 122 members of undergraduate departments of colleges and universities. These constituent members offer courses with social welfare content on the preprofessional level. Persons who complete this undergraduate training are qualified to go either into graduate social work training or to take junior social work positions in agencies. Another aim of this program is to provide social welfare content in the liberal education of students to aid in promoting good citizenship.

On the graduate level there are presently sixty-three schools of social work in the United States and Canada which are affiliated with the Council on Social Work Education and which offer a Master's degree in social work. Their graduate training programs take two years and combine classes in instruction with actual field work practice in agencies. Most graduate schools operate on the concurrent plan wherein they offer academic classes and field work training simultaneously. Several schools use the *block* plan which provides for academic training at the beginning of the total program, followed by intensive five-day-a-week field instruction for several months, and finally culminates in additional academic seminars and other integrative instructional activities. Nearly all of the health and welfare agencies are utilized for field instruction including psychiatric, medical, school, correctional, settlement, public welfare, child welfare, and group work agencies.

The basic program for the Master's degree includes the three core areas of human behavior and social environment (formerly titled Human Growth and Behavior), social services and social policies, and the methods courses. Earlier, considerable emphasis was placed upon *specialization* in certain fields such as psychiatric social work, medical social work, and school social work. Today the training is on a generic base, with students taking the two-year training program to become social workers qualified to work in any agency. In addition to the three core areas there is considerable work offered in research, and schools require either an individual or group thesis or a research project for graduation. Elective courses provide a well-rounded program for the person who is going to practice as a professional social worker.

Several schools now offer a third-year program which provides for a deepening and intensification of study regarding casework, group work, administration, research, community organization, or some other aspect of the total service program. Certificates are awarded at the completion of the third year.

Some graduate schools have introduced Doctoral programs. In 1962 there were seventeen schools (two in Canada) offering post-Master's programs, either a third-year or Doctoral program, or both. Enrollment in these programs during 1962–63 amounted to 176 full-time students.

For some time the profession has been gravely concerned about the shortage of social workers. Various plans have been suggested to cope with this situation. An innovation which will likely receive considerable attention was presented at the annual meeting of the Council on Social Work Education in Boston in 1963. The director, Dr. Ernest Witte,[11] presented a proposal developed by the Council staff which would, if carried out by the schools, provide a six-month training program for persons who had graduated from college and who were interested in social welfare and social work. Upon graduation they would enroll in a ten-week, summer, noncredit course, organized and offered by a graduate school of social work. After successful completion of this study, they would begin three months of in-service training in a participating agency under competent direction. A weekly seminar would be held concurrent with the field experience for which the school and the agency would be jointly responsible. Upon successful completion of the program, in January, a certificate would be awarded to the trainee, with the designation *social welfare aide*.

RESEARCH

Within the past decade social work has begun to blossom in the area of research, which, of course, is basic to professional development. Most schools of social work have one or more research projects or grants which they are sponsoring. Grants are awarded not only from federal and state government sources, but also from foundations and from private business and other corporations. More and more people are coming to social workers, requesting help to study human social behavior, the helping processes, and related activities.

A recent development which is augmenting research in social work is that many agencies, public and private, are now sponsoring research projects of their own. Various kinds of studies are being financed from regular agency budgets to ferret out facts regarding social problems and what might be done about them. A concrete example of this trend is the recent allocation of $17,000 by one state welfare department to a Community Services Council to conduct a study of working mothers—with the aim of ascertaining the pertinent facts and implications related to family problems and their solutions.

Another contribution, research-wise, is the work being done by the 2,500 students who graduate each year with their MSW degrees. Each is

11 "CSWE Proposes Plan for Training Social Welfare Aides," *Social Work Education*, Vol. 11 (February, 1963), pp. 4–5.

required to participate in a research study, individually or in groups. Some of these studies are making significant contributions toward new knowledge about human behavior and social work education and practice.

PRIVATE PRACTICE

One of the interesting developments in recent years has been the increase in the amount of private practice by persons with training in social work. Many social workers have joined forces with doctors or psychiatrists in providing services for patients. Others have set up their "shingle" in an office by themselves. Numerous questions have arisen and several leaders in social work have made vitriolic accusations against this development. However, the fact is that many qualified social workers are in private practice and recent articles and studies reflect that this development seems to be another move toward full-fledged professionalization. Siporin observes that the NASW Commission on Social Work Practice has considered the question of private practice and has decided that it does fall "within the present definition of social work practice." He recognizes that there are safeguards and limitations to be kept in mind regarding private practice and then summarizes: [12]

Private practice fills an institutional gap in meeting the pressures for social work service from an important and large segment of the community. It extends and realizes social work's purpose as an institution to serve the interests of the total community, and marks the attainment of professional maturity and status. Its contributions bring certain problems to which the profession has already begun to address itself. As an instrument for social control and change, the social worker, in private as well as in agency practice, needs to carry—and to be helped to carry—his obligations and mission with secure balance and with good will.

A different point of view is illustrated by Merle who states: [13]

At this juncture in our professional history, agencies should seriously consider the arguments given by some social workers entering private practice that certain agency routines (recording practice, never ending supervision, inability to practice creatively, salary scales, and the like) need careful review. The agencies should examine carefully the whole range of possibilities that may be pushing their most competent practitioners in a direction that is to be viewed with alarm.

In December, 1962, a workshop on private practice was held in Cleveland, Ohio, immediately prior to the 1962 Delegate Assembly of the National Association of Social Workers. Considerable difference of

[12] Max Siporin, "Private Practice of Social Work: Functional Roles and Social Control," *Social Work*, Vol. 6 (April, 1961), p. 60.
[13] Sherman Merle, "Some Arguments Against Private Practice," *Social Work*, Vol. 7 (January, 1962), p. 17.

opinion was presented, but the overall conclusion was that, with certain safeguards, private practice does seem to fit into the total realm of professional social work. Following hours of spirited debate, the Delegate Assembly adopted interim minimum standards for NASW members engaged in private practice of social work. They agreed that no NASW member may enter private practice unless: [14]

1. He is a graduate of a school of social work accredited by the Council on Social Work Education or its predecessor organizations.
2. He is a member of the Academy of Certified Social Workers.
3. He has five years of acceptable full-time experience in agencies providing supervision by professionally trained social workers, of which two years were in one agency consecutively under such supervision, while giving direct service and using the method or methods to be used in the practice contemplated.

The Assembly, in adopting these standards and recommendations, pointed out that the qualifications should "not be construed as an endorsement of the competence of any individual member who meets the standards but rather be viewed as minimum criteria under which the form of practice would be sanctioned."

PUBLICATIONS

Another criterion of a profession is that it produces professional publications. *Social Work* has been published monthly by the National Association of Social Workers since 1955 and is recognized as a respectable, worthwhile professional journal. This same organization publishes *NASW News,* monthly, which keeps professional social workers up-to-date on current developments, and also *Personnel Information,* bimonthly, which calls job openings and opportunities to the attention of social workers.

The Council on Social Work Education publishes, on a bimonthly basis, *Social Work Education* which keeps its membership abreast of current developments in social work education, at home and abroad. This Council is also in the formative stages of planning for a professional journal in social work education.

Numerous professional books are appearing in social work and many articles written by social workers are being published in professional and scientific journals, particularly those related to social functioning and the treatment of human interactional problems.

SALARIES AND JOBS

One of the first official activities of NASW was to establish a policy regarding salaries. The Association recommended that the beginning salary be a minimum of $5,400 per annum and suggested that social

[14] *NASW News,* Vol. 8 (February, 1963), p. 5.

workers should be able to look forward to receiving $10,000 per annum after ten years of experience. In 1962 this minimum was adjusted upward and listed at $6,000 with a recommendation that annual increments be awarded at the rate of 5 to 7 percent each year.

The number of current job openings for trained, qualified social workers is tremendous, estimated around 15,000 in the United States. Vacancies exist in all parts of the country and in practically every kind of agency.

One of the fascinating aspects of social work practice is that it can take place in a variety of settings or agencies. Job opportunities are available in almost every kind of endeavor for helping mankind individually, family-wise, or on a community basis. Positions are offered in settings such as psychiatric clinics and hospitals, medical hospitals, schools, prisons, YMCA's, public welfare, child welfare, and adoption agencies.

IMAGE OF SOCIAL WORK

Kadushin [15] and others have studied the present status of social work, particularly in relation to other professions. They have found that social work has been moving upward but still has some distance to go. Apparently in the past two or three years there has been considerable advance in the prestige and status of the profession of social worker, even in light of some intense criticism of public welfare and other related activities.

One current development which gives promise to help in raising the image and status of social work is the increase in the number of males entering the profession. In 1931–32 only 6 percent of those who received the Master of Social Work degree in the United States were males. In 1960–61 the number of men receiving the MSW degree in schools in the United States and Canada amounted to 42.4 percent. Men go into social work at an earlier age than women and stay in it longer. This tends to stabilize the profession and give increased status to it.

TEAM APPROACH

One of the current professional developments of social work is that the social worker is becoming an extremely important member of the professional team working with human problems. The minimum team consists of the psychiatrist, social worker, and psychologist, and oftentimes involves the nurse, other doctors, the physical therapist, and additional qualified personnel. The social worker often assumes the pivotal position, acting as the coordinator of the team when cases are presented and helping staffing plans to materialize.

15 Alfred Kadushin, "Prestige of Social Work—Facts and Factors," *Social Work,* Vol. 3 (April, 1958), pp. 37–43.

SUMMARY

Social work is a rapidly developing, emerging profession. Its charity and social welfare roots reach back for many centuries. The history of civilization reflects a sincere attempt to provide welfare services for people, families, and communities with problems. Particularly since the turn of the twentieth century, there have been more formalized programs to professionalize the social welfare helping process.

In order to train qualified social workers, numerous schools of social work have been introduced; currently there are sixty-three in the United States and Canada. Professional organizations were created to help dedicated, welfare-minded individuals to join forces and support each other in providing humanitarian services for mankind. These associations provided effective services over a period of years. In 1955 came the uniting and integration of seven professional social work organizations into the unified National Association of Social Workers. This organization has made significant contributions within its first years of existence.

In the field of education, the Council on Social Work Education, established in 1952, has likewise made important strides in upgrading standards of education, in furthering recruitment, in offering consultation services, and in interpreting to the public what social work really is and can be.

Research, publications, and private practice all point to an ongoing profession of social work. The new Code of Ethics outlines the "right" goals of this helping profession and presents worthwhile guidelines for the dedicated persons who join. Advance educational programs beyond the Master's degree are on the increase, and are providing opportunities for further education, greater knowledge, better skills, and mature professional attitudes.

QUESTIONS FOR DISCUSSION

1. What are the basic criteria of a profession?
2. Is social work a profession? Discuss.
3. Outline briefly some of the significant historical developments in social work.
4. What role has the National Conference on Social Welfare played in the development of social work?
5. What are the main purposes and activities of the Council on Social Work Education?
6. Evaluate the origin and contributions of the National Association of Social Workers.
7. What are some examples of social work operating on an international base?
8. Evaluate the Code of Ethics of the National Association of Social Workers.

9. Since there is such a shortage of trained social workers with a Master's degree, would you favor lowering the standards and granting a degree at the end of one year's graduate training? Or giving such a degree at the time of undergraduate graduation?

10. How important is research for a profession?

11. What safeguards would you recommend for social workers who want to go into private practice?

12. How might the prestige of social work be increased?

SPECIAL ACTIVITIES

1. Interview a psychiatrist, lawyer, or teacher and discuss with him the status of social work as a profession. Report your findings to the class.

2. Invite a psychiatrist, social worker, and psychologist to present a panel before the class with the "professional team" as the theme.

3. Interview representatives of three different generations and ask their opinions of social work. Report your findings to the class.

SELECTED REFERENCES

BISNO, HERBERT, "How Social Will Social Work Be?" *Social Work,* Vol. 1 (April, 1956), pp. 12–18.

BOEHM, WERNER W., *Objectives of the Social Work Curriculum of the Future,* Curriculum Study, Vol. I (New York: Council on Social Work Education, 1959).

COCKERILL, ELEANOR, "The Interdependence of the Professions in Helping People," *Social Casework,* Vol. 34 (November, 1953), pp. 371–378.

EATON, JOSEPH W., "Whence and Whither Social Work: A Sociological Analysis," *Social Work,* Vol. 1 (January, 1956), pp. 11–26.

GOLDSTEIN, LOUIS, "Professions and Professional Associations," *NASW News,* Vol. 7 (August, 1962), pp. 9–12.

GREENWOOD, ERNEST, "Attributes of a Profession," *Social Work,* Vol. 2 (July, 1957), pp. 45–55.

KADUSHIN, ALFRED, "Prestige of Social Work—Facts and Factors," *Social Work,* Vol. 3 (April, 1958), pp. 37–43.

REISSMAN, LEONARD, "Life Careers, Power and the Professions," *American Sociological Review,* Vol. 21 (April, 1956), pp. 215–221.

YOUNG, DONALD, "Sociology and the Practicing Professions," *American Sociological Review,* Vol. 20 (December, 1955), pp. 641–648.

CHAPTER 19

Social Work and Prevention

One evening a group of doctors were on their way to a meeting in a bus. As they neared a turn they noticed that an automobile had slid off the road on an icy curve and been involved, apparently, in a serious accident. Twenty-three of the twenty-four doctors ran to the vehicle which had left the highway to administer medical aid, if needed. The other physician, viewing the total situation, located a flashlight, ran up the road, and flagged down approaching automobiles. He felt it was particularly important to warn approaching motorists and prevent additional accidents in view of the slippery condition of the highway. His action was entirely different from that of the other twenty-three doctors. Was it important? Of course, the answer is obvious.

Police officials report that most automobiles that are stolen by teenagers have the keys in the ignition and a few even have the engines running. If something were done to educate adults to remove the keys from their automobiles and to lock their cars when they park, the number of auto thefts would likely decrease. In thinking about human behavior, and especially about social problems, is it not possible to reduce and prevent them? Social work is very much interested in this approach.

DEFINITIONS

Prevention is a word which is used in many different ways. It indicates action which staves off something from happening. Stated positively, it is the process of action taken so that antisocial behavior or personal, family, or community problems are minimized or do not arise at all. Theoretically, it means the doing of something so that personal and social pathology will not develop. The National Commission on Social Work Practice of the National Association of Social Workers defined prevention in social work as "activities which have merit in averting, or discouraging the development of, specific social problems, or in delaying or controlling the growth of such problems after they have presented beginning symptoms."

Broadly speaking, prevention in relation to social work may be regarded in two ways: first, proper action which is taken so that the personal, family, or community problems do not arise at all; and secondly, action taken so that personal, family, and community problems are not repeated, so that recidivism does not occur, even though such problems existed at the outset. Prevention is concerned with keeping the vase intact, rather than trying to repair the broken pieces. It is interested in keeping human personalities and human interrelationships operating on an integrated and mature level, rather than in gluing together human parts which may have been cracked, broken apart, or splintered.

The field of public health in medicine has offered many helpful concepts and specific terminology in regard to prevention, and social workers have borrowed from this field several interesting ideas and principles. Five levels of prevention in public health which are commonly accepted in preventive medicine, are: (1) health promotion, (2) specific protection, (3) early diagnosis and treatment, (4) disability limitation, and (5) rehabilitation.[1]

The field of public health also describes the levels of prevention as primary, secondary, and tertiary. Leavell and Clark [2] explain that primary prevention includes health promotion and specific protection, that secondary prevention encompasses early diagnosis and prompt treatment, and that tertiary prevention includes disability limitation and rehabilitation. Health promotion concerns the general health and well-being of the population and is not directed at any particular disease or disorder. Health education and motivation are particularly important on this level of prevention. Examples of this level would include promotion of adequate housing, selective periodic health examinations, and health promotional activities which aim toward the realization of optimal personality development. Specific protection would include such measures as immunization, sanitation, and sound nutrition.

In regard to secondary prevention, early diagnosis and prompt treatment are particularly important. This level stresses case findings and handling of disruptive problems. The aim, of course, is to relieve distress and to shorten duration of the illness, minimize contagion, and reduce symptoms. Tertiary prevention is focused mainly on the chronic and serious illnesses and includes attempts to reduce pain and suffering.

---

[1] Hugh R. Leavell, and E. Gurney Clark, *Preventive Medicine—For the Doctor in His Community* (New York: McGraw-Hill Book Co., Inc., 1958), p. 31.
[2] *Ibid.*, pp. 21–39.

Disability limitation includes delaying the consequences of clinically advanced diseases. The preventive measures are primarily therapeutic and are directed toward the patient in order to arrest the disease process and to prevent further complications. Rehabilitation is "more than stopping a disease process; it is also the prevention of complete disability after anatomic and physiologic changes are more or less stabilized. Its positive objective is to return the affected individual to a useful place in society and make maximum use of his remaining capacities." [3]

Rapoport claims that the concept of prevention, evolved largely from the public health field, is often used in "a distorted and confusing manner in the social work framework." [4] Wittman [5] observes that we, in the field of social work, are presently devoting our main effort to areas of secondary and tertiary prevention and are doing very little on the primary level. We need to become more interested in and focused upon enhancing the well-being of individuals, families, and communities and helping to bring about an enrichment in daily living. We need to look at the socially healthy people as well as the disabled. In order to assist on the broad basis of health promotion, we need to do more on the positive side by working with normal people and increasing the long-range values of social work to the community. We need to consider the "points of entry" where preventive social work may be particularly effective. Social work may help especially in relation to obstetrics, the nursery school, kindergarten, with adolescence, and at time of marriage. "All can provide points of departure for constructive preventive social services." [6]

Wittman suggests that until there is some extension of service coverage to the total population, rather than to the present social work clientele as we now know it, we must remain committed mainly to the secondary and tertiary levels of prevention. The major concern for the near future should be "to develop adaptations of current practice which will reach more of the healthy segment of the population and may thereby retard the rising incidence of social pathology." [7]

SOCIAL WORK FOCUS ON PREVENTION

Parad explains that there are many problems and significant implications related to preventive casework. At the Annual Forum Meeting of

---

[3] *Ibid.*, p. 27.

[4] Lydia Rapoport, "The Concept of Prevention in Social Work," *Social Work,* Vol. 6 (January, 1961), p. 3.

[5] Milton Wittman, "Preventive Social Work: A Goal for Practice and Education," *Social Work,* Vol. 6 (January, 1961), p. 23.

[6] *Ibid.*, p. 24.

[7] *Ibid.*, p. 27.

the National Conference on Social Welfare in 1961, he proposed a three-fold thesis as follows: [8]

1. A carefully focused "retail" program of short-term, person-to-person casework intervention with families under stress should be systematically and comprehensively included in our total spectrum of social services to implement and bolster the effectiveness of "wholesale" methods of preventing family breakdown.

2. Such an approach, when located in a range of preventive social work activities, may be appropriately labeled "early secondary prevention" since its preventive component outweighs its remedial aspects.

3. More rational organization of family-oriented social services will enable us to identify, reach, and serve a larger number of families in acute stressful situations with an increasingly effective, planned type of preventive intervention which makes more meaningful use of limited professional resources of time and staff.

At present there is considerable interest in prevention in social work practice; and this interest is filtering into the educational process. Some individuals think this emphasis is entirely new to social welfare and social work; the pages of history depict otherwise.

At the Twelfth Annual Session of the National Conference of Charities and Correction, held in Washington, D.C., June, 1885, a considerable amount of the conference was devoted to *preventive work*. In fact, more than sixty pages of the proceedings were concerned with various papers and discussions in this area, which included such topics as: "Thirty Years' Experience in Nursery and Child Hospital Work," "The Shady Side of the 'Placing-Out System'," "Methods of Industrial Training for Girls," "The Kindergarten as a Character Builder," and "Compulsory Education." Indicative of pioneer thinking was a report which follows of one discussion in this field.[9]

Mr. Caldwell thought the method of trying to get rid of crime by attacking the adult criminal was like trying to restore a tree to health by binding up the branches, when the real trouble was in the root. The way to get rid of pauperism and crime is to take care of the children, and to begin with them as early as possible. As John Plowman says about breaking a colt, "The work will thrive, if you start before he's five." Not only the children, but the homes need reforming.

Within recent years social work educators and practitioners have developed considerable interest in prevention and have conceptualized some of their ideas. Boehm, in a paper on the nature of social work, describes the functions of social work as threefold: [10]

8 Howard J. Parad, "Preventive Casework: Problems and Implications," *The Social Welfare Forum, 1961*, Official Proceedings, National Conference on Social Welfare (New York: Columbia University Press, 1961), p. 179.

9 *Proceedings of the National Conference of Charities and Correction*, at the Twelfth Annual Session held in Washington, D. C., June 4–10, 1885 (Boston: Press of Geo. H. Ellis, 1885), p. 462.

10 Werner W. Boehm, "The Nature of Social Work," *Social Work*, Vol. 3 (April, 1958), pp. 16–17.

1. Restoration—which function seeks to identify and control or eliminate those factors in the interactional process which cause breakdown or impairment of social relationships. It aims at a return to a maximum level of functioning. This function is essentially curative and rehabilitative.

2. Provision of resources—which is concerned with the creation, enrichment, improvement and better coordination of social resources, and the mobilization of existing, but inoperative, individual capacity for interaction in the physical, intellectual, emotional, and spiritual realms. This function is essentially developmental and educational.

3. Prevention—which consists of early discovery, control, and elimination of conditions which potentially could hamper effective social functioning. It consists of (a) prevention of problems in the area of interaction between individuals and groups, and (b) prevention of social ills, through the study of "social infection" and "social contamination."

This same classification was presented in the Curriculum Study, Council on Social Work Education, which gives great emphasis to the importance of prevention in the total field of social work.[11]

Indicative of the increasing support of prevention in social work is the statement made by Hamilton: "One way of expressing the objective of psychosocial adjustment would be to say that the caseworker is interested in preventing social breakdown, in conserving strengths, in restoring social functions, in making life experiences more comfortable or compensating, in creating opportunities for growth and development, and in increasing the capacity for self-direction and social contribution." [12]

The National Association of Social Workers has likewise been very much interested in the whole area and process of prevention. In 1962, a report on "Prevention and Treatment" contained a pertinent statement with an introduction as follows: [13]

The basic concern of social work with prevention arises out of the profession's service commitment. If the social pathology with which most social workers deal could be prevented, then many individuals would be spared destructive experiences and society would benefit. This in itself is important enough to justify greater efforts toward the further development of effective prevention. If, for example, it is possible to prevent the disintegration of families rather than merely aiding members of the disintegrated family group to deal with affects of separation, who would deny the worthiness of the preventative effort?

After considerable discussion of some of the issues and problems related to prevention, the report concluded that "NASW, as the single

11 Werner W. Boehm, *Objectives of the Social Work Curriculum of the Future,* Curriculum Study, Vol. I (New York: Council on Social Work Education, 1959), pp. 51–52.

12 Gordon Hamilton, *Theory and Practice of Social Casework,* 2nd ed. (New York: Columbia University Press, 1951), p. 239.

13 Bertram M. Beck, "Prevention and Treatment," based on the work of the Subcommittee on Trends, Issues and Priorities of the NASW National Commission on Social Work Practice, 1962, p. 1; mimeographed.

professional membership association with the authority and responsibility to speak for social work, needs, through the democratic process, to evolve its position concerning the issue of prevention and then implement that position in communities throughout the nation." [14]

Several current developments on the political and economic scene have given additional interest and emphasis to the area of prevention. President Kennedy, in the first presidential message wholly on the subject of welfare, in 1962, told Congress, "Public welfare must be more than a salvage operation, picking up debris from the wreckage of human lives. Its emphasis must be directed increasingly toward prevention and rehabilitation." In 1961, the U.S. Congress passed a law for the prevention and control of juvenile delinquency which provided ten million dollars annually to encourage demonstrations, experimentations, and training activities which would help to meet this problem and prevent it.

In February, 1963, President Kennedy, in the first presidential address to Congress specifically on mental health, asked Congress to consider this disastrous national problem and to appropriate money to increase facilities, particularly community mental health centers for reducing and preventing mental illness. He suggested we must first "seek out the causes of mental illness and of mental retardation and eradicate them." He warned that we need to prevent thousands of new cases of mental illness and mental retardation and recommended appropriations of several millions of dollars to help establish additional community mental health centers and provide staff and other activities which would help in this total preventive and rehabilitative movement.

The 1962 Amendments to the Social Security Act include a new emphasis on prevention as well as protection and rehabilitation. Theoretically, the act has been changed to help remove some of the personal, family, and community conditions which are conducive to the breeding of social pathology. For example, one of the purposes was designated to "maintain and strengthen family life for children."

PROBLEMS INVOLVED

Several factors exist which cloud the preventive scene. First is the complexity of human behavior. Final answers have not been acquired regarding what causes social problems or the best solutions. Thus, it is very difficult to plan action and to predict what the outcome will be in regard to a specific personal or social situation. A legitimate question arises: If we do not know the precise causes of a social problem, can we prevent the problem? In medicine and other fields, even though we do not know the exact causal relationships of phenomena, we are able to produce situations which seem to bring about desired results. We do not

14 *Ibid.,* p. 31.

know for sure what electricity is, but we are able to control it. In medicine, we are not aware of the exact cause of the common cold, but there are precautions and activities which can be practiced which seem to prevent colds and reduce the number.

Another problem is that our knowledge and skills in relation to human behavior and social functioning are just in the beginning stages. We can ask many more questions than we can answer. Thus, it becomes a genuine challenge to increase and utilize knowledge and skills in the prevention of social malfunctioning.

Another problem is the difficulty of evaluation. How do we know for sure that the action we have taken has brought the results we desired? With so many factors involved in human behavior, it is especially difficult to be objective in evaluating what takes place and why.

Buell,[15] before the Eighty-sixth Annual Forum of the National Conference on Social Welfare, posed the question, "Is prevention possible?" In his discussion he came to the conclusion that there are six key words or phrases which need to be considered: (1) epidemiology, (2) family, (3) systematization, (4) differential classification, (5) aggressiveness, and (6) evaluation. He explained that epidemiology refers to the synthesis of knowledge which is practically applicable to communitywide prevention and control of a given problem. The family unit is not only the key in a reporting system, but the use of the family as a uniformly consistent base for diagnosis, treatment, record keeping, and all administrative practice is desirable. Systematization is needed to underpin the whole series of therapeutic processes so that what takes place can be uniformly recorded. To bring this about, each step in the process must be taken with conscious intellectual awareness, and the judgments must be systematically guided and recorded for future reference.

The fourth phrase, differential classification, refers to the value of classifying agency caseloads by relative potentialities for rehabilitation or prevention and the levels of social service required to meet this goal. Aggressive casework is important in attempting to break down resistance to social service workers and in discovering positive motivations and family strengths on which to build. The sixth and last factor is that of a careful evaluation of the whole process. Buell, after careful consideration of some of the factors and challenges in relation to prevention, answered his own question by saying that prevention is possible, according to project experiences of Community Research Associates: [16]

1. *If* the community's key agencies accept and implement a problem-solving goal

2. *If* planning is done on the basis of community-wide facts

15 Bradley Buell, "Is Prevention Possible?" Eduard C. Lindeman Memorial Lecture (New York: Community Research Associates, Inc., 1959), pp. 15–19.
16 *Ibid.*, p. 20.

3. *If* services are coordinated and integrated to prevent family breakdown through:

the systematization of therapeutic processes

the differential classification and assignment of cases in relation to rehabilitation potentiality; and finally,

4. *If* there is objective, periodic evaluation of results.

EXAMPLES OF PREVENTION

Several examples of prevention are presented to illustrate some of the possibilities and potentialities involving social work.

Premarital counseling is illustrative of an attempt at primary prevention on the part of social workers and other counselors. Within family service agencies, marriage and family counseling bureaus on university campuses, and in private marriage counseling clinics many individuals are interviewed by professionally trained social workers in an attempt to help them to understand themselves better in relation to marriage and their mates. Theoretically, this is an attempt to help them to gain the most from marriage, to prevent problems which might arise, and to guide them toward meaningful positive relationships on the marital journey. A case taken from a university setting illustrates some aspects of this process.

PREMARITAL COUNSELING

Mr. C, age 26, majoring in biology, and Miss T, age 23, majoring in English, came to the Bureau in the spring of the academic year and stated that they planned to marry in June, after Mr. C had received his Master's degree and Miss T had completed her undergraduate studies. They said that they had come to the Bureau because they had heard that marriage counseling would provide an opportunity for them to learn more about each other and about marriage. They themselves had no major problems. Although they had differed on many things during the two years of their courtship, they had been able to work through their disagreements to the satisfaction of each.

A caseworker interviewed each of them three times and then saw them together for one final interview. Each was given an opportunity to take the Marriage Prediction and the Personality Inventory tests. The results of these tests were favorable and indicated that each had a mature personality.

In the individual interviews with the caseworker, Miss T discussed a few of her fears about marriage, particularly in relation to childbearing. She also indicated some concern about the differences in religious belief and activity between herself and Mr. C, although both of them belonged to the same denomination. She had many other questions related to courtship and the future marital relationship. She talked about how she and Mr. C might improve their ability to communicate with each other and to solve differences that seemed to arise. Mr. C also raised several questions that he seemed anxious to discuss with the worker. He, too, was worried about religious differences, but felt that these could be worked out satisfactorily. He was concerned about money management, and he wondered whether he was being fair and realistic in going ahead with marriage at this time in view of his desire to continue graduate work.

In the joint interview, Miss T and Mr. C's religious differences, their financial planning, and other matters were discussed, and the couple seemed to develop greater understanding of each other and some helpful insights regarding their relationship. They felt definitely that they would like to go ahead with their plans for marriage. At the close of this interview Mr. C said, "I feel that counseling has helped us to understand ourselves, each other, and what marriage is all about as we never have before." Miss T added, "Talking to the worker has removed some fears I have had. I think it has opened the door for us to know each other better, to communicate with each other better, and to learn how to solve problems that are bound to come up in marriage." [17]

A summarization of functions by three marriage counselors who work in a university agency further describes the emphasis on and the methods of prevention through premarital counseling: [18]

1. Through interviewing, provide an opportunity for prospective marriage partners to discuss concerns regarding their approaching marriage. Questions frequently focus on personality differences, wedding plans, the honeymoon, physical adjustment, housing plans, religious differences, money and its management, emancipation from family, adjustment to new friendships, and in-laws.

2. By giving factual information directly or by suggesting appropriate reading material.

3. Through the use of personality tests, inventories, and other tools.

4. By giving counselees an opportunity to ventilate fears, doubts, and wishes regarding marriage and each other, so that they recognize how important inner feelings are in a marital relationship.

5. By encouraging the couple to go to a physician for medical examination and conference which includes a pelvic examination for the girl.

6. By referral, if indicated, to other specialists or agencies for needed assistance.

7. Through the counselor's conferring, if the situation warrants, with other counselors or consultants in his own agency, or with other specialists in the community regarding the problems of the counselees.

[17] Milton G. Thackeray and Rex A. Skidmore, "Casework Service in a University Setting," *Social Casework*, Vol. 43 (February, 1962), p. 69.

[18] Rex A. Skidmore, Hulda Van Steeter Garrett, and C. Jay Skidmore, *Marriage Consulting—An Introduction to Marriage Counseling* (New York: Harper & Row, Publishers, 1956), pp. 339–340.

8. By acquainting the couple with the resources of marriage counseling so if later they are confronted with problems they feel unable to handle alone they will seek professional help.

9. By assisting the couple to build and strengthen a realistic, positive philosophy toward marriage. The counselor encourages the couple to discuss their basic goals and values; he aids them to realize that no marriage is perfect, all have conflicts, and all require effort, compromise, and adjustment. The counselor helps the couple to leave the counseling situation with "eyes open" to the somewhat uncertain path ahead but with a firm conviction that a happy and successful marriage is worth working for.

In Family Service Societies, there are many activities which are sponsored to assist on a preventive level. Staff members give talks before service clubs, PTA groups, Family Life Institutes, and other groups of people. These are presented with the purpose of helping members of society to better understand marriage and family relationships and to adjust more adequately in these relationships.

PREVENTIVE MENTAL HEALTH

An interesting example of prevention was the project in preventive mental health conducted at the Family Counseling Service of the Child Study Association of America in New York City. McClure and Schrier [19] described such preventive counseling with parents of young children. Such counseling is offered on an individual basis to parents when it is believed that the child's difficulties will respond positively to an alteration in the parents' attitude or mode of handling. The basic premise is that such counseling may prevent future pathology in the child by influencing the interrelationship between parent and child through direct help to the parent. Preliminary evaluations show that after one year of time in 51 percent of the cases the counselors judged that the "service enabled family or individual to handle the situation better." In 10 percent of the cases this was judged not to be so. In 39 percent of the cases, the counselors were unable to make an evaluation.

MATERNAL AND CHILD HEALTH

Another program in prevention which is related to maternal and child health was instigated in Boston with the establishment of the Family Health Clinic, a service-study program for health supervision of mothers and infants. This clinic offered complete service in prenatal, postnatal, and well-child care to 116 families having first babies. As a member of the clinic team, the social worker usually saw the patient eight to ten times in the prenatal clinic, monthly at the well-child clinic, and also

[19] Dorothea McClure and Harvey Schrier, "Preventive Counseling with Parents of Young Children," *Social Work*, Vol. 1 (April, 1956), pp. 68–80.

made other visits to the home or offered consultation at the office when necessary. There was at least one ward visit made during the eight-day period of hospitalization. The casework interviews were primarily unstructured, allowing the patient to initiate the problems and matters to be discussed. The usual techniques of ego support, clarification, and modification of the environment were used. In addition, educational methods were applied to advantage and included anticipatory guidance. Cyr and Wattenberg reported that the Family Health Clinic "has demonstrated the value of having several professions join together for the guidance of families on the threshold of parenthood. Special emphasis was placed on the promotion of good mental and physical health through incorporation of preventive measures." [20]

FAMILY COUNSELING

An additional example of the preventive aspects of social work comes from the files of the Family Service Association of America. The following case glimpse was presented in an interpretive publication to illustrate its procedures and services, and was taken from the files of a Southern Family Service Agency.

Mr. Wilson, an airline pilot, came to Family Service stating he was at the end of his rope. For the last six months he had been struggling to find a way to help his wife control her drinking. He felt she was becoming an alcoholic and he feared not only what she was doing to herself, but also what might happen to their son. *He found himself, he said, "pushing his plane on the home journey."*

There had been no apparent problem for either of the Wilsons until about a year before. The trouble started when Mrs. Wilson always wanted "just one more" at parties and "just one more" after she got home. Mr. Wilson began to lose his temper because she didn't stop drinking until she passed out. He wasn't sure how much drinking she did while he was away, but she was almost always in a bad state when he arrived home. When he tried to talk to her about it, she just became quieter and more depressed. Then she would say, "get the divorce you want and leave me alone." He couldn't get across to her that he didn't want a divorce—he wanted her as his wife—the wife she had been—not the one she was now. Both Mr. and Mrs. Wilson received family counseling for a period of six months.

Strangely enough, Mrs. Wilson's pattern of drinking was related to her husband's presence in the home. While he was away—she did not drink—but as his return became imminent, she began to drink

---

[20] Florence E. Cyr, and Shirley H. Wattenberg, "Social Work in a Preventive Program of Maternal and Child Health," *Social Work*, Vol. 2 (July, 1957), p. 39.

heavily. This pattern was further related to a major source of friction —Mrs. Wilson's almost irrational involvement with her younger brother and sister, their resentment of her, and their dislike and criticism of Mr. Wilson.

Mrs. Wilson was the oldest of the three children in her family. The parents had died when the children were quite young and the family was divided. Mrs. Wilson had tried desperately to meet her own needs for a family by attempting to care for the other children. As soon as she began working, she had sent money to the next oldest. She assumed more responsibility than was appreciated, and her strivings and ambitions for her brother and sister were not met by them. Currently, Mrs. Wilson's superior financial, educational, and social status, and her constant effort to "help" them achieve more, were further irritants to them.

They felt that Mr. Wilson, too, saw himself as better off than they were. They were openly critical and suspicious of him, and they insinuated to Mrs. Wilson that her husband probably was paying attention to other women on his trips out of town. She began to believe this.

Mr. Wilson was impatient and concerned about the way in which Mrs. Wilson was continually frustrated in her attempts to "mother" her younger brother and sister, because they were irritated rather than appreciative of her help. He had been openly critical about this and he had been increasingly critical of Mrs. Wilson's housekeeping, her care of their child, and her unwillingness to be his wife. He said if she didn't straighten out—the marriage couldn't continue.

In the course of family counseling, Mrs. Wilson was helped to give up her attempted control over her brother and sister. She became more independent of them and allowed them to be themselves. As she was able to separate herself from her assumed "mother role," she was better able to view her own marriage and her role as a wife and mother.

When Mr. Wilson was able to face the fact that her drinking was related to the relationship between himself, his wife, and her relatives, and to realize that it did not represent a hopeless alcoholic pattern, he was able to relax some of the pressures he had placed on Mrs. Wilson.

Although the beginning of success in talking together and listening to each other came in the caseworker's office, later on they were more truly "communicating" with each other when they were alone, and at home. Mr. Wilson became more accepting of his wife's need to talk out her frustrations about her brother and sister, and he was better able to let her manage his life in little ways. Mrs. Wilson, who has gained a better understanding of herself and a truer self-concept, doesn't need to escape by drinking.[21]

RELIGIOUS LEADERS

Recently, a social worker was invited to meet with religious leaders in a rural community. He talked for some time about understanding parent-child relationships and behavior of people and then questions were invited to help the people to gain more understanding and some insights regarding what causes personal and social problems and what might be done about them. The whole focus was to assist these people in a positive manner to understand more about human relationships and how they can assist in preventing problems. The first session was considered to be so profitable by all the participants that they agreed to hold a series of six more meetings in which the social worker was the enabler, assisting these religious leaders to increase their knowledge and skills and, consequently and hopefully, to aid them in working with their clientele to prevent personal and social problems.

PREVENTION OF MENTAL DISORDERS

The Sub-Committee on Tertiary Prevention of the Program Area Committee of Mental Health of the American Public Health Association published a pamphlet, *The Prevention of Disability in Mental Disorders*,[22] which outlines various activities which can and should be adopted if mental disorders are to be reduced. The report gives several general trends and suggests these should be considered as part of the design for reducing disabilities associated with mental disorders. They include (1) unlocking of wards, removal of other restraints, and general development of the open hospital; (2) a growing interest in including families in treatment, particularly in its rehabilitative phases; (3) wider use of community resources, which brings the *community* into the hospital through relatives and volunteers; (4) significant new focus on post-hospital experience of patients and growth of resources to continue the gains made; that is, better aftercare programs including halfway houses, clubs for former patients, and vocational rehabilitation; (5) the genuine interest of many psychiatrists in the social world of the patient and in how to make this social world more therapeutic; (6) general concern about making it easier to enter and leave mental hospitals, and in turning these hospitals into *therapeutic* or *rehabilitative* communities, rather

21 "An Airline Pilot Who Was Pushing His Plane," *Family Service HIGHLIGHTS*, September–November, 1960 issue, Vol. XXI, pp. 114–115. Published by Family Service Association of America.

22 *The Prevention of Disability in Mental Disorders* (Washington, D.C.: U.S. Department of Health, Education, and Welfare, Public Health Service, 1962).

than deprived islands of custodial care.[23] Social workers, of course, can and do play important roles in these current developments related to reduction and prevention of mental illness.

DELINQUENCY PREVENTION

In a metropolitan community in the Eastern United States, some years ago, there was a dilapidated area with poor housing and a high degree of social disorganization. Delinquency rates were very high. Some enterprising, dedicated community leaders decided to take some action. Through the efforts of public-spirited citizens and some professional helpers who involved the youth, a recreational center was established. In the next year, only three arrests were made among the teen-agers in comparison with more than a hundred and fifty which had been made the year before. What had happened? Had this concerted action prevented delinquency? The answer seems to be rather obvious, because the only apparent change in this slum community had been the introduction of a recreational center, accompanied by trained and interested personnel who did what they could to provide *wholesome* recreational opportunities for the youth.

FAMILIES IN CRISES

Rapoport [24] reports a demonstration in working with families in crises where an exploration in preventive intervention was utilized. The study involved eleven families, considered to be in a state of crisis because of the birth of a premature infant in each family, and comprised a total of sixty interviews all of which were held in the home.

Her conclusion was that preventive intervention with the families studied consisted of a range of activities related to prevention which were: keeping an explicit focus on the crisis through helping the families to consciously perceive what a crisis means to them; helping with doubts of feminine adequacy, guilt, and self-blame; helping with grief and mourning in relation to feelings of loss and emptiness stimulated by separation from the infant; and helping with anticipatory worry work and anticipatory guidance. Another service was the offering of basic information and education regarding child development and child care; and a final contribution consisted of creating a bridge to community resources, opening pathways of referral, and intervening in communication failures and in problems of stereotyping and misinterpretation of

23 *Ibid.*, pp. 37–38.
24 Lydia Rapoport, "Working with Families in Crisis: An Exploration in Preventive Intervention," *Social Work*, Vol. 7 (July, 1962), pp. 48–56.

motivation and need. There appeared to be a meaningful number of direct accomplishments through these activities in relation to prevention.

Cohen and Bernard [25] describe a relevant two-year demonstration and research project among direct relief recipients in Washtenaw County, Michigan. The results of this study indicate that there was a considerable reduction of dependency significantly related to prevention. The overall conclusion was that experience with the project caseload shows that most of the cases studied benefited from intensive treatment. Half of the thirty cases increased their self-support; seventeen improved their family relationships and individual adjustment; and twenty improved their use of community resources. Twenty-five cases showed improvement in one or more of these three areas; four showed no gain; and only one case deteriorated during the course of the project.

Numerous other cases exist which show the effective result of social work in regard to prevention of future personal and family problems. The caseloads in public assistance are filled with examples like the one of Harry Smith. Harry was 35 years of age, married, and had two children. He lost his job due to illness. When his small reserves had been spent he went to the County Department of Public Welfare for assistance. He was unskilled, had never held jobs which paid much, and even these had been irregular. He and his family were given financial assistance and, even more important, a social worker helped him to make effective plans for becoming trained in bricklaying. The worker also helped him to develop a desire, accompanying his skill, to work and support his family. Today this man is the successful manager of a construction company and is making significant contributions to himself, his family, and his community. In all probability, if he had not been assisted by a social worker, or someone else, he would have difficult personal and family problems today and would be a liability to the community in which he lives.

In Marin County, California, close to the Golden Gate Bridge, a demonstration project [26] was sponsored in 1956 which indicated rather clearly that through professional services and selected, limited caseloads, persons who were on relief could be assisted to become independent, self-controlling individuals. If these services were multiplied considerably, recidivism in public assistance would undoubtedly be lessened. This is a concrete example of what social workers might do in regard to prevention.

[25] Wilbur J. Cohen and Sydney E. Bernard, *The Prevention and Reduction of Dependency* (Ann Arbor, Michigan: Washtenaw County Department of Social Welfare, 1961), pp. 1–94.

[26] "Building Services into a Public Assistance Program Can Pay Off," A Study of Marin County, California (State of California: Department of Social Welfare, n.d.g.).

SUICIDE PREVENTION

A recent innovation which involves social workers in the area of prevention, is the Suicide Prevention Center, established in Los Angeles, California, 1958. This center was set up for the evaluation, referral, treatment, follow-up, and overall prevention of suicidal behavior. It was established under the purview of a five-year grant from the U.S. Public Health Service and is administered through the University of Southern California. The goals of the center are (1) to save lives, (2) to demonstrate that such a center can play a vital role in the health and welfare activities of a large metropolitan community, and (3) to collect and collate heretofore unavailable data regarding suicidal phenomena and to employ this information in developing and testing hypotheses concerning suicide. Hopefully, this procedure will "lead to more accurate prediction and, hopefully, will lead ultimately to lower suicide rates." Social workers are integral members of the professional team which includes psychiatrists and psychologists.

PERSONAL AND FAMILY RESOURCES

Otto [27] has been doing some pioneering research in the areas of personal and family resources. His approach is particularly related to health promotion and the advancement of the general well-being of individuals, families, and society. It attempts to focus on the positive factors and potentialities inherent in personal and family relationships. The interest is in studying and stressing the dynamics of the so-called healthy or normal family or individual and to develop understanding regarding the basic elements of healthiness or strength in an individual or family, so as to tap these resources for enriching living and for preventing and reducing personal and social pathology. Another major purpose of this research is to develop methods, instruments, and techniques which will enable individuals and families to make better use of their potentialities and strengths. His basic hypotheses include the following:

1. Every individual and family has resources or strengths which can be identified and recognized, and these resources can be used to build still further strengths.
2. Every individual and family has emotional and other creative resources which are not being fully utilized, or which are as yet undiscovered, or not recognized.

[27] Herbert A. Otto, "The Personal and Family Resource Development Programmes: A Preliminary Report," *The International Journal of Social Psychiatry,* Vol. 8, No. 3 (1962), pp. 185–195.

3. The average or healthy individual or family is capable of making a survey or inquiry of strengths and on the basis of this survey is able to select specific areas for the purpose of development and utilization of resources and strengths.
4. The process of discovering the topography of individual and family strengths is in itself strengthening.

IMPLICATIONS OF PREVENTION IN SOCIAL WORK

With the current interest and emphasis on social work, it is apparent that considerable time and talents must be spent in thinking through the relationship of professional social work to the preventive process. Several implications stand out.

If social workers are really going to tap the resources of prevention, they must spend more time and effort in creative thinking and activity. They will need to go beyond and extend the present boundaries and activities of practice. What can be done by social workers to prevent personal, family, and community problems is one of the great challenges of today.

It is apparent that all three of the basic methods, casework, group work, and community organization, will need to be utilized, as well as the processes of research and administration, if prevention is to become more effective. The caseworker, the group worker, and the community organizer can all play important roles in the preventive process. Many times through working together, they can assist each other in accomplishing desired goals. One challenge seems to be, then, a closer cooperation and coordination among workers who are skilled in the different methodologies.

One great need is for more objective research and evaluation of activities and projects related to prevention. We need to quantify and objectify our procedures. We need to know in advance what we are doing, what we hope to accomplish, and then to be able to measure afterwards what has actually taken place.

There should be special focus on the *before* in relation to prevention. In other words, if we can utilize our professional knowledge and skills to prevent problems from arising on the horizon of daily living, this seems to be particularly important. The educational and consultation processes seem to be especially significant in this area of social work.

We will need to anticipate problems which might arise in advance of their occurrence. This calls for even greater understanding of human behavior, interrelationships, and social phenomena.

Experimentation is needed as never before. We must try new techniques, skills, and plans to see if they will work in preventing personal and social problems. In the educational field, additional interest in prevention will necessitate increased offerings regarding this process in the curriculum of the professional schools. Principles regarding prevention and case examples will need to be introduced into the core areas and specific classes, and probably diffused directly and indirectly throughout the total curriculum. In the future, there may well be seminars, probably on an elective basis, available for those who are particularly interested in this phase of social work endeavor.

Social work practice needs to be broadened to include more emphasis on consultation, family life education, and related activities. Social workers must become more community-minded and more family-minded. They need to ferret out the principles and knowledge which will help families and communities to anticipate problems and to prevent them. They need to broaden their skills so that they can utilize a variety of techniques and methods to help bring about desired results preventionwise.

SUMMARY

The old adage, "An ounce of prevention is worth a pound of cure," is emphasized today as never before in the helping professions. In particular, medicine has led with its public health programs.

Within the past few years, prevention has come to the fore in social work and is now recognized as a major function. There is still considerable uncertainty and lack of clarity regarding the roles of social work in relation to prevention. Nevertheless, various demonstrations and experiments indicate that the social worker can anticipate social problems and can help to avert them. Additional study, experimentation, and research are much needed in this area.

QUESTIONS FOR DISCUSSION

1. Trace briefly the history of the emphasis on prevention in social work.

2. Evaluate the three functions of social work presented in the Curriculum Study.

3. Define, describe, and illustrate prevention in relation to social work.

4. Do you think that social work can help to enrich daily living? Give an example to illustrate your answer.

5. How important is evaluation as part of the prevention process?

6. Evaluate Bradley Buell's six factors related to prevention.

7. How can social workers develop more creativity in relation to prevention?

8. What can social workers do to anticipate problems in social functioning before they happen?

9. How might family life education play a significant role in preventing social problems?

10. Do you agree that prevention should be given more emphasis in social work? Discuss.

SPECIAL ACTIVITIES

1. Visit a social welfare agency in your community and ask one of the staff to describe preventive services which it offers.

2. Evaluate a current radio or TV program in relation to prevention of a social problem.

3. Have a debate before the class on the subject "Resolved: Prevention is a Major Aspect of Social Work."

SELECTED REFERENCES

BOEHM, WERNER W., *Objectives of the Social Work Curriculum of the Future,* Curriculum Study, Vol. I (New York: Council on Social Work Education, 1959).

BUELL, BRADLEY, "Is Prevention Possible?" (New York: Community Research Associates, Inc., 1959).

Public Health Concepts in Social Work Education (New York: Council on Social Work Education, 1962).

RAPOPORT, LYDIA, "The Concept of Prevention in Social Work," *Social Work,* Vol. 6 (January, 1961), pp. 3–12.

RAPOPORT, LYDIA, "Working with Families in Crisis: An Exploration in Preventive Intervention," *Social Work,* Vol. 7 (July, 1962), pp. 48–56.

WITTMAN, MILTON, "Preventive Social Work: A Goal for Practice and Education," *Social Work,* Vol. 6 (January, 1961), pp. 19–28.

THACKERAY, MILTON G., and SKIDMORE, REX A., "Casework Service in a University Setting," *Social Casework,* Vol. 43 (February, 1962), pp. 65–70.

CHAPTER 20

Education for Social Work

Social work education is a phenomenon largely of the twentieth century. Its prominence today among the professions results from community demands for trained staff to administer social services. An affluent society, having made the decision to organize for human improvement, has declared in effect that the work of helping people with personal and social problems must be handled with professional regard, understanding, and skill, if it is not to do more harm than good.

The first agencies trained their own staff in the "fundamental theory and practice of charity." The early schools of social work were the outgrowth of pressures and demands from agencies for competent personnel. To a large extent these schools were sponsored by the agencies themselves. Classwork was practice-oriented and intended to prepare staff for work in particular agencies.

It was through the efforts of the Charity Organization Society of New York that the first course of instruction was established in 1898 for society workers. Thirty students were enrolled for three months. This summer school of "philanthropic workers" continued until 1904, when the course was reorganized on an eight-month basis to become the New York School of Philanthropy, now the Columbia University School of Social Work.

In addition, at the turn of the century, an Institute of Social Science was established as a part of the Extension Division of the University of Chicago. In response to efforts of practicing social workers in the Chicago area, the Institute became an independent School of Civics and Philanthropy and was later incorporated into the University of

Chicago and the School of Social Service Administration. "Similar developments were taking place in Boston where a school was established under the joint auspices of Harvard University and Simmons College (now the Simmons College School of Social Work) and in Philadelphia where a short training course expanded to become the Philadelphia Training School for Social Work (now the University of Pennsylvania School of Social Work)." [1]

By 1919, a sufficient number of schools had been established to justify the formation of an Association of Training Schools for Professional Social Work, through which the schools could gain "recognition and exchange views and experience." This Association was the forerunner of The American Association of Schools of Social Work and the present, Council on Social Work Education, which came into being July 1, 1952. Membership of the first association of schools was open to practically any school that maintained a course of training covering at least one academic year and substantial field and class work.

The early schools saw their purpose largely in terms of vocational and narrow apprenticeship training. The courses offered reflected this purpose and the primary interest of students and teachers alike was to learn how to do the jobs entrusted to social workers in specific agencies.

A minimum curriculum was adopted by the schools in 1932, which became the yardstick for determining membership in the American Association of Schools of Social Work. This minimum curriculum framework was Association policy from 1932 to 1944, and a standard for one year of training only. "The new demands made upon social work in the depression era, the new opportunities opened up by the social legislation of the 1930's, the new status accorded schools of social work by the requirements that professional education be offered within a university and on the graduate level—these and many other factors combined to extend the scope of social work education beyond the narrow limits of the 1932 curriculum." [2]

In a mobile society, social work graduates, like other Americans, are on the go. They move from one agency to another, from one part of the country to another. For these graduates and the public they serve, it is important that their education—their professional equipment—be exportable. Professional education, which becomes too highly individualistic or narrowly structured to accommodate the practice demands of a particular agency cannot serve a society on the move. Mobility places a premium on flexibility and the free exchange of manpower, intelligence, knowledge, and skill. Thus, today, in planning the curriculum schools take into consideration the fact that their graduates will be employed in agencies widely dispersed throughout the country, repre-

---

1 *Social Work Yearbook, 1954* (New York: American Association of Social Workers, 1954), p. 170.
2 *Ibid.,* p. 173.

senting not one, but many fields of practice. Fortunately, because of the timely and forward-looking action on the part of schools, graduates completing their training have the assurance that their mental endowments and professional skills can be put to the service of the profession anywhere in the United States, in Canada, or elsewhere. Moreover, it is possible for graduates who receive part of their training in one school to transfer to another school to complete their course without being subjected to the tyranny of highly individualized program requirements.

SCHOOLS OF SOCIAL WORK

Sixty-three schools of social work in the United States and Canada are accredited to offer the graduate program leading to the master's degree.

"Seventeen schools (two of which are Canadian) are currently providing graduate social work education at the post-Master's level. Enrollment in these programs for 1962–63 is 176 full-time students, a nine percent increase over last year's figure of 164." [3]

All accredited schools provide a two-year sequence of class and field instruction in social casework. In addition, a substantial number of the schools provide sequences in social group work, community organization, and opportunity for related class and field instruction in administration and in research.

During the school year 1931–32, 166 students completed the second-year program in schools of social work in the United States and Canada. The number of graduates with Master's degrees in 1962 was 2,476. Of these, 158 were graduates of Canadian schools and 2,318 were from the United States. In 1962, the number of full-time faculty in schools of social work was 935.

Graduates of schools of social work were employed in a wide variety of public and private health, welfare, correctional, and educational institutions. It is conservatively estimated that 15,000 trained social workers are needed to fill existing vacancies. The new group of graduates each year hardly does more than take care of the annual manpower loss caused by death, retirement, marriage, and transfer of workers to positions outside the field.

Graduates are in a seller's market and can choose from among many positions at beginning salaries for those with a Master's degree of approximately $6,000, or more. The average beginning salary of twenty-seven graduates from one school in 1962 was $6,178. A mean salary of $7,592 was reported for 286 graduates recently surveyed. The median annual salary for five graduates possessing doctorates was $12,166. [4] These same graduates, in the main, reported that they were working

---

3 *Social Work Education*, Vol. 10 (December, 1962), p. 28.

4 R. Reid Davidson, "Social Work Graduates, University of Utah, 1938–1962" (unpublished Master's thesis, June, 1963), pp. 26, 30.

in casework positions in psychiatric agencies, hospitals, schools, child-placing and family agencies, in the field of correction, in public assistance offices, or in some supervisory or administrative capacity.

PREPROFESSIONAL TRAINING

An increasing number of colleges and universities are developing courses and content in social welfare for undergraduates.

"There are now 122 undergraduate departments which are members of the Council. A number of them are developing social welfare sequences along the lines suggested in the Council's guide, *Social Welfare Content in Undergraduate Education.*" [5]

Traditionally, the notion was that undergraduate preparation for the vocations and professions should be broadly *liberal* and cultural rather than vocational. However, this view differs somewhat from what appears to be a trend in American education toward the inclusion of both specialized, vocational-oriented courses and courses of a preprofessional and professional character, along with the traditional liberal arts education. Bisno [6] asks, "*Can an undergraduate program which specifically focuses on social work and is viewed as part of the total process of preparation for social work fit within the framework of a liberal arts college?*" He states that there is a positive answer to the question depending on the "character of the social work program" and whether it meets the requirement of being liberal. "The conclusion we have come to is that there should be an interweaving of liberal and professional education and that there is no inherent reason why a liberalizing professional education should not be accommodated within the structure of the present day liberal arts college."

Whether undergraduate work is *liberal* or vocational will be decided by various social and economic pressures and the demands which the public makes upon the colleges and universities. The writers' view is that the aims and purposes of liberal education and preprofessional social work are not incompatible and that the dichotomy between the two is arbitrary and unrealistic.

TRAINING OBJECTIVES IN SOCIAL WORK EDUCATION AT THE MASTER'S DEGREE LEVEL

The basic aim of a school's educational program is to help students who plan to engage in the important profession of social work to de-

[5] *Social Work Education, op. cit.*, p. 28.

[6] Herbert Bisno, *The Place of the Undergraduate Curriculum in Social Work Education*, Curriculum Study, Vol. II (New York: Council on Social Work Education, 1959), pp. 36, 37.

velop sound knowledge, adequate skills, and professional attitudes. Illustrative of specific student objectives are the following:

1. To achieve, through two years of graduate training, competence to begin social work practice within the structure of a social work agency, with major ability in either casework, group work, or community organization, and an introductory knowledge and skill in the other social work methods: casework, group work, community organization, administration, and research.

2. To develop a sensitive knowledge of people and human behavior in relation to social environment, of society's methods of meeting needs including the role of the social work profession in planned social change, and of methods of social work practice.

3. To develop the capacity to use knowledge analytically and through class discussions and field experience—integrated and involving case studies of individuals, groups, and communities—in order to develop the skills to formulate treatment or action plans based on sound social study and diagnosis.

4. To gain an understanding of their own emotional responses and the ability to direct their feelings to constructive ends, to minimize or eliminate bias or prejudice which would thwart their efforts to help others, and to acquire other attitudes which will insure the development of a professional capacity to be helpful.

5. To gain appreciation for and understanding of social research, and in the second year to plan and carry out a research project individually or within a group.

6. To acquire an understanding and acceptance of the contribution of other professions and ability to work with them on common problems.

7. To establish an identification with the profession of social work and to become a professional person.

THE PROFESSIONAL CURRICULUM

The graduate program includes a basic core curriculum with method concentrations in casework, group work, and community organization. Social work education is generic; i.e., students enrolled in graduate schools of social work take courses which equip them basically for practice in any field of social work practice. The training consists, in the main, of classroom instruction and field work. Educational content and subject matter for social work consists of knowledge, principles of method, tools and techniques, values, community services, and research.

The curriculum is divided into main core areas: Social Welfare Policy and Services, Human Behavior and Social Environment, Social Work Methods, and Field Work.

SOCIAL WELFARE POLICY AND SERVICES

The social services curriculum consists of a series of classes at the graduate level which focus on the various ways in which society seeks to meet its responsibility for the social welfare of its members. This content area is designed to help students acquire:

1. An acquaintance with a broad variety of social problems, their extent, and their cost to society in terms of human suffering as well as financial loss.

2. A feeling for and understanding of the people whose unmet needs make up the social problem, and of the social forces which contribute to their misfortune.

3. An understanding and appreciation of the decision-making process by which society develops policy for preventing, ameliorating, or resolving such problems.

4. Knowledge of major policy decision as reflected through such legislation as the Social Security Act, and the National Mental Health Act.

5. Knowledge and understanding of social agency structure and function, programs, and services as provisions for implementing social policy.

6. A beginning skill in a systematic method of evaluating social agencies and social welfare services.

7. Recognition of the role of social work in the prevention of social problems and enrichment of social relationship functioning.

8. An appreciation of and a beginning sense of responsibility for the leadership role which social work should assume in consideration of social issues and planned social change.

HUMAN BEHAVIOR AND THE SOCIAL ENVIRONMENT

Human Behavior and the Social Environment is a second major division of the social work curriculum. The primary purpose of this sequence is to develop within students a sensitive knowledge of people and understanding of human behavior. A corollary purpose is that of developing professional attitudes, self-awareness, and a beginning understanding of the thinking and feeling of students toward a wide range of people-centered situations consonant with the theory and practice of modern professional social work. This sequence is designed to help students to:

1. Gain a knowledge of the functioning of the individual in continually interacting biosocial dimensions.

2. Obtain an understanding of the behavior and functioning of individuals at each developmental stage based on current theory and tested assumptions about physical maturation, emotional growth and change, and the socialization process.

3. Become aware of the concept of health and illness as a continuum, that a person may be in fact healthy and unhealthy at the same time, and that there is fluidity in the concept of health; know psycho-physiological states and the mind-body concept.

4. Understand that every healthy individual has the potential for

becoming ill. Understand the meaning of stresses which weaken healthy defenses and strengthen pathological ones.

5. Understand that the individual whose behavior is pathological, including the most regressed patient, may have ego potential and may use professional help to improve his social functioning. The student learns that he will meet people with pathology wherever he may be working.

6. Learn that although behavior under stress may resemble pathological behavior, disturbed behavior is not always pathological; gain the knowledge to assess stress and understand the adaptations used in coping with stress.

7. Be able to evaluate ego strengths and potential, while recognizing the role of the defenses in maintaining equilibrium under stress.

8. Gain some self-awareness without undue anxiety or identification with pathology. The student is expected to modify attitudes and develop feelings appropriate to practice with the mentally ill, the mentally retarded, and other disabled, the delinquent and adult offender, and with individuals in families who require the help of a social worker through an organization or institution provided by society.

As stated by Butler in the Curriculum Study of the Council on Social Work Education, the five major educational objectives, or knowledge areas, of the growth and behavior sequence, are: [7]

I. Understanding Endowment as the Source of the Potential for Human Functioning.

II. Understanding Environmental Forces Which May Enhance or Endanger the Potential for Social Functioning.

III. Understanding Interaction of Endowment and Environmental Forces as Enhancing or Endangering the Potential for Social Functioning.

IV. Understanding the Person's Response to Change and Stress.

V. Understanding Assessment of the Potential for Social Functioning.

METHODS OF SOCIAL WORK

A third major area of the social work curriculum comprises the methods of social work practice. These consist of casework, group work, and community organization, and, in addition, such enabling methods as administration and research. In general, methods courses are designed to help students to: [8]

Understand the relation of knowledge, value, and method in the appraisal

[7] Ruth M. Butler, *An Orientation to Knowledge of Human Growth and Behavior in Social Work Education,* Curriculum Study, Vol. VI (New York: Council on Social Work Education, 1959), p. 31.

[8] Official Statement of Curriculum Policy for the Master's Degree Program in Graduate Professional Schools of Social Work (New York: Council on Social Work Education, 1962), pp. 5–6.

of problems or situations for social work intervention and in the provision of professional service.

Develop the self-awareness requisite to disciplined performance as a social worker.

Recognize and appreciate the similarities and differences in the helping roles and problem-solving processes associated with service to individuals, groups, and communities.

Understand the responsibility and role of the social worker in contributing from professional knowledge to the prevention of social problems and to the improvement of social welfare programs, policies, and services.

The specific objectives of the methods courses are designed to help the student acquire:

1. Knowledge of social work principles, the professional relationship, referral procedures, the family, community, social values, the philosophy of social work, and the scientific method of problem solving.

2. Skill in the application of knowledge to specific situations, the uses of the processes of group work, casework, and community organization, the skill and the application of techniques—interviewing, recording, letter writing, etc.—skill in helping clients use personal and other resources, use of agency structure and function, and skill in the use of the relationship and the scientific process.

3. Appropriate attitudes, beliefs, and feelings about people that would include oneself as a professional person with awareness of one's own values and biases and how these affect practice; respect for the dignity and worth of people and their differences; appropriate attitudes about the community and various social agencies and services; the values, the goals, and the methods of the various processes of social work; and appropriate attitudes about objectivity and scientific inquiry.

Instruction on administration is given and is designed to help the student to: [9]

Understand and accept the concept of accountability of the social worker as a professional practitioner, agency employee, and agency representative.

Become familiar with administrative organization and method, particularly in relation to the functions of policy formation, decision-making, program-planning, supervision, and consultation.

Understand administrative process as it relates to social work purposes and values, and become familiar with administrative principles that make possible the effective provision of social welfare services.

Research instruction has the objective of helping students to:

Understand the nature and function of social work research and its relationship to the advancement of professional knowledge and improvement of professional practice.

Understand the relationship of research to the helping and problem-solving tasks of social work, and strengthen habits of disciplined thought and performance.

Become familiar with the application of principles of scientific inquiry to

[9] *Ibid.*, p. 6.

social work practice and to the prevention, treatment, and control of social problems.

Develop capacity to undertake or participate in studies and research, and to evaluate and use the results of research in social work practice.[10]

Student research culminates in a written study, project, or thesis.

FIELD WORK

Field work receives a strong emphasis in social work education. It is the social work *practicum* or *internship*. Field work takes place in agencies and provides practical experiences for the application of classroom theory. In field work the student is responsible for carrying a limited load of clients, patients, or groups under careful supervision in an approved social agency or institution. Field work parallels course work in most schools and is directed by the school staff in conjunction with the field instructor.

The field work experience supplements and reinforces not only the student's theoretical knowledge of principles and techniques, but also his understanding of human behavior, and his knowledge of a broad array of social services. It is different from merely carrying on the function of the agency. The student is helped to recognize general principles and theoretical concepts in specific practice situations, to become conscious of skills he uses intuitively, and to apply purposively the techniques he learns intellectually. The field work experience is an integral part of a comprehensive educational program.

The field work experience and curriculum stress those learning experiences and objectives that will enable students to:

1. Form and sustain meaningful professional relationships.

2. Develop self-awareness and self-discipline in professional relationships.

3. Develop a useful understanding of multiple positive factors in behavior, and to acquire skill in use of the available body of professional knowledge pertaining thereto.

4. Develop the ability to work knowingly and effectively within agency structure, function, and philosophy.

5. Develop an effective knowledge and use of community, state, and national resources.

6. Develop a knowledge and use of social work methods (casework, group work, community organization, research, and administration) as an integral part of social work practice, including professional competence with one method and an awareness of and some skill with the other four methods.

[10] *Ibid.*, p. 7.

7. Develop an awareness of the need for social action and the desire and capacity for leadership in such action.

8. Establish an identification with the profession of social work, and to become a professional person.

9. Gain competence in the scientific method of study, diagnosis, and treatment in all areas of social work practice.

ADMISSION TO SCHOOLS OF SOCIAL WORK

Students admitted to schools of social work are carefully screened. The door is open to candidates who have received their undergraduate degrees and who possess the potential for practice in the profession of social work. Men and women are accepted for training irrespective of race, creed, or color who can meet the personal and academic qualifications which usually include:

1. Evidence of superior ability, character, and personality.

2. Academic credentials attesting above average scholarship and satisfactory completion of four full years of collegiate work with a baccalaureate degree from an accredited college.

3. Suitable undergraduate background in the arts and sciences with some emphasis in the social sciences, i.e., sociology, psychology, political science, social ethics, anthropology, economics, and education.

4. A genuine interest in working with people.

5. An admissions interview with a member of the Admissions Committee.

A nationwide panel of professional interviewers constitutes a valuable adjunct to the screening of candidates for social work education. This panel is comprised of professional social workers strategically located throughout the United States and Canada. Qualifications of panel members are determined by the Council on Social Work Education followed by certification to the schools. Upon request from a school, a panelist will conduct an interview with an applicant, who is usually a person living within the same area as the interviewer, submit a record of the interview, which, together with other application material, is then used by the school in its admission decision. Panelists are not paid for their work, but they perform a service of incalculable worth to the profession.

Social work education makes high financial and personal demands upon the student and the community, and it would be a great disservice to both for a school to be lax in screening and selecting applicants. The personal and financial loss to the student who has to be "counseled out" is considerable. This becomes a disappointing, frustrating experience, frequently viewed as failure by the student. Moreover, the student who enrolls and then withdraws, has occupied a berth and required school and faculty time which might have been used more advantageously by other more promising students. Because of the sequential nature of the learning pattern of social work education, substitutions cannot be made easily; thus, fewer students can be trained for the field, which is serious indeed, considering the large unmet need for trained and qualified personnel.

The policy of schools of social work, which is reflected in their admission procedures, is to select only those college graduates who combine native endowment, relationship capacity, maturity, imagination, industry, motivation, and such other physical, social, emotional, and spiritual qualities which lend themselves to excellence in helping others.

The policy of some schools is not to admit students who have reached middle age, although many do not place an age limit on admission policies. Increasing numbers of students are admitted from foreign countries representing cultures which are radically different from American communities. Special problems often ensue in the training of foreign students, as would be expected, and this matter has received searching study from the profession which now has guidelines for schools admitting and training students from other countries. The profession is jealous of maintaining and improving its public image. It is constantly upgrading and seeking to improve the quality of its services to the public. Schools of social work are often the vanguard of this striving and have made notable advances in their educational contributions.

FINANCING STUDENT TRAINING

Social work education, as all quality professional education, is costly. Fortunately, it has received considerable encouragement in its efforts by various gifts, endowments, grants, and money for trainees. Many social agencies, public and private, assist students financially to obtain graduate social work education. Work study plans, provision for educational leave, and loans to students are a few of the more common arrangements.

An example of financial support for social work education is the program of the National Institute of Mental Health. Following the passage of the Mental Health Act in 1946, NIMH embarked upon a program of extending and improving psychiatric social work training in already established schools of social work. Under this program, schools of social work became eligible to apply for and receive training grants-in-aid. As the program matured, and its merits were demonstrated, Congress increased appropriations for training. Today grants-in-aid are available to schools for training in psychiatric social work, school social work, the field of corrections, and in other selected fields. These grants are substantial amounts and pay for instructional salaries and stipends, clerical help, and for such indirect costs as administration. In 1960–61, seven and eight-tenths million dollars went to schools of social work training in psychiatric social work alone. Of this amount "39 percent was on stipends, 37 percent on instructional salaries, 10 percent on other direct costs, and 14 percent on indirect costs." [11]

Stipends to students from the National Institute of Mental Health range from $1,800 to $3,600 plus tuition for each academic year of training. The first year cost of graduate training is defrayed by the amount of $1,800; second year, $2,000; third and fourth years, $3,600. Tuition is paid in addition to these amounts.

For fiscal years 1948–1961, 4,854 stipends were awarded to schools of social work, amounting to $10,662,263. Total training grants to schools of social work numbered 764 for fiscal years 1948–1961, for a total of $20,158,513.[12]

Grants-in-aid under the aegis of the National Institute of Mental Health have been highly effective in increasing the quality and number of trainees in virtually every school of social work in the United States. Statesmanship of the very highest quality has characterized the relationship between the National offices and the schools. The least intervention with the educational function commensurate with responsible administration of funds has keynoted more than fifteen years of social work education under this program.

The Vocational Rehabilitation Administration (VRA), in a way similar to NIMH, has stimulated sound educational developments in social work through providing considerable financial support for teaching and numerous stipends for students. The Veterans Administration has also adopted a work-study plan of payments to trainees which substantially assists approximately 300 students each year with their social work training. The new Public Welfare Administration, Washington, D.C., with an eye to improving staff performance, has embarked upon a substantial program of training which includes stipends for students, money with which to hire competent qualified field instructors, work-study plans, and various educational leave arrangements for eligible staff.

This program augments and accelerates previous efforts on the part of the federal and state governments to make stipends, scholarships, and educational leave provisions available for the training of child welfare and public assistance personnel.

The number of trained social workers in the public welfare field

[11] *Survey of Funding and Expenditures for Training of Mental Health Personnel, 1960–1961* (Washington, D.C.: U.S. Department of Health, Education and Welfare, 1963), p. 3.

[12] Roger L. Robertson and Eli A. Rubinstein, *Training Grant Program, Fiscal Years 1948–1961* (Washington, D.C.: Department of Health, Education, and Welfare, n.d.g.), pp. 20, 55.

is small; not more than 5 percent in public welfare and 26 percent in the child welfare field possess Masters' degrees. The burden of their task is demanding and to do the job efficiently and well, training is definitely required.

Many private agencies have invested some fraction of their gift dollars in training, and in so doing have encouraged a greater excellence on the part of staff. Notable among these have been federated fund-raising organizations many of which, as policy, set aside 1 percent of their gift money for the training and recruiting of staff.

In no other profession is there greater evidence of public support for training than in social work where 82.5 percent of all full-time students received financial aid in some form in their training during the academic year 1961–62.[13] Some schools report that every eligible candidate can be assured of some financial support to defray cost of social work education at the graduate level of training.

The community appears increasingly willing to invest funds in education in order to make certain that the clientele of social work agencies will be helped by those having requisite knowledge, skill, and scholarship.

COUNCIL ON SOCIAL WORK EDUCATION

Social work schools have greatly improved their offering to students and to the public. They have raised their standards of training, tightened admission requirements, and shifted from narrow practice specialization to a generic approach emphasizing broad basic principles and concepts, values, and philosophy.

The Council on Social Work Education, created by the schools in 1952 as an upgrading, standard-setting, and a maintaining arm of the profession, certifies the program of schools and accredits training. An important Council objective is to continuously improve professional education in all schools of social work. Curriculum standardization is general and allows for considerable experimentation and flexibility. Accreditation is based on a generic two-year program.

Notable also is the institution of periodic accreditation reviews (at ten-year intervals) to insure that all schools of social work are keeping abreast of changing educational requirements. Accreditation standards are more and more expressed in terms of educational goals to be achieved and less and less in terms of fixed absolutes. The process of accreditation is one that is increasingly shared by the Commission through ongoing cooperation with the six regional accrediting bodies and the National Accrediting Commission.[14]

13 *Social Work Education, op. cit.,* p. 28.
14 *Social Work Year Book, 1960* (New York: National Association of Social Workers, 1960), p. 226.

The Council is a coordinating force. It is a rallying point for educational institutions which train social workers. It brings members of its organization together for meetings, and provides various other important services to schools and groups. The major functions of the Council include: [15]

Continuous review, formulation, and reformulation of educational standards for social work.

Accreditation of the program of graduate schools based on established educational standards.

Evaluation and re-evaluation of graduate programs of social work education.

Maintenance of working relationships, in the interests of social work education, with national and regional accrediting organizations and with other educational bodies.

Formulation of curriculum policy, development of curriculum content, and provision of consultation on curriculum organization in content to graduate schools, undergraduate departments, social work agencies, government departments, and other organizations.

Consideration of the nature and content of undergraduate education for social work.

Development of sound curriculum plans for post-master's education.

Development, publication, and distribution of publications, including informational materials, proceedings, brochures, and pamphlets on all phases of social work education at the undergraduate, graduate, and post-master's levels.

Selection and publication of teaching materials for use in graduate schools, undergraduate departments, and staff development programs.

Provision of an annual national meeting on social work education (held in January of each year), and sponsorship of occasional regional meetings, special workshops, and conferences.

Provision of educational services relating to (a) the administration of schools of social work, (b) more adequate financing of social work education, (c) teaching methods, (d) development of scholarship and fellowship programs, and (e) equitable distribution of educational facilities.

Sponsorship of research on educational questions and issues at all levels of social work preparation.

Increasing the quantity and competence of social workers, particularly through organizing and conducting a national recruitment program, study of admission procedures, and development of methods for evaluating educational results.

Encouragement of and participation in programs of international exchange and cooperation.

Making the knowledge about social work education as developed in Canada and the United States available to other countries.

SOCIAL WORK EDUCATION AND THE FUTURE

There have been many significant developments in social work education during the past half century. Graduate schools have been established and social work given status within the university setting. Schools

[15] *Ibid.*, pp. 225–226.

have successfully formed themselves into an association of schools whose mandates, rules, and educational standards they established, and which in turn they accept as binding upon themselves.

Social work is forging the tools for keeping pace with rapid social change. The Council on Social Work Education, with foundation financial support, recently sponsored a curriculum study. Referred to as the Social Work Curriculum Study, this thirteen volume analysis

is a milestone in the development of effective educational programs for professions which are in the midst of profound changes. Since World War II, the rapid increase in population and its great mobility, the marked changes in the economy with the consequent shifts in occupations and employment, and the changes in the expectations and attitudes of the American people have set new conditions in which and with which the social services must function. At the same time, the sharp acceleration of demand for personnel in all professions creates severe shortages in social work and increases the need for educational programs that can effectively prepare highly competent social workers who can function productively under these new conditions. The educational programs developed in earlier years for a different set of conditions required rethinking and replanning.[16]

Four framework statements produced by social work in a period of forty years have in turn guided curriculum building in all approved institutions. The latest, adopted in 1962, although offering guidelines for schools as they forge ahead, is not the final word. Changes occur in programming at the very moment framework statements are being drafted, and some schools have already gone beyond the 1962 statement in curriculum building.

No school is tightly bound by framework statements. The profession seeks to achieve standards of performance and to improve the quality of education. It is not interested in rigid conformity and schools have been encouraged to use the reports and policy statements of the standard-setting bodies in ways germane to their circumstances and needs in achieving excellence.

Each curriculum statement has been built upon its predecessor, and it can be assumed that successive curriculum framework statements will follow and schools will probably continue to build solidly upon the experiences, knowledge, and accomplishments of the past.

Plans for reviewing, evaluating, and reevaluating of graduate programs have been formulated, and the machinery for implementation securely augmented by procedures, timetables, and competent Council staff. The impetus and far-reaching changes in social work education resulting from all these efforts are incalculable.

[16] Werner W. Boehm, *Objectives of the Social Work Curriculum in the Future*, Curriculum Study, Vol. I (New York: Council on Social Work Education, 1959), p. xiii.

SUMMARY

From small beginnings as independent institutions of learning, social work education has become established in leading colleges and universities. Practice-oriented courses have been supplanted by more academic theory and concept-related schooling.

The profession has created a Council on Social Work Education for the United States and Canada comprised of schools of social work, practice organizations, and social work agencies to establish educational standards, accredit programs, evaluate and reevaluate programs of training, and to otherwise address its efforts to strengthening and improving social work education.

The curriculum for the Master's degree in social work consists basically of course work in three core areas: human behavior and social environment, social services, and social work methods, including research and opportunity for supervised field instruction. Theory is taught and learned in the classroom. Field instruction typically occurs in a variety of social agencies where broad representative experiences are sought for and by the student.

Admission policies of schools are aimed at screening students and admitting those who show promise for practice in the field of social work. They have been carefully worked out by schools of social work and consist of such techniques as the written application, autobiographical material, interview, transcript of credits, and other screening examinations and admission procedures designed to assure the student and the school of a sound educational investment.

Schools receive funds for part of their faculties from grants and foundations, and a high percentage of students enrolling in schools can and do depend upon financial aid in the form of scholarships and stipends. Among the more prominent of the stipend arrangements are those administered by state welfare departments, by the National Institute of Mental Health, the Vocational Rehabilitation Administration, and the Veterans Administration.

Social work education is carefully scrutinized by its leaders who are dedicated to excellence of training. Educators work assiduously on the curriculum and the thirteen volume *Social Work Curriculum Study* attests to the seriousness with which social work training is viewed by the profession.

The future of social work education is promising in the light of developments in schools and the profession. The profession has created the machinery for maintaining standards and increasing the quality and effectiveness of the educational effort. The field is aware of the need to improve its services to the public and works energetically at it.

QUESTIONS FOR DISCUSSION

1. Explain the concomitant development of social work education and the social services.

2. In what manner has the Council on Social Work Education served the welfare of clients who are made recipients of professional social work service?

3. What is meant by a *core area* of the curriculum?

4. What is the rationale for a core area of curriculum consisting of knowledge of behavior, methods, and services?

5. What are the values of field work instruction?

6. Defend the logic of education which combines both theory and practice.

7. Evaluate the importance to social work education of financial support of graduates in training.

8. What, if any, is the provision of your college or university for the interweaving of preprofessional social work instruction and training?

9. Make an estimate of the future of social work education in a changing world.

SPECIAL ACTIVITIES

1. Write a prospectus on the philosophy of the traditional liberal arts view of undergraduate education and how this view differs from the approach to vocational and professional training at your university or college.

2. Prepare a five-minute talk on the history of social work education in the United States.

SELECTED REFERENCES

BISNO, HERBERT, *The Place of the Undergraduate Curriculum in Social Work Education,* Curriculum Study, Vol. II (New York: Council on Social Work Education, 1959).

BOEHM, WERNER W., *Objectives of the Social Work Curriculum of the Future,* Curriculum Study, Vol. I (New York: Council on Social Work Education, 1959).

BUTLER, RUTH M., *An Orientation to Knowledge of Human Growth and Behavior in Social Work Education,* Curriculum Study, Vol. VI (New York: Council on Social Work Education, 1959).

HOLLIS, ERNEST V., and TAYLOR, ALICE L., *Social Work Education in the United States* (New York: Columbia University Press, 1951).

LURIE, HARRY L., *The Community Organization Method in Social Work Education,* Curriculum Study, Vol. IV (New York: Council on Social Work Education, 1959).

MENCHER, SAMUEL, *The Research Method in Social Work Education,* Curriculum Study, Vol. IX (New York: Council on Social Work Education, 1959).

MURPHY, MARJORIE, *The Social Group Work Method in Social Work Education,* Curriculum Study, Vol. XI (New York: Council on Social Work Education, 1959).

PUMPHREY, MURIEL W., *The Teaching of Values and Ethics in Social Work Education,* Curriculum Study, Vol. XIII (New York: Council on Social Work Education, 1959).

ROBERTSON, ROGER L. and RUBINSTEIN, ELI A., *Training Grant Programs Fiscal Years 1948–1961* (Washington, D.C.: U.S. Department of Health, Education, and Welfare, n.d.g.).

WEISSMAN, IRVING, *Social Welfare Policy and Services in Social Work Education*, Curriculum Study, Vol. XII (New York: Council on Social Work Education, 1959).

WITTMAN, MILTON, *Scholarship Aid in Social Work Education* (New York: Council on Social Work Education, 1956).

CHAPTER **21**

Social Work and the Future

We live in a rapidly changing world which idolizes speed and automation. Newspapers flash the latest scientific inventions, and trips to the
moon appear possible within the foreseeable future. As satellites and
astronauts encircle the globe, and TV and other broadcasts become
worldwide, many questions arise regarding the part that people and
human relationships play in the total scheme of things.

Indicative of the prospects of the future and the rapidly changing
world was a suggestion of Dr. Mortimer Adler that the most important
cabinet position in the United States Government in the future could
well be the "Secretary of the Future." [1] He then suggested that two major
problems face future generations. First, "Can the masses obtain the intellectual, cultural, and comfortable levels which in the past were held only
by a few aristocrats?" Second, "Could it be that man isn't up to enjoying
too much free time, power, comfort and wealth which technological advances will undoubtedly realize in the next thousand years?" [2]

In this fast moving, push-button age, where is social work likely to
find itself? In the years ahead, how will social work fit into the total
scheme?

If it were possible to look into a crystal ball and to see exactly what
is ahead, we would likely be surprised in many ways. Since this is impossible, the next best action is to look at the past and the present and
to make projections and predictions based upon available knowledge

[1] Lecture by Dr. Mortimer Adler at the University of Utah, February 18, 1963.
[2] *Utah Chronicle*, February 19, 1963, p. 1.

regarding what is likely to happen. This chapter is an attempt to consider some of the likely developments in social work in the years ahead.

INCREASE IN SERVICES

Present-day facts in social welfare indicate that social work services will increase in the future. Leaders in welfare estimate that within the next ten years, 44,500 additional trained social workers will be needed. In child welfare alone it is predicted that about 12,000 new social workers will be wanted, along with 21,000 for public assistance and family services, and 11,500 more for juvenile delinquency services.

Not only are the demands increasing for trained social workers on the federal governmental level, but also on state and local levels. State mental health departments, for example, are asking for more trained personnel. State hospitals, industrial schools, medical hospitals, state prisons, and other state institutions are seeking additional trained social workers.

On the local level, school districts, hospitals, mental hygiene clinics, and many other agencies and institutions are seeking additional trained social workers, and the demand is likely to increase in the years ahead.

Private agencies are reaching out and asking for more social workers. There are shortages in family service societies, children placement agencies, neighborhood houses, YMCA's, Girl Scouts, and in many other local and national private agencies.

Numerous reasons exist for the increased demands for social workers. People today are more aware of resources for helping with personal, family, and community problems; thus, they reach out for competent practitioners when serious problems arise. Thousands of persons and families have tasted the help which they can receive from qualified personnel and have told their relatives and friends about these services. When personal and social problems strike, the guideposts point toward those who can be of assistance. A wife whose marriage has been "saved" by the Family Service Society tells her close friend, with enthusiasm, about this agency when the friend divulges she is having serious marital difficulties which are shattering her family circle.

It is likely in the future that in addition to expansions of social work in traditional agencies, both governmental and private, there will be innovations. Some business leaders are beginning to hire social workers to assist in personnel work, recognizing that employees who have difficult personal or family problems are not the best workers. The basic premise is that qualified social workers can help employees to solve their personal and family problems and consequently to become more effective and efficient on the job. An interesting current development involves a leading hotel in Miami Beach, Florida, which advertises that it provides a qualified marriage counselor—available for guests at the hotel, particularly those on their honeymoons—if they need assistance with marital and family problems. The possibilities are almost unlimited in respect to the avenues along which social work services may develop. Since personal, family, and community problems affect all people, directly or indirectly, social work services which help people to meet these problems are likely, in the years ahead, to expand and to move into virgin areas of service.

It is estimated that there are at least twelve to fifteen thousand vacancies for qualified social workers at present in the United States. With the 1962 Amendments to the Social Security Act and other developing services in governmental and private agencies, it is likely that there will be additional demands for qualified social workers in the years ahead.

PROFESSIONAL IDENTIFICATION

One of the challenging problems of the emerging profession of social work has been the need to develop a stronger professional identification. A few decades ago there were many dedicated social workers and several independent, semiprofessional associations, all of which at times seemed to be striking out in different directions. A most significant step took place in 1955 with the amalgamation of seven of these independent associations into the National Association of Social Workers. This Association has already made major contributions to the development of professional interest and identification. Through its staff and various committees, it has helped practitioners, educators, lay citizens, and students to realize that social work is an important profession which calls for the best in people, including integrity, maturity of personality, and specific professional graduate training. The Association has helped considerably to assist social workers to identify with their profession, and to interpret to non-social workers the role of social work in this nuclear age.

Graduate students are encouraged to become student members in this Association and to identify with its purposes and activities prior to embarking upon practice. Two thousand seven hundred and ninety-nine joined in 1962. They have an opportunity to study the Code of Ethics and to understand its professional implications. They also have excellent opportunities for association with professional persons, self-expression, and professional identification. In the years ahead it is likely that this Association will continue to bolster, build, and strengthen the profession, both on a national and local level. Its membership is increasing each year and is likely to continue to do so. In 1961 the membership totaled 34,494. By the end of 1962 it had increased to 36,741.

On a local chapter basis, it is probable that members of NASW will devote more of their time and talents to strengthening their profession, improving practice, expanding recruitment, and participating in other professional activities. NASW chapters are sponsoring worthwhile programs as they have never done before; and this momentum is likely to continue in the years ahead.

The Council on Social Work Education which was established in 1952, with its special emphasis on training, has been another major force in leading social workers to a stronger professional identification. The Council began with a minimum personnel and now has several full-time staff and professional consultants. Its annual Conference has increased in stature so that it had a paid attendance of 969 at its 1963 meeting in Boston. These persons came from colleges and universities with graduate training programs in social work, from undergraduate programs in preparation for social work, as well as from various fields of practice. The participants joined together with serious intent to understand social work better and to improve the training programs resulting in more effective practice in social work. Various projects and activities of the Council are providing many opportunities for strengthening the total profession. In the years ahead, it is likely that the Council will grow stronger and provide even more services related to social work education on the undergraduate, Master's, and Doctoral levels.

Apparently, one of the fundamental needs in social work is for stronger professional identification and maturity; and it appears from every indication that in the years ahead these will be realized.

LICENSING

Within the past decade several steps have been made toward licensing in social work. For a field to become a full-fledged profession, it is almost imperative that some kind of official control and licensing be in operation. Doctors must pass an examination and be issued a license in the state in which they practice. Lawyers qualify by taking state bar examinations to become properly licensed. Until a few years ago, there was little attempt to control social work standards and practice. However, within the past several years there have been assertive activities in some states related to certification or licensing.

California, for example, for several years has had a system of *registered social workers* which has attempted to help separate the trained social workers from the untrained. This has been basically a voluntary system, and yet, across the years, has apparently been effective in helping to raise standards and to aid the people in training to do the jobs required of them.

In 1961 the National Association of Social Workers inaugurated a movement to strengthen social work practice. Provision was made for a voluntary system of registration, resulting in *certified social workers*. An Academy of Certified Social Workers was established and practicing workers were invited to apply for membership. Membership was contingent upon a person's having had two years of paid social work employment and two years of NASW membership. Stipulations were that future applicants must not only have a Master's degree in social work, but also at least two years of experience in social work under qualified supervision by a member of the Academy of Certified Social Workers. This plan has been approved with considerable enthusiasm by professional social workers as a major step forward toward licensing. In 1963, there were more than 20,000 persons who had applied for certification and who had been awarded membership in the Academy of Certified Social Workers. As a result of this movement, social workers everywhere now add *ACSW* after their names on letters, just as persons of other professions give designations which display professional meaning.

In the years ahead it is entirely likely that social work will take another step forward—licensing of social workers will become an accomplished fact. There are already attempts in some states in this direction. California, for example, has proposed bills before the Legislature which would make this possible. In other areas, efforts are being made to bring about licensing of qualified social workers. As states establish provisions for licensing social workers, undoubtedly the status of social work will be enhanced and the roles and functions of those who are adequately trained will be more clearly identified.

Several beneficial effects will likely accrue as licensing becomes a reality. Such a program will minimize the number of charlatans and others who are unqualified to help people with personal, family, and community problems. Second, such a program will increase the professional status of social work and make its services even more effective. Licensing also would probably cull out the few trained social workers who are not able to do a satisfactory job in practice.

Estimates differ regarding licensing and when it will become established. Some think it will become popular within a few years; others believe it may be a decade or two before becoming a reality in many states.

CLARIFICATION OF "SOCIAL WORK ASSOCIATE"

In the years ahead it is likely that there will be clarification regarding the roles played and services performed by those with preprofessional training in social welfare and social work. During the past several years there has been a movement to originate a name for those who have completed an undergraduate sequence in social welfare, but who have not continued toward a Master's degree in social work. The Curriculum Study, Council on Social Work Education, recommended that the words *Social Work Associate* might be used to describe persons who had completed a satisfactory undergraduate program in social welfare, which includes study of basic knowledge, principles, goals, institutions, and agencies. Emphasis would not be on techniques and skills but rather on gaining a broad, overall view of social welfare, institutions, and social functioning of people. This proposal was an attempt to recognize that there are persons in social welfare and social work who have different amounts of training and that there are various jobs which can be handled adequately by persons with different levels of training.

The general conclusions of the Curriculum Study described the underlying philosophy and proposals for more recognition of undergraduate social welfare training programs: [3]

On the basis of assumptions we postulated and the preceding analyses of the shortage of social workers, the difficult competitive position of social work in regard to recruitment, and the possibilities of effective differentiation among social work functions, we conclude as follows:

1. Social work education at the undergraduate level should have as one goal the preparation of students for employment in social work upon graduation.

2. Such undergraduate education might appropriately aim at the preparation of "social work associates." It should not and need not fail to prepare students simultaneously for advanced training and full professional standing.

3. "Legitimatizing" a category of "social work associates" would necessitate, as a minimum, specification of relatively attainable, definite, but limited educational requirements, and appropriate recognition of this occupational status by the professional association.

Inclusion of educational preparation for an occupation within a college or university goes a long way toward legitimatizing it. For social work associates, it would imply that they are being prepared in at least a minimally adequate manner for the positions they will hold, in contrast with the present view of them as less than adequately prepared substitutes for presently unattainable professional social workers. Of course, professions are not static and it is possible that in the future other levels may be developed. With such further differentiations, social work associate and "social worker" might be upgraded, or even merged.

4. The probability is that legitimatizing the social work associate category would result in an overall upgrading of social work standards, greater adequacy of service, and improved personnel morale, as well as raising the societal evaluation of social work, provided the following minimum conditions were met: (1) clear recognition . . . that certain social work positions, because of their defined functional characteristics, need to be filled by professional social workers with completed graduate education; (2) the availability of a reasonably adequate number of social workers to fill such positions; (3) establishing of salary and other status differentials commensurate with the various levels of preparation; (4) a quality of job performance by social workers and social work associates that reflects the differential value of their training in comparison with persons with less or no special education.

5. A conclusion that follows logically from the preceding one is that students who qualify, upon graduation, for the status of social work associate, should

---

[3] Herbert Bisno, *The Place of the Undergraduate Curriculum in Social Work Education,* Curriculum Study, Vol. II (New York: Council on Social Work Education, 1959), pp. 77–78.

be granted employment preference for appropriate types of social work positions over those without such training.

6. While the development and expansion of agency in-service training programs is highly desirable, such programs constitute an inappropriate method, in principle, of meeting the need for more social workers. Such programs should be used to complement formal social work education rather than to substitute for it at any level. Conversely, specific training for performance in particular settings *is* appropriately included in in-service training programs but is not a legitimate function of an undergraduate college.

At the annual meeting of the Council on Social Work Education held in Boston in 1963, the director, Dr. Ernest Witte, in a major address, proposed that a new program be established and approved to help provide more workers with limited training, who could assist in meeting the tremendous demand for workers in social welfare. He suggested the designation should be *social welfare aide* and that a person could be given this kind of certification upon the completion of an adequate undergraduate sequence in social welfare, plus six months of additional training and experience upon graduation. This would involve a training program of ten weeks of classes under the leadership of graduate schools of social work, followed by three months of in-service training in a participating agency. During the agency experience, these workers-in-training would participate in a weekly seminar sponsored jointly by the school and the agency. At the end of this time, a certificate would be awarded which would give the official stamp of the social work profession, recognizing this as a limited kind of approval, but would qualify a person to perform many services in social welfare. This would help to bring people who had some training experience into jobs where, at the present time, individuals are handling them who have very little or no training or experience in social welfare.

It is felt by many—and perhaps by most social workers—that there is a definite need to provide undergraduate emphasis and preprofessional training programs. This seems particularly significant in light of the fact that of the 105,000 persons employed in social welfare in 1960, only about one in five had had two years of graduate work in a school of social work. The question arises: Is it not better for persons working in social welfare programs to have some training than to have none?

At the Council meetings in Boston there was considerable discussion about the title to be used in the six months training programs. In addition to the designation *social welfare aide, social work aide* and *social work associate* were proposed. It was felt by many that persons working in social work agencies should have the term *social work* attached to their title rather than *social welfare*.

Although the proposal mentioned above was made by the Council staff and board, there is nothing binding upon the affiliated schools to carry it

out. In the years ahead, however, it is likely that many schools will experiment with the provision of some kind of program for *social work
aides* or *social work associates,* with particular emphasis on undergraduate and/or a few months of postgraduate training and experience for
these certifications. It is possible, also, that the Council on Social Work
Education may take a more definite stand on such training programs as
part of the offerings of the schools of social work in the United States and
Canada.

Along with training programs related to undergraduate offerings and
the Master's degree level, the future will undoubtedly bring further clarification of the roles which each of the workers is to perform on the job.
Attempts are being made at present to clarify and spell out explicitly
role specifications and job expectations, depending upon the training and
experience of those who are participating. Undoubtedly, further clarification will take place in the future.

DEVELOPMENT OF TRAINING PROGRAMS

Schools of social work are bombarded from every angle by employers
who wish to interview and to hire their graduates. With a current shortage of at least 12,000 persons with Master's degrees, it seems imperative
that, if the demand is ever to be met, there will need to be more schools
of social work. At present there are sixty-three schools in the United
States and Canada, and the number of graduates earning MSW degrees is
only about 2,500 a year. This number would need to be more than
doubled to begin to meet the demands for trained social workers.

Many schools of social work are operating at full capacity at present.
A major limiting factor is the number of field work placements available.
However, as the number of trained workers increases, the number of
potential field instructors expands accordingly. This should open the
door to more trainees in the future. Furthermore, there are some schools
of social work which are not operating at capacity. If applicants who
want training can be encouraged to attend these schools, this will be
helpful in increasing the total number of graduates.

New schools of social work are being founded at the rate of about one
or two a year. These, of course, will assist in increasing the number
of qualified social workers.

Probably no other field or profession has as many scholarships provided for its students as does social work. Wittman, in his study of 820
social work students (a 22 percent sample as of November, 1953), found
that 69 percent of the students received financial grants, yet only 46 percent reported this aid as the primary source of income. It was of interest
to note that 524 of the students (64 percent) reported that they knew of

others who might have entered social work education if scholarship aid funds had been available. Wittman concluded: [4]

> Scholarship aid is an essential part of the educational system in social work. With over two-thirds of the students receiving grants, and half of the students reporting they could not enter the professional school without the help they were receiving, it is quickly perceived that the role of aid is a sustaining and crucial one to the student group.

In 1962, according to the Council on Social Work Education, 82.5 percent (5,501) of all full-time students enrolled in graduate schools of social work were receiving financial aid in some form during the academic year. The actual number of grants rose from 5,355 in 1961 to 6,231 in 1962.

The federal government, through its training programs sponsored by the National Institute of Mental Health, the Vocational Rehabilitation Administration, the Children's Bureau, and other agencies, is offering hundreds of scholarships, work-study grants, and other financial assistance to social work students. The typical grant is $1,800 plus tuition for the first year and $2,000 plus tuition for the second year. The Veterans Administration also provides about three hundred work-study grants which vary in amount from about $1,400 to $2,400 a year, depending upon background, experience, and hours spent in field work. It is likely that in the future these stipends and financial assistance programs will be maintained and even increased because of the need to induce additional, capable students into training, and to fill national and local needs for social workers.

A recent development in social work education, which will likely increase, is the doctoral program. Seventeen schools of social work at present provide post-Master's training which can lead to a third-year certificate, a Doctor of Social Work degree, or a Ph.D. degree with a major in social work. These doctoral programs vary considerably, and so far there have been no specific standards established by the Council on Social Work Education regarding them. However, within a few years there will probably be some recommendations and minimum requirements formulated.

Most of the Doctoral programs in social work require the students to take courses taught by the social work faculty and also to enroll in related graduate departments which can help them to enrich their understanding of human behavior and of the helping processes. Some of them offer additional field work experience.

In all probability, most of those who obtain a Doctoral degree will go into schools of social work and become teachers themselves. Some will undoubtedly enter practice in key administrative positions in hospitals, mental hygiene clinics, or other social work agencies.

[4] Milton Wittman, *Scholarship Aid in Social Work Education* (New York: Council on Social Work Education, 1956), p. 79.

Another development which will likely increase is the third-year program. This is an offering which helps persons to specialize and to become more adept in a particular social work method or process, for example, casework, group work, community organization, research, or administration. Persons who enroll in this kind of program and who receive a third-year certificate upon completion of their studies, participate in a considerable amount of field work related to a particular method as well as appropriate class work.

INTERDISCIPLINARY COLLABORATION

At the present time, social workers cooperate with representatives of many other professional disciplines, and the future will most likely intensify these relationships. The professional team will probably become even more effective in trying to work with the total individual, the total family, and the total problems through interdisciplinary cooperation.

The professional team, including particularly the psychiatrist, social worker, and psychologist, is beginning to be utilized in many agencies and services other than in the traditional mental hygiene clinic or hospital setting where this team has been in operation for years. For example, the professional team is being used in public welfare services, in schools, in family service societies, and in many other public and private agencies, both for diagnosis and treament services. Many juvenile courts and adult probation and parole programs are now taking advantage of professional team work to improve their services.

The team relationship implies a two-way process. This means that each profession provides ideas, skills, and suggestions for the team and also receives these from the others. This working together in sharing of knowledge, attitudes, and skills is one of the cogent reasons that the use of the professional team approach is likely to be expanded to provide services for people with personal, family, and community problems.

DEVELOPMENT OF ROLE OF CONSULTANT

Within the past few years, social workers have not only used consultants from the disciplines of psychiatry, psychology, medicine, and other areas, but have become consultants themselves. Many social workers are now spending their full time in the role of consultant. For example, in one school district in California, two social workers spend their entire working day, every day, in a consultative capacity. They talk with teachers, principals, counselors, and other professional people about their problems in working with the boys and girls and their families. The basic aim is to help teachers, counselors, and others to understand themselves better and what they are doing in relation to assisting the boys and girls with personal or family troubles.

Social workers are used as consultants in a variety of settings, and are likely in the future to be used by additional agencies. They are hired as consultants not only in schools and in mental hygiene clinics, but in family service societies, in YW and YMCA's, in Girl Scout groups, in hospitals, and in numerous other kinds of agencies.

In the role of consultant, the social worker acts mainly as a catalyst who unlocks the door to bring about better understanding, information, and procedures which may be helpful to other professional people. In this capacity the social worker does not instruct the others as to what to do, but helps them to understand what different lines of action are possible and then leaves the choices to them. As a consultant, the social worker does not have authority over those with whom he consults. He acts as an advisor and one who assists them to understand more about social dysfunctioning and what can be done about it.

MORE RESEARCH

Social workers are the first to recognize that they can ask more questions about human behavior and the solution of human problems than they can answer. This immediately implies, of course, the tremendous need for additional scientific research and study regarding social functioning of people and how to deal with it.

The future seems to hold almost unlimited challenges for research regarding people, their relationships, and reduction of social malfunctioning.

A few years ago, almost nothing was spent upon research regarding human relations. Today, millions of dollars are being appropriated both by government and private foundations and agencies to encourage and sponsor worthwhile research projects.

Two main kinds of studies are sponsored in particular. One is the objective evaluation of current activities, both from a pure and applied research point of view. The other is provision for experimental or demonstration projects which are accompanied by built-in evaluation programs to keep careful account of what transpires. In the field of juvenile delinquency control alone, Congress in 1961 authorized ten million dollars for each of three fiscal years, to encourage experimentation and evaluation of projects in order to try to better control and prevent delinquency in this country.

Several large foundations have appropriated millions of dollars to study human relations, social problems, and what can be done about the problems.

In addition to governmental and foundation grants, many agencies, both public and private, are now including in their regular budgets appropriations for research so that they can evaluate what they are doing. Public welfare departments are supporting research along with family service societies and other agencies. Community welfare councils and united funds, in particular, are hiring trained, qualified researchers to become integral parts of their staffs. In one large community, twelve staff members are spending their full time in research activities related to community problems and their solution.

Human behavior and social problems are extremely complex. This means, then, that we must keep whittling away if we are to find answers to the questions about social relationships and solutions of social problems. In the future research will certainly become even more important than it has been in the past.

INCREASED STATUS

The future undoubtedly portends greater status for the social worker than the past or present. When social work was coming into its own during the early decades of the twentieth century, many people "raised their eyebrows" regarding it and were very critical. Some claimed social work was all wrong because it abolished independence. Others declared social work was synonymous with socialism, and even communism. A minority thought of social work as merely the process of handing out a dole to the poor and transient.

In the last two decades tremendous shifts in attitudes have taken place. While community leaders were previously sometimes critical of social work and its practices, today many of these same leaders are making referrals of relatives and close friends to social work agencies. The general attitude has changed so much that most citizens today look upon social work as a beginning profession which has many *solid* services to perform. These changes are evident in the increased demand for social workers, not only in regard to well-established social work services, but in the creation of new agencies and services to help to meet personal, family, and community problems.

Probably the main reason for the favorable shift in attitude has been because millions of individuals, families, and numerous communities have benefited from social work services. As people have been helped with their personal and family problems, to face them, work them through, and go on to an enrichment of living, they have become ardent exponents of social work and its services.

In the years ahead this trend is likely to continue. As training is increased and differentiation within jobs evolves, total social work practice will probably become even more effective and worthwhile. As this takes place, undoubtedly the position of the profession will continue to rise in public esteem. Although today, according to some studies, there are several professions which have higher prestige and status ratings than does social work, the movement seems to be gradual and substantial toward an elevation of its position. Increased salaries and improved working conditions, along with fringe benefits, are indicative of this development.

A significant factor in the increased status of social work is the *emergence of the male social worker*. Traditionally, the social worker was a woman who was a dedicated humanitarian. In recent years a considerable shift has taken place in the number of men attending graduate schools and graduating. For example, for the academic year 1931–32, there were only 10 (6 percent) male graduates [5] among the 166 obtaining second-year degrees. By 1950 the number had increased to 543 (29 percent) out of a total of 1,857; and by 1961 there were 980 (42 percent) men who received their Master's degree in social work, compared to 1,330 (58 percent) women.

The increased number of men entering the field of social work has had, and will likely continue to have, a salutary effect on the status of the social worker. Men usually receive higher salaries than women. They tend to stay in their positions for longer periods of time and add stability to a profession. Many people still regard women as *supplementary wage earners*. Public awareness of more men entering the field aids in the recruitment of both men and women. Men hold more top administrative and research positions, relatively speaking, than do women. All of these implications augur well for bringing about an increased status in social work in the future. Of course, social work is a profession for both men and women, and one in which both can serve with dedication and distinction.

HIGHER SALARIES

During the Great Depression of the 1930's, many social workers were hired for as little as $60 to $100 a month. Most of them were untrained. Many persons who wanted to enter into social work did not do so because they felt that salaries were too low. In the 1940's there was a considerable change in the salary pattern, although incomes were still in a relatively low position compared with other professions.

In the 1950's, salaries took a definite turn for the better. In 1950, the median salary for a social welfare worker in the United States was $2,960. By 1960, according to the survey by the U.S. Department of Labor, it had increased to $5,220.

The National Association of Social Workers originally recommended

[5] Rex A. Skidmore and Milton G. Thackeray, "Male Social Workers—On the Increase," *Personnel Information,* Vol. 6 (May, 1963), p. 33.

a minimum beginning salary for a person with an MSW degree of $5,400 and, hopefully, a wage scale that would allow for $10,000 after ten years of experience. Within a few years, this beginning salary was achieved and now NASW has raised its minimum recommendation to $6,000 beginning salary for a person with a Master's degree and no experience. Salaries are continuing to improve so that more social workers are now earning $10,000 or more a year, and the hope is for additional workers to reach the five-figure class after they have been in practice for some years.

Salaries, of course, vary considerably and some agencies pay a minimum. On the other hand, there are many social workers who make considerably more than $10,000 a year; and there are some in key administrative positions in the larger cities who receive an annual income of $25,000 or more. Since the demand for social workers is critical, it is likely that the salaries will continue to increase.

Higher salaries will probably attract more men and women of excellent backgrounds and dedicated interests in people. This, again, will provide an effective chain reaction for improving the status and prestige of the profession. As salaries increase, better people apply for training, which results in more effective social work services. More effective services help to bring about increases in salaries. From nearly every direction the prospect looks encouraging for higher salaries and enhanced status in social work.

STRESS ON COMMUNITY ORGANIZATION

With the approval, as specified in the 1960 Curriculum Policy Statement, of community organization as one of the three basic methods in social work, has come a sanction and recognition of the importance of this method. Traditionally, the emphasis has been upon casework and group work. Today, and in looking ahead, there is increased emphasis on the community approach to social problems, human interaction, and social functioning. Many leaders today believe that the community approach is the one with the greatest potential in facing and solving the ills of society. Experimentation has indicated that sometimes, through a single community-sponsored project, hundreds of personal and family problems can be alleviated or prevented.

This new emphasis on community organization does not mean that casework and group work are methods of the past. In fact, they are just as important, or more so, as before. Individuals will always need individual help. The group as a tool will undoubtedly always be effective in working with small groups or segments of the population. However, the community approach, with its focus on large numbers of people, has many potentialities for trying to solve social problems, enrich living, and better mankind.

To illustrate, the problem of juvenile delinquency is being viewed today particularly from a community point of view. The Mobilization for Youth Project in New York City is an attempt in this direction. It is focusing on the total problems and resources within a disadvantaged area in lower Manhattan, with the goal of mustering the community resources available to help the community to raise its standard of living and its social functioning, and consequently to minimize the existing degree of antisocial behavior. Attempts are being made to provide jobs for teen-agers—many of whom have never worked—to support their attendance at school, to provide additional recreational facilities, and to help in many ways to improve the total functioning and well-being of the populated area.

The overall proposal is based primarily upon the

belief that no effort to prevent juvenile delinquency can succeed which does not provide young people with *genuine* opportunities to behave differently—especially through creative educational and exciting work programs, and which does not involve local residents directly in the effort to improve the social and economic opportunities which their community affords to young people.[6]

An important side effect of the new emphasis on the community approach is the involvement of more citizens and community-minded individuals. As additional people become interested in social services and their operation, there is likely to be increased interest in social work and in multitudinous community projects for building and strengthening various communities. These people will not only become aware of social problems which exist, but will likely increase their understanding of ways to solve these problems. They will also probably become more interested in helping to bring about effective solutions.

IMPROVED PUBLIC RELATIONS

There are many who believe that one of the major weaknesses of social work at present is its inadequate public relations. Especially in the past, social work has done very little to paint a favorable public image. Today there is considerable interest in this kind of activity and many social workers and agencies are spending time and energy in improving their public relations policies and activities.

The strengthening of public relations will probably arise through two main avenues. The first involves increased interest and activity among the social workers themselves. There is additional interest in

[6] "Mobilization for Youth, A Proposal for the Prevention and Control of Delinquency by Expanding Opportunities" (New York: Mobilization for Youth, Inc., 1962), p. 3; mimeographed.

studying knowledge and skills of public relations in the graduate schools of social work. There are also more social workers "on the firing line" who feel that they must take more interest and participate more fully in improving their public image.

A second approach, just coming to the fore, is one that will probably be tapped more in the future. This is the hiring of public relations experts as consultants to social work agencies and social workers. Social workers are beginning to recognize that they are not experts in public relations and that if they are going to obtain the best professional services available, they will need to pay for these services, to employ those who are especially trained. Why should not social workers hire experts in public relations just as they hire consultants in psychiatry, psychology, and other related disciplines? There are many examples extant which indicate that this procedure has been most effective in improving the public image of social work and social work agencies and programs. This trend, undoubtedly, will continue in the future.

PREVENTION

The Curriculum Study of 1959, of the Council on Social Work Education, stressed prevention as one of the three basic functions of social work practice. This gave added impetus to the preventive movement. Recent professional conferences and meetings have nearly all included one or more talks and discussions on the importance of prevention in social work.

Certainly in the years ahead there will be more stress placed upon prevention. "An ounce of prevention is worth a pound of cure." Is it not really better to try to prevent personal, family, and community problems from happening in the first place, rather than to cure or treat them? Is it not more effective to spend time and talents in action which will prevent problem situations from taking place? Many believe that the intrinsic powers and contributions of social work in the years ahead lie in preventive approaches.

One of the main services of social work is that of marriage counseling. Dr. Abraham Stone, often regarded as the father of marriage counseling in the United States, suggests that [7]

. . . the chief task of marriage counseling of tomorrow . . . will be to further marital stability by preventive measures. In medicine as well as in the social sciences the emphasis today is increasingly on prevention. This approach is particularly applicable to the field of marriage counseling. Instead of dealing merely with ailing marriages, marriage counseling will be concerned with the broad principles of constructive education and preparation for marriage and

[7] Abraham Stone, "Marriage Counseling Today and Tomorrow," *Marriage and Family Living*, Vol. 12 (Spring, 1950), p. 40.

family life, which will be a part of the individual's general preparation for life in our society.

SUMMARY

The people of today live in a fast-moving, jet-propelled world which has many implications for the rapidly developing profession of social work. In the years ahead, what pathways will social work be likely to follow?

Several trends and developments seem to be in the offing as projections are made into the future of social work: more research, increased status, higher salaries, more emphasis upon the community organization approach, improved public relations, more training centers, and additional stress on prevention.

The potentialities in the years ahead seem almost unlimited for social work and social workers. Professional training and services are likely to be improved, increased, and strengthened.

QUESTIONS FOR DISCUSSION

1. What, in your opinion, is likely to be the most significant development in social work in the future?

2. Evaluate some of the factors which will probably help to bring about a stronger professional identification in social work in the years ahead.

3. Compare and contrast the values of certification and licensing of social workers.

4. What suggestions do you have for improving interdisciplinary collaboration including social work on the professional team?

5. Spell out the functions of the social worker as a consultant.

6. Why is there likely to be more research performed by social workers in the future?

7. What might help to bring about improved status of social workers?

8. What is your opinion of the increased stress on the community organization approach by social workers?

9. Do you agree that social work agencies should hire public relations experts to assist with their programs?

10. What part do you think prevention will play in social work in the years ahead?

SPECIAL ACTIVITIES

1. Visit your local Community Welfare Council and discuss with the director a current community-focused project. Give an oral report on this to your class, with your own evaluations.

2. Interview a doctor who is either a member of a medical department in preventive medicine or who is very much interested in preventive medicine, and discuss with him the role of prevention in medicine. Evaluate this information in relation to social work and report this to your class.

3. Assuming you had a million dollars at your disposal, formulate a written plan for reducing juvenile delinquency in your community through the use of the community approach and prevention.

SELECTED REFERENCES

BISNO, HERBERT, *The Place of the Undergraduate Curriculum in Social Work Education,* Curriculum Study, Vol. II (New York: Council on Social Work Education, 1959).

BOEHM, WERNER, *Objectives of the Social Work Curriculum of the Future,* Curriculum Study, Vol. I (New York: Council on Social Work Education, 1959).

FERGUSON, ELIZABETH, *Social Work, An Introduction* (Philadelphia: J. B. Lippincott Co., 1963).

Social Work as Human Relations—Anniversary Papers of the New York School of Social Work and the Community Service Society of New York, Part III: "Vistas in Human Relations" (New York: Columbia University Press, 1949), pp. 197–285.

Social Work Yearbook, 1960 (New York: National Association of Social Workers, 1960).

SKIDMORE, REX A., and THACKERAY, MILTON G., "Male Social Workers—On the Increase," *Personnel Information,* Vol. 6 (May, 1963), pp. 1, 33–36.

WITTMAN, MILTON, *Scholarship Aid in Social Work Education* (New York: Council on Social Work Education, 1956).

Name Index

Subject Index